Basic Language
Messages and Meanings

Text and Grammar Handbook

Authors: **Harry A. Greene**

Kate Ashley Loomis

Norma W. Biedenharn

Pauline C. Davis

Basic Language Coordinator:

Norma W. Biedenharn

CALIFORNIA STATE SERIES
Published by
CALIFORNIA STATE DEPARTMENT OF EDUCATION
Sacramento, 1975

Illustrations by Muriel and Jim Collins

Standard Book Number 06-530100-5

Some of the material in this book was previously published under the titles oı
*Building Better English 7 Torch Edition, The New Building Better English 7
Fourth Edition, The New Building Better English 7, Building Better English 7,
Building Better English in Every Way;* copyrights © 1972, 1968, 1965, 1961,
1958, 1952, 1947, 1944 by Harper & Row, Publishers, Incorporated.

PREFACE

In the Basic Language: Messages and Meanings series, the authors and the publishers reaffirm their belief that effective instruction in English must be founded upon a basic-skills approach.

In line with that belief, the grammar chapters have been designed to incorporate valuable principles and practices of modern linguistic grammar. All linguistic-grammar material included was chosen because it does one or both of these things:

1. It offers useful new terms, explanations, or practices that can be of tangible help to the students who will use the books.

2. It brings to light certain interesting or unusual facts about English grammatical structure that are worth including for their own sake.

Another notable feature of this series is an outstanding treatment of the area of composition.

Certain other features that distinguish this series are listed below.

1. The content shows careful, logical organization; and that organization is clearly apparent. Piecemeal, hit-or-miss instruction has no place in the Basic Language series. Further, the content shows an orderly, definite progression from one book of the series to the next. Finally, the arrangement of material is such as to make it readily adaptable to varied types of curricula.

2. Each of the large areas of communication—speaking, listening, reading, and writing—receives ample treatment, not merely token recognition.

3. Instruction is clear and specific, with rules, definitions, and guides easily distinguishable from introductions and exercises. The practice material is useful, varied, and appealing; it makes provision for individual differences. There is consistent maintenance of skills throughout. In addition, there is available a thorough testing program that covers the mechanics of expression.

4. An integral part of the texts is concrete provision for applying English skills to the student's work in all subjects and to his life outside school.

5. The content makes sense to the students who use the books. It is the belief of the makers of this series that young people do not object to hard work if they understand what they are to do and how they are to go about it.

Even a brief examination of Basic Language: Messages and Meanings will reveal how closely these books adhere to the preceding criteria. A careful analysis should bring the conviction that students and teachers who use this series will find the study of English a productive and pleasurable experience, not a dreary chore.

The Publishers

CONTENTS

Section I: Speaking and Listening

Section II: Reading

Section III: Writing

Section IV: Grammar Handbook—Building Sentences

Chapter 14   Grammar: The Code of Language   271

Chapter 15   Using Verbs in Building Sentences   279

Speaking and Listening

THE ENGLISH LANGUAGE: PLACE NAMES IN THE UNITED STATES

THINK IT OVER...

To someone who does not live there, "Likely" may seem a strange name for a town. To the residents of Likely, however, *Soso* or *Yellville* or *Hasty* or *Sopchoppy* or *Floydada*—or the name of *your* town—may seem just as strange.

The United States, you see, is rich in unusual names. Where do they come from? This chapter will lead you to explore some of the sources.

3

Examine the following list of place names; then separate them into five groups by what you think they have in common. In one group, for example, put such names as "Loyal"—ones, in other words, that express an opinion. Separate the others into groups named for (*a*) famous persons, (*b*) foreign places, (*c*) a natural resource, (*d*) a geographical or natural feature.

Riverside	Happy Camp	Fair Play	Vienna
Plentywood	Lake City	Supreme	Hustle
Niceville	Coal City	Columbus	Holland
Copper City	Jefferson	Paradise	Dickens
New London	Superior	Franklin	Big Pine
Clearbrook	Iron Mountain	Aimwell	Seward
Granite Falls	Darkharbor	Hudson	Athens
Alexandria	Valparaiso	Leadville	Gas
Opportunity	Napoleon	Lisbon	Soso
Weeping Water	Challenge	Anchorage	Rimrock

1. The Names on a Map

"WIRDLEY, IF YOU COULD NAME A TOWN, WHAT WOULD YOU CALL IT?"

"I'D NAME IT WIRDLEY! NO OTHER PLACE HAS THAT NAME!"

If you were to have the chance to name a new town, what would your choice be? Would *you* be tempted to give it your own name? Would you want to honor your favorite athlete or television star, your best friend, some great hero, a character in a favorite book? Would you search for some descriptive name so unusual that you could be fairly sure no other place would have it?

Place names come from all the sources in the above paragraph and from many others, as you have already discovered. Sometimes the names have an unusual and interesting history.

The county seat of Knox County, Nebraska, for example, is named "Center." That name came about because the two largest towns in the county were competing to become the county seat. The matter was finally settled by having surveyors locate the exact center of the county. It turned out to be in a farmer's cornfield—and there the county seat was built! Since that spot *was* the center of the county, "Center" was a natural choice for the name.

Some places are even named through a mistake. On an early map of Alaska, for instance, the mapmaker marked the location of a certain town but failed to write in a name. Later, someone who was examining the map noticed the omission and then wrote "Name?" beside it. *Name* was misread as "Nome," and the place has had that name ever since.

America itself, as you may have learned, received its name through a mistake. Amerigo Vespucci, an Italian navigator who voyaged to the New World several years after Columbus, wrote letters about the lands he had explored. In 1507 a German map maker, evidently thinking that Vespucci was the first to explore these new lands, proposed that they be named "America" in honor of Americus [Amerigo]. As a result, that name was put on the maps of the New World—and it stuck!

LEARNING ACTIVITIES IN INTERESTING PLACE NAMES

Use encyclopedias, atlases, or road maps in doing these activities.

A. Choose one state. Examine a map of it or go over the list of place names accompanying the map. Write down four of what seem to you the most interesting names, along with their location and their population. Share your lists in class.

B. Using the same state as in *A,* find and list at least one example probably named for each of the following: *a famous American, a famous foreigner, a foreign city, a geographical feature, a woman* (first name). Compare lists in class or in your small groups.

ENRICHMENT

A. For one of the interesting names that you found in *A* above, or for one of those listed below, write an imaginary story about how that place came to be named. Pretend, for example, that you were one of the original settlers and that you are telling your small grandson all about it. The Guides for Telling a Story, page 240, will help you.

Bumble Bee	Embarrass	Flasher	Rescue
Show Low	Sleepy Eye	Riddle	Tigerville
Yellville	Peculiar	Windfall	Ten Sleep
Cash	Twodot	Nodaway	Indian Neck
Hideaway Park	Colts Neck	Scarville	Lost Cabin
Slaughter	Mocksville	Hazard	Mousie

B. The very sound of some place names is like music: *Avalon, Duluth, Fontanelle, Loma Linda,* ... Other place names are appealing because of what they suggest: *Blooming Prairie, Pearblossom, Silver Star, Still Pond,* ... Have fun by writing a two-line rhyme about one name or more that you like especially. Here are some examples that suggest the sort of thing you might do:

> I like its sound! Who wouldn't go a
> Long way to settle in Shenandoah!

> Though you search town names the country over,
> You'll find none prettier than *Clover!*

> I'd love to live in Apple Valley—
> *That* town sounds right up my alley!

> How could anyone ever forget a
> Place with the name of *Alpharetta!*

> What a lovely sound has *Mountainair!*
> I'm sure that I could be happy there.

Choose from the following names or find on a map others that you like.

Spangle	Violet Hill	Fontana	Rockaway	Daisy
Lightfoot	Dewdrop	Pretty Prairie	Juanita	Ivy
Blue Hill	Butterfly	Cherry Tree	Echo Lake	Roselle
Honeydew	Castle Gate	Half Moon Bay	Fallen Leaf	Far Hills
Moon Run	Silver Plume	Bloomingrose	Rising Star	Shadow
Florissant	Birchleaf	Summer Shade	Merry Hill	Sunset

2. Names from Europe

READ AND DISCUSS

Imagine yourselves as having come to this country with the first Spanish, English, or French settlers. You would have no maps naming rivers or harbors, lakes or mountains in this new land. There would be no towns until you made them. How would you be likely to try to make yourself "feel at home"? If you look at a map of the United States, how can you tell that those first settlers actually did do just as you would have done?

As you discovered, one way the early colonists tried to get a feeling of home was to give familiar names to their new surroundings. In many cases, they simply borrowed place names from home; in Connecticut, for example, both the city of New London and the Thames, the river on which it is located, are such borrowed names. In other cases, the settlers honored their king or queen, some other titled person, or a great leader; Jamestown, Virginia, for instance, the first permanent English colony, was named for James I, who was then ruling England. The two Carolinas were named for an English king, too: Charles II, from the Latin name "Carolus."

Those names and similar ones were given to geographical places in the United States over three hundred years ago. As the colonies grew larger, and after they had won their independence from Great Britain, settlers moved farther and farther westward. Over and over the same names were applied to the places where they settled. California, on the shores of the Pacific Ocean, has both a Plymouth and a Jamestown. Twenty-three states besides Massachusetts, where the first Salem was founded, have places with that name. In addition, five states have a New Salem. (Not all those Salems were named directly for the one in Massachusetts, but in one way or another they can be traced back to it.)

LEARNING ACTIVITIES IN NAMES FROM EUROPE

A. The list that follows contains names of United States cities, all of which had their source in England. (1) In an encyclopedia find for whom or what each city was named. For some names in the list, the encyclopedia will give more than one city. Choose the one that was founded earliest. (2) Discover how many of the names are also to be found in your home state. To find out, use the listings of place names on a road map of the state or after the state map in the encyclopedia.

Baltimore	Cambridge	New Bedford	Reading
Bath	Charleston	New Haven	Richmond
Birmingham	Charlotte	New York	Williamsburg
Boston	Haverhill	Pittsburgh	Worcester

B. Spanish explorers and settlers left their mark mainly on names in Florida and the Southwest. California is particularly rich in such names. Many of the following cities are in that state or in Florida; the others are in Arizona, New Mexico, or Texas. (1) Identify the state for each city. (2) All these names are descriptive. Use an English-Spanish dictionary or the glossary at the back of a Spanish language textbook to help you discover what each name actually means. Compare your findings in class.

Arroyo Grande	El Campo	La Puente	Montebello
Boca Grande	Hermosa Beach	Las Cruces	Naranja
Boca Raton	Islamorada	Los Gatos	Portales
Casa Grande	La Feria	Los Nietos	Punta Gorda
Cuero	Laguna	Molino	Socorro

C. Most states have at least a few place names of French origin. Two states, Louisiana and Michigan, have a great many. Some of those given below are in Louisiana; the others, in Michigan. (1) Find out in which state each belongs. (2) With the aid of the encyclopedia or of *Webster's Biographical Dictionary,* discover which of the cities were named for persons. (3) All the other names are descriptive. Find out what each one means in English. Use a French-English dictionary or the glossary section of a French-English language textbook. Check your findings by going over your answers in class.

Allouez	Duplessis	Grosse Ile	Lafitte
Baton Rouge	Grand Blanc	Grosse Tete	Mer Rouge
Cadillac	Grand Coteau	Iberville	Plaquemine
Charlevoix	Grand Marais	L'Anse	Vacherie

D. The following place names come from sources other than English, Spanish, or French. (1) Copy the list; then find and identify on your paper the source of each name. (2) Check to see how many states have places so named.

Belgrade	Damascus	Genoa	Naples	Syracuse
Berlin	Delhi	Hamburg	Norway	Troy
Bethlehem	Dresden	Hanover	Pulaski	Utica
Cairo	Dublin	Madrid	Rome	Venice
Canton	Florence	Milan	Sparta	Verona
Carthage	Geneva	Moscow	Stockholm	Warsaw

ENRICHMENT

Prepare a little mystery quiz containing statements about one of the European cities named in Activity D. Read your statements to the class one at a time. See how long you can keep your classmates guessing. Select your facts from an encyclopedia account of the city. Keep until last the best-known facts about the city; for example, if you chose Venice, you certainly would wait until the end to say, "This city has canals instead of streets" or "In this city there are boats called 'gondolas.'" Either of those remarks, you see, practically gives away the name of the city.

3. Biblical Names

"MOUNT ARARAT — I WONDER WHO THOUGHT UP A NAME LIKE THAT!"

"I DON'T KNOW, BUT MY DAD SAYS THAT NOAH'S ARK LANDED ON TOP OF IT."

READ AND THINK ABOUT

Would *you* have known that "Ararat" is a name that has its source in the Bible?

Why do you think that early settlers in this country sometimes gave their new homes Biblical names?

Many of those first settlers in the Thirteen Colonies came to the New World for religious reasons. It is only natural that they would name settlements after places or characters in the Bible, especially if those names had some special meaning that seemed to fit the new home or their hopes for it. "Bethel," for example, is the name of a town founded in Connecticut in 1700. It means "house of God."

Other place names with a religious origin are those named for saints, such as St. Augustine, San Francisco, Santa Barbara. California leads all states with such names, but Texas, Florida, New Mexico, and Louisiana also have a good many.

LEARNING ACTIVITIES IN BIBLICAL NAMES

A. With the help of an adult encyclopedia or a Bible dictionary, find out the significance of the following names that led settlers in the Thirteen Colonies to choose them for their new homes. (Disregard the word "Beach" and the ending "ville" in the first and the last names on the list.) Tell also whether the names are from the Old, or the New, Testament. Compare your findings in class.

Bethany Beach, Delaware	Goshen, Connecticut
Bethlehem, Pennsylvania	Hebron, Maryland
Calvary, Georgia	Jordan, New York
Cana, Virginia	Sharon, Massachusetts
Canaan, New Hampshire	Zionville, North Carolina

B. All the following places are named for saints. (1) Check road-map listings or the encyclopedia listings for the states of California, Florida, Louisiana, New Mexico, and Texas to locate the places by states. (2) Use encyclopedias, the *Reader's Encyclopedia,* or *Webster's Biographical Dictionary* to help you identify the saints.

St. Augustine	San Francisco	San Pedro	Santa Margarita
San Antonio	San Marcos	Santa Barbara	Santa Monica
San Bernardino	San Mateo	Santa Clara	Santa Rosa

C. The Old Testament has in it many interesting persons for whom places in at least one state have been named. With the help of encyclopedias, Bible histories, or other special reference books, prepare a short oral or written report about one or more of the following Biblical characters. Include in your report what actions or qualities of a character you think might have influenced settlers to name their new home in that person's honor.

Aaron	Eli	Joseph	Samson
Abraham	Elijah	Joshua	Sarah
Benjamin	Gideon	Laban	Saul
Daniel	Job	Rachel	Seth
David	Jonah	Ruth	Solomon

ENRICHMENT

The state of Louisiana has "parishes" instead of "counties." Use the resources of the library to carry out the following activity about their names. Report to the class or to your small group.

The French settlers of Louisiana gave the names of saints to eight of the parishes. Find out (1) the names of those parishes, and if possible, (2) the identity of the saints so honored. All eight parishes are in what part of the state?

4. Historical, Mythological, and Literary Names

"WHOEVER NAMED THAT TOWN MUST HAVE BEEN A BASEBALL FAN!"

HOMER — 6 mi.

TALK IT OVER

What is the most probable source for the name "Homer"?
Why would anyone be likely to choose that name?

What is true of "Homer" is true of many other place names in the United States; they are "classical" names that come from the history, mythology, or other literature of ancient Greece and Rome. The settlers who chose such names were likely to be men who had studied Greek or Latin—or both. In those days, you see, an educated person was expected to know at least one of those languages. It was only natural for them to name their new homes for the persons, places, or gods about whom they had read so much.

There are places named for great heroes of the Trojan War in the Greek poet Homer's *Iliad*. One hero was Achilles, whose mother had dipped him, as a baby, in the River Styx. Doing so made him invulnerable except in the heel by which his mother had held him. It was a wound there that killed him.

There are towns or cities named for ancient places: Crete, for instance, where the monstrous Minotaur of mythology destroyed his victims. There is Thermopylae, named for the mountain pass in Greece where a handful of Spartans died in a heroic stand against a great force of invading Persians. There are places named for Roman gods and goddesses; as examples, Mars, the god of war; Venus, the goddess of love and beauty.

The settlers also knew later literature and history, as many a place name indicates. Here are some examples.

Romeo (Colorado, Michigan): named for the hero in one of
Shakespeare's plays
Shelley (Idaho): named for Percy Bysshe Shelley (1792-1822), an
English poet

LEARNING ACTIVITIES IN HISTORICAL, MYTHOLOGICAL, OR LITERARY NAMES

A. Copy these twenty place names in a column: *Arden, Argo, Aurora, Avalon, Cicero, Dante, Elaine, Elsinore, Euclid, Helen, Grasmere, Leonidas, Maud, Medusa, Merlin, Minerva, Neptune, Nottingham, Stratford, Thor.* Use encyclopedias and dictionaries to match each of the following identifications with the right place name.

1. Heroine of Tennyson's long poem by that name
2. Roman god of the sea
3. Greek mathematician; the father of geometry
4. Forest where most of Shakespeare's play *As You Like It* takes place
5. Scandinavian god of thunder
6. Famous Italian poet, born A.D. 1265
7. Heroine of one of the King Arthur stories
8. Roman goddess of the dawn
9. Woman over whom the Trojan War was fought
10. Sorcerer in the King Arthur stories
11. Roman goddess of wisdom
12. Shakespeare's birthplace
13. Ship of the legendary Greek hero Jason
14. Spartan king who died a hero's death
15. Home of the English poet Wordsworth (1770–1850)
16. According to legend, where King Arthur was taken after his death
17. Famous Roman orator, author, and statesman
18. Location of the castle in which Shakespeare's *Hamlet* takes place
19. Horrible snaky-haired monster in Greek legend
20. Territory of the sheriff who was Robin Hood's enemy

B. Below are listed the names of Roman gods or goddesses after whom places in various states have been named. With the help of encyclopedias or books of mythology, prepare reports on those deities. Divide the names among the members of the class so that at least two people research each one. Make the reports oral. Use the Guides for Making a Short, One-Source Report, page 134, as you plan what you will say. Include your own ideas about why the names might have been chosen.

Mercury	Athena	Diana	Juno	Pluto
Ceres	Mars	Flora	Pomona	Vesta

C. Most states have some places named, directly or indirectly, for famous authors. Here are the names of some well-known books or other writings. Each is by a different famous author, one whose name has been given to a place in one state or more. Find out (1) who those authors are and (2) whether any are represented in your state.

1. *Great Expectations*
2. *The Count of Monte Cristo*
3. *Knickerbocker's History of New York*
4. *Quentin Durward*
5. *Snow-Bound: A Winter Idyl*
6. *The House of the Seven Gables*
7. *Robinson Crusoe*
8. *Paradise Lost*
9. *The Prisoner of Chillon*
10. *Tam o'Shanter*
11. *The Pied Piper of Hamelin*
12. *The Murders in the Rue Morgue*
13. *Ode to the West Wind*
14. *She Stoops to Conquer*
15. *The Decline and Fall of the Roman Empire*
16. *Essay on Criticism*
17. *The Vision of Sir Launfal*
18. *The Stones of Venice*
19. *Puck of Pook's Hill*
20. *History of the French Revolution*

ENRICHMENT

Some place names honor famous battles or sieges. Examples are the place names listed below. Use adult encyclopedias to help you find the following facts about those conflicts: (1) dates, (2) the cause, (3) the opposing forces, (4) the victor. Check road atlases or other geographical references to see whether your own state has in it any of the places.

1. Sedan	3. Sebastopol	5. Marengo	7. Hastings	9. Shrewsbury
2. Lepanto	4. Philippi	6. Waterloo	8. Marathon	10. Syracuse

5. Indian Names

READ AND THINK ABOUT

Some of the most interesting and beautiful names in this country have an Indian origin. Lydia Howard Sigourney (1791-1865) once wrote a poem about such Indian names. Here it is, on this page and the next one.

INDIAN NAMES

Ye say, they all have passed away,
   That noble race and brave;
That their light canoes have vanished
   From off the crested wave:
That, 'mid the forests where they roamed,
   There rings no hunter's shout;
But their name is on your waters,—
   Ye may not wash it out.

'Tis where Ontario's billow
   Like Ocean's surge is curled;
Where strong Niagara's thunders wake
   The echo of the world;
Where red Missouri bringeth
   Rich tribute from the West,
And Rappahannock sweetly sleeps
   On green Virginia's breast.

Ye say, their cone-like cabins,
   That clustered o'er the vale,
Have fled away, like withered leaves
   Before the Autumn gale;
But their memory liveth on your hills
   Their baptism on your shore,
Your everlasting rivers speak
   Their dialect of yore.

Old Massachusetts wears it
   Within her lordly crown,
And broad Ohio bears it
   Amid his young renown;
Connecticut hath wreathed it
   Where her quiet foliage waves,
And bold Kentucky breathes it hoarse
   Through all her ancient caves.

Wachusett hides its lingering voice
    Within its rocky heart,
And Allegheny graves its tone
    Throughout his lofty chart;
Monadnock, on his forehead hoar,
    Doth seal the sacred trust;
Your mountains build their monument,
    Though ye destroy their dust.

DISCUSSION ACTIVITY: EXPLORING THE POEM

1. In the seventh line of the first stanza, the poet says: "But their name is on your waters." She goes on, in the second stanza, to name four of those waters. Identify each of them as to what kind of body of water it is.
2. The third stanza speaks of "everlasting rivers" that have Indian names. What ones can you suggest in addition to those that the poet has named?
3. All the names in the fourth stanza are those of states. In the fifth stanza, all the proper nouns are names of what kind of *natural feature*? What additional ones that have Indian names can you add to that group?
4. "Your" and "ye," in the last two lines of the poem, refer to whom? Who is meant by "their"? Interpret what you think the poet means by those two lines.

As the poem brings out, many natural features in this country have Indian names. In the activities that follow, you will be looking for such names as well as for those of cities or other places.

LEARNING ACTIVITIES IN INDIAN NAMES

A. Find out how many of the state names in this country are of Indian origin. List the names of those states. Beside each, give (1) its source and (2) the meaning of the name, if you can find it. Use encyclopedias, almanacs, dictionaries, or other special references to help you find the answers.

B. How many large rivers in the United States can you find that have the same names as the states listed in Activity A? Use your classroom dictionary, a geographical dictionary, or an almanac in carrying out your research.

C. Using a state atlas, a road map, or an encyclopedia, make a list of places in your own state that you think probably have Indian names. Compare lists in class.

The place names in the following list are the personal names of famous Indians. Using atlases or encyclopedias, find out how many states have places with these names. Then prepare a brief oral report on one of the Indians in the list.

Cochise	Hiawatha	Pocahontas	Powhatan	Samoset	Tecumseh
Geronimo	Osceola	Pontiac	Red Cloud	Satanta	Tuscaloosa

6. Names of American Leaders

While the colonies were growing and developing, many people distinguished themselves as leaders in government. Others became famous as explorers, writers, Indian fighters. After the colonies became the United States, patriotic citizens honored its great leaders by naming places after many of them. This principle of naming places after heroes still goes on. Since the first successful orbital flights by United States astronauts, for example, streets and parks have already been named or renamed to honor these pioneers of space.

A. Almost every state has places named for Washington and Lincoln. The names of other famous Americans also have been honored by being given to towns or counties in various states. The following list includes such names. (1) How many of these are to be found in your own state or in some other state that interests you? (2) For each place that you find, write a sentence identifying the person for whom it probably was named.

Audubon	Burbank	Edison	Hoover	Jefferson	Perry
Austin	Clark	Emerson	Houston	Lewis	Revere
Boone	Crockett	Fremont	Jackson	Marion	Sheridan

B. Using a book that is a history of your state, make a list of its outstanding leaders. Have any cities or counties in the state been named for them? Report your findings to the class, including a brief description of the leaders so honored. The Guides for Making a Short, One-Source Report, page 134, will help you to plan what you will say.

7. Descriptive Names

Time brings changes!

Often you will find that a name on the map of the United States was chosen because for some reason or another it just seemed to fit the place to which it was given. The name *Greenfield,* for example, sounds like a pleasant place to live. *Newborn* sounds as though whoever named it was rejoicing over his new home. It is altogether likely that those names did express the feeling of the namers. How do you think *Appleton, Church Creek, Junction, Rocky Ford,* or *Landing* might have been named?

Americans like to feel that they have a good sense of humor. That humor certainly shows in some of the unusual-sounding place names: Antler, Bad Axe, Battiest, Decoy, Nail, Peculiar, and Zigzag, for instance. Some such names were changed later on, probably because of a feeling that the old name was undignified. Luckily, some oddly named places kept their original name.

The name of a place may have been suggested by an incident, by something observed in the vicinity (often an animal of some kind), by a definite feeling or impression, or by an industry or some other local activity. You can find on the map, for example, a Wounded Knee, an Otter Creek, a Smile, a What Cheer, and a Deadwood.

As you can see, names can be colorful as well as descriptive!

LEARNING ACTIVITIES IN DESCRIPTIVE NAMES

A. The missing words in the following place names are natural features of the locality. Use encyclopedia listings or those on road maps or in road atlases to find out what those natural features are. In some cases, you will find more than one place name with a natural feature that fits the blank.

1. Big ...., Michigan
2. Big Stone ...., Virginia
3. Black ...., Arizona
4. Cold ...., Alaska
5. Dry ...., Kentucky
6. Fair ...., North Carolina
7. Gold ...., Oregon
8. Golden ...., Louisiana
9. Grand ...., Washington
10. Grass ...., Wyoming
11. Great ...., Pennsylvania
12. Green ...., Massachusetts
13. High ...., Florida
14. Little ...., New York
15. Long ...., Nebraska
16. Pleasant ...., Wisconsin
17. Red Boiling ...., Tennessee
18. Round ...., Maine
19. Sun ...., Montana
20. Three ...., Texas

B. Using any of the references named in *A*, locate in your own state as many places as you can that are named for a natural feature. (If you prefer, choose some other state that interests you.) For any of the places with which you are familiar, tell whether you think the name still fits.

C. Several of the following places sound as though they were named by someone with a good sense of humor. Some show how the namers seem to have felt about the places. Still others seem to show both humor and opinion. Decide into which group each fits; then find names in your state that fall into those groups. Make this an oral activity.

Accident, Maryland	Lugoff, South Carolina
Admire, Kansas	Luck, Wisconsin
Bell Buckle, Tennessee	Maybee, Michigan
Bobo, Mississippi	Oblong, Illinois
Bowlegs, Oklahoma	Panacea, Florida
Delight, Arkansas	Pepper Pike, Ohio
Dusty, New Mexico	Plush, Oregon
Early, Iowa	Ritzville, Washington
Eek, Alaska	Rocky Comfort, Missouri
Frozen, West Virginia	Sleepy Eye, Minnesota
Goodway, Alabama	Stillmore, Georgia
Hardburly, Kentucky	Toast, North Carolina
Hygiene, Colorado	Wink, Texas
Igo, California	Winner, South Dakota
Jigger, Louisiana	Wynot, Nebraska

D. Many descriptive names have come from French or Spanish settlers. (1) Check to see whether any of the following are represented in your state or in a neighboring one. (2) Translate as many as you can into their English meanings. Some may be in your dictionary; for the others, use a French-English or a Spanish-English dictionary or textbook.

Alta Loma	Chula Vista	La Junta	Palo Alto
Amarillo	Coeur d'Alene	Las Vegas	Prairie du Chien
Beaufort	Corona	Loma Linda	Puerto de Luna
Bellevue	Culdesac	Montevideo	Rochelle
Belmont	Del Rey	Ojo Caliente	Terre Haute
Caliente	Fond du Lac	Palacios	Tres Pinos

ENRICHMENT

A. Here is a chance to try your hand at choosing some unusual descriptive place names.

Copy the paragraph that follows on page 21, filling in each blank with names or descriptive details as needed. Use your imagination by making up the names, select them from maps, or pick ones listed in the encyclopedia, in road-map listings, or in other reference sources.

Read your completed stories in class or in your small groups. If you like, vote on the paragraphs that you think have the most unusual names.

In English class the other day, we were talking about the birth-places of our parents or other relatives. Bill Gray's father, we learned, was born in .... City, so called because of the .... near it. Mrs. Gray was not born there, but in the town of ...., named for its .... Lori Allen said that both parents and all four grandparents were born and grew up in ....field, which probably took its name from the .... that you can still see there. Don Farley's greatgrandfather was a pioneer who helped to found the town of ...., named for the .... that had taken place there. Some of the other descriptive names that I thought were either really funny or appealing are .... Valley, ... Bay, ... Point, and .... Corners. As for me, I've decided that if I ever have the chance to name a place, I'll call it ...., even if there isn't a .... anywhere near it!

B. As a special research project, investigate names that begin with the names of *fruits, plants, trees, animals, flowers, minerals* or *precious stones, building materials*. Proceed as follows:

Go to your local post office and ask to see a copy of the *Directory of Post Offices*. With the help of the Table of Contents, turn to the section that contains in one alphabetical list all the post-office names in the entire country. By checking that list, you can have an enjoyable time finding the answers to one or more of the following questions.

Use what you learn as the basis of an oral or written report. You might call it "Would You Believe . . . ?" In your report, you need not name the states where these places are found; just give all the different names that begin with the words you are researching. Skip ones that are merely plurals; for example, if you are checking *Cedar,* you need not list both *Cedar Bluff* and *Cedar Bluffs.*

1. What different place names can you find that begin with *Peach?* with *Apple?* with *Orange?* with *Lemon?* with *Plum?*
2. What ones can you find beginning with *Wheat?* with *Grain?* with *Hay?* with *Grass?* with *Meadow?*
3. What places can you discover that begin with *Horse?* with *Deer?* with *Bear?* with *Beaver?*
4. What names can you find that begin with *Elm?* with *Maple?* with *Cedar?* with *Pine?* with *Birch?*
5. How many different places can you find that begin with *Rose?* with *Clover?*
6. What names can you discover that begin with *Gold?* with *Silver?* with *Diamond?* with *Iron?* with *Copper?*
7. How many different place names begin with *Wood?* with *Stone?* with *Marble?* with *Granite?*

8. Place Names with Suffixes

THINK IT OVER...

The travelers reading the road sign in the illustration might really feel confused. All the names *do* sound similar, for they have a common base, *Rock*. Look at them carefully, though. Note that each name has a different suffix, or *word ending,* that will keep the travelers from going to *Rockfield* when their real destination is *Rockford*.

Many place names have such suffixes. Sometimes if you look up the origin of a suffix, you can pretty well guess where the persons who named a place came from. The meaning of the suffix also may suggest something about the nature of the land on which the town was located. You will not be able to tell for sure, though, for the namers may simply have liked the sound of the name. Perhaps they may have named it for their old home, with the result that a place called Mount Pleasant, for example, may be in country that is as flat as a pancake.

A number of suffixes mean "city" or "town." Among them are the Saxon (*early English*) *-ham, -ton, -wich,* as in *Birmingham, Dayton, Norwich.* Others are the Danish *-by,* as in *Canby;* the French *-ville,* as in *Bienville;* the German *-dorf,* as in *Allendorf;* and the Greek *-polis,* as in *Indianapolis.*

LEARNING ACTIVITIES IN PLACE NAMES WITH SUFFIXES

A. How many cities in your state can you find that end in suffixes meaning "city" or "town"? Compare your findings in class.

B. In your state, there are probably some city names that begin with a common root word, such as *Rock* in the illustration, but that end with different suffixes, *-dale, -point, -port,* or *-view,* . . . Using an encyclopedia, (1) make a list of such place names in your state; (2) tell which root word was used most often in making these place names; (3) list the different suffixes that have been used. Be sure that you count only true suffixes, as in *Riverside,* and not two-word place names, such as *River Side.*

C. Use dictionaries in this activity. (1) Find from what language each of the following suffixes comes. (2) Give the English meaning of each suffix. (3) Make a list of cities in your state that end with any of these suffixes.

-borough (berg, burg)	*-down*	*-holm*	*-stead*
-dale	*-field*	*-kirk*	*-thorpe*

9. Summary

Many of the motives that led the early settlers in naming their new homes still hold good. Today, however, namers no longer have complete freedom, for most place names that are to be put on official maps must have the approval of the United States Department of the Interior. It is still true, though, that names of streets, suburbs, and communities that are not official Post Office addresses may be left up to the local government.

Now that you have studied the ways that many place names in this country came about, carry out the following activity. It gives you the chance to do some naming of your own!

LEARNING ACTIVITY

Make this a class activity. Pretend that you have just discovered a new region in the United States. You are the ones who must find names for (*a*) a new state, (*b*) twenty counties, (*c*) ten rivers, (*d*) a mountain range, (*e*) three lakes, and (*f*) any other natural features that the region has. When you have chosen all those names, go on to name the capital, the twenty county seats, and two national parks.

Climax the project by having a committee draw a map of the region, including all the natural features and place names that you have chosen. Post the map on the bulletin board, or, if possible, display it in the school office or library.

Go on exploring the resources of the library for more information about the history of place names in the United States. You will find that special books have been written about place names in this country. Some states even have books all about their particular place names.

The first two books in the following list cover place names in the United States as a whole; the others concern the individual states named in their titles.

Names on the Land by George R. Stewart
Nicknames of Cities and States of the United States by Joseph N. Kane and Gerald L. Alexander
Arizona Place Names by Byrd H. Granger (*editor*)
California Place Names: Their Origin and Meaning by Erwin G. Gude
Indian Place Names of New Jersey by Donald W. Becker
Introduction to a Survey of Missouri Place Names by Robert L. Ramsay
Louisiana–French by William A. Read
Maine Place Names by Ava H. Chadbourne
Nebraska Place Names by Lilian Fitzpatrick; edited by G. Thomas Fairclough
Nevada Place Names: Their Origin and Significance by Rufus W. Leigh
New Mexico Place Names by T. M. Pearce
Oklahoma Place Names by G. H. Shire
Oregon Geographic Names by Lewis A. McArthur
Our Storehouse of Missouri Place Names by Robert L. Ramsay

If your state is not one of those named in the preceding list, you can explore its names through other books. You are pretty sure to find at least one state history as well as a guidebook or handbook about the state. Such books often contain interesting information about places and their names.

BUILDING GOOD LISTENING HABITS

1. Learning to Listen

READ AND THINK ABOUT

It would seem that there are some people who have never learned to listen. They can be a real problem to their friends and family, as well as to anyone else who tries to talk with them.

Such people are so wrapped up in what they have to say that they cannot be bothered with listening to anyone else. You, like others, probably have learned that it is not much fun trying to carry on a conversation with someone who does not listen. Remember that fact the next time you are doing the listening, and really listen!

Listening is a skill. Because it is a skill, you must practice if you are to become really good at it. There is a difference between hearing and listening, though that idea may never have occurred to you before. Think about this, for instance: you can hear a new song being sung, but if you want to learn the words, you must really listen with your mind as well as with your ears. Listening means giving your full attention to a sound, whether that sound is an assignment by a teacher, directions from your mother, a play being called by a quarterback, or the song of a cardinal or a thrush. Hearing is, in other words, mostly a matter of the ear; listening, of the ear *and* the mind.

GUIDES TO GOOD LISTENING

1. Think of the other person; keep your mind on what he is saying, and not on your own affairs.
2. Listen not only with your ears, but with your mind. As you listen, ask yourself such questions as these:
    a) What points or facts is the speaker trying to express?
    b) Is he sticking to those points?
    c) If someone should ask me later what he said, what things would I want to remember to tell?
    d) Where did the speaker get his information?
    e) Do I agree with what he says? If not, why not?
    f) What questions would I like to ask? (When you have a chance, ask them!)
3. Show interest, even when you do not agree with what is being said. The interest expressed on your face will help the speaker to do a better job than he can do if you just sit back with a polite smile.
4. Do not try to listen and do something else at the same time. Listening needs your full attention.

Learn about words!

You will find the above heading often as you study this book. Each time it calls your attention to certain words in the lesson—words with interesting histories. The history, or source, of a word is shown in the dictionary in brackets, like this: [ ] Here are the first words for you to trace. They are taken from *C* of the Learning Activities. With which word is the drawing connected?

aisle   cadet   velvet

LEARNING ACTIVITIES IN LISTENING

A. Choose two members of the class to dramatize the conversation on page 25. Discuss what a person might do to become a better listener. (Guides 3 and 4 of the Guides for Holding Discussions, page 33, will help you to have a good discussion.)

B. Discuss in class this question: *Are there times when it is all right to interrupt?* If you think so, be ready to give an example and to tell how the interruption might be made courteously.

C. Write on a piece of paper a sentence containing facts about yourself or members of your family. Take turns at reading the statements aloud; read each sentence only once. Call on a classmate to repeat the statement word for word. This sentence may help you think of an idea.

> Mary Lou, dressed in white velvet, looked down the aisle and smiled at the handsome cadet, her husband-to-be.

ENRICHMENT

A. Make a list of kinds of work that require good listening ability. Explain to the class why each of them requires listening skill.

B. (1) Write an account of how you once got into difficulty by not listening. For help in paragraphing, turn to the guides on page 214. (2) *Proofread your paper for errors in capitalization, punctuation, and spelling.* (3) Using the Guides for Reading Aloud, page 57, prepare your story and read it to the class.

C. Prepare a short oral or written report on *sound*. You may need to use reference books and science books to get the information. If so, see the Guides to the Use of References, page 124. Let the Guides for Making a Long Report, page 135, aid you in preparing the report.

2. Listening to Learn

TALK IT OVER . . .

What "attention getters" besides those pictured above can you think of? How do teachers get your attention when they want you to listen?

Have you ever asked questions like these:

"What was the assignment, Miss Jones?"
"What time did you say we should be there, Mother?"
"Where did the scoutmaster say we should meet?"
"Are we supposed to do all these problems?"

If you often ask such questions, something is wrong with your listening habits.

How much learning, do you think, comes through listening? Well, you learn when you listen to radio or television programs. You learn as you listen to reports or to announcements in class or in assembly. You learn a person's name when you are introduced to him. (How many times have you only heard a name and not really listened to it?) You learn as you listen to teachers giving directions and making explanations. You learn as you listen during class and group discussions, as well as during club meetings. You learn as you listen in conversations with your friends and family.

Yes, much learning comes—or can come—through listening. If your own learning is handicapped by poor listening, let the following guides help you to form the habit of careful listening.

GUIDES FOR LISTENING TO LEARN

1. Listen carefully to oral directions and explanations.
   a) Take notes; they will help you to remember.
   b) Ask questions if necessary. If you are courteous, the speaker is not likely to mind being interrupted.
   c) Know the order in which directions are to be carried out.

2. Listen with full attention to assignments. Write in your notebook as much about the assignment as you can.
   a) Know the purpose of the assignment.
   b) Know how much material is to be covered.
   c) Know exactly how you are to do the work.
   d) Know when the assignment is due.

3. As reports are given in class, keep your mind on what is being said. Jot down anything that you want to be sure not to forget.

4. When an announcement is made, think about what it means to you in particular and to your class as a group.

5. During discussions, think about the ideas that are being presented. Apply guide 2 of the Guides to Good Listening, page 26.

LEARNING ACTIVITIES

A. In class, discuss the poor listeners who are pictured on this page. Think of names for each, such as "Slumbering Slouch." List these on the board; add other types of poor listeners.

B. In your small groups, make a list of situations, in school and out, in which you are a listener. Compare the lists in class.

C. For the rest of the day, be alert for ways that people attempt to get and hold your attention. Watch your classmates, teachers, members of your family, and radio and television speakers for examples that you can bring to class tomorrow. List the ways on the board.

D. (1) In a social studies or science book, find a paragraph containing five or six different facts. (2) Prepare a question dealing with each fact. (3) Read the paragraphs in your small groups. (4) Call on students to jot down answers to your questions as you read them. (5) Exchange papers for checking to see how many in your audience really listened.

USING ENGLISH IN ALL CLASSES

Listen carefully to the next lesson assignment in one of your other classes. Afterwards, try to write out exactly what the teacher said in making the assignment.

ENRICHMENT

Write a paragraph describing a situation in which a person can hear many sounds but must listen to only one or a few of the sounds. For instance, tell how you must sometimes "sift" sounds to get your homework done. If you prefer, tell how one of the following might need this skill: *astronaut, hunter, doctor, detective.* For help with the writing, see the Guides for Writing a Paragraph, page 214. Read the paragraphs in class.

3. Building Good TV, Radio, and Film Habits

INTRODUCTORY ACTIVITY

Suppose that a boy or a girl from some foreign country were to visit you for a month or so. Naturally you would want that visitor to get a good impression of you, your home, your home town, and your country. What radio, television, and film entertainment would you feel proud to offer?

Think about that question; then, on a sheet of paper, list the following:

1. Three radio or television programs (aside from news broadcasts) that you honestly think would be worth your visitor's attention.

2. Three motion pictures that you feel would give a true-to-life idea of America. (Many foreigners think that this country is made up largely of gangsters, juvenile delinquents, and Wild West outlaws.)

List only programs or films that you yourself have seen.

When they have been completed, have the lists read and then written on the board. Before talking them over, read carefully guide 4, page 33.

GUIDES FOR GOOD LISTENING AND VIEWING

1. See what newspaper critics say about motion pictures, television shows, and radio programs. These critics are likely to be more dependable than the advertising previews are.

2. Think critically about a program after you have heard it. Did it give you real pleasure or useful and interesting information; or did it leave you feeling let-down, discontented, bored?

3. Branch out; see what entertainment is being offered that you do not know about. Get variety into your listening and viewing.

LEARNING ACTIVITIES

A. Make a list on the board of the television and radio programs that members of the class follow regularly. Discuss the list in terms of variety or lack of variety. Call on students who listen to little-known programs to tell about them.

B. In small groups discuss motion pictures that members have attended. Use guides 3 and 4 of the Guides for Holding Discussions, page 33. Make a group list of the reasons given for liking some films and disliking others. Be sure to write the reasons in complete sentences; see the facts about sentence fragments on page 337. Choose one person from each group to read the lists to the class. How much agreement is there?

C. (1) Bring to class newspaper clippings reviewing television shows, radio programs, and motion pictures. For comparison, clip also the advertisements for the same shows or programs. Have the clippings mounted on the bulletin board. (2) Write a paragraph pointing out the differences between a critic's review and the advertisement. If you saw the performance, tell whether you agree with the advertisement or the critic. (3) Check your work by the Guides for Writing a Paragraph, page 214. *Proofread your paragraph for errors in capitalization, punctuation, and spelling.* (4) Exchange paragraphs for criticism.

ENRICHMENT

See whether you can find in the library the results of surveys made to determine the most popular radio and television programs during the past year. Try the *World Almanac* and the *Readers' Guide.* (See page 123.) Your librarian will help you find the information. Compare the top programs with the list of programs that you regularly listen to and watch.

TALKING WITH AND TO OTHER PEOPLE

1. Holding Discussions

"WE'RE GOING TO HAVE A ROUND-TABLE DISCUSSION. WHY NOT A SQUARE TABLE?"

THINK IT OVER ...

Can *you* answer the question? Is a table needed at all?
What *is* needed for a round-table discussion?

One of the best ways to practice good discussion habits is to have a round-table discussion. You do not need a round table, though. "Round-table" just means that the talking circulates about the group, and that everyone has a part in it. Sitting in a circle or around a table seems to help, probably because everyone has a chance to see everyone else as he speaks.

Although the words "conversation" and "discussion" are often used as if they mean the same thing, there are differences:

A *conversation* is usually just an exchange of information about people or events.

A *discussion* usually involves (1) a difference of opinion and (2) an attempt to solve a problem.

Many times, of course, a conversation will turn into a discussion.

GUIDES FOR HOLDING DISCUSSIONS

1. Select a topic.
   a) Be sure that it is of interest to the group.
   b) Choose a topic on which members of the group (1) have opinions and (2) can find information.

2. Choose one person to act as leader of the discussion. If you are the leader, follow these special guides:
   a) Call upon the various members of the group. (You may want to prepare a list of questions to ask them.)
   b) Keep the discussion moving.
   c) Hold the speakers to the point.
   d) Keep the discussion from becoming an angry argument.

3. Plan your part as a member of the group. Know what you will say and how you will say it.
   a) Jot down what you know about the topic.
   b) Look over your list and pick out the ideas that seem most important and most interesting.
   c) Arrange these ideas in the order in which you will speak of them. (The Guides for Outlining, page 99, will help you.)
   d) Do not memorize what you will say.

4. Have the discussion.
   a) Be a good listener. (See the guides on page 26.)
   b) When you talk, speak plainly so that everyone can understand your words.
   c) Speak up with your ideas, but do not take more than your share of the time.
   d) Be thoughtful.
      (1) Do not interrupt a speaker.
      (2) If you disagree, do so politely. For example, say, "John, I agree with you on most things, but . . ."

LEARNING ACTIVITIES IN HOLDING DISCUSSIONS

A. Divide the class into groups of seven or eight students. Have each small group get together in a corner of the classroom and, after choosing a leader, carry on a short round-table discussion on this topic: *How much control should parents have over the selection of television programs in the home?* After the discussions, the leaders will report the conclusions of their groups to the class. (Use the Guides to Speaking Clearly and Correctly, page 43.)

B. Let each small group plan, outside class, a ten-minute round-table discussion to carry on before the class. Use the guides both in planning and in holding your discussion. Choose one of the following topics, unless you can think of another one that you would rather use.

After each discussion, take two or three minutes for the audience to point out good and bad features.

1. How many school activities should seventh graders take part in?
2. Why do some people have trouble making friends?
3. How can we help students who are new in our class or our school?
4. What are the biggest problems in getting along with one's family?
5. What does it mean to be a "good sport"?

USING ENGLISH IN ALL CLASSES

A. Perhaps your social studies teacher will let you have a round-table discussion in his class on some topic of current interest or on one connected with whatever you are studying now. Plan the discussion carefully. Afterwards rate yourself and others by the Guides for Holding Discussions and also by the Guides to Good Listening, page 26.

B. Science class is another good place for a round-table discussion if the teacher is willing. Plan it according to the Guides for Holding Discussions. Afterwards, talk over in English class and rate this discussion. Be sure to point out good features as well as poor ones.

FOLLOW-UP

If you really want to make sure that you are a good citizen in class or group discussions, keep a record in your notebook of how you rate yourself on the items in point 4 of the Guides for Holding Discussions, page 33. Grade your performance, using marks such as *A, B, C, D.* Try to check yourself once a week on a discussion in one of your classes or in one held outside school.

2. Building Good Conversation Habits

READ AND THINK ABOUT

Have you ever had a cold so bad that you lost your voice for a while? If so, you cannot have forgotten how hard on you it was to be able to speak only in a whisper. Why? The reason is that talking is the best way that you have of expressing yourself to other people, the best way of getting acquainted with them.

You cannot tell just by looking at a person that he enjoys swimming or has a Polaroid camera or has been to Hawaii or builds model airplanes. But through talking, you may learn all those bits of information and many others that will make you want to know him better. You may find out, too, that a person who had made a poor first impression on you really is very much worth knowing.

GUIDES FOR CARRYING ON CONVERSATIONS

1. Never say things that might hurt or embarrass people around you.

2. If you disagree with something that is said, do so courteously.

3. Be patient; that is, do not interrupt a speaker. If you do not understand something that is said, wait until the speaker has finished and then ask a courteous question.

4. Include everyone in the group in your conversation. Look at each person in your group, not at just one or two of them.

5. Ask questions that will bring out the special interests of the others in your group; they may not care very much about *you* as a topic.

Learn about words!

The following words, taken from *A* of the Learning Activities, have interesting histories. Use your dictionary to find the story behind each word. With which word is the drawing connected?

aunt   plan   ukulele   walk

LEARNING ACTIVITIES IN CONVERSATIONS

A. Among the worst conversation habits you can have is that of being thoughtless of other people. Read silently and then dramatize the following three conversations.

Conversation 1:

SUE: Mary and I went on a three-mile hike out in the country this morning.

JENNIE: Where did you go?

MARY: We went to Hipple's Grove.

JENNIE: To Hipple's Grove? Well, then you didn't walk three miles. Don't you know that Hipple's Grove is just one mile west of the schoolhouse corner? I thought everyone knew that.

MARY: Yes, we know it.

JENNIE: Well, then you walked only *two* miles, one out and one back.

SUE: But we didn't start from the schoolhouse corner; we started and finished at Mary's house. That's a half mile east of the schoolhouse.

JENNIE: Oh!

Conversation 2:

JACK: Did you see the ball game yesterday afternoon?

RAY: Yes, I went with Dick and Fred. That pitcher for Salem was really good. He's the best pitcher I've ever seen.

JACK: You thought Simmons was good? I guess you haven't seen many real ball games. Why, he's terrible! He doesn't even have a good curve ball. Anybody should be able to tell that!

Conversation 3:

(*The place is the school playground on Friday morning. The characters are Jean, Alice, Marie, Helen, Ruth, Evelyn, Martha, Anne.*)

JEAN: Don't forget our plan for tomorrow, Alice. You and Marie and Helen come over to my house about ten, and we'll start from there.

ALICE: I hope it's cool. I'd like to wear the new red jacket my aunt sent me.

MARIE: If you wear your jacket, I think I'll wear my red sweater.

HELEN: Mother said she'd make some bread-and-butter sandwiches, and then we can buy some wieners.

RUTH: Are you girls going on a hike?

JEAN: I'll bring my ukulele, and don't you forget to bring your camera, Alice. Maybe we can take some pictures.

ALICE: I won't forget it. Come on; there's the bell .

B. Think about the following questions. Then discuss your answers in class. Be sure to keep in mind point 4 of the Guides for Holding Discussions, page 33.

1. In the first conversation, how does Jennie impress you? In what way is she thoughtless? How could Jennie have disagreed about the distance and yet done so courteously?

2. In the second conversation, what do you think of Jack? What is thoughtless in his remarks? How could Jack have shown courteously that he did not agree with Ray's opinion of the pitcher?

3. In the third conversation, what is thoughtless on the part of Jean, Alice, and Marie? Why do you suppose that Evelyn, Martha, and Anne kept still? (*Clue:* What happened to Ruth?)

C. Act out the conversations again, only change them so that the *thoughtless talkers* become *thoughtful talkers*. They may still disagree or doubt what is being said, but they will do so courteously.

D. Discuss the following questions in class. Be careful to apply point 4 of the Guides for Holding Discussions on page 33.

1. Why do you think that people often are less considerate when they are talking with their families than when talking with friends? Are they justified? If not, what can be done to improve the situation?

2. Do you ever have trouble in finding something to talk about to certain people? Why? What do you think you can do to get over that trouble?

E. Separate the class into small groups and hold conversations in which you compare your experiences in connection with one or more of the following topics. Keep in mind the Guides for Carrying On Conversations.

Picnics	Playing Badminton	Earning Money
Visits	Fourth of July Parade	Nicknames
Camping	Working on a Farm	New Classmates
Trips	Differences in Schools	Pets
Brothers	Mispronunciations of Names	Vacations
Sisters	Likes and Dislikes	Company

FOLLOW-UP

Think about the conversations that you have had today, at home or at school. Rate yourself as *good, fair,* or *poor* on each of the Guides for Carrying On Conversations. Write in your notebook any that you need to work on; then concentrate on those points. From time to time, rate yourself again to see whether you are improving.

3. Facing an Audience Alone

Only one of the above speakers illustrates good posture. Which one is it?

Which speakers are doing things that probably would keep an audience from paying close attention to what they are saying?

The human mind and body work closely together. If either one is not under control, the other is affected. A speaker who has not learned to feel "at home" before an audience cannot keep his mind on what he is saying. What is more, he cannot expect his audience to pay much attention to his words.

Feeling at ease as a speaker—being poised—is something that can be learned. The following activities provide help toward that goal.

LEARNING ACTIVITIES IN FACING AN AUDIENCE ALONE

A. (1) When the teacher has called your name, or when you have volunteered for your turn, walk to the front of the room at an ordinary rate of speed. If you sit near the front of the room, walk to the back of the room first and then to the front of the room, going down one aisle and up the next. (2) When you get to the front of the room, turn to face the audience, but do not say anything. (3) Stand there for one minute and look at the different people in the audience. Your teacher or someone else will tell you when the minute is up. Giggling will indicate that you do not have control over your mind and body. (4) Then, still taking your time, walk back to your seat. (5) After you sit down, list on a piece of paper as many things as you can remember noticing as you stood looking at the class. Do not look around; write from memory. Jot down such things as who had a red ribbon in her hair, how many people were wearing glasses, and so on. Write until the next person has reached the front of the room. Then stop at once. Turn your paper face down. (6) After everyone has had his turn, compare your lists in class.

B. Repeat activity A, only add to it. As you turn to face the audience this time, follow these additional instructions: (1) Let your hands drop easily to your sides. Do not put them behind you, or people may think either that you have something hidden in them or that they need washing. (2) Stand with one foot slightly ahead of the other, and at a slight angle to it, like this:

Standing in this way will mean that your weight is evenly distributed so that you will not seesaw from side to side. Do not get behind or near furniture; there is too much temptation to use it for support. Do not lean against the wall or the blackboard; leaning makes you look frightened and unsure of yourself. (3) When you are standing according to those directions, take a good look at the audience. Looking at them will also give the audience a chance to get a good look at you.

C. Repeat *B,* only this time let yourself be an "answer man." As you stand before your classmates, let them ask you three or four questions about yourself. Each person who wishes to ask a question will raise his hand, and you will call upon anyone you choose, one after the other. Keep the following points in mind.

1. People who do not know you very well will probably ask the best questions, since they really will want to learn things about you that your best friends already know. Those friends will co-operate by keeping their hands down while you are the speaker.

2. The audience should not ask questions to which they already know the answers.

3. The questions should be of the sort that you can answer at once, without having to stop to think: *when your birthday is, how old you are, how many brothers and sisters you have, who your nearest neighbors are, what pets you have, what your hobby is* . . . In other words, they should be *fact* questions about you and your family.

4. In asking questions, be sure that you never ask any that you yourself would not like to answer. (In other words, be courteous and kind.)

5. Include the question in your reply. Do not say, "Jack Allen Smith." Say, "My full name is Jack Allen Smith."

After you have answered the questions, return to your seat. Take your time. Be careful not to start for your seat until you have finished speaking.

D. Actions help to make clear or more definite what a speaker is saying. Demonstrate that fact by showing what facial expressions and actions would fit the following lines. *Do not say the lines;* let the class decide which ones you are illustrating. Which line fits the drawing?

1. Please, won't you help me?
2. Hey! Come on back!
3. What is that up there?
4. Hello there! I'm delighted to see you.
5. How do you like my new dress?
6. Now, see here, young man! You listen to me!
7. What a mess this is!
8. I don't want anything to do with it!
9. Boy! Am I tired!
10. Who? You mean *me?*

ENRICHMENT

In old magazines find pictures to illustrate five or more of the lines in activity D. Mount these pictures and under each of them write the line that applies. Perhaps your work can be displayed on the bulletin board.

4. Using Your Voice Well

MAKING YOUR OWN VOICE PLEASING AND EFFECTIVE

TALK IT OVER...

In class or in your small groups, discuss this question: "If you could trade your speaking voice for that of some radio or television performer, whose voice would you choose, and why?" Keep in mind that this would be the voice that you would have to use *all the time,* not just for a few minutes before an audience. In your discussion, be sure to apply guides 3 and 4, page 33. List on the board the different reasons given for liking certain voices. What conclusions can you draw?

One of the best things about the human voice is that it is *flexible.* In other words, it can go up and down; it can shift from loud to soft, and from fast to slow; it can vary in tone so that it shows the speaker's feelings.

GUIDES TO A PLEASING, EFFECTIVE VOICE

1. Really open your mouth so that full, round tones can come out. (Your music teacher can help you.)

2. Avoid shrill, high-pitched tones. They are easily heard, but they are hard on the listener.

3. Avoid hoarse, harsh tones. They, too, bother the listener.

4. Vary your tone, emphasis, loudness, and speed in whatever ways will (*a*) make your meaning clear and (*b*) have on your listeners the effect that you want.

LEARNING ACTIVITIES

A. (*This exercise may be done at home.*) If your school does not have a recording machine, test the sound of your voice in this way: (1) Stand facing into a corner of a room, with your hands cupped behind your ears. (2) Speak a few words, perhaps your name, age, grade, and address. The way that your voice sounds to you will then be much the way that it sounds to other people. What you hear may surprise you. (3) If you do not like what you hear, try speaking in different tones.

B. Here are some sentences that make different impressions, depending upon how the lines are spoken. Take turns reading the sentences to indicate the feelings suggested in parentheses. (Do not tell your listeners which feeling you have in mind; let them decide.)

1. Don't leave. (*anger, fear, worry, sarcasm, sympathy*)
2. He turned out to be a fine friend. (*satisfaction, disgust, surprise*)
3. I wouldn't say that. (*indignation, worry, embarrassment, sarcasm*)
4. There they go. (*fear, envy, surprise, relief*)
5. He didn't believe a word I said. (*surprise, indignation, anger*)
6. She's my best friend. (*sarcasm, pride, satisfaction*)
7. I wonder what he meant. (*worry, puzzlement*)

C. Notice this sentence: *Give me that red apple.* By emphasizing a different word each time, say that sentence to give the following ideas:

1. I haven't the money to pay for it.
2. Don't give it to anyone else.
3. I want that one, not the one next to it.
4. I don't want the yellow one.
5. I'm not interested in the plums.

ENRICHMENT

In your reading or literature book, find a short poem or paragraph to read aloud to the class. Practice beforehand several times so that your delivery will show you know and understand the Guides to a Pleasing and Effective Voice, page 41. If you choose a poem, the guides on page 46 may be helpful.

USING ENGLISH OUTSIDE SCHOOL

If you would like to improve the sound and range of your voice, practice much at home. Try saying the notes of the scale up and down, as high and as low as you can go without straining your voice. Repeat, using the words of a sentence, such as "I want to see what I can do." Listen to radio or television voices that you think are especially pleasing; practice imitating them.

SAYING WORDS CLEARLY AND CORRECTLY

"TRY IT AGAIN!"

"I SAID, 'SLEEP SHOULDN'T SHEEP IN A SHACK: SEEP SHOULD SHEEP IN A SHED.'"

READ AND DO

Do *you* know the troublesome tongue twister? If so, write it on the blackboard.

How good are your own speech habits? Test your enunciation; that is, the clearness or distinctness with which you pronounce words. To do so, try repeating quickly several times the above tongue twister or one of the following:

> A big black dog bit a big black bear.
> Two tall boys bought two toy boats.

You will discover that the faster you say the words, the more mistakes you make.

GUIDES TO SPEAKING CLEARLY AND CORRECTLY

1. Use tongue, lips, and teeth to make your words come out plainly. Lazy lips turn "didn't you" into "dincha" and "want to" into "wanna," for example. (Only a ventriloquist should speak with his mouth nearly closed.)

2. Breathe regularly and smoothly. Take a breath when you pause for punctuation.

3. Do not let your voice fade at the end of a sentence.

4. Finish one word before you begin the next, or your listeners may misunderstand you. For instance, you may think that you are saying, "He works on an iceboat," but your listener may hear this: "He works on a nice boat."

5. Be careful to pronounce words correctly. Make the dictionary your right-hand helper in checking and improving your pronunciation. (Pages 109–118 tell you how to use the dictionary.)

Learn about words!

The following words, taken from *D* of the Learning Activities, have interesting histories. Use your dictionary to find the story behind each word. With which word is the drawing connected?

rage   polite   worry   charge

LEARNING ACTIVITIES IN SAYING WORDS CLEARLY AND CORRECTLY

A. Careless speech is especially noticeable when a word that ends in *d* or *t* comes just before "you" or "your." (1) With a partner, practice the following combinations until you are sure that you are speaking each word separately. (2) Take turns in class at giving oral sentences containing these words.

didn't you	(not *didncha* or *didnchoo*)
can't you	(not *cuncha* or *canchoo*)
won't you	(not *woncha* or *wonchoo*)
don't you	(not *doncha* or *donchoo*)
did you	(not *dija* or *dijoo*)
had you	(not *haja* or *hajoo*)
told you	(not *tolja* or *toljoo*)

B. Many little words are mispronounced because of a wrong vowel sound. The nine numbered words below are such words. (1) Practice pronouncing them in unison. (2) Take turns at reading the sentences that follow the words. (3) Make, and then practice saying, sentences of your own, using at least three of the words in each sentence.

	Rhyme	*Not a Rhyme*
1. can	ran	tin
2. catch	match	stretch
3. for	war	her
4. get	let	hit
5. just	must	best *or* list
6. meant	bent	hint
7. such	much	rich *or* stretch
8. when	den	chin
9. our	power	car

(*Practice sentences*)

1. *Can* you *catch just* one game *for our* team?
2. *Such* a plan would have *meant* that we could *get* there *when* you did.

C. In your literature book or in a library book, find a short sentence (one of about ten words) that has several words ending in *d, g* (but not *ing*), *k,* or *t* sounds. When you are called upon, go to the front of the room, turn your back to the class, and read your sentence in your ordinary speaking voice. If persons at the back of the room can repeat the sentence exactly, you are speaking fairly plainly.

D. If the italicized words in the following sentences are not separated clearly, what might the listener think the speaker is saying? Take turns at reading the sentences. Your listeners will tell whether they think that your reading might be misunderstood.

EXAMPLE: Ted has *a name* like mine. (Ted has *an aim* like mine.)

1. I have *a notion* of my own.
2. *Her rage* really surprised me, but I tried to be polite.
3. I'd worry if I had to live in *an icehouse.*
4. *Our rally* is open to the public, free of charge.
5. Would you like to trade *your ache* for a different one?
6. *What all* people need is friendship.
7. May I have *some more?*
8. I have *an arrowhead.*
9. My name is *Ellen Elson.*
10. I should like you to meet *Stan LeRoy.*

E. (1) Read aloud and as fast as you can this "poem." (2) Perhaps you know where you can find other tongue twisters. (3) Bring them to class; recite them; then give them to someone else to read.

Betty Batter bought some butter.
"But," she said, "this butter's bitter.
If I put it in my batter,
It will make my batter bitter."
So she bought some better butter,
And she put the better butter in the bitter batter,
And made the bitter batter better.

ENRICHMENT

Write a tongue twister of your own. Your teacher may let you put it on the board for class practice.

5. Enjoying Choral Reading

INTRODUCTORY ACTIVITY

If you are lucky, you have already had fun with *choral reading;* that is, you have read poetry aloud as a class or in smaller groups. In that case, you know that poetry can do many things for you. A poem may hold you breathless with excitement as it tells an action-filled story. It may sing a song that keeps repeating itself in your mind. Sometimes, as in the old, old poem that follows, the aim is merely to tickle your funnybone. Read the poem together as marked, applying the italicized directions at the right.

WHISTLE, WHISTLE

Boys
Whistle, whistle, old wife,
  And you'll get a hen.

[*Speak in coaxing tones.*]

Girls
I wouldn't whistle, thank you, sir,
  If you could give me ten!

[*Toss heads scornfully.*]

Boys
Whistle, whistle, old wife,
  And you'll get a coo.*

[*Draw out* "whistle." *Let the sound show the meaning.*]

＊ coo: cow.

Girls
I wouldn't whistle, thank you, sir,   [*Speak still more scornfully.*]
   If you could give me two.

Boys
Whistle, whistle, old wife,   [*Speak slowly and importantly.*]
   And you'll get a gown.

Girls
I wouldn't whistle, thank you, sir,   [*Keep scornful tones.*]
   For the best one in town.

Boys
Whistle, whistle, old wife,   [*Pause importantly before
   And you'll get—a man!*   "a man."]

Girls
Wheeple, whauple, thank you, sir!   [*Try to whistle the first two
   I'll whistle if I can!*   words. Speak very eagerly.*]

   You can have fun reading poems together even if doing so is
new to you. Following the simple guides below will help you to
get real satisfaction out of reading together.

GUIDES FOR CHORAL READING

1. Talk over what you think the basic mood of the poem is.

2. Break a poem into as many group and solo parts as will help you
   to express it well.

3. Let your voices show the mood of the poem.
   a) Speak sad, gloomy, or serious lines, as a rule, in low-pitched
      tones and at a slow rate.
   b) Speak light, amusing, or exciting lines with a higher pitch
      and at a faster rate.

4. Speak clearly; do not run words together.

5. Practice.
   a) Make sure that each solo or group comes in on time.
   b) Work to get the "feel" of the poem. If you do, it will show in
      your voices.

A. (1) Divide the class into two equal groups. (2) In each group, study the following picture poem to get the "feel" of it. (3) Assign the solo parts and practice reading the poem, following the suggestions at the right of the lines. (4) Listen carefully as the other group reads. (5) Discuss the performances critically but courteously. (See guide 4 on page 33.)

FIVE EYES*

Walter de la Mare

Boys
In Hans' old mill his three black cats   [*Slowly. Low pitch,*
Watch the bins for the thieving rats.   *all one tone.*]

Girls
Whisker and claw, they crouch in the night,   [*High and fast.*]
Their fire eyes smouldering green and bright: [*Draw out "green."*]

Solo Girl 1   *Solo Girl 2*
Squeaks from the flour sacks,   squeaks from where   [*High, quick voices.*]

Boys
The cold wind stirs on the empty stair,   [*Slow and deep.*]

Girls
Squeaking and scampering, everywhere.   [*High and fast.*]

Solo Boy 1   *Solo Boy 2*
Then down they pounce,   now in, now out,

Girls
At whisking tail, and sniffing snout;

Boys
While lean old Hans he snores away   [*Draw out "snores."*]

Girls
Till peep of light at break of day;   [*High and soft.*]

Boys
Then up he climbs to his creaking mill,   [*Make it "creak."*]

Girls
Out come his cats all grey with meal—   [*Quickly.*]

Solo Boy 1   Solo Boy 2   Solo Girl 3
Jekkel,   and Jessup,   and one-eyed Jill.   [*Pause between solos.*]

*"Five Eyes" from *Peacock Pie: A Book of Rhymes* by Walter de la Mare. Published by Constable and Company Ltd., 1921, London. Reprinted by permission of The Literary Trustees of Walter de la Mare, and The Society of Authors as their representative, London.

B. Here is a good "mood" poem. As you read it, your hearers should feel the depth and the mystery of a great river. Read it as marked. Practice until you can say it from memory.

TIDE IN THE RIVER *

Eleanor Farjeon

Boys
Tide in the river,   *[Make it deep and slow.]*
Tide in the river,
Tide in the river runs deep.

Girls
I saw a shiver   *[Say the first two lines*
Pass over the river   *lightly and quickly. Make*
As the tide turned in its sleep.   *the last line slow and soft.]*

C. Here is a merry tale that you may believe or not, just as you choose. It tells what happened to a woman who enjoyed washing and scrubbing (of all things!) so much that she would not stop, even on Easter Sunday. The famous Salem witches came sailing up the Hudson, saw her scrubbing away, and—but find out the story for yourselves. Read the poem silently first; then assign the parts and read it aloud.

TUBBY HOOK †

Arthur Guiterman

Girls
Mevrouw ‡ von Weber was brisk though fat;   *[High and quick.]*

Solo Girl 1   *Solo Girl 2*
She loved her neighbor,   she loved her cat,

Solo Girl 3   *Boys*
She loved her husband;   but, here's the rub—   *[Boys' voices slower*
Beyond all conscience she loved her tub!   *and lower.]*

Solo Boy 1
She rubbed and scrubbed with strange delight,   *[Faster.]*

Solo Boy 2
She rubbed and scrubbed from morn till night;   *[Still faster.]*

---

* "Tide in the River" from *Gypsy and Ginger* by Eleanor Farjeon; copyright 1920, 1948 by Eleanor Farjeon. Reprinted by permission of Harold Ober Associates Incorporated, New York.

† "Tubby Hook" from *Ballads of Old New York* by Arthur Guiterman; copyright 1920 by Harper & Brothers; copyright renewed 1943 by Vida Linda Guiterman. Reprinted by permission of Vida Linda Guiterman.

‡ **Mevrouw** (mev′rou): Mrs.

Boys
Her earthly hope
Was placed in soap;

[*Slowly.*]

Solo Girl 4
Her walls and chimneypiece fairly shone,

[*Quickly.*]

Solo Girl 5
Her skirts were starched till they stood alone!
By mop and duster and broom she swore.

Girls
She scrubbed the floor
Until she wore
The oak in channels from door to door.

[*Faster, little
by little.*]

Boys
The flood she reveled in never ebbed,

[*Slowing down.*]

Solo Boy 3
And hill to dale

[*Importantly.*]

Solo Boy 4
Retold the tale

Boys
That both her hands and feet were webbed!

[*Slow, solemn tones.*]

Girls
Now Hans, her husband, was mild and meek;
He let her scrub through the livelong week;

[*Meek, hopeless
tones.*]

Boys
But when the suds of her washboard churned
On Easter Sunday!—the earthworm turned.

[*Indignant voices.*]
[*Pause after* "Sunday."]

Solo Boy 5
"Nay, vrouw,"* quoth he,
"Let labor be!
This day when all the world's at feast
Thou'lt wash no more—in my house, at least!"

[*Angrily and quickly.*]

Girls
She stopped her toil at her lord's command.

Solo Girl 1
Without a sound
She flaunted round
And took her tub to the river strand,

[*Quickly and
indignantly.*]

---

* **vrouw** (vrou): wife.

Solo Boy 1
Where Hans, who followed in dark dismay,   [*Puzzled and*
    Could hear her vow,   *worried tone.*]
    His angry vrouw,

Solo Girl 2
"I'll wash and wash till Judgment Day!"   [*Defiantly.*]

Boys
Along a river that leaped in flame   [*Quickly.*]

Girls
The Sailing Witches of Salem came.

Boys
(They ride the waters, that evil crew,   [*Deeply and*
Whenever the Duyvil* hath work to do.)   *mysteriously.*]

Girls
And every witch in a washtub sat,   [*Slowly.*]

Boys
And every witch had a coal-black cat   [*Impressively.*]
That steered the course with a supple tail,

Solo Girl 3
    A shift for sail,   [*Faster.*]

Solo Girl 4
    A shell to bail,

Boys
A thread to reef when the wind blew strong,

Girls
A broom to whurry the bark along.

Boys
They hailed the vrouw on her spit † of sand;   [*Loudly.*]

Girls
She waved them back with a soapy hand.   [*Indignantly.*]

Solo Boy 2
Cried one whose face was a Chinese mask,   [*Quickly.*]

Solo Girl 5
"This dame is sworn to a goodly task!   [*High and shrill.*]
Come, friends that ride on the crested swell,
We'll charm the spot with a lasting spell

* **Duyvil** (dĭ′vəl): Devil.
† **spit:** long, narrow point of land.

That here she'll stay
And scour away,
And never rest till the Judgment Day!"

Girls

With cries to Satan and Beelzebub,*   [*High, quick tones.*]
They shaped the cape like an upturned tub!—

Boys

Beneath its dome and the shifting sands   [*Slowly and*
That busy vrouw at her washtub stands,   *importantly.*]

Solo Boy 3
While day and night   [*Quickly.*]

Solo Boy 4
She bends her might

Boys
To scrub the fur of a black cat white!   [*Slowing down.*]

Girls
When down the river the norther † scuds,   [*Quickly.*]
The waves are flecked with the rising suds.

Boys
When clouds roll black as a Dutchman's hat,   [*Gloomily.*]

Girls
You'll hear the wail of the injured cat!   [*Draw out* "wail."]

Solo Boy 5
So heed her fall,   [*Warningly.*]
Good housewives all,

All
And take this truth from a ragged song—   [*Slowly and*
That super-cleanliness *may* go wrong!   *solemnly.*]

D. Here is a longer poem, one that almost says itself. (1) Read the introduction; (2) read the poem silently; (3) assign parts; (4) practice reading the poem.

[*Sir Francis Drake was a great English fighter who defeated the Spanish in many sea battles during the early days of settlement in the New World. Drake was a pirate, but he loved England. When he lay dying, far away from home, he said to his men, "Take my drum to England. Hang it in Plymouth on the old sea wall. If England needs me, no matter when, strike that drum—*

*Satan and Beelzebub (bi el′zə bub): the Devil and his right-hand helper.
†norther: north wind.

51

and I'll come, living or dead!" More than two hundred years later, England was fighting for her life against the French. A new hero, Lord Horatio Nelson, with a shriveled arm and only one eye, came to England's rescue and won a great sea battle over the French. . . . Or WAS it really Lord Nelson?]

The Admiral's Ghost *

Alfred Noyes

Boys

I tell you a tale tonight
  Which a seaman told to me,
With eyes that gleamed in the lanthorn † light
  And a voice as low as the sea.

[*Softly, slowly, mysteriously.*]
[*Draw out "gleamed."*]

Girls

You could almost hear the stars
  Twinkling up in the sky,

[*Very softly; slowly.*]

Boys

And the old moon woke and moaned in the spars,
  And the same old waves went by,

[*Draw out "moaned."*]

Girls

Singing the same old song
  As ages and ages ago,

[*Slowly and smoothly.*]

Boys

While he froze my blood in that deepsea night
  With the things that he seemed to know.

[*Low; draw out "froze."*]

Girls

A bare foot pattered on deck;

[*Quickly.*]

Boys

Ropes creaked—then all grew still,
And he pointed his finger straight in my face
  And growled, as a sea dog will.

[*Pause after "creaked."*]

Solo 1

"Do 'ee know who Nelson was?
  That pore little shriveled form
With the patch on his eye and the pinned-up sleeve
  And a soul like a North Sea storm?

[*Half-whisper.*]

[*Strongly.*]

*Choral arrangement of "The Admiral's Ghost" adapted from Collected Poems in One Volume by Alfred Noyes; copyright 1906, copyright renewed 1934 by Alfred Noyes. Reprinted by permission of J. B. Lippincott Company, New York, and John Murray (Publishers) Ltd., London.
† **lanthorn:** old spelling of *lantern.*

52

Solo 2

"Ask of the Devonshire * men!
   They know, and they'll tell you true;
He wasn't the pore little chawed-up chap
   That Hardy † thought he knew.

[*Slowly and
seriously.*]

Solo 3

"He wasn't the man you think!
   His patch was a dern disguise!
For he knew that they'd find him out, d'you see,
   If they looked him in both his eyes.

[*Faster.*]
[*Mysteriously.*]

Solo 4

"He was twice as big as he seemed;
   But his clothes were cunningly made,
He'd both of his hairy arms all right!
   The sleeve was a trick of the trade.

[*Seriously.*]
[*Pause after
"made" and
"right."*]

Solo 5

"You've heard of sperrits, ‡ no doubt;
   Well, there's more in the matter than that!
But he wasn't the patch and he wasn't the sleeve,
   And he wasn't the lace cocked-hat.

[*Mysteriously
and very
seriously.*]

Girls

"*Nelson was just—a Ghost!*

[*Half-whisper.*]

Boys

You may laugh! But the Devonshire men
They knew that he'd come when England called,
   And they know that he'll come again.

[*Show that you
really believe
the lines.*]

---

* **Devonshire** (dev′ən shir): Sir Francis Drake's home was in that
part of England.
† **Hardy:** He was Nelson's flag-captain on the *Victory* in the Battle
of Trafalgar, the fight referred to in the introduction.
‡ **sperrits:** spirits; ghosts.

Solo 6

"I'll tell you the way it was   [*Confidentially.*]
   (For none of the landsmen know),
And to tell it right you must go a'starn
   Two hundred years or so.

. . . .

Solo 7

"The waves were lapping and slapping   [*Slowly and*
   The same as they are today;   *softly.*]
And Drake lay dying aboard his ship   [*Solemnly.*]
   In Nombre Dios Bay. *

Girls

"The scent of the foreign flowers   [*Softly and*
   Came floating all around;   *lightly.*]

Boys

'But I'd give my soul for the smell of the pitch,'   [*Emphatically.*]
   Says he, 'in Plymouth Sound. †

" 'What shall I do,' says he,   [*Seriously.*]
   'When the guns begin to roar,   [*Make them roar!*]
An' England wants me, and me not there   [*Anxiously.*]
   To shatter her foes once more?'

Solo 8

("You've heard what he said, maybe,   [*Quietly and*
   But I'll mark you the points again; ‡   *seriously.*]
For I want you to box your compass right
   And get my story plain.)

Boys

" 'You must take my drum,' he says,   [*Slowly and*
   'To the old sea wall at home;   *solemnly.*]
And if ever you strike that drum,' he says,   [*Faster; pause*
   'Why, strike me blind, I'll come!   *after* "blind."]

" 'If England needs me, dead   [*Do not drop*
   Or living, I'll rise that day!   *voices or pause*
I'll rise from the darkness under the sea   *after* "dead."]
   Ten thousand miles away.'   [*Draw it out.*]

Solo 9

"That's what he said; and he died;   [*Pause after*
   And his pirates, listenin' roun'   "said."]
With their crimson doublets and jewelled swords   [*Draw out* "crimson"
   That flashed as the sun went down,   *and* "jewelled."]

***Nombre Dios** (num'brə dyōs') **Bay:** bay on north coast of Panama.
†**Plymouth Sound:** Plymouth was Drake's home port.
‡**I'll mark you the points again:** I'll tell you again.

Solo 10

"They sewed him up in his shroud   *[Make the*
  With a round-shot top and toe,   *picture sharp*
To sink him under the salt sharp sea   *and clear.]*
  Where all good seamen go.

Boys

"They lowered him down in the deep   *[Slowly and*
  And there in the sunset light   *solemnly.]*
They boomed a broadside over his grave,   *[Make it* "boom."*]*
  As meaning to say 'Good night.'

Girls

"They sailed away in the dark   *[Softly.]*
  To the dear little isle they knew;

Boys

And they hung his drum by the old sea wall   *[Slowly and*
  The same as he told them to.   *seriously.]*

   .   .   .   .

Solo 11

"Two hundred years went by,   *[Draw it out.]*
  And the guns began to roar,   *[Make them roar.]*
And England was fighting hard for her life,
  As ever she fought of yore.

Girls

" 'It's only my dead that count,'   *[Seriously.]*
  She said, as she says today;
'It isn't the ships and it isn't the guns
  'Ull sweep Trafalgar's Bay.'*

Solo 12

"Do you guess who Nelson was?   *[Mysteriously;*
  You may laugh, but it's true as true!   *pause after the*
There was more in that pore little chawed-up chap   *first* "was."*]*
  Than ever his best friend knew.

Girls

"The foe was creepin' close   *[Softly and*
  In the dark to our white-cliffed isle;   *breathlessly.]*

Boys

They were ready to leap at England's throat,   *[Make them* "leap."*]*
  When—O, you may smile, you may smile;   *[Pause after* "when."*]*

---

*Trafalgar's (trə fal′gərz) Bay: off the southeast coast of Spain; the scene of the naval battle (1805) in which the British defeated the French and the Spanish fleets to make Britain ruler of the seas. Nelson met his death here.

Girls
"But—ask of the Devonshire men;   [*Mysteriously;*
   For they heard in the dead of night   *pause after* "But."]

Boys
The roll of a drum, and they saw *him* pass   [*Draw out* "roll."]
   On a ship all shining white.   [*Draw out* "shining."]

Solo 13
"He stretched out his dead cold face   [*Make it* "dead"
   And he sailed in the grand old way!   *and* "cold."]
The fishes had taken an eye and an arm,
   But he swept Trafalgar's Bay.

All
"Nelson—was Francis Drake!   [*Triumphantly;*
   O, what matters the uniform,   *long pause*
Or the patch on your eye or your pinned-up sleeve, *after* "Nelson."]
   If your soul's like a North Sea storm?"

FOLLOW-UP

Set aside at least part of one English or literature period a week for
enjoying poems through choral reading. Let a different committee be
responsible each week for choosing a selection and planning how it is to
be read. Use poems from your literature book or others that you find.
Here are the titles of some poems that are fun to do. The card catalogue
in the library (see page 128) will help you find these poems.

"The Mouse That Gnawed the Oak Tree Down" by Vachel Lindsay
"P. T. Barnum" by Rosemary and Stephen V. Benet
"The Microbe" by Hilaire Belloc
"Rhyme of Johnny Appleseed" by Nancy Byrd Turner
"The Sniffle" by Ogden Nash
"Casey at the Bat" by Ernest L. Thayer
"Matilda" by Hilaire Belloc

6. Reading Aloud

READ AND THINK ABOUT

Did you ever daydream about holding an audience spellbound?
Not everyone can be an audience spellbinder, but anyone who can
read to himself can learn to read aloud to others. The following
guides contain suggestions to help you become a better oral reader.

GUIDES FOR READING ALOUD

1. First read the material silently; be sure that you understand the meaning. Notice the punctuation marks, for they are clues to meaning. (They also indicate good places to catch your breath.)

2. Use the dictionary to check the pronunciation of any words that you are not sure of. Say them over until you *are* sure.

3. If possible, get a friend or a relative to hear you practice.

4. Except for some special purpose, read at a medium rate. You may read easy material faster than hard. Remember, though, that the faster you read, the more distinctly you must say each sound.

5. In reading to entertain—for instance, if you are reading to a little brother or sister—be as dramatic as you can.
   a) Look for words that are clues to the impression the author wants to make. Say those words in a way that will help to give the right effect.
      (1) Make the sound suggest the meaning. For example, let your voice suggest a growl when you say the word "growl."
      (2) Use a big, deep voice for "big" words like *huge, giant, shout;* use a little, high voice for "little" words like *tiny, wee, whisper.*
   b) Speak in a different voice for each character.
   c) Suit your speed to the mood. Speed up for exciting action; slow down for gloomy or peaceful scenes.

6. If you get "stuck," just stop—and then go on. Do not back up or say the same words over and over.

7. Hold the book or paper so that the audience can see your face as you read. Look at them, or they will feel that you are reading only to yourself.

LEARNING ACTIVITIES IN READING ALOUD

A. Here are some famous lines from literature. (1) Talk them over in class or in your small groups to decide what point the author is making. (2) Take turns reading the lines aloud. (3) Listen closely so that you can express an opinion about one another's performance and can offer suggestions for better bringing out the author's meaning. Remember to look first for what is good about a classmate's reading.

1. A cow is a very good animal in the field; but we turn her out of a garden.—SAMUEL JOHNSON
2. He that falls in love with himself will have no rivals.
   —BENJAMIN FRANKLIN
3. Live always in the best company when you read.—SYDNEY SMITH
4. He that wrongs his friend
   Wrongs himself more, . . .—ALFRED TENNYSON
5. A community is like a ship; everyone ought to be prepared to take the helm.—HENRIK IBSEN
6. The reward of a thing well done, is to have done it.
   —RALPH WALDO EMERSON
7. Nature has given us two ears but only one mouth.
   —BENJAMIN DISRAELI
8. Give what you have. To someone, it may be better than you dare to think.—HENRY WADSWORTH LONGFELLOW
9. Every man is the builder of a temple, called his body.
   —HENRY DAVID THOREAU
10. Any coward can fight a battle when he's sure of winning; but give me the man who has courage to fight when he's sure of losing.
    —GEORGE ELIOT
11. Parents are apt to be foreigners to their sons and daughters.
    —GEORGE WILLIAM CURTIS
12. Some people are so fond of ill-luck that they run half-way to meet it.—DOUGLAS JERROLD
13. What small potatoes we all are, compared with what we might be!
    —CHARLES DUDLEY WARNER
14. A sharp tongue is the only edge tool that grows keener with constant use.—WASHINGTON IRVING
15. A wrong-doer is often a man that has left something undone, not always he that has done something.—MARCUS AURELIUS

B. Examine the following paragraph from Robert Louis Stevenson's *Treasure Island.* (1) Look first for any unfamiliar words; find out what they mean. (2) Look for words that give clues to the impression that the author wants to give. (3) Note the punctuation; see how it helps you to get the meaning. (4) Decide which words or sentences should be spoken faster than the rest. (5) Take turns at reading the paragraph aloud.

> . . . I suddenly put my hand upon my mother's arm; for I had heard in the silent, frosty air a sound that brought my heart into my mouth—the tap-tapping of the blind man's stick upon the frozen road. It drew nearer and nearer, while we sat holding our breath. Then it struck sharp on the inn door, and then we could hear the handle being turned, and the bolt rattling as the wretched being tried to enter; and then there was a long time of silence . . . At last the tapping recommenced, and to our indescribable joy and gratitude, died slowly away . . .

C. All the paragraphs in this activity are taken from *Treasure Island*. Choose one paragraph and prepare to read it to the class. (1) By yourself study the paragraph, as the class did in *B*. (2) Practice at home until you can look often at your audience. (3) Read the paragraphs in class or in your small groups. (4) Talk over the various readings, naming their good points as well as ones that could be strengthened. (Keeping your eyes closed as you listen to the readings will help you to judge them well.)

1. I remember him as if it were yesterday, as he came plodding to the inn door, his sea chest following behind him in a hand-barrow; a tall, strong, heavy, nut-brown man; his tarry pigtail falling over the shoulders of his soiled blue coat; his hands ragged and scarred, with black, broken nails; and the saber cut across one cheek, a dirty, livid-white. I remember him looking round the cove and whistling to himself as he did so, and then breaking out in that old sea-song that he sang so often afterwards:

Fifteen men on the dead man's chest—
Yo-ho-ho, and a bottle of rum!

in a high, old tottering voice . . .

2. So things passed, until, the day after the funeral, and about three o'clock of a bitter, foggy, frosty afternoon, I was standing at the door for a moment, full of sad thoughts about my father, when I saw someone drawing slowly near along the road. He was plainly blind, for he tapped before him with a stick, and wore a great green shade over his eyes and nose; and he was hunched, as if with age or weakness, and wore a huge, old tattered sea cloak with a hood, that made him appear positively deformed. I never saw in my life a more dreadful-looking figure.

3. My heart was beating finely when my mother and I set forth in the cold night . . . A full moon was beginning to rise, and peered redly through the upper edges of the fog, and this increased our haste, for it was plain, before we came forth again, that all would be as bright as day, and our departure exposed to the eyes of any watchers. We slipped along the hedges, noiseless and swift, nor did we see or hear anything to increase our terrors, till, to our relief, the door of the "Admiral Benbow" had closed upon us.

4. In I got bodily into the apple barrel, and found there was scarce an apple left; but, sitting down there in the dark, what with the sound of the waters and rocking movement of the ship, I had either fallen asleep, or was on the point of doing so, when a heavy man sat down with rather a clash close by. The barrel shook as he leaned his shoulders against it, and I was just about to jump out when the man began to speak. It was Silver's voice, and, before I had heard a dozen words, I would not have shown myself

for all the world, but lay there, trembling, for from these dozen
words I understood that the lives of all the honest men on board
depended upon me alone.

D. Poetry is especially full of good "picture" words that suggest the
mood or feeling that the author wants to give. (1) Study the following
quotations from famous authors, noting especially the picture words.
(2) Take turns reading the lines. (3) Listen with closed eyes; be ready
to say what you think the reader feels are the picture words.

1. . . . and over them the sea-wind sang
    Shrill, chill, with flakes of foam.—ALFRED TENNYSON

2. The days were like hot coals; the very ground
    Was burned to ashes; . . .—HENRY WADSWORTH LONGFELLOW

3. We buried him darkly, at dead of night,
    The sods with our bayonets turning;
    By the struggling moonbeam's misty light,
    And the lantern dimly burning.—CHARLES WOLFE

4. There spread a cloud of dust along a plain;
    And underneath the cloud, or in it, raged
    A furious battle, and men yelled, and swords
    Shocked upon swords.—EDWARD SILL

5. Over the cobbles he clattered and clashed in the dark inn-yard,
    And he tapped with his whip on the shutters, but all was
    locked and barred.—ALFRED NOYES

6. Deep asleep, deep asleep,
    Deep asleep it lies,
    The still lake of Semmerwater
    Under the still skies.—WILLIAM WATSON

7. Strong gongs groaning as the guns boom far,
    Don John of Austria is going to the war, . . .
    —GILBERT KEITH CHESTERTON

ENRICHMENT

Begin a special section in your notebook in which you put lines of
poetry that make you see pictures or that appeal to you for their sound.
Reread them often—and soon they will be in your memory to stay.

USING ENGLISH IN ALL CLASSES

When you study at home, read aloud the hard points of any lesson.
Many times such reading will make the lessons easier to understand. In
addition, reading aloud will help you to remember.

7. Making and Using a Speech Chart

Make and file in your notebook a speech chart similar to the following one. Draw as many columns as your sheet of paper will allow. For the time being, you will be expected to score only the first seven points on the chart.

(Do not write in this book.)

Speech Chart

Name Date						
Speech Number	1	2	3	4	5	
1. Waited until audience was ready?						
2. Looked at the audience?						
3. Stood properly?						
4. Knew what to do with hands?						
5. Finished before starting to seat?						
6. Spoke in a pleasant voice?						
7. Spoke distinctly and not too fast?						
8. Used correct pronunciation?						
9. Had interesting material?						
10. Knew material well?						

RATING THE SPEAKER

Prepare a supply of slips of paper about 2½ x 3 inches. Keep them on hand for use as follows:

1. When a person gives a talk, write his name at the top of a slip.
2. Write on each slip the words and numbers shown on the left-hand sample on page 63.

3. When a speaker begins, put your pencil down and *listen*.

4. When he has finished, rate him on the slip.
    a) Use the following key: *G*—good; *F*—fair; *P*—poor. Remember, be as fair and accurate as you can. It does not help to mark a friend *good* when you know that he is poor.
    b) Jot down at the bottom of the slip any special comments.
    c) Sign your name or your initials at the foot of the slip. The right-hand example shows how a marked slip will look.

5. Pass the slips to the speaker when he has finished. He should not look at them, but should place them in a neat pile, face down on his desk.

Speaker _____		Speaker *Roger* _____	
1.	6.	1. G	6. P
2.	7.	2. G	7. P
3.	8.	3. F	8.
4.	9.	4. F	9.
5.	10.	5. G	10.
Comments:		Comments:	
		You are doing better at looking at the audience.	
			N.C.

MARKING AND USING YOUR SPEECH CHART

Your teacher will probably give you the last five minutes or so of the period for marking your Speech Chart.

1. Take the slips handed to you and go over them carefully

2. Use them as a guide in rating yourself on your own Speech Chart. For example, if you had ten *G*'s, eight *F*'s, and no *P*'s on one point, mark yourself *F+*.

3. When you next prepare a speech, choose and work on one point on which you received a low mark.

4. Next time, choose another weak point and work on that. Practice to master one weakness at a time.

Never compare your record with that of others. Always compare your score with your own past record, and work hard for improvement. If you are improving, you are doing well.

LEARNING ACTIVITIES IN USING THE SPEECH CHART

A. You will be given five minutes in which to plan a short talk about yourself. Jot down such things as your favorite color, foods, sports, hobbies, pets, and so on. At the end of the five minutes, you will be called upon to talk. Remember to take your time, to look at the audience, and to stand correctly. Go over the Guides to a Pleasing, Effective Voice, page 41.

Members of the audience should rate each speech by the first seven items on the Speech Chart, and then pass the slips of paper to the speaker. When you are given time, mark your Speech Chart. Notice where you need to improve.

B. Prepare a short talk on a book that you have read or a motion picture that you have seen recently. Work especially on some point that your Speech Chart shows you are weak in. Mark your chart again after this talk, as in *A*. In what ways have you improved? If you have not improved, do not be discouraged. You *can* improve if you keep trying.

SPEAKING IN LIFE SITUATIONS

1. Making Clear Explanations

Last Saturday a boy was out in the back yard showing a friend the willow whistle that he had just made. When asked how he had done it, he said, "Oh, it's easy. You just take a piece of green willow, cut a slot in one end of the stick, slide the bark off, deepen the slot, and slide the bark back on. That's all there is to it."

The following day the friend came back. He complained, "I can't make a whistle like yours. The bark keeps splitting."

The whistle maker said, "It's easy, but maybe I didn't give enough details. I'll try again and draw a few pictures.

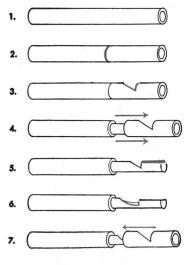

"(1) Cut a piece of green willow about five inches long and a half-inch thick. (2) With your knife, cut around the stick about two inches from one end. Cut just through the bark, no deeper. (3) Cut a slanting notch as shown in drawing 3 one inch from the same end. (4) With the handle of your knife, tap the bark lightly on the short end of the stick until you have loosened the bark enough to slide it off the stick all in one piece. (5) Slice a layer about an eighth of an inch thick from the short end to the notch, as in drawing 5. (6) Deepen the notch as shown in drawing 6. (7) Moisten the stick, slide the bark back on, and your whistle is ready."

In what ways is the second explanation more helpful than the first one?

Many times you will need to explain something orally. The suggestions in the guides that follow will aid you in making clear, concise explanations that will satisfy your listeners.

GUIDES FOR GIVING CLEAR ORAL EXPLANATIONS

1. Be sure that you yourself understand and see clearly the thing that you are trying to explain. If you do not have all the facts necessary for a clear explanation, find them.

2. Make an outline that includes *in the right order* every necessary step or detail. (See page 99 for help in outlining. A topic outline probably will be easiest to make and use.)

3. Put your explanation into words that your hearers can understand. Explain any words that you think may be puzzling.

4. As you give the explanation, follow your outline *exactly*.

5. Use drawings or charts wherever they will help.

6. In explaining orally, give listeners a chance to ask questions.

LEARNING ACTIVITIES IN MAKING EXPLANATIONS

Directions: Here are some exercises in making explanations. Activity **A** will test how well you can make explanations right now. The others offer practice in improving your ability to make explanations.

A. Below is a list of topics. You probably know something about most of them. Choose a topic and prepare to explain it at the end of ten minutes. Rate the explanations by the Speech Chart, page 61.

Explain how one of these is handled in your school. You may prefer to explain something else suggested by this list.

1. Absences and tardinesses
2. The school library
3. The grading system
4. Vacations and holidays
5. The seating arrangement of your classroom
6. The school band
7. The school patrol
8. Bells and buzzers
9. Gym classes
10. Clubs
11. The school paper
12. Fire drills
13. Assembly periods
14. The lunch hour
15. The playground

B. In an oral explanation, tell how to make one of the items listed below, or something suggested to you by the list. *Choose something that you actually have made*. Plan and practice the explanation at home. Make an outline to help you (see the Guides for Outlining, page 99). If possible, try the explanation on someone at home before you give it to the class. Apply the Guides to a Pleasing, Effective Voice, page 41, as you practice.

1. A neckerchief slide
2. An apron
3. Hand puppets
4. A birdhouse
5. A kite
6. A pocket telescope
7. A toy or puzzle
8. A knife sheath
9. A pair of stilts
10. An Indian tepee
11. A stencil design
12. A dog bed
13. A relief map
14. A rabbit pen
15. A crystal radio
16. A crossword puzzle

C. In your small groups, explain how to do one of the things listed or something suggested by the list. Be certain that you know what each step is and just how one step follows another. Make a topic outline to help you, using the Guides for Outlining, page 99. If possible, try your explanation first on someone at home. The listeners should rate the explanations by the Speech Chart, page 61.

1. Raising rabbits, chickens, pigeons, hamsters, . . .
2. Playing a certain game
3. Cleaning fish
4. Developing a roll of film
5. Earning merit badges in scouting
6. Repairing a bicycle tire
7. Blazing a trail
8. Teaching a dog tricks
9. Setting a dinner table
10. Tying different kinds of knots
11. Making a bed
12. Cooking with charcoal
13. Traveling in a Pullman
14. Building a campfire
15. Using a light meter
16. Preparing a seed bed

ENRICHMENT

Give an oral explanation of the important information from one of the graphs on page 205. Be sure to follow the guides for this lesson. Review, also, the Guides to Speaking Clearly and Correctly on page 43.

USING ENGLISH IN ALL CLASSES

If you must soon write an explanation of some problem or experiment in social studies, science, or arithmetic, let your English class help you to prepare a really good report. Use the Guides for Giving Clear Explanations, page 65. Practice the explanation in English class; ask your classmates to suggest improvements that you might make before you give it in your other class.

2. Giving Oral Directions

A special explanation that you often need to make is the kind in which you give directions for reaching a certain place. If you have ever been lost, you know how important good directions are.

GUIDES FOR GIVING ORAL DIRECTIONS ACCURATELY

1. Find out first of all whether the person has his directions straight. *North, south,* and so on will not mean a thing to him if he is turned around. Instead of telling such a person to turn *north* at a certain corner, tell him to turn *right* or *left,* as the case may be.

2. Begin the instructions from the spot where the person will start.

3. Take each step in order.

4. Mention any landmarks or buildings that will serve as guides.

5. Make a sketch if you can do so clearly and accurately.

6. When giving oral directions, ask the person to repeat the directions after you to see that he has understood them correctly.

7. Give directions only if sure of the way. If not, say so politely.

LEARNING ACTIVITIES IN GIVING DIRECTIONS

A. Think about the following questions. Find answers to them and be ready to discuss them in class.

Which of the two sets of the following directions would be easier to follow? Which set follows the guides above? Which guides does the other fail to follow? Be definite, and point out examples.

1. Our picnic will be in Turner's Woods. To get there from the schoolhouse, leave by the main door and drive to the right. The first stop street you will come to is Route 58. Turn left onto Route 58 and stay on it for about three miles, until you cross Salt Creek. A half mile farther on, you will reach a dirt road that goes to the right. This is not a crossroad. Take this dirt road for a half mile. The entrance to Turner's Woods is on the left side of the road and is marked.

2. Our picnic will be in Turner's Woods. To get there from the schoolhouse, drive toward Route 58. Stay on Route 58 for quite a while, going east. Oh, no, I mean *north.* At last you will come to a dirt road. Take this till you come to Turner's Woods. Oh, I forgot to tell you, you'll cross Salt Creek when you're on Route 58.

B. Divide the class into pairs and let each pair choose one of the places listed below. Have each member of the pair, working by himself, get ready to give directions to that place. Ask one member of the pair to leave the room while the other gives his directions. Then call in the second person to give his directions. The class will then discuss the two sets of directions in the light of the Guides for Giving Directions Accurately. Be critical but courteous; apply the points under guide 4, page 33.

1. The public library
2. A certain bank
3. The post office
4. A hospital
5. A nearby town
6. A neighboring farm
7. A certain church
8. The school nearest yours
9. The nearest filling station
10. Your own home
11. A park
12. The nearest doctor
13. The police station
14. A certain picnic spot
15. A bus or railway station
16. The nearest drugstore

3. Following Oral Instructions

"I THOUGHT I DID JUST WHAT MOM TOLD ME."

THINK IT OVER . . .

You have just spent some time in learning to *give* careful instructions and directions. It is just as important, and sometimes harder, to know how to *follow* instructions.

GUIDES FOR FOLLOWING ORAL INSTRUCTIONS

1. Be sure that you understand the purpose of the instructions.

2. Listen carefully. See guides 1 and 2 of the Guides for Listening to Learn, page 29.

3. Be sure that you understand exactly what you are to do, and how you are to do it. Ask questions if you do not understand.

4. Check every step to be sure that you did it correctly.

For one week keep a daily record for each piece of work that you are given instructions for doing. Put a star beside each one that you completed exactly according to instructions. Your list need not be detailed. Something like this should be enough:

> January 17
> *arithmetic assignment
> science experiment
> errand for Mother
> *gym exercises

Follow the same plan the next week. Then compare the two lists to see whether you have improved. If not, keep on with the plan. Bring your lists to class and compare them.

4. Using the Telephone

READ AND THINK ABOUT

Late one night Jim Reynolds, who lives in a small town, awoke to the sound of his mother's voice calling him faintly. When he went to her room, he found her moaning with pain. "Jim," she said, "it's my neuralgia again. Since Dad is out of town, you'll have to call Dr. Blake. Ask him whether he can come over. This pain is driving me wild."

Jim hurried to the telephone. He took time, however, to look up Dr. Blake's number; then he made his call.

JIM: (dialing) 623-4085

. . . .

DR. BLAKE: Dr. Blake speaking.

JIM: Dr. Blake, this is Jim Reynolds, Dale Reynolds's son. I'm sorry to call you so late at night, but Mother has a bad attack of neuralgia, and she'd like you to come over if you can.

DR. BLAKE: I'll be there in fifteen minutes.

JIM: Thank you, Doctor. I'll be waiting at the door for you. The porch light will be on. Good-by.

When he made that call, Jim showed that he had learned good telephone habits. Guides for building such habits are listed here. How well do you follow them?

GUIDES FOR TELEPHONING

1. Be sure that you give the right number to the operator. On a dial telephone, be careful to dial the right numbers. It is rude to make someone answer the telephone unnecessarily.

2. Speak clearly and slowly enough so that everything you say can be understood correctly. Keep your mouth about a half-inch from the mouthpiece.

3. Tell who you are.

4. Know beforehand exactly what you are going to say so that you will not waste time. Especially on a party line, keep calls short.

5. Be polite. Say "I'm sorry" and "Thank you" and "Please" and "You're welcome."

6. Be pleasant. Never lose your temper either with the person you are calling or with the operator.

7. Call at times that will be convenient for the person whom you are telephoning. Try not to interrupt his work, his sleep, or his meals.

8. When you answer the telephone and the call is for someone who is out or is unable to come to the telephone, say, "May I take a message?" Keep a pencil and a pad of paper near the telephone. After jotting down the information, repeat it to check whether you have taken the message accurately.

9. Turn down the radio or TV before using the telephone.

Telephoning is conversing. How to improve conversation skills is covered in section 2 of Chapter 3, pages 35–37. Summed up, the guides for telephoning would repeat what is emphasized in that section on conversing: "Be thoughtful of others."

LEARNING ACTIVITIES IN USING THE TELEPHONE

A. Read Jim's telephone conversation again. Which guides for telephoning did he follow? How can you tell? Which ones did he not follow? Did he have good reasons? Discuss those questions in class.

B. Plan a short explanatory talk on telephone manners. In your planning, review the Guides to Speaking Clearly and Correctly, page 43. Apply the Guides for Giving Clear Explanations, page 65.

C. Working in small groups, dramatize one or more of the following calls, or any others that you would like to practice. In each call, use three persons: the operator, the person calling, and the one being called. Each group should also be a committee to discuss the performance of one other group. The performers should be rated by the Guides to a Pleasing, Effective Voice, page 41, as well as by the Guides for Telephoning.

1. You are at home alone when a friend of your mother's calls to say that their club meeting has been postponed. She tells why the change has been made, when and where the meeting actually will take place, and the time at which she will call for your mother. She adds, "Tell your mother to call me this afternoon if she has any questions." Jot down the information as she gives it. Afterwards repeat the message to see whether you have forgotten anything.

2. Your family plans to drive to a near-by park for a picnic supper. Call a friend and invite him or her to go with you. Be ready to supply any information that your friend may need, such as when you are going, when you will return, what you plan to wear, . . .

3. Call someone to make arrangements for a class trip. Be sure to write down all the details so that you can report accurately.

4. Call one of the following to get or to give some necessary information. If you are calling for information, jot down before you call exactly what you want to ask. Take down what you are told so that there will be no chance for a mistake.

a) A dry cleaner or a laundry	*f*) Your dentist
b) A railway or bus station	*g*) Your doctor
c) A motion-picture theater	*h*) A newspaper office
d) The electric light company	*i*) A garage
e) A camera store	*j*) The zoo

ENRICHMENT

If you can, bring to class copies of any telephone directories. Notice their organization, the instructions for placing calls, and any other information given on the introductory pages. Read those pages carefully now, and then quiz one another until you are familiar with the help that they offer.

USING ENGLISH OUTSIDE SCHOOL

In class, work out a chart covering good telephone methods and manners. Make a copy for yourself. Fasten this above the telephone at home on a level with your eyes as you are telephoning. Seeing those points listed right there can help make good telephone manners a habit.

5. Introducing and Being Introduced

THINK IT OVER...

It is unnecessary to feel embarrassed when introducing people or being introduced, for the proper ways to make and to respond to introductions are simple. The following guides will help you to feel at ease in all introductory situations.

GUIDES FOR MAKING INTRODUCTIONS

1. Say *first* the name of the person you wish to honor.
   a) *Mother,* this is Shirley Smith. (*A young person is introduced to an older one.*)
   b) *Mr. Jones,* may I present Don Scott? (*This style is formal.*)
   c) *Miss Smith,* I'd like you to meet my father. (*A man is introduced to a woman.*)
   d) Jack, this is our new classmate, Ted Brown. Ted, this is Jack Evans. (*These two boys are about the same age; either name may come first.*)

   Notice that in *a* and *c,* the speaker need not give his mother's or father's last name, since it will be taken for granted that their name is the same as his. In *d* he must give both last names.

2. Say each name so plainly that there will be no excuse for anyone to say, "I'm sorry, but I didn't hear your name."

3. If you are being introduced, listen carefully for the other person's name. Try to use it in your conversation.

4. If you are introducing two people who will be expected to go on talking for a time, help them to get the conversation started.
   For example, in connection with *d* above, you might say, "Ted shares your hobby, Jack. Tell him about the model plane I saw you making last night, Ted."

5. When you are introduced, say, "How do you do." It is a good idea to add the person's name to show that you understood it correctly, as "How do you do, Mr. Blackmore." If you like, say, "I've been hoping to meet you," or something similar.

6. If you are a boy or a man, shake hands when you are introduced to another boy or man.

7. If you are a boy, rise for all introductions. (Girls need to rise only when they are introduced to older people.)

8. Never say, "Jane, meet Fred Smith," or "Jack, shake hands with Mary Brown," or "Pleased to meet you."

9. Never point to the people whom you are introducing.

A. In groups of three, dramatize the following introductions. In some of the introductions, have one of the persons seated.

1. Your father and a teacher (woman)
2. Your mother and a teacher (man)
3. Your cousin and your best friend
4. Your grandmother and one of your friends
5. A boy and a girl near your own age

The audience will judge each introduction. Did the people being introduced say and do the right things? Did the person who was making the introductions do so correctly? Be courteous and helpful.

B. If you feel that you need more practice, write possible introductions on slips of paper. Exchange these with your neighbors and make the introductions, choosing the people that you need to take the various parts. Perhaps you would have fun using the names of famous sports, radio, television, or film stars.

6. Holding Club Meetings

Well-run club or class meetings are likely to follow what are known as the rules of *parliamentary procedure*. Use the following section as a guide to help your class or club hold successful meetings.

Step 1

"The meeting will come to order. Will the secretary please read the minutes of the previous meeting."

"The Speakers Club held its weekly meeting on January 27, 1958, in room 37 of Willard Junior High School. The meeting was called to order at 10:05 A.M. by Gary Hill, president. The secretary, Susan Brown, read the minutes of the January 20 meeting. They were approved. Steve Bell, program committee chairman, reported that Captain Ames of the fire department would be unable to speak at our February 3 meeting, but would come on February 17. Sue Ellis moved that the club write a thank-you letter to Mr. Smith, Mildred's father, for his help with last week's program. The motion was carried. A committee of three—Sue Ellis, Jack Wilson, and Bob Brown—was appointed to write the letter. The program for the day was a choral-reading presentation of the poem 'The Height of the Ridiculous.' The meeting was adjourned at 10:45 A.M. Signed, Susan Brown, Secretary."

Step 3

"Are there any corrections to the minutes? . . . The minutes stand approved as read. Are there any committee reports? . . . If not, is there any old business? . . . Since there is no old business, we shall take up new business. Since this is the first Monday of the month, it is time to elect new officers. Nominations are now in order for president."

Step 4

"Mr. President."

"Helen."

"I nominate Sue Ellis."

"Sue Ellis has been nominated."

"Mr. President."

"Jack."

"I nominate Judy Higgins."

"Judy Higgins has been nominated."

Step 5

"Mr. President."

"Fred."

"I move that nominations be closed."

"I second the motion."

"It has been moved and seconded that nominations for president be closed. Those in favor say aye.... Those opposed say no....The motion is carried. The secretary will pass out slips of paper. Write on the paper the name of the person you want for president."

Step 6

"Sue Ellis has been elected president."

"Nominations are now in order for vice-president."

After the vice-president has been elected, a new secretary is elected. A new officer takes over his duties as soon as he is elected. The newly-elected president, Sue Ellis, took over as chairman of the meeting illustrated here. The new secretary, when elected, will take over the minutes from the past secretary.

GUIDES FOR ELECTING OFFICERS

1. Vote for a person because of his fitness for the job, not just because he is a good friend.

2. Choose a president who can carry out his duties well. Know what those duties are.
   a) To call the meeting to order
   b) To give all members an equal chance to talk
   c) To state motions and put them to a vote
   d) To vote only if his vote will make a tie or break a tie
   e) To appoint committees
   f) To keep out of the discussion

3. Since the vice-president takes charge when the president is absent, choose a vice-president who would make a good president.

4. Choose an efficient secretary, keeping in mind what his duties are.
   a) To take clear, exact notes of meetings, and to put those notes into clear, exact minutes
   b) To read the minutes at the beginning of the meeting
   c) To carry on club correspondence

5. Vote secretly by ballot.

   NOTE: A majority of all the votes cast is needed to elect an officer. **(DEFINITION) A majority is more than half of all the votes cast.** A candidate may receive more votes than anyone else but still may not have a majority. For example, suppose John has 16 votes; Tom, 10; and Phil, 7. John has more votes than anyone else, but he does not have over half the total number of votes cast (33). He would need 17 for a majority.

LEARNING ACTIVITIES IN HOLDING CLUB MEETINGS

A. Go over the following questions in class. On the board, write complete answers. To check, turn back to the drawings on pages 73–75.

1. When during the meeting does the president stand?
2. What is the correct order in which to take up *committee reports, old business, reading of minutes, new business?*
3. How does a person get permission to speak? How does the chairman give that permission?
4. Does a member stand, or sit, while making a nomination?
5. Are nominations seconded?
6. Does a member stand, or sit, to make a motion?
7. With what three words does a motion begin?
8. When does a member not need to get permission to speak?
9. How is voting for officers done?
10. How is voting on a motion done (in the sample meeting)?

B. Using your answers in *A* as a guide, plan and dramatize an election of officers for an imaginary club.

HOLDING CLUB MEETINGS—*Continued*

The sample meeting illustrated on pages *73–75* is continued here. The new officers have taken over the running of the meeting.

Step 7

"Is there any more new business?"

"Madam President."

"Wirdley."

"I move that we ask Mrs. Richard Aiken to show her movies of Europe at our next meeting."

"I second the motion."

"It has been moved and seconded that we ask Mrs. Richard Aiken to show her movies of Europe next week. Is there any discussion?"

The club members take turns at giving reasons for being for or against the motion. Then the chairman asks, "Are you ready for the question?" If someone calls out, "Question!" the chairman puts the motion to a vote. ("Question!" means "Let's vote on it.")

"Question!"

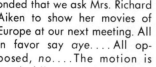

"It has been moved and seconded that we ask Mrs. Richard
Aiken to show her movies of
Europe at our next meeting. All
in favor say aye.... All opposed, no....The motion is
carried."

"Madam President."

"Karen."

"I move that the meeting be adjourned."

"I second the motion."

"It is moved and seconded that
the meeting be adjourned. All
in favor say aye.... All opposed, no....The meeting is
adjourned."

● **THESE ARE THE FACTS ABOUT CONDUCTING CLUB MEETINGS**

1. The chairman usually sits except when (*a*) calling the meeting to order and (*b*) stating the motion and calling for a vote.

2. As a rule, a member must rise and get permission to speak. He may, however, remain seated and speak without permission when he (*a*) seconds a motion or (*b*) calls for a vote by saying, "Question!"

3. A meeting should follow this order:
   a) Call to order
   b) Reading and approval of the minutes
   c) Committee reports
   d) Unfinished business
   e) New business
   f) Program (if any)
   g) Adjournment

4. The commonest method of voting is by saying "Aye" or "No." (*Aye* is pronounced "eye" and means "yes.")

LEARNING ACTIVITIES IN CARRYING ON CLUB WORK

A. Assign parts and dramatize the club meeting that is illustrated on pages 73–78. Be sure to rise and to sit at the right times.

B. (1) Write the minutes for the pictured club meeting. (2) *Proofread your paper for careless mistakes in capitalization, punctuation, spelling, and sentence sense.* (3) Compare your minutes in class. (4) Decide whether each set of minutes has included all the information needed.

C. Dramatize a meeting of your own in which at least six motions are made and voted on. Afterwards have the minutes read.

Reading

READING AND LEARNING

"I READ THE LESSON, BUT I DON'T REMEMBER A THING ABOUT IT!"

TALK IT OVER...

Is the student really inaccurate in saying that she "read" the lesson? In other words, should reading involve more than the eyes? If so, what else should she be using?

Is it important to be able to read? Teachers have told you that it is, ever since you entered the first grade. How well have they convinced you? If you still have doubts, consider the following facts.

If you did not know how to read, most street and highway signs would be a mystery to you. You could have no really personal mail, because someone else would have to read your letters to you. You could not look up anyone's telephone number. You would miss many good television and radio programs because you would be unable to read the schedules. You would miss the point in most cartoons, and even comic books would puzzle you. What other situations can you think of that call for the ability to read?

1. Reading for Different Purposes

Though you may never have thought about the matter, you read for different purposes.

1. Sometimes you read for fun—just to enjoy a story. This usually is *rapid reading*. It is likely to be easy for you.
2. Sometimes you do not read a whole page but just glance over it to find some definite piece of information. This kind of reading is called *skimming*. Here you focus your eyes only on certain words, dates, or numbers. For example, suppose you want to find out in what year Babe Ruth hit his greatest number of home runs. You do not read all that the encyclopedia tells about him; instead, you run your eye quickly down the page, stopping only when you see a date.
3. Sometimes you read to get *all* the information from a page. This is *careful reading* and will go much more slowly than the other two types. You need to do this kind of reading often when you study.

The suggestions in this chapter can help you to do your studying faster and to remember better what you study. If you use these suggestions regularly, you should find that you have more time for extra activities, and that your school grades are improving.

LEARNING ACTIVITIES IN READING FOR DIFFERENT PURPOSES

A. In an oral discussion, decide which kind of reading would probably be the chief type to use in each of the following cases. Be sure to apply guides 3 and 4 of the Guides for Holding Discussions, page 33.

1. Using a telephone directory
2. Carrying out a science experiment
3. Reading a mystery novel
4. Cutting out a dress
5. Making a list of important dates in a biography
6. Finding a word in the dictionary
7. Reading the comics
8. Preparing one's income tax statement
9. Using a new cookbook recipe
10. Reading magazine stories

B. Here is an activity to carry out in the class period. It will give you practice in skimming. Your teacher will allow you ten minutes only. (1) Number your paper from 1 to 10. (2) By skimming the indicated pages of this book, find and jot down the answers to the following questions. (3) Go over the questions orally. If you failed to find all or most of the answers, you need practice in skimming.

1. How many capital letters are there on page 106?
2. According to the Index, on what page are prepositions defined?
3. Skim the Table of Contents to learn the title of the tenth chapter of this book.
4. How many lines are there in the poem that begins on page 45?
5. In the Index, how many main entries are there between "Agreement" and "Auxiliary verbs"?
6. How many commas are there on page 81?
7. Which spelling rule on page 187 deals with words that end in *o*?
8. Which item on the Speech Chart, page 61, deals with the hands?
9. What book title is mentioned on page 58?
10. How many questions do you find on page 88?

2. Improving Reading Habits

Although you have been reading for years, you may have some bad habits that need correcting. How well do you follow each of the following guides?

GUIDES TO BETTER READING

1. Do not point to the words as you read. Pointing slows you down, because you read single words instead of groups of words.

2. Try to avoid moving your lips or your throat muscles.

3. Practice to increase the number of words that your eyes can see at a time.

4. Read with your mind as well as with your eyes; that is, think about the meaning of what your eyes see.

LEARNING ACTIVITY IN IMPROVING YOUR READING HABITS

Turn to a page in a book that you have not read before. Begin reading the page to yourself. Have a partner watch you as you read to see (1) whether at any time you point to words, (2) whether you tend to move your lips or throat muscles, (3) whether your eyes move rapidly or slowly, and (4) whether your eyes make many or few pauses per line.

After your partner has checked your reading habits, change places with him and watch him in the same manner.

FOLLOW-UP

If you have any of the bad habits mentioned in the Guides to Better Reading, you should begin at once to practice overcoming them. Be sure to check yourself as well as you can every time that you are reading. At home, ask your mother or someone else to check you, too. Moving the lips and pointing to words are crutches. Make up your mind that you will not be a reading cripple.

3. Getting the Central Thought

READ AND TALK ABOUT

The other day Miss Adams overheard two boys arguing about paragraphs. Here are a few of the things that they said. Which of their remarks are not true?

"A paragraph has to have at least three sentences."
"A paragraph should not have more than a hundred words."
"Paragraphs are there just to make reading look easier."
"Every paragraph has to have a topic sentence."

As a matter of fact, every one of those four remarks is untrue.

The boys need not have argued if they had learned the following things about paragraphs.

1. A paragraph is a unit of writing that is built around one main idea. That idea is the *central thought* of the paragraph. It often, but not always, is expressed in one sentence of the paragraph.

   (DEFINITION) Often, especially in explanations and descriptions, the central thought of a paragraph *is* stated in one sentence, called the *topic sentence,* or the *topic statement.*

2. Usually, as in the following paragraph, the topic sentence comes at the *beginning* of a paragraph. Note the details in the other sentences.

   In the meantime the seasons gradually rolled on. The little frogs that had piped in the meadows in early spring croaked as bullfrogs during the summer heat, and then sank into silence. The peach tree budded, blossomed, and bore its fruit. The swallows and martins came, twittered about the roof, built their nests, reared their young, and then winged their flight in search of another spring. The caterpillar spun its cocoon, dangled in it from the great buttonwood tree that shaded the house, turned into a moth, fluttered with the last sunshine of summer, and disappeared. Finally the leaves of the buttonwood tree turned yellow, then brown, then rustled one by one to the ground, and whirling about in little eddies of wind and dust, whispered that winter was at hand.*

3. Sometimes the topic sentence comes *last* in a paragraph. Notice that all other sentences in this example lead up to the topic sentence.

   On the moon there is no wind to wear the mountains away. There is no water to freeze in the cracks and break off big boulders. There are no plants to help break up the rock into soil. There are no rivers of ice to carve valleys in the sides of the mountains. *The mountains of the moon come close to being "everlasting hills."* †

4. Once in a while the topic sentence may be in the *middle* of a paragraph.

   A very common idea is that certain crops must be planted in the dark of the moon, while others must be planted in the full moon. *Scientists have not been able to find that the moon has anything to do with crops.* It makes no difference to plants whether the moon is shining or not.†

---

*From "Wolfert Webber, or Golden Dreams" from *Tales of a Traveller with Selections from The Sketch Book,* edited by George Philip Krapp, Ph.D.; copyright 1901 by Scott, Foresman and Company, Glenview, Illinois.

†Adapted from *The Earth's Nearest Neighbor* by Bertha Morris Parker; copyright © 1959, 1950, 1947, 1941 by Harper & Row, Publishers, Incorporated, Evanston, Illinois.

Learn about words!

The following words, taken from *A* of the Learning Activities, have interesting histories. Use your dictionary to find the story behind each word. With which word is the drawing connected?

country   trunk   area   calm

LEARNING ACTIVITIES

A. Volunteer to read any one of the following paragraphs aloud to the class. Reviewing the Guides for Reading Aloud, page 57, will help you. Decide for yourself what the topic sentence is. After a paragraph has been read, talk it over. Name the topic sentence and show how each sentence in the paragraph has a connection with it.

1. Members of an Indian family did not work all the time. Little girls played with dolls. Boys spun tops, flew kites, and enjoyed games of tag, hide-and-seek, and blindman's buff. Boys became expert swimmers and learned to throw a spear and shoot an arrow. They learned to imitate the call of birds and the cry of wild creatures that lived in the forest.*

2. Insects that are our friends do not deserve any credit for being helpful. Neither do insects that are our enemies deserve blame for harming us. Insects live their own lives, and in doing so, simply happen to interfere with us human beings. The cockroach that comes into our kitchens is not trying to take our food away from us—it is simply getting the food that it needs for itself. The honeybee that stores up honey is laying away food for its own use, and not for ours.†

3. When man began to cultivate the dry grasslands, he made conditions better for the grasshopper than they had been before. At the same time, he made conditions worse for such natural enemies of the grasshoppers as prairie foxes and many kinds of birds. He killed great numbers of them and disturbed the homes or nesting sites of others. If man had not upset the balance of nature by cultivating the dry grasslands, the grasshopper might never have become a serious pest.†

*Adapted from *The Old World* by Mabel Rockwood Grimm and Matilda Hughes; copyright © 1955, 1953, 1948 by Row, Peterson and Company, Evanston, Illinois.
†Adapted from *Insect Friends and Enemies* by Bertha Morris Parker and Robert E. Gregg; copyright © 1959, 1952, 1947, 1941 by Harper & Row, Publishers, Incorporated, Evanston, Illinois.

4. If the 1849 gold seeker did not go to California by sea, there were several land trails that might be taken. First, there was the trail to Oregon. This well-known trail led from Independence, Missouri, to the present state of Idaho. From there, the traveler could then turn southward to California. Another trail led from Independence to Santa Fe, crossed what are now New Mexico and Arizona, and entered southern California. Still other trails went through Texas to El Paso and crossed southern New Mexico and Arizona. All the trails crossed desert country and were difficult and dangerous. Before the end of 1849, these desert trails were marked by bleaching bones of horses and cattle that had died on the way.*

5. One calm summer evening an Illinois family was eating supper when a tornado struck the area suddenly. It lifted the roof and walls of the house away but did not disturb the supper table. In Arkansas a family sitting on the front porch of their house saw the house blow away while the porch stayed behind. In Minnesota a tornado blew a trunk full of clothes from one house to the attic of another house two blocks away. Whenever there are tornadoes, one will hear of strange and almost unbelievable results of these storms.†

6. The early English explorers alone could never have made America an English country. There was, though, a young Englishman who saw clearly what must be done. English men and women and children must make their homes in the land if it was ever to belong to England. This young gentleman, whose name was Sir Walter Raleigh, wanted to start a settlement in the New World. To do so, he needed the approval and help of Queen Elizabeth.‡

B. Choose a paragraph from one of your other schoolbooks and read it to the class. Look over the Guides for Reading Aloud, page 57, before doing the reading. Call on a classmate to tell what the central thought is and to give his reasons for thinking so. Use the Guides to Good Listening on page 26.

---

*Adapted from *The Story of Our Country* by Clarence L. Ver Steeg; text copyright © 1965 by Harper & Row, Publishers, Incorporated; pictures, maps, and diagrams copyright © 1965 by American Heritage Publishing Co., Inc.

†Adapted from *Ways of the Weather* by Bertha Morris Parker; copyright © 1957, 1952, 1947, 1941 by Row, Peterson and Company, Evanston, Illinois.

‡Adapted from *Our New Land* by Eugene C. Barker, Frances Cavanah, and Walter P. Webb; copyright © 1961, 1955, 1949, 1948 by Row, Peterson and Company, Evanston, Illinois.

4. Using Key Words as a Study Help

READ AND THINK ABOUT

What do *you* think the "key" words in a paragraph are?

You have been studying topic sentences, the sentences that tell you what a paragraph is about. Not every paragraph, however, has a topic sentence. Stories, for example, have many paragraphs without a sentence that states the central idea. In such a paragraph, you must figure out the central idea for yourself. To do so, you need to be able to find and use the *key words* in the paragraph.

What are key words? If you stop to think what a door key does, you can figure out what key words are. Keys unlock doors; key words unlock paragraph meaning. If you have those key words, you can get along without the rest of the words in the paragraph and still be able to know and tell the main information in it.

Read the following paragraph, paying special attention to the italicized words.

> In the summer of *1847*, Captain John Augustus *Sutter* decided to build a sawmill. He *hired* James Wilson *Marshall* to *build* a *mill* on the banks of the American River in *California*. The mill rose without incident until the next year, *1848*. One January evening, Marshall turned the water from the millpond into the tailrace to wash the channel free of loose dirt. In the morning, when he returned, his eye was caught by the gleam of *yellow metal* at the bottom of the clear *water*. When he pounded this soft metal, it flattened easily like *gold*.*

In the preceding paragraph, the words in italics might be called key words. They are *1847, Sutter, hired, Marshall, build, mill, California, 1848, yellow metal, water, gold.*

The paragraph has no topic sentence, but the key words suggest this central thought: "Gold was discovered in California in 1848." If you want to add a bit more than the central thought, the key words will even help you to recall important details:

> The discoverer, Marshall, built the mill for his employer, Captain Sutter, in 1847.

---

*Adapted from *The California Gold Rush* by the Editors of *American Heritage;* copyright © 1961 by American Heritage Publishing Co., Inc., New York.

The following guides will help you to review and remember the important information in lessons that you read.

GUIDES FOR USING KEY WORDS AS A STUDY HELP

FOR PARAGRAPHS WITHOUT TOPIC SENTENCES

1. Skim each sentence in a paragraph that has no topic sentence.
2. Jot down the most important words; that is, the *key words.*
3. Build a sentence that gives the central thought suggested by those words.
4. Go back over the paragraph to see whether your central thought is accurate.
5. Under the central thought write brief sentences giving any important details also suggested by the key words.

FOR PARAGRAPHS WITH TOPIC SENTENCES

1. Copy the topic sentence.
2. Jot down the other key words in the paragraph.
3. Build short sentences that give the important details suggested by those key words.

Learn about words!

The following words, taken from the guides above, have strange or interesting histories. Use your dictionary to find the story behind each word.

jot   skim   suggested   accurate

LEARNING ACTIVITIES IN USING KEY WORDS

A. The five paragraphs in this activity do not have topic sentences. (1) Find and jot down what you think are key words in each paragraph. (2) Write a topic sentence for each one, using as many of your key words as you need. (3) Write another sentence, giving main details suggested by the key words. (4) Compare work in class or in your small groups. Some key words you choose in a paragraph may differ, but each of you should express the same *idea* in your topic sentence for that paragraph.

1. Some of our states have state police systems. In those states the job of these officers is to hunt criminals who are roaming through the state. But most of our state governments depend upon city police and the county sheriffs to enforce the law. In the early days, when thieves went on foot and bandits rode on horseback, the local police could catch most criminals. But now, in the days of gangsters with high-speed motor cars, it is hard for the city police or the county sheriff to capture them. Modern aids in catching criminals are costly, too costly for small cities and rural counties. The state police can afford to have especially trained men and radio-equipped automobiles that cruise around and can get to the scene of a crime swiftly.*

2. On a frosty winter day in 1673, a lone rider galloped out of Manhattan to the ferry which took him across the Harlem River. He was loaded with leather packs. Travelers did not know that he was the first postman in the New World to follow a regular postal route. The lone rider had told no one that he was a personal messenger of Francis Lovelace, governor of the Colony of New York. Lovelace, finding it hard to keep in touch with the governors of other American Colonies, tried to overcome part of this difficulty by dispatching a rider on a regular monthly service to Boston. This service resulted in a closer understanding between the two colonies.†

3. In the tropics, there is very little change in the weather. On the other hand, in such regions as the western plains of the United States and Canada, the only thing certain about the weather is that it will be uncertain. The summers are often very hot, and the winter temperatures may go down to fifty or sixty degrees below zero. Some years there will be in these regions a fair amount of rain, but these may be followed by five or six years of drought.‡

4. The first houses in Plymouth were very quickly built and probably looked like the wigwams of the Indians. As soon as they could, the Pilgrims began to cut down trees and saw them into

---

*From *State Government* by Helen Hanford, Romance C. Koopman, Karyl Kanet Chipman; copyright 1941 by Row, Peterson and Company; copyright © 1968 renewed by Western Publishing Company, Inc., Racine, Wisconsin.

†Adapted from *Our Federal Government* by Benjamin Brodinsky; copyright 1941 by Row, Peterson and Company; copyright © renewed 1969 by Western Publishing Company, Inc., Racine, Wisconsin.

‡Adapted from *Balance in Nature* by Bertha Morris Parker and Ralph Buchsbaum; copyright © 1958, 1952, 1941 by Row, Peterson and Company, Evanston, Illinois.

beams and boards. They used these to build houses, the first of them just shacks. The roofs were made of brush and straw, and the floors of dirt. Solid shutters, without glass, formed the doors and windows. When they were closed, the only light came through the cracks.*

5. None of the houses of the Pilgrim settlers had bathrooms; in fact, none even had running water. Windows and doors were without screens, and in the summertime flies and mosquitoes swarmed everywhere. There were, of course, no gas stoves and no electricity. People lighted their houses with whale-oil lamps and pine knots, or with tallow candles that they made at home.*

B. (1) Reread each of the six paragraphs on pages 86–87. (2) Copy each topic sentence. (3) Under it, jot down the key words in the rest of the paragraph. (4) Build a sentence or more that states important details based upon these key words. (5) Compare work in class. Apply points 3 and 4 of the Guides for Holding Discussions, page 33.

C. (1) Read the first paragraph of "The Importance of Clear Thinking," page 94. As you read, jot down on a piece of paper the key words. (2) Close your book, and, using the key words, reconstruct the paragraph in your own words. (3) *Proofread your paragraph for careless mistakes in capitalization, punctuation, spelling, and sentence sense.* Use the Writing Chart, page 172. (4) Before reading your paragraphs in class, review the Guides for Reading Aloud, page 57.

ENRICHMENT

As would be expected, the list of key words in a paragraph will vary somewhat from student to student. Even though *most* conscientious students will include the same words, *some* students will include more words than are really necessary. Following is such an "overcomplete" list.

Using your imagination, write a paragraph suggested to you by these key words:

Winter ... 1777–78 ... Washington ... soldiers ... starved ... froze ... Valley Forge ... log huts ... little protection ... cold winds ... many ... rags ... uniforms ... worn out ... hundreds ... no shoes ... some ... wrapped ... rags ... others ... barefoot ... bloody footprints ... snow ... many ... sick ... died.

If two or more in the class do this assignment, your teacher may let you read your paragraphs aloud to show how they may differ in details. If so, prepare by practicing as suggested in guides 3–7, page 57.

---

*Adapted from *Our New Land* by Eugene C. Barker, Frances Cavanah, and Walter P. Webb; copyright © 1961, 1955, 1949, 1948 by
Row, Peterson and Company, Evanston, Illinois.

A. Here is an assignment that will test your reading ability and the listening skill of your audience. (1) In your social studies or history or geography book find a paragraph that has no topic sentence. (2) Read it to the class. (In preparing to read, be sure to apply guides 3–7 on page 57.) (3) Ask classmates to jot down what they think are the key words and the central thought. (4) When you have finished, call on someone to read his list of key words and his statement of the central thought. If there is disagreement, take time to go over the paragraph again. Apply guides 3 and 4 of the Guides for Holding Discussions, page 33.

B. If you have a reading assignment in some other class for tomorrow, try, as you read, to pick out the central thought in each paragraph. (If there is a topic sentence, copy that; if there is none, use key words to help you frame your own central thought.) This is a very good way to study a lesson. Jot these central thoughts down on paper to see whether they tell you the main points in the assignment.

If some of you have the same assignment, compare the central thoughts that you jotted down. If you do not agree, go over the paragraphs together to see whether you can reach an agreement.

5. Learning By Summarizing

"WELL, TO MAKE A LONG STORY SHORT..."

"NOW HE'S SUMMARIZING HIS SUMMARY."

THINK IT OVER...

What is a "summary"?
How would you go about making one?

Probably at one time or another, you, like the man in the drawing, have said, "To make a long story short . . ." That is exactly what a summary is: telling in a few words the most important points of a story or an article.

You have had practice in finding central thoughts and key words. Making a summary is based upon those two things—central ideas and key words. The guides that follow explain how to use them sensibly in summarizing material made up of several paragraphs.

GUIDES TO MAKING A SUMMARY

1. Pick out the main idea of each paragraph. Let topic sentences and key words help you.
2. Write each main idea in your own words, being as brief as possible.
3. Put all the main-idea sentences together in one paragraph.
4. Go back over your paragraph. Cut any words or ideas that are not important.

Learn about words!

The following words, taken from the Learning Activities, have interesting histories. Use your dictionary to find the story behind each word. With which word is the drawing connected?

boil   awards   rescue   patrol

LEARNING ACTIVITIES

A. Go over the following article, "The Importance of Clear Thinking," and its summary carefully. Then check the summary, using the Guides to Making a Summary. In class, decide (1) whether all the main ideas are included in the summary, (2) whether any unimportant ideas are included, and (3) whether the summary could be boiled down even more. In the article, paragraphs are numbered. In the summary, sentences are numbered to show which sentences come from which paragraphs.

1. A panther can run much faster than a man on foot. A lion can fight better than a man without a gun. A bird can fly by flapping its wings. But there is one big advantage that man has over these and all other known creatures: he has a superior brain.

2. With this superior brain he is able to organize complex sounds into meaningful speech to communicate ideas to other men. He can write and print these ideas on paper and transmit them to others. He can think about these ideas and put them together in different ways to obtain new information or to draw a conclusion about things he is unable to see, hear, or touch. In other words, he can *reason*.

3. Man's reasoning power, plus his ability to speak and to use his hands skillfully, has made it possible for him to invent automobiles that travel faster than any panther, airplanes that leave the fastest birds far behind, and cranes, derricks, and shovels that lift hundreds of times more weight than any animal.

4. Using his reasoning power, man has mastered the secrets of making many new foods, learned how to fashion clothes from newly created fibers, and developed ways of building giant bridges, skyscrapers, factories, homes, and many kinds of special structures for a variety of purposes. He has dug rock out of the earth and changed it into iron, aluminum, lead, copper, tin, and other metals. He has learned how to burn fuels in safe ways to heat his homes and drive his vehicles.

5. Reasoning power has made it possible to create our modern civilization, cure disease, and extend life. This same power has enabled man to fling vehicles out into space and to embark on the conquest of the difficult problems of surviving on inhospitable planets. He has devised complex instruments to probe the secrets of the atom. Then he has used these secrets to develop new ways of producing electricity, as well as to manufacture devastating nuclear weapons. Reasoning power will be needed to prevent the destruction these weapons can bring.*

SUMMARY OF "THE IMPORTANCE OF CLEAR THINKING"

(1) Man's big advantage over other creatures is his superior brain. (2) With his superior brain, man can reason. (3) Using his reasoning power, man can out-perform any animal. (4) With his reasoning power, man can create things and develop natural resources. (5) By means of his reasoning power, man has created modern civilization and the means to extend it or destroy it.

*From *Clear Thinking* by Hy Ruchlis; copyright © 1962 by Hyman Ruchlis. Harper & Row, Publishers, New York.

B. There is some needless repetition in the summary sentences for "The Importance of Clear Thinking," page 94. Condense the thoughts of the summary into three sentences, two sentences, or (possibly) one sentence. Study the summary sentences carefully first; do not omit necessary information.

C. (1) Divide the class into several discussion groups, with four or five people in each group.

(2) Read silently through the article below to get the general idea.

(3) Then in your small groups, read the article aloud. Check one another's reading by guides 4–7 of the Guides for Reading Aloud, page 57. For some words that are new to you, you may find clues in the way that they are used. (See the Guides for Getting Meaning from Context, page 105.) If other words give no clues, use the dictionary. Decide in your group which meaning makes the best sense in the sentence that you are reading. Use the Guides to Finding the Right Meaning, page 118.

(4) Go back over the article together, but this time pick out the important information and put it into as many sentences as you need to tell it clearly. Have someone act as secretary to write the sentences as they are made. Let the Guides for Improving Expression, page 453, help you.

(5) Choose one person to read your summary to the class. As the various summaries are read, listen carefully to see whether all groups agreed on what is the important information in the article. Use the Guides to Good Listening, page 26.

THE OLYMPIAN GAMES

1. Long ago only Greeks were allowed to take part in the Olympian games, which today are called the Olympic games. If the ancient Greeks were fighting when it came time for the games, the war was halted for one month. This month of truce gave men time to go to the games and return. The games were important to the Greeks, even more important than war.

2. The young men who were to compete were chosen by their city-states. They went to Olympia early to receive their final hard training. Before the games began, each athlete took an oath to play fair and to obey all the rules.

3. On the first of the five days that the games lasted, sacrifices were offered to the god Zeus. In this solemn ceremony, the representatives rode in chariots to the god's temple. There each one approached the great gold-and-ivory statue of Zeus and gave him a gift.

4. The athletic events began on the second day. Very early in the morning, the visitors hurried to the stadium to get their seats. Here they watched young men run foot races, wrestle and box, jump, throw the javelin, and hurl the discus. Those last three

events were done to the music of a flute. Most exciting of all were the chariot races, which were held on a special track called the "hippodrome."

5. The awards to the winners were made on the fifth day. Wreaths, made of leaves cut from an olive tree, were the victors' crowns. A herald called the names of the winners. As a winner stepped forth, his father's name and the name of his city-state were announced by the herald. Then one of the judges placed the crown of olives on the young man's head. That was a proud moment for the victor and for his home city.

6. There were other honors waiting for the victor. Poets wrote poems about him, and sculptors made statues of him. Often special honor was done him by his own city. Sometimes, for example, part of its wall was torn down so that the victor could enter by a route over which no man had ever before walked. One city, Athens, gave each winner the privilege of eating at the table where only the men who ruled the city ate.

7. The Olympian games were so important to the Greeks that they marked time by them. The time between the games was called an "Olympiad." Each Olympiad was four years long. The famous Battle of Marathon, which we say took place in 490 B.C., was dated by the Greeks as having occurred in the third year of the seventy-second Olympiad.*

D. Now try your hand at making a summary alone. (1) Again read carefully through the directions in *B,* only this time do everything by yourself. (2) Then summarize the following article. (3) *Proofread your paragraph for careless errors in capitalization, punctuation, spelling, and sentence sense.* (4) Be prepared to read your summary to the class. Use the Guides for Reading Aloud, page 57.

*Adapted from *The Old World* by Mabel Rockwood Grimm and Matilda Hughes; copyright © 1955, 1953, 1948 by Row, Peterson and Company, Evanston, Illinois.

A flood is a terrible thing. There comes a short, frantic warning by telephone or radio, and people are forced to flee for their lives. Their homes, their furniture, their beds must be left to the mercy of muddy, oily water. A few people refuse to leave their homes and stay staunchly to meet the flood. Busily they move their furniture to the second floor. As the water rises, they are forced to climb out on the roof.

The icy flood pushes in the windows and doors. Sometimes, groaning and crumbling, the house caves in, dumping its occupants into the swirling waters with little chance of rescue. The people who were prudent enough to escape to the hills are crowded into schools, churches, and refugee camps.

Hourly, the coast guard brings additions to this miserable company. Many are ill from exposure; some have been injured. Doctors and nurses work day and night. After dark, emergency operations must be performed by the light of a candle or a lantern. There is no electricity: the floodwaters have covered the power plants.

The greatest problem is drinking water. In all this sea of water, people cannot find a drop to drink. Even without floods, the river is so poisoned with sewage that no one would dare to drink from it. Now with dead animals floating past and with purification plants under water, to drink from the river would be suicide. Pure water must be brought in; yet transportation over railroads and highways is paralyzed. Epidemics of disease threaten.

Because desperate men from downstream may try to dynamite the levees and spread the floodwaters in an effort to save their homes, in some places national guards and special deputies patrol the levees, shooting strangers on sight.

After the flood there comes the dirty, disgusting job of cleaning up. Merchants, returning to their stores, find their stock ruined. People, returning to their homes, may find a barn on their front lawn or a dead horse against the kitchen door. Inside, the wallpaper has peeled, glued chairs and tables have fallen apart, the rug oozes with slime, and the mattress is saturated with filthy water.

Wells must be cleaned, and for weeks their water will be unfit to drink. Automobile motors and the machines of factories will have to be taken completely apart and cleaned of caked mud and rust. The decaying bodies of dead animals will have to be gathered and burned. Yes, the flood is a terrible thing.*

* Adapted from *Soil, Water, and Man* by Murl Deusing; copyright 1941 by Row, Peterson and Company; copyright © renewed 1968 by Western Publishing Company, Inc., Racine, Wisconsin.

E. Bring to class a short article from a magazine or an editorial from a newspaper. Write a summary of it, letting the Guides to Making a Summary help you. Check your paper by the Writing Chart, page 172. Read the summaries in your small groups. As a listener, be sure that you understand clearly what each article is about. If you do not, tell the one who wrote the summary what you think needs to be made clearer.

USING ENGLISH IN ALL CLASSES

In preparing your next reading assignment in science or social studies, make a summary of the lesson. If some of you have the same assignment, compare your results. Discuss them if you do not agree. You will find that what you study is much easier to understand and remember if you make a summary of the important facts.

USING ENGLISH OUTSIDE SCHOOL

Listen carefully to a talk on television or on radio, to the minister's sermon next Sunday, or to any other speaker that you have a chance to hear. Write a summary and read it to the class or to your small group. Call upon someone to tell in his own words what you have said.

6. Outlining: a Help to Clear Thinking

Have you ever watched the building of a house? If you have, you know that a framework is built upon a firm foundation, and that the walls, floors, ceilings, and roof are fastened to that framework. You do not see the framework in the finished house, but it is there.

In the same way, a well-written paragraph, story, or article has a framework. *Making an outline* of the material that you read will help you to understand that material. By making an outline of the material, you are finding its framework.

There are two kinds of outlines: (1) *sentence outlines,* in which every point is a complete sentence, and (2) *topic outlines,* in which there are no sentences at all. A sentence outline really summarizes what the writer says and is therefore more useful than a topic outline whenever you must refer to it sometime in the future. A topic outline, on the other hand, just states the topics about which the writer says something; it is most useful when it is to be used soon after it has been made.

GUIDES FOR OUTLINING

1. Read carefully through the material to be outlined.

2. Decide what the main idea of each paragraph is. State it as a topic or as a sentence. (Look for topic sentences, central thoughts, and key words.)

3. Use these main ideas as chief points; label them *I, II,* and so on.

4. Decide whether there are at least two points that give important information about a main point. Such points are *subpoints.*

5. List these subpoints under the right main point and label them *A, B,* and so on.

6. Decide whether at least two details tell more about a subpoint.

7. List these details under the right subpoint and label them *1, 2,* and so on.

8. Remember, never put only one subpoint under a main point or one detail under a subpoint.

9. Capitalize and punctuate properly.
   a) Use a period after each division number or letter.
   b) Capitalize the first word of each point.
   c) Use a period after each point in a sentence outline; use no period after a point in a topic outline.

10. Use only sentences *or* topics, not both, in the same outline.

Sentence Outline	Topic Outline
I. This is a main point.	I. Main point
A. This is an important subpoint.	A. Important subpoint
B. This is an important subpoint.	B. Important subpoint
1. This is a detail.	1. Detail
2. This is a detail.	2. Detail
3. This is a detail.	3. Detail
II. This is a main point.	II. Main point

Read the following selection concerning fur trappers; then study the *sentence outline* and the *topic outline* that come immediately after it. Notice that there are three main points in the outline, one for each paragraph of the selection, and that they are marked by Roman numerals. Note that the subpoints are indicated by capital letters and that details are set off by small numbers.

Note also that every main point has at least two subdivisions. Each numeral and each letter is followed by a period, as in the forms under guide 10, on page 99. Observe how the main topics, subpoints, and details "line up" in both outlines. *The only difference is that one is made up of sentences; the other is not.*

Study the differences between the information given in the two outlines. Under the first main point (I), for example, notice that the sentence outline makes clear what might happen to the trapper: *He might be killed by . . .* The topic outline merely indicates dangers; it does not mention what might happen.

Always remember that a topic outline merely *suggests* ideas; a sentence outline actually *states* the ideas. It will be as useful a month or a year later as when it was first written. The topic outline may be a real puzzle after a month or more has gone by.

Fur Trappers

Death was always close beside the fur trapper. He might be attacked by hostile Indians, swept away by a flood or a snowslide, or torn beyond recognition by grizzly bears.

Yet, because trapping held a fascination for him, he continued to trap. This was his procedure. Slipping along the shore, softly in the grainy snow of early spring, he looked for likely places to set his traps. Having found a runway or a dam, he stepped into ice-cold water, carrying his cocked trap and a long, sharpened stick. Putting the trap into the water so the surface came a hand above the trigger, he drew the chain to its full length and secured it by driving the sharpened stick into the stream bed. Back at the bank he found a willow twig, peeled it, and dipped it into the antelope horn at his belt in which he carried the bait he called "medicine"— a musky secretion taken from a dead beaver. He set the bait twig in place over the trap.

Just before sunup the trapper came out of the lodge he had made by stretching skins over saplings and went to collect his pelts. A full-grown beaver weighed thirty to sixty pounds, and the pelt, when ready, weighed from a pound and a half to two pounds. Usually the trapper skinned the beaver on the spot, saving the bait gland, and usually taking the tail back to camp to be charred on the fire and then boiled for good eating. The pelt was scraped by the trapper, by his Indian wife—if he had one—or by camp-tenders in large company brigades. It was stretched on a willow hoop and set in the sun for a day or two, then folded with the fur inside and kept dry until delivery at rendezvous time.*

* Adapted from *Trappers and Mountain Men* by the Editors of *American Heritage;* copyright © 1961 by American Heritage Publishing Co., Inc., New York.

Here is the sentence outline of the selection.

FUR TRAPPERS

I. The fur trapper lived close to death.
   A. He might be killed by Indians.
   B. He might be killed by a flood or a snowslide.
   C. He might be killed by grizzly bears.
II. The fur trapper followed a certain procedure.
   A. He found a place to set his trap.
      1. It might be a runway.
      2. It might be a dam.
   B. He fastened the trap in the water.
   C. He baited the trap.
III. The trapper collected his pelts each morning.
   A. The trapper usually skinned the beaver on the spot.
      1. A beaver weighed from thirty to sixty pounds.
      2. A pelt weighed from one and a half to two pounds.
      3. The trapper saved the bait gland.
      4. He usually saved the tail to eat.
   B. The trapper or his wife or a camp-tender scraped the pelt.
   C. He stretched the pelt in the sun to dry.
   D. He folded the pelt with the fur inside.

Here is the topic outline of the selection.

FUR TRAPPERS

I. Dangers to trappers
   A. Indians
   B. Floods and snowslides
   C. Bears
II. Trapping procedure
   A. Trap sites
      1. Runways
      2. Dams
   B. Setting traps
   C. Baiting traps
III. Collecting pelts
   A. Skinning beaver
      1. Weight of beaver
      2. Weight of pelt
      3. Bait gland saved
      4. Tail saved
   B. Scraping pelt
   C. Stretching pelt
   D. Folding pelt

A. Read the following article. Then study the outline that follows it. In class, discuss the form of the outline, as well as such questions as these: (1) How many paragraphs are there in the article? How many main divisions are there in the outline? (2) Why do *I* and *II* have no subdivisions? (3) Are all the points and subpoints in proper order?

How Animals Protect Themselves

Animals, like other forms of life, have enemies from which they must find ways to protect themselves. The following paragraphs tell about some of those ways.

Being able to move fast is the best way that many animals have of protecting themselves from their enemies. Some animals—the swallow for one—have no other way.

Many animals have what is known as "protective coloring"; that is, their color changes to match their surroundings. Some animals, the arctic foxes, for example, change color with the seasons. Other animals change oftener. The common tree toad is one of these that do. It changes from gray to green, for example, if it moves from the trunk of a tree to a green leaf.

The walking-stick insect is protected by its resemblance to a twig. The dead-leaf butterfly escapes being seen by its enemies because it looks like a dried leaf. This means of protection is called "protective resemblance."

Many animals wear armor of one kind or another. Shellfish such as clams, oysters, and scallops, are enclosed in shells. So are beetles and turtles. The tough hide of the elephant and the hippopotamus is not easily penetrated. The armadillo has its head and body encased in armor made up of many small bony plates.

Some animals carry weapons. The spines, or quills, of the porcupine can inflict painful wounds. The swordfish has a long, dangerous, swordlike beak. Lions, tigers, and leopards have deadly claws. Other animals protect themselves by poison. The sea anemone, for instance, has poison darts. Bees and wasps inject poison with their stings. The black widow spider poisons as it bites. Some animals protect themselves by giving out a bad odor. The skunk is a good example.

Animals may have habits that help protect them from their enemies. The opossum, for instance, plays dead. The hog-nosed snake protects itself in the same way. Many animals escape their enemies by doing their hunting at night.*

---

*Adapted from *Adaptation to Environment* by Bertha Morris Parker; copyright © 1959, 1952, 1949 by Harper & Row, Publishers, Incorporated, Evanston, Illinois.

How Animals Protect Themselves

I. Animals must be able to protect themselves from enemies.

II. Some animals, such as the swallow, must depend on their speed.

III. Some animals have protective coloring.
  A. The arctic foxes change color with the seasons.
  B. Some animals, such as the tree toad, change oftener.

IV. Some animals have protective resemblance.
  A. The walking-stick insect looks like a twig.
  B. The dead-leaf butterfly looks like a dead leaf.

V. Many animals have armor.
  A. Shellfish, turtles, and beetles have protective shells.
  B. The elephant and hippopotamus have tough hides.
  C. The armadillo has strong bony plates.

VI. Some animals carry weapons.
  A. The porcupine has spines.
  B. The swordfish has its sword.
  C. Lions, tigers, and leopards have claws.
  D. Some use poison.
    1. The sea anemone shoots out poison darts.
    2. Bees and wasps inject poison with their stings.
    3. The black widow spider's bite is poisonous.
  E. Some animals, such as the skunk, give out a bad odor.

VII. Animals have habits that protect them.
  A. The opossum and the hog-nosed snake play dead.
  B. Many animals escape enemies by hunting at night.

B. In your small groups, make a sentence outline of "The Olympian Games," page 95. Have outlines put on the board and compared.

C. Now make an outline by yourself. (1) Turn to the article on page 97 ("Floods") and make a sentence outline of the important information in it. (2) *Proofread for careless errors in capitalizing and punctuating.* (3) Have several outlines put upon the board or read in class.

D. (1) Find an interesting article, a page or so long, in a magazine. (2) Make a topic outline of the article and then prepare a talk based upon that outline. (3) Examine your Speech Chart, page 61, to see which points need special work on your part. (4) Practice this talk before a mirror at home, and then ask someone there to listen to you. (5) As each speech is given in class, rate it on a speech slip (page 62). (6) Afterwards mark your own Speech Chart.

USING ENGLISH IN ALL CLASSES

As you study your next assignment in any class, outline the important facts. If any of you have the same assignment, compare outlines.

103

LEARNING NEW WORDS

"IF THESE WORDS ARE ENGLISH, I MUST BE READING THEM UPSIDE DOWN."

READ AND THINK ABOUT

What do you do in your reading when you come to words that you do not know?

What are you doing to improve your vocabulary?

If you have ever been out in a heavy fog, you will remember that everything around you was blurred and hard to make out. When the fog lifted, everything looked different, so clear and plain that you could not possibly mistake one thing for another.

In the same way, the things that you read may be blurred and hard for you to understand, just because you come across words that puzzle you. To get a clear idea of what you read, you must know what the words mean.

1. Learning Words from Context

Sometimes you can guess correctly at the meaning of a word from its *context;* that is, from the other words used with it in the sentence or in nearby sentences. The following guides will help you to use context clues in your reading.

GUIDES FOR GETTING MEANING FROM CONTEXT

1. Watch for a word that explains or defines the unfamiliar word.

    I found the old man waiting on the **gallery**, or, as it is called here, the *porch.*

    On the tree trunk, I noticed a strange **excrescence**, a gray, thorny *lump.* (*Lump* is an appositive. See Rule 4, page 153.)

2. Watch for a word that gives a clear hint as to the meaning of the unfamiliar word.

    It seemed that nothing could **slake** his *thirst.*

    ("Thirst" suggests that "slake" probably means "satisfy.")

3. If no single word gives a clue, look (*a*) at the sentence as a whole, or (*b*) at a sentence or sentences nearby.

    a) The **famished** man seized the loaf of bread and began to gnaw on it hungrily.

    (The whole sentence suggests that "famished" means "starving.")

    b) The man stared at me **wrathfully**. I could see that he was *hot-tempered.*

    ("Hot-tempered" suggests that "wrathfully" means "angrily.")

LEARNING ACTIVITIES IN USING CONTEXT CLUES

A. (1) Read the following paragraph, paying special attention to the words in italics. (2) Copy the paragraph, but for the italicized words select substitutes from the list that follows the paragraph. The paragraph has in it context clues that should help you to choose the right words. (3) Compare your choices in class. (4) Point out context clues that helped you to choose certain words.

The Hurons stood *aghast* at this sudden *visitation* of death on one of their band. But, as they regarded the *fatal* accuracy of an aim which had dared to *immolate* an enemy at so much *hazard* to a friend, the name of La Longue Carabine burst *simultaneously* from every lip and was succeeded by a wild and a sort of *plaintive* howl. The cry was answered by a loud shout from a little thicket, where the *incautious* party had piled their arms; and, at the next moment, Hawk-eye, too eager to load the rifle he had regained, was seen advancing upon them, *brandishing* the clubbed weapon, and cutting the air with wide and powerful sweeps.*

1. appearance	4. all at once	7. reckless
2. horrified	5. deadly	8. shaking
3. danger	6. sacrifice	9. mournful

B. Using any context clues that you can find, decide what you think is the meaning of each italicized word in the following sentences, all taken from *A Tale of Two Cities* by Charles Dickens. Make this an oral activity.

1. The air among the houses was of so strong a *piscatory* flavor that one might have supposed that sick fish went up to be dipped in it, as sick people went down to be dipped in the sea.
2. They had not *traversed* many steps of the long main staircase when he stopped, . . .
3. No crowd was about the door; no people were *discernible* at any of the many windows; . . .
4. But Miss Pross suddenly became *afflicted* with a twitching in the head and body, and retired into the house.
5. Mr. Lorry was already out when Carton got back, and it was easy to *surmise* where the good old man was gone.
6. It was as if the wind and rain had *lulled* at last, after a long and fearful storm.
7. "I would ride over any of you very willingly, and *exterminate* you from the earth."
8. The *wicket* opened on a stone staircase, leading upward.
9. "Now, I told you so," said the spy, casting a *reproachful* look at his sister; "if any trouble comes of this, it's your doing."

C. (1) Rewrite the following paragraph, replacing each word in italics with one word or more suggested to you by context clues. (2) *Proofread for careless errors in copying.* (3) In class, compare your work. (4) List on the board the various words substituted for the italicized ones. With the help of the dictionary, if necessary, decide which substitutes best give the meaning intended.

A sudden thought struck me how I might *extricate* myself from the bandit's *clutches.* I was unarmed, it is true, but I was *vigorous.* His companions were at a distance. By a sudden pull, I might *wrest* myself from him and spring up the staircase, *whither* he would not dare follow me by himself. The idea was put into

*From *The Last of the Mohicans: A Narrative of 1757* by James Fenimore Cooper. Perennial Classic Edition, Harper & Row, Publishers, Incorporated, New York.

action as soon as *conceived*. The *ruffian's* throat was bare; with my right hand I seized him by it; with my left hand I grasped the arm which held the carbine. The suddenness of my attack took him completely *unawares;* and the *strangling* nature of my grasp paralyzed him. He choked and *faltered*. I felt his hand relaxing its hold and was upon the point of jerking myself away and darting up the staircase before he could recover himself, when I was suddenly seized from behind.*

ENRICHMENT

Use context clues to unlock the meaning of the italicized words in the lines of poetry below.

1. As a feather is *wafted* downward
   From an eagle in his flight.—LONGFELLOW

2. And he *smote* upon the door again a second time;
   "Is there anybody there?" he said.—WALTER DE LA MARE

3. The bride kissed the goblet; the knight took it up,
   He *quaffed* off the wine, and he threw down the cup.—WALTER SCOTT

4. The waves beside them danced; but they
   Outdid the sparkling waves in glee:
   A poet could not but be gay,
   In such *jocund* company.—WORDSWORTH

USING ENGLISH IN ALL CLASSES

In class, examine your science or social studies text. When you find an unfamiliar word that is made clear by its context, raise your hand. If called upon, say the word; then read the sentence. Ask a classmate to give the meaning suggested by the context and to tell what words are clues.

2. Using Root Words, Prefixes, and Suffixes

TALK IT OVER . . .

What are *root words, prefixes,* and *suffixes?* What is their relationship? If you do not know, find what the dictionary says about them.

*From "The Painter's Adventure" from *Tales of a Traveller with Selections from The Sketch Book,* edited by George Philip Krapp, Ph.D.; copyright 1901 by Scott, Foresman and Company, Glenview, Illinois.

Many words in the English language come from Greek or Latin sources. Knowing even a few Greek and Latin root words, prefixes, and suffixes will unlock for you many English words.

GUIDES FOR USING WORD PARTS TO UNLOCK MEANING

1. Learn common *roots, prefixes,* and *suffixes* such as these.

PREFIXES	ROOT WORDS	SUFFIXES
anti (against)	**aud** (hear)	**able, ible** (able to, able to be)
in, im, il, ir, un (not)	**graph** (write)	**er, or** (one who, that which)
	meter (measure)	**ion, sion, tion** (act of,
mis (wrong)	**sens** (feel)	condition of)
pre (before)	**vid, vis** (see)	**itis** (inflammation of)
re (back, again)	**vit, viv** (life,	**less** (without)
tele (far)	live)	**ness** (condition of being)

2. Look for familiar parts. Perhaps the only new thing about a word is a prefix or a suffix. For example, in "imperfect," you can spot "perfect." If you know that *im* is a prefix meaning "not," you will see quickly that *imperfect* means "not perfect."

3. In applying the meanings of prefixes, roots, and suffixes, change the form of the root definition if necessary. For example, in the word "vision," *vis* is "see," and *ion* is "act of." "Act of see" is what you get when you put the two together; so you change that to "act of see*ing*."

4. Remember that context clues will give you extra help in unlocking words. For example, if you met the word "illegible" by itself, you would know from *il* and *ible* that it means "not able to be" something or other, but without knowing the meaning of the root (*leg*), you would be stumped. If the word were in a sentence, the context might give you the clue to that root:

Because the ink had faded, most of the words were *illegible.* "Faded" is the clue that you need to decide that *illegible* means "not able to be read."

LEARNING ACTIVITIES IN USING ROOTS, PREFIXES, AND SUFFIXES*

A. (1) Go over the following words in class. Give the meaning of each word and show how knowing the prefixes, root words, and suffixes helps to figure out the meaning. (2) Name other words with the same roots.

* There is more practice in the dictionary activities, page 121.

1. inaudible	6. sensation	11. revive
2. telegrapher	7. auditor	12. visionless
3. invisible	8. tonsillitis	13. mismanage
4. preview	9. television	14. audition
5. sensible	10. audiometer	15. senselessness

B. Many words begin with the following prefixes: *uni, trans, sub, non, auto,* and *pro.* Take turns at giving words that begin with the prefixes. Write the words on the board; see how long a list you can make.

C. (1) Copy the following sentences, supplying prefixes and suffixes from the lists on page 108 to complete the words that have letters missing. (2) Exchange papers for checking. (3) *Proofread for careless errors, especially in spelling.*

1. The operat...... of the filling sta...... told me that his best custom...... always uses the same kind of ......knock gasoline.
2. A reason...... man would admit that my search for the lost mine is use......, but my stubborn...... keeps me going.
3. The weatherman is ......dicting some ......cipita...... for tonight. Most of his forecasts are reli.......
4. My chief competit...... in the race had just ......covered from an appendic...... opera.......
5. You ......judge Charles. I have watched his ......casts on WNBQ count...... times, and I have never yet ......ceived any ......informa...... from them.

ENRICHMENT

Using the prefixes, root words, and suffixes in guide 1 on page 108, invent new words. For instance, you might make "sensometer" and "regrapher." Ask the class to decide what they think your words mean.

3. Using the Dictionary

READ AND THINK ABOUT

Once upon a time Mark Twain, who wrote *The Adventures of Tom Sawyer,* sat in the United States Senate listening to a friend make a long speech. Mark Twain decided the next day to have some fun with this friend.

"Do you know, Senator," he said, "I was surprised at your speech yesterday. You may not believe it, but I own a very old book which has every word of that speech in it!"

The senator was indignant. "That speech," he shouted, "was entirely my own! I'd like to see the book, old or new, that contains it!"

A few days later he received a copy of a much-used dictionary!

Of course that book had every word the senator had used. In fact, if it was an unabridged dictionary, it had all the words that anyone who speaks and writes English uses to express his ideas.

Context clues and a knowledge of word parts often help you to figure out word meanings. When you need further help, the place to look first is in the dictionary. Perhaps you already have the dictionary habit; if not, now is a good time to get it. Using the dictionary regularly will help you (1) to understand better what you hear or read and (2) to express yourself better.

PART ONE: FINDING THE WORD

"LET'S SEE ---- a b c d e f g h i j k l m n o p q r s t HERE IT IS --- t."

THINK IT OVER ...

Is it true to say that he is wasting time?

What does he need to learn before he will be able to find words quickly in the dictionary?

How good are *your* dictionary habits?

To find words quickly, you must know the alphabet. Really knowing the alphabet means more, however, than just being able to say it through quickly from *a* to *z*. It means, for example, knowing, without having to say half the alphabet through first, that *s* comes after *r* and before *t;* that *j* comes before *k,* and *k* before *l.*

GUIDES FOR INCREASING SKILL IN USING THE ALPHABET

1. Learn to say and write the alphabet in sections: *abc, bcd, cde, def, efg, fgh,* and so on through the alphabet. When you can speed through them, go on to groups of four: *abcd, bcde,* and so on.

2. Skim not only the first letter of a word, but the second, third, and so on. For example, suppose you want to find "minimum."
   a) Find the *m's.*
   b) Skip over all the "ma" and "me" words.
   c) Skip over all the words that begin with "mic," "mid," and so on until you reach "min."
   d) Skim the "min" words until you reach "mini."
   e) Skim those "mini" words (there will not be many) until you find "minimum."

3. Use the guide words to help you skim. These guide words are the big black words at the top of each page. The guide word at the top of the left column tells the first word on the page. The one above the right column tells the last word on the page.

4. Use the thumb index, if your dictionary has one, to help you turn quickly to the right letter.

LEARNING ACTIVITIES IN USING THE ALPHABET

A. (1) In this exercise, think of the two letters that come *just before* and the two letters that come *just after* each letter given below. (2) Have someone read the letters as given here, while you write them, as rapidly as you can, with the two letters that come before and the two letters that come after them. In other words, for the letter *p* you would write **n, o, p, q, r.** (3) Exchange papers for checking.

1. _ _ c _ _	6. _ _ m _ _	11. _ _ t _ _	16. _ _ f _ _
2. _ _ r _ _	7. _ _ w _ _	12. _ _ e _ _	17. _ _ p _ _
3. _ _ u _ _	8. _ _ h _ _	13. _ _ s _ _	18. _ _ g _ _
4. _ _ j _ _	9. _ _ o _ _	14. _ _ k _ _	19. _ _ l _ _
5. _ _ d _ _	10. _ _ i _ _	15. _ _ v _ _	20. _ _ n _ _

B. (1) In your dictionary, locate the following words. (2) Write down (*a*) the number of the page containing each word and (*b*) the guide words on that page. (3) Check work in your small groups.

1. mischief	6. nozzle	11. shank	16. attend
2. porch	7. foundry	12. salable	17. whether
3. expense	8. increase	13. kernel	18. tragic
4. pilot	9. correct	14. earnest	19. restrict
5. wrought	10. quest	15. glove	20. humidor

C. Write these words in the order in which they would appear in the dictionary. When you have finished, exchange papers for checking.

1. carrot	7. grumble	13. graduate	19. candy
2. forgive	8. daughter	14. memorize	20. frighten
3. shoulder	9. shower	15. friendship	21. soldier
4. foreign	10. candidate	16. career	22. memory
5. camera	11. friendliness	17. milling	23. graduation
6. solid	12. millionaire	18. darkness	24. should

PART TWO: LEARNING WHAT THE DICTIONARY TELLS ABOUT A WORD

Here are some kinds of information that the dictionary gives about words. The numbers on the following page are keyed to this list.

1. Spelling
2. Pronunciation: (*a*) respelling; (*b*) key
3. Division into syllables
4. Meanings
5. Part of speech
6. Derivation (history of the word)

7. Irregular forms
   a) Of plurals
   b) Of verbs
   c) Of adjective and
      adverb comparisons
8. Illustrations

LEARNING ACTIVITY

On the sample dictionary page that follows, find the answers to these questions. Make this an oral activity.

1. What kind of photograph is American English in origin?
2. Which word comes from the Latin word for "fear"?
3. Give the location and size of the island of Timor.
4. The name of what coarse grass is derived from a proper noun?
5. Tintoretto was a native of what city? What was his profession?
6. What President of the United States was given the campaign nickname of a river?

Ti mor (tē′môr or ti môr′), *n.* island in the East In-dies. Part belongs to Indonesia and part to Portugal. 800,000 pop.; 13,090 sq. mi.

tim or ous (tim′ər əs), *adj.* easily frightened; timid. [< Med.L *timorosus* < L *timor* fear] —**tim′or ous ly,** *adv.* —**tim′or ous ness,** *n.*

Timor Sea, sea between Timor and N Australia.

tim o thy (tim′ə thē), *n.* a kind of coarse grass with long, cylindrical spikes, often grown for hay. [Am.E; named after *Timothy* Hanson, early American cultivator]

Tim o thy (tim′ə thē), *n.* **1.** a disciple of the Apostle Paul. **2.** either of the two books of the New Testament written as letters by Paul to Timothy.

tim pa ni (tim′pə nē), *n. pl. of* **tim pa no** (tim′pə nō). kettledrums. [< Ital. *timpani,* pl. of *timpano* < L *tympanum.* See TYMPANUM.]

tim pa nist (tim′pə nist), *n.* person who plays the ket-tledrums.

tin (tin), *n., adj., v.,* **tinned, tin ning.** —*n.* **1.** a metallic element resembling silver in color and luster but softer and cheaper. *Symbol:* Sn **2.** thin sheets of iron or steel coated with tin. **3.** any can, box, pan, or other container made of tin: *a pie tin.* —*adj.* made of tin. —*v.* **1.** cover with tin. **2.** *Brit.* put up in tin cans or tin boxes; can. [OE]

tin a mou (tin′ə mü), *n.* a South Amer-ican bird somewhat like a partridge, quail, or grouse. [< F < Carib]

Tinamou (about 14 in. long)

tinct (tingkt), *Poetic.* —*adj.* tinged. —*n.* tint; tinge. [< L *tinctus,* pp. of *tingere* tinge]

tinc ture (tingk′chər), *n., v.,* **-tured, -tur ing.** —*n.* **1.** solution of medicine in alcohol: *tincture of iodine.* **2.** trace; tinge. **3.** color; tint. —*v.* **1.** give a trace or tinge to. **2.** color; tint. [< L *tinctura* < *tingere* tinge]

tin der (tin′dər), *n.* **1.** anything that catches fire easily. **2.** material used to catch fire from a spark. [OE *tynder*]

tin der box (tin′dər boks′), *n.* box for holding tinder, flint, and steel for making a fire.

tine (tīn), *n.* a sharp projecting point or prong: *the tines of a fork.* [OE *tind*]

tin foil, a very thin sheet of tin, or tin and lead, used as a wrapping for candy, tobacco, etc.

ting (ting), *v.* make or cause to make a clear ringing sound. —*n.* a clear ringing sound. [imitative]

tinge (tinj), *v.,* **tinged, tinge ing** or **ting ing,** —*v.* **1.** color slightly: *A drop of ink will tinge a glass of water.* **2.** add a trace of some quality to; change slightly: *Sad memories tinged their present joy.* —*n.* **1.** a slight color-ing or tint. **2.** a very small amount; trace. [< L *tingere*]

tin gle (ting′gl), *v.,* **-gled, -gling,** *n.* —*v.* **1.** have a feeling of thrills or a pricking, stinging feeling: *He tingled with excitement on his first train trip.* **2.** cause this feeling in: *Shame tingled his cheeks.* **3.** be thrilling: *The newspaper story tingled with excitement.* —*n.* **1.** a tinkle; jingle. **2.** a pricking, stinging feeling. **2.** a tinkle; jingle. [probably var. of *tinkle*]

tink er (tingk′ər), *n.* **1.** man who mends pots, pans, etc. **2.** unskilled or clumsy work; activity that is rather useless. **3.** person who does such work. —*v.* **1.** mend; patch. **2.** work or repair in an unskilled or clumsy way. **3.** work or keep busy in a rather useless way. [? ult. < *tin*]

tin kle (ting′kl), *v.,* **-kled, -kling,** *n.* —*v.* **1.** make short, light, ringing sounds: *Little bells tinkle.* **2.** cause to tinkle. **3.** move with a tinkle. **4.** call, make known, etc., by tinkling: *The little clock tinkled out the hours.* —*n.* series of short, light, ringing sounds: *the tinkle of sleigh bells.* [ult. imitative]

tin man (tin′mən), *n., pl.* **-men.** **1.** man who works with tin. **2.** dealer in tinware.

tin ner (tin′ər), *n.* **1.** person who works in a tin mine. **2.** person who works with tin. **3.** *Brit.* a canner.

tin ny (tin′ē), *adj.,* **-ni er, -ni est.** **1.** of tin; containing tin. **2.** like tin in looks or sound. —**tin′ni ness,** *n.*

tin-pan alley, district frequented by musicians, song writers, and song publishers.

tin plate, thin sheets of iron or steel coated with tin. Ordinary tin cans are made of tin plate.

tin sel (tin′sl), *n., v.,* **-seled, -sel ing** or *esp. Brit.* **-selled, -sel ling,** *adj.* —*n.* **1.** glittering copper, brass, etc., in thin sheets, strips, threads, etc., used to trim Christmas trees, etc. **2.** anything showy but having little value. **3.** a thin cloth woven with threads of gold, silver, or cop-per. —*v.* trim with tinsel. —*adj.* of or like tinsel; showy but not worth much. [< F *étincelle* spark < L *scintilla.* Doublet of SCINTILLA.] —**tin′sel like′,** *adj.*

tin smith (tin′smith′), *n.* person who works with tin; maker of tinware.

tint (tint), *n.* **1.** variety of a color: *The picture was painted in several tints of blue.* **2.** a delicate or pale color. —*v.* put a tint on; color slightly. [earlier *tinct* < L *tinctus* a dyeing < *tingere* to dye]

tin tin nab u la tion (tin′tə nab′yə lā′shən), *n.* the ringing of bells. [Am.E; ult. < L *tintinnabulum* bell]

Tin to ret to (tin′tə ret′ō), *n.* 1518-1594, Venetian painter.

tin type (tin′tīp′), *n.* photograph taken on a sheet of enameled tin or iron. [Am.E]

tin ware (tin′wār′), *n.* articles made of tin.

ti ny (tī′nē), *adj.,* **-ni er, -ni est.** very small; wee. [ME *tine;* origin uncertain] —**Syn.** little, minute, microscopic.

-tion, *suffix.* **1.** act or state of ____ing, as in *addition, opposition.* **2.** condition or state of being ____ed, as in *exhaustion.* **3.** result of ____ing, as in *apparition.* [< L *-tio, -onis* < *-t-* of pp. stem + *-io* (cf. *-ion*)]

tip¹ (tip), *n., v.,* **tipped, tip ping.** —*n.* **1.** the end part; end; point: *the tips of the fingers.* **2.** a small piece put on the end of something. —*v.* put a tip on; furnish with a tip. [ME] —**Syn.** *n.* **1.** extremity.

tip² (tip), *v.,* **tipped, tip ping,** *n.* —*v.* **1.** slope; slant: *She tipped the table toward her.* **2.** upset; overturn: *He tipped over his glass of water.* **3.** take off (a hat) in greeting. **4.** empty out; dump. —*n.* a slope; slant. [origin uncer-tain] —**Syn.** *v.* **1.** tilt, incline, lean. **2.** capsize.

tip³ (tip), *n., v.,* **tipped, tip ping,** *n.* —*n.* **1.** a small pres-ent of money: *He gave the waiter a tip.* **2.** piece of secret information: *Fred had a tip that the black horse would win the race.* **3.** a useful hint, suggestion, etc. **4.** a light, sharp blow; tap. —*v.* **1.** give a small present of money to. **2.** give secret information to. **3.** give a tip. **4.** hit lightly and sharply; tap. **5.** tip off, *Informal.* **a.** give secret in-formation to. **b.** warn. [origin uncertain]

tip-off (tip′ôf′ or tip′of′), *n. Informal.* **1.** piece of se-cret information. **2.** a warning.

Tip pe ca noe (tip′ə kə nü′), *n.* **1.** river in NW Indiana, flowing into the Wabash River. 200 mi. **2.** campaign nickname giv-en to William H. Harrison, ninth president of the United States.

Tip per ar y (tip′ər ār′ē), *n.* **1.** county in the S part of the Irish Republic. **2.** town located there. 5000.

tip pet (tip′it), *n.* **1.** scarf for the neck and shoulders with ends hanging down in front. **2.** a long, narrow, hanging part of a hood, sleeve, or scarf. [probably < *tip¹*]

Tippet (def. 2)

tip ple (tip′l), *v.,* **-pled, -pling,** *n.* —*v.* drink (alcoholic liquor) often. —*n.* an alcoholic liquor. [origin uncertain. Cf. Norwegian *tipla* drip, tipple]

tip pler (tip′lər), *n.* a habitual drinker of alcoholic liquor.

tip staff (tip′staf′ or tip′stäf′), *n.* **1.** staff tipped with metal, formerly carried by constables and other officers of the law. **2.** official who carried such a staff.

tip ster (tip′stər), *n. Informal.* person who makes a business of furnishing private or secret information for use in betting, speculation, etc. [< *tip* a hint + *-ster*]

tip sy (tip′sē), *adj.,* **-si er, -si est.** **1.** tipping easily; un-steady; tilted. **2.** somewhat intoxicated but not thoroughly drunk. [probably < *tip³*] —**tip′si ly,** *adv.* —**tip′si-ness,** *n.*

tip toe (tip′tō′), *n., v.,* **-toed, -toe ing.** —*n.* **1.** the tips of the toes. **2.** on tiptoe, **a.** walking on one's toes. **b.** eager. **c.** in a secret manner. —*v.* walk on the tips of the toes.

tip top (tip′top′), *n.* the very top; highest point. —*adj.* **1.** at the very top of highest point. **2.** *Informal.* first-rate; excellent. [< *tip* end + *top*]

hat, āge, cāre, fär; let, bē, tèrm; it, īce; hot, gō, ôrder; oil, out; cup, pút, rüle, üse; ch, child; ng, long; th, thin; ℞H, then; zh, measure; ə represents *a* in about, *e* in taken, *i* in April, *o* in lemon, *u* in circus.

When you run into an unknown word in your reading, one of the things that you want to know is how to pronounce the word. In such a case, the dictionary is ready to help you. Examine the sample page and notice the following aids to pronouncing words.

1. Syllable divisions are shown by (*a*) accent marks or (*b*) by a space.

2. The pronunciation of a word is shown in parentheses after the word.

3. The main accent is shown by a heavy mark (′). It tells which part of a word of more than one syllable gets the most emphasis, as in *excerpt* (*n.* ek′serpt; *v.* ek serpt′).

4. In some longer words, two syllables may be accented, with one syllable being emphasized more than the other and therefore being shown by the heavy accent mark. The lighter accent is shown by a lighter mark (′), as in *energetically* (en′ər jet′-ik li).

5. How the various letters are pronounced is shown in the key at the foot of the page; for example, ā is the marking for the sound of *a* as in *dare;* ė, as in *her;* ô, as in *order.* These marks are known as *diacritical marks.* (In some dictionaries, the *short* sound (˘) of vowels, as in *hat,* is marked.)

LEARNING ACTIVITIES IN PRONUNCIATION

A. (1) In the key at the foot of the sample dictionary page, find these words: age, hat, far, equal, let, term, ice, it, open, hot, cup. (2) Copy those eleven words in a column. (3) Beside each word, write one or more other words containing the same sound as that of the marked vowel. For *āge,* for example, *gate, crane,* and *maple* have the same sound of *a.* (4) Compare work in class.

B. (1) Using the key at the foot of the pages in your dictionary, indicate the vowel sounds in each of the following words. (2) Exchange papers. (3) Check by looking up the vowel markings of each word as given in your dictionary.

1. foot	5. meal	9. paid	13. wear
2. bone	6. weigh	10. blind	14. turn
3. tool	7. farm	11. meat	15. goal
4. hall	8. seize	12. war	16. rule

C. Find in the dictionary the answers to the following questions. Each question has to do with the respellings and markings that the dictionary gives in the parentheses after the words italicized in the questions. Make this an oral activity.

1. What happens to the *g* in *gentle?*
2. What happens to the *y* in *say?* to the *e* in *late?*
3. What happens to the *ey* in *they?*
4. What takes the place of the *t* in *whistle?* What happens to the *e?*
5. What happens to the *i* in *first?*
6. What happens to the *nk* in *think?*
7. What happens to the *i* and the *a* in *field* and *meat?*
8. What happens to the *c* in *cent?*
9. The respellings of *hallow* and *halo* contain the same four letters. How do their markings differ?

D. (1) Copy each of the following words, putting them all into one column. (2) In your dictionary, find and copy the respelling of each word. (3) Mark the sound of each vowel, and put in the accent marks. (4) Pronounce the words in class to show that you know what the marks mean.

1. invulnerable	4. stabilize	7. tonsorial
2. culinary	5. decorum	8. harbinger
3. masticate	6. multitudinous	9. turbulent

FOLLOW-UP

Notice the words "Used correct pronunciation" on your Speech Chart, page 61. From now on, pay special attention to this point.

USING ENGLISH IN ALL CLASSES

Check through a lesson in another subject to see whether any sentences contain words that you are not sure you can pronounce. Find the words in the dictionary and figure out the pronunciation. Then practice reading the sentences until you are sure of the pronunciation of every word.

PART FOUR: DIVIDING WORDS INTO SYLLABLES

As shown in point 1 on page 114, dividing words into syllables is a help in pronunciation. Knowing how to divide words into syllables is also helpful in all your written work, since you often find yourself needing to break a word at the end of a line.

GUIDES TO DIVIDING WORDS INTO SYLLABLES

1. If you are uncertain where to divide a word, use your dictionary. *Thorndike-Barnhart High School Dictionary* (see the sample on page 113) shows syllable divisions by accent marks and by spaces.

    EXAMPLE: par tic i pa tion (pär tis′ə pā′shan)

2. In written work, use a hyphen at the end of the line to show that a word is divided. (See guide 7 on page 140.)

3. Divide only between syllables, but never leave a single letter at the end of a line or at the beginning of the next line.

    WRONG: He turned his face ǎ-
    way. [Do not divide the word.]

    WRONG: We shall need *man-*
    χ helpers. [Do not divide the word.]

LEARNING ACTIVITIES IN DIVIDING WORDS

A. Divide the class into two equal groups. Then see which group can (1) find the most words of more than one syllable in the following paragraph, and (2) divide them correctly. Omit the proper nouns.

I had heard of some giant bats in the Chillibrillo Valley in Panama, creatures with a wing spread of a yard. They had originally been described by Linnaeus, and a few preserved specimens were in museums, but no living example had ever been exhibited. I engaged some young Hindus in Trinidad, who were keen woodsmen. They found tails of rats and feathers at the hollow bases of giant silk-cotton trees. Such trees average twenty feet in diameter at the ground, and taper up to towering, cylindrical trunks. In the broadened portion they are usually hollow to a height of about twenty-five feet. Investigation by flash-lamps disclosed that these tree chambers were the homes of single pairs of giant bats, and that these bats were flesh-eaters. When I arrived, I went to the inhabited trees. The beam of the searchlight in each hollow shaft revealed a pair of hanging bats whose bodies looked almost as big as those of opossums. With spliced bamboo poles we dislodged the bats toward us. As we grasped them in heavily gloved hands, their big wings wrapped around us like folds of a thin raincoat. I captured three pairs.*

---

*Adapted from *Animal Kingdom: The Way of Life in a Zoo* by Raymond Ditmars; copyright 1941 by Row, Peterson and Co., Evanston, Illinois.

B. For further drill, turn back to pages 211–12 and copy one of the paragraphs there. Keep as even a margin as you can at the right (one-half inch or more). Doing so will mean that you must divide some words at the end of a line. To help you decide where the divisions come, pronounce the words to yourself so that you can hear each syllable clearly. Exchange papers and check by using the dictionary.

USING ENGLISH IN ALL CLASSES

Go over the most recent paper that you have written for some other class. Look at each word that you divided at the end of a line; decide whether you did so correctly. If the word is not divided right, make the necessary corrections.

PART FIVE: FINDING THE RIGHT MEANING

"IT SAYS HERE THAT THE SHIP WAS FLEET. HOW CAN ONE SHIP BE A WHOLE FLEET?"

THINK IT OVER...

What does the student need to know about the word "fleet"? What is the intended meaning of the word here?

As you should have discovered before now, most words have more than one meaning; some words have many, many meanings. When you look up a word that you have met in your reading, you need to choose one meaning out of the different ones given in the dictionary. Here are some guides to help you.

GUIDES TO FINDING THE RIGHT MEANING

1. Read through the various meanings.
2. Try out those meanings.
3. Choose the meaning that makes the best sense in the sentence where you found the word.
4. If the word you are looking up is a verb that ends in *ed* or *ing,* drop the ending and find the base word. Choose the best meaning and add *ed* or *ing,* whichever your word had. For example, look at this sentence:

> John's work had been *deteriorating* for weeks.

The dictionary may give no definition for *deteriorating;* so you look up *deteriorate.* You find that one meaning is *grow worse.* You add *ing* to *grow* and substitute that meaning:

> John's work had been *growing worse* for weeks.

LEARNING ACTIVITIES IN CHOOSING RIGHT MEANINGS

A. Here are some sentences using words that are defined on the sample dictionary page (page 113 of this book). Decide which of the numbered meanings is needed in each sentence. Make this an oral activity.

1. Across from me sat a little boy who made my heart *tingle.*
2. Our calf *tipped* over the water pail.
3. She poured the fudge into the *tin.*
4. The bells *tingled* on the icy air.
5. We trimmed the tree with *tinsel.*
6. That hotel gives *tip top* service.

B. (1) Rewrite the following paragraphs, using other words for the words in italics. Use your dictionary to help you pick out for each word the meaning that makes the best sense. (2) *Proofread for careless errors in copying.* (3) Read several paragraphs in class or in your small groups. (See that you apply the Guides for Reading Aloud, page 57.) (4) List the various words substituted for the italicized ones. (5) Decide which words give the meaning best.

1. The real Texas Ranger was no *swaggering* hero. Before enlisting he had probably been a cowboy, a son of one of the pioneer families that had been in the state before the *influx* of bad men. He knew cattle and horses, and following a trail had always been a part of his business. Usually he was quiet, soft-spoken, *deliberate,* and gentle of manner. *Bullies* were not wanted in the force. Courage he had to have, but that was something most men

brought up on the wild frontier, close to danger, possessed in abundance. Other qualities as necessary were integrity, good judgment, knowledge of character, and *tact* in dealing with people.*

2. During the Lincoln County cattle war in New Mexico, Billy the Kid was the leader of the McSween *faction*. The story of that struggle is one of ambush, cold-blooded murder, and *pitched* battles. The war died down at last only when the principals on both sides were dead or their *resources* exhausted. General Lew Wallace was appointed governor to patch up a peace between the *feudists*. Billy the Kid refused to promise good conduct in the future, and instead *resumed* practice as a *rustler* and killer. Within ten days of the time Governor Wallace had personally pleaded with him to *desist* from crime, he *wantonly* killed an Indian agency clerk named Bernstein, for no reason except that the young man had seen him stealing horses.*

USING ENGLISH IN ALL CLASSES

(1) From the next day's assignment in any class, choose and copy a paragraph that has in it at least five unfamiliar words. (If necessary, take more than one paragraph.) (2) Underline the words that puzzle you. Find each word in the dictionary and then select the meaning that fits. (3) Above each puzzling word write the meaning that you chose.

FOLLOW-UP

As you study each day's lessons, form the habit of looking up in the dictionary any puzzling words. Use context clues (see page 105) to help you select the right meaning for each word.

---

*Adapted from *45-Caliber Law: The Way of Life of the Frontier Peace Officer* by William MacLeod Raine; copyright 1941 by Row, Peterson and Co., Evanston, Illinois.

FINDING AND USING SOURCES OF INFORMATION

"LIBRARIES ARE FOR PEOPLE WHO KNOW A LOT."

"THAT'S WHERE YOU'RE WRONG. THEY'RE FOR PEOPLE WHO WANT TO LEARN A LOT."

THINK IT OVER...

What do *you* do when you need information on any topic?

With what "special sections" of the dictionary are you acquainted?

With what reference books besides dictionaries and encyclopedias are you acquainted?

What do you know about the *Readers' Guide?*

1. Exploring Special Sections in the Dictionary

Pages 109–19, in Chapter 6, explain how to find words in the dictionary and tells what different kinds of information it gives about the words. Some dictionaries have certain special sections.

Most dictionaries include brief sections on "How to Use This Dictionary." Such sections are of specific help in getting the most out of dictionary study. Here, for instance, are the main items included in the "How to Use This Dictionary" section of the *Thorndike-Barnhart High School Dictionary*:

How to Find a Word
How to Use This Dictionary for Spelling
How to Use This Dictionary for Pronunciation
How to Use the Inflected Forms
How to Use the Definitions
How to Use the Etymologies
How to Use the Synonyms and Antonyms
How to Use the Usage Notes

ACTIVITIES IN USING SPECIAL INFORMATION IN THE DICTIONARY

A. Referring to the pronunciation chart in your dictionary (in the Thorndike-Barnhart High School Dictionary, this chart is opposite "How to Use This Dictionary for Spelling"), copy the various spellings for the following sounds.

1. the $\bar{u}$ sound	3. the $\bar{o}$ sound	5. the n sound
2. the *schwa* (ə) sound	4. the g sound	6. the z sound

B. A dictionary entry may include a number of *idioms* in which the entry is included. An *idiom*, as defined by the *Thorndike-Barnhart High School Dictionary*, is a "phrase or expression whose meaning cannot be understood from the ordinary meanings of the words in it: '*How do you do?*' and '*I have caught cold*' are English idioms."
Write down all the idioms that you find listed under "hand."

C. (1) In your dictionary, find the following abbreviations. Some have more than one meaning. (2) Write the abbreviations and their meanings on a sheet of paper. (3) Go over papers orally.

1. agt.	3. amt.	5. bal.	7. chap.	9. dpt.	11. N.C.O.
2. alt.	4. b.	6. bbl.	8. chm.	10. fr.	12. pk.

D. In your dictionary, find answers to the following questions. Write each answer in a complete sentence. *Proofread for careless mistakes in spelling, capitalization, and punctuation.* Exchange papers for checking as the answers are read aloud. If you think that an answer on a classmate's paper is a fragment instead of a complete sentence, mark *F* in the margin.

1. When was Abraham *Lincoln* born?
2. Where and what is *Vesuvius?*
3. When was James *Madison* President?
4. For what is Roald *Amundsen* famous?
5. What is another name for *Nippon?*
6. How far below sea level is the *Dead Sea?*
7. Which English king named *Edward* was murdered in the Tower of London?
8. How many square miles are there in the *Hawaiian Islands?*
9. How many *Henrys* were French kings?
10. What two high offices did William Howard *Taft* hold?

2. Exploring Other Sources of Information

READ AND THINK ABOUT

You have seen how much information the dictionary can give you. Sometimes, however, you want to know more than the brief facts given in the dictionary. What do you do in such cases?

Knowing where to look for information is important, for then you are pretty sure to find what you need—and are likely to find it quickly. Among the references that will be most useful to you are (1) almanacs, (2) atlases, (3) encyclopedias, (4) the *Readers' Guide,* and (5) books on special subjects.

YEARBOOKS OF FACTS, OR ALMANACS

Yearbooks of facts, called also *almanacs,* contain up-to-date information about many things, such as the name of the football team that won the Rose Bowl game last year, the name of the state that leads in the production of corn, and so on. Two of the best-known almanacs are listed here.

Information Please Almanac   *World Almanac and Book of Facts*

ATLASES

An *atlas* is a book of maps and other geographical information. It contains not only maps that show the location of countries, cities, and so on, but maps that show natural resources, population facts, temperature and rainfall, surface, and many other things. The following are atlases especially prepared for school use.

Denoyer's School Atlas   *Hammond's World Atlas for Students*
Rand McNally's World Atlas, Goode's Edition

ENCYCLOPEDIAS

Encyclopedias usually are sets of books. They give information about thousands of people, places, things, and events. Those listed here are found in many schools.

Britannica Junior   *Compton's Pictured Encyclopedia*
World Book Encyclopedia

READERS' GUIDE

The *Readers' Guide to Periodical Literature* (usually shortened to *Readers' Guide*) is an index naming all the articles published in more than a hundred important magazines. (Magazines are called *periodical* literature because they come out at regular periods.)

Here is part of a page from the *Readers' Guide,** showing some of the information given for various topics. The abbreviations that are used are explained at the front of each issue.

	LIGHT tables. (See Drawing boards, tables, etc.)	— *cross*
page numbers	LIGHTING fixtures Kitchen lighting pointers. Bet Hom & Gard (50:168+)N '72	*reference*
	LIGHTSEY, Ralph. See Lanier, D. jt. auth.	
author entry	LILIES Lilies, a glory; with photographs by I. Penn. Vogue 160:166-9 D '72	*title of*
	(LIN, Yutang) Scrutable Chinese. il por (Newsweek) 80:128-9 D 4 '72 *	*magazine*
subject	(LINCOLN, Abraham) Lincoln's lost love; letter. April 1, 1838. (il) por Am Heritage 23:110-11 Ap '72	*illustrated*
	LINCOLN, George A. Winter fuel shortage: how serious? interview. il por U.S. News 73:73-6(D 11 '72)	*date of* *publication*
	LINCOLN Center for the performing arts, New York (Opera house)	*subtopic*
title of article	(Touring backstage.) L. Levant. il Opera N 37:32-3 D 23 '72	

BOOKS ON SPECIAL SUBJECTS

Books on special subjects, textbooks, for example, contain information about some particular field of knowledge.

*From *Readers' Guide to Periodical Literature,* January 10, 1973, Vol. 72, No. 20; copyright © 1973 by The H. W. Wilson Company, New York. Reprinted with permission.

GUIDES TO THE USE OF REFERENCES

1. Get acquainted with the way that encyclopedias are organized. Like the dictionary, the entries in encyclopedias are arranged alphabetically and have guide words at the top of each page. Look for the last name of a person, as in the telephone book.

   a) The first volume of *Britannica Junior* is a ready reference index, alphabetically arranged, of all the different topics covered. It lists for each topic all pages in the entire set that contain information about that topic. The letter *a* after a page number indicates that the information is in the left-hand column; *b,* in the right-hand one.

   b) *Compton's Pictured Encyclopedia* has at the back of each volume an index that lists all the items covered in that volume, plus references to other volumes that also have information on that topic.

   c) *World Book* has no such index as the other two, but a special volume, *Reading and Study Guide,* accompanies the set. It is organized alphabetically under many subject-matter heads.

2. Learn to use the index that you will find at the back of most atlases, almanacs,* and books on special subjects.

3. Get acquainted with the organization of the *Readers' Guide.*

   a) Main entries give (1) subjects or (2) names of people.

   b) Subheads break subjects into smaller topics. Under "Phonograph records," for example, you might find such entries as "Folk music," "Jazz music," "Opera."

   c) Names of people may refer to (1) authors or (2) people about whom someone has written articles.

LEARNING ACTIVITIES IN USING SPECIAL REFERENCES

A. Check your classroom. Has it a set of encyclopedias, an atlas, and any special subject books besides your regular textbooks?

Hold a discussion about ways to make good use of the reference books in your classroom. Have a chairman in charge. He should keep his book open to guide 2 of the Guides for Holding Discussions, page 33.

B. If your school has a library, arrange to take a period or more to find out how many of the references listed on pages 122–23 are contained there. Make note of other special reference books. List on the board all these sources. Decide how they can best be used.

* The index of the *World Almanac* is at the front of the book.

C. Let someone volunteer to telephone to the public library to see whether your class may arrange for a visit there. Before telephoning, review the Guides for Telephoning, page 70.

After the visit, discuss in class the sources of information that you found at the library.

Write a letter thanking the librarian for allowing you to visit. Follow the Guides for Writing Thank-You Letters, page 262, and use the form for business letters, page 265. Choose and mail one of the best letters.

D. In which kind of reference book, other than books on special subjects, could you probably find answers to the following questions? Make this an oral discussion. To have a good one, follow guides 3 and 4 of the Guides for Holding Discussions, page 33.

1. Where and when was the atom first split?
2. Which baseball player won the American League batting championship last year, and what was his batting average?
3. Which countries of the world lead in coal production?
4. What river forms part of the boundary between Uruguay and Argentina?
5. Who is the United States Secretary of State now?
6. Who first played the game of lacrosse?
7. Have there been any important new discoveries in medicine in the past few months?
8. What countries of the world have a very light rainfall?
9. How many voyages to the New World did Columbus make?
10. How are diamonds mined?

E. Here are some entries from the *Readers' Guide*. With the help of the sample on page 123, tell all the information given in each entry. Make this an oral activity. Magazines that you might not know are *New Catholic World* and *National Parks and Conservation Magazine*.

MALI
    Native races
    Nomads of the Niger. J. P. Imperato. il Natur Hist 81:60-9+ D '72
MALITS, Elena
    Yoga is a spiritual discipline. il New Cath World 215:249-51+ N '72
MALLIOS, Harry C.
    Symbolic expression: the new battle facing school administrators. bibliog Intellect 101:117-18 N '72
MALPRACTICE
    Yogurt cure; treatment at Feminist women's health center in Los Angeles. Newsweek 80:44 D 18 '72
MAMMOTH CAVE NATIONAL PARK
    Mammoth Cave. Holiday 52:26 N '72
    Mammoth Cave: a model plan. R. A. Watson. il Nat Parks & Con Mag 46:13-18 D '72

F. In finding answers to the following questions, which is the key word to look for in the encyclopedia or in the index of some other book?

Number your paper from 1 to 10 and beside each number write the word or words that you would look for first. Compare words in class; then find the answers to the questions.

1. What is the motto of the state of Kentucky?
2. What is the area of Scotland?
3. Which baseball league came first, the National or the American?
4. Who discovered the Hawaiian Islands?
5. What country first tried to dig the Panama Canal?
6. When did the United States Military Academy at West Point first begin training soldiers?
7. What new volcano appeared in Mexico in 1943?
8. In what year did the United States set up standard time zones?
9. Can a living person be elected to the Hall of Fame?
10. Who invented the game of basketball, and when?

USING ENGLISH OUTSIDE SCHOOL

Have you a hobby? If so, use the *Readers' Guide* to find magazines or magazine articles about it. In reading them, you may discover people with whom you would like to correspond. In that case, follow the letter-writing guides on pages 253, 256, and 258.

3. Finding Books in the Library

"I THINK IT'S A BIG RED BOOK. BUT THESE SHELVES ARE FULL OF BIG RED BOOKS!"

THINK IT OVER . . .

What better way of locating that book might Wirdley use?

Examining everything on the library shelves in search of a particular book probably is a harder job than you would care to tackle. Luckily, that kind of search is not necessary, for most libraries are arranged in a special way that makes finding books easy.

The plan used by most libraries is the *Dewey Decimal System.*

1. **The Dewey Decimal System divides books into ten large classes, such as** *Religion, Social Sciences, History.*

2. **Each class is assigned a special set of numbers.** Every book about religion, for example, will be marked with a number somewhere between 200 and 299. All those books will be put together in one section of the library.

3. **The class number of a book is part of what is known as its "call number."** The call number has two parts:

   a) The upper part is the class number.

   b) The lower part begins with a letter, the first letter of the author's name.

   The call number is put on the backbone of the book so that it can be seen as the book stands on the shelf.

4. **Books are arranged on the library shelves in regular order from left to right, beginning with the lowest call numbers.** When the upper part of the call number of two or more books is the same, the books are arranged in order by the lower part, as shown by the 373.6 books in the drawing.

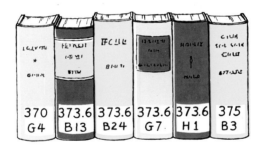

| 370
G4 | 373.6
B13 | 373.6
B24 | 373.6
G7 | 373.6
H1 | 375
B3 |

LEARNING ACTIVITY

Arrange in a column the following call numbers in the order that books so marked would be found on the library shelves. Make this a chalkboard activity.

702.4 H5	717.3 D2	722.44 M16	717.4 F5	717.1 F2
792 A6	717.4 C3	722.1 R3	792.1 A21	722.1 R14

* All books except fiction (storybooks) are arranged on the shelves according to this system.

As you can see, once you know the call number, you will know where to look for a certain book. To find the call number itself, you should look in the *card catalogue.*

● THESE ARE FACTS ABOUT THE CARD CATALOGUE

1. The card catalogue is contained in a cabinet with drawers about the size of shoe boxes.
   a) On the front of each drawer is a label telling what part of the alphabet the cards in it cover.
   b) In the drawer are cards, arranged alphabetically, that give the call number of every book in the library.

2. Every book except fiction (storybooks) has three cards: (*a*) an *author* card, (*b*) a *title* card, and (*c*) a *subject* card.

3. Books of fiction have only two cards: (*a*) an *author* card and (*b*) a *title* card.

4. Each card carries the call number of the book, in the upper left-hand corner. Fiction may have no call number, or may have only the lower part, perhaps with *F* (for *Fiction*) above it.

AUTHOR CARD

The first word on the top line is the *author's last name.* This card is filed alphabetically by that last name.

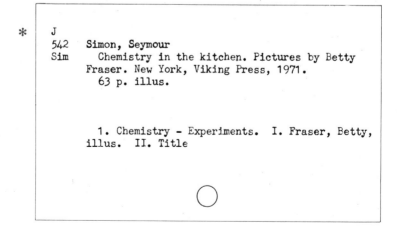

*The J in front of the call number indicates that the book is juvenile literature.

The *title card* is the same as the author card, except that the *title* of the book is typed at the top of the card, above the author's name. The title card is filed in the card catalogue alphabetically by the first word on that top line, unless the first word of the title is *a, an,* or *the.* In that case, it will be filed by the second word. For example, for a book named *The Lost Island,* you would look under *L,* not *T.*

```
J          Chemistry in the kitchen
542      Simon, Seymour
Sim           Chemistry in the kitchen. Pictures by Betty
          Fraser. New York, Viking Press, 1971.
              63 p. illus.



              1. Chemistry - Experiments.  I. Fraser, Betty,
          illus.  II. Title
```

SUBJECT CARD

The *subject card* is the same as the author card, except that the top line tells the *subject* dealt with in the book, such as *baseball* or *butterflies.* There will be a card for each book that the library has on that particular subject.

```
J          CHEMISTRY - EXPERIMENTS
542      Simon, Seymour
Sim           Chemistry in the kitchen. Pictures by Betty
          Fraser. New York, Viking Press, 1971.
              63 p. illus.



              1. Chemistry - Experiments.  I. Fraser, Betty,
          illus.  II. Title
```

LEARNING ACTIVITY IN READING CATALOGUE CARDS

Write answers to the following questions, all based on the card below. Make each answer a complete sentence. (See page 337 to help you avoid sentence fragments.) *Proofread for careless errors.* Exchange papers for checking as you go over the questions in class.

```
595.7   Swan, Lester A.
Swa         The common insects of North America, by
        Lester A. Swan and Charles S. Papp. Illus-
        trated by Charles S. Papp. New York, Harper
        & Row [1972]
            750 p. illus.
            Bibliography: p. 693-710.

            1. Insects - North America.  I. Papp,
        Charles S., jt. auth.  II. Title
```

1. Who is the author?
2. What is the title?
3. How many pages has the book?
4. Who illustrated the book? How do you know?
5. Who published the book? When?
6. Under what subject would the book be catalogued?
7. Why is there no *j* preceding the call number?

GUIDES FOR LOCATING BOOKS IN THE LIBRARY

1. Go to the card catalogue.
    a) If you want a book and know its title, look for that title.
    b) If you want a particular book and know only the name of the author, look for that author's name.
    c) If you are looking for no particular book but want books on a special topic, such as *Circuses,* look under that word.

2. Copy the call number, the title of the book, and the author's name.

3. Find the shelf that holds books with the upper number that is on the book that you want.

4. Look at the lower part of the call number, which begins with an initial and has a number after it.

A. (1) Decide whether you would look for an author card, a title card, or a subject card in each of the following cases. (2) Use the card catalogue to help you locate the books indicated. Copy and read to the class the call numbers, authors, and titles of the books that you find.

1. You are recommending to a friend a book called *Going into Space,* but you have forgotten the author's name.
2. You have heard that a man named Ogden Nash has written several amusing books of poetry.
3. Chemistry is your hobby. You would like to know what books your library has in that field.
4. You want to get some information about helicopters.
5. You want to find some new books by Walter Farley.

B. In the card catalogue, look up the author of a book that you have read this year. Note whether your library has any other books by that person. Report to the class the name of the book that you read, the name of the author, and the call number. Give also the call numbers and titles of other books that the author has written.

C. (1) Using the card catalogue, make a list of six books that the library has on one of these subjects: *aviation, forests, poetry, art, television, politics, stars, inventions, music, travel, photography, physical education.* Copy the title, the name of the author, and the call number of each book. (2) See whether you can locate the books. (3) Leaf through the books to decide on several that you would like to read. (4) Put a star beside each such title on your list. (5) Compare lists in your small groups.

D. The following authors write (or have written) fiction enjoyed by boys and girls. Find out what books the library has by these authors. To do so, divide the names among the class. (If your class is large, two people may report on the same author.) Go over the lists in class. File in your notebook the names of books that you might want to read.

Louisa May Alcott	Marguerite Henry	Howard Pyle
Jane and Paul Annixter	Annabel and Edgar	Armstrong Sperry
Howard M. Brier	Johnson	Robert L. Stevenson
Betty Cavanna	Rudyard Kipling	Mary Stolz
Bruce Carter	James M. Kjelgaard	Geoffrey Trease
B. J. Chute	Florence C. Means	John R. Tunis
Elizabeth Coatsworth	L. M. Montgomery	Robb White
Walter D. Edmonds	Rutherford Montgomery	Phyllis Whitney
Elizabeth J. Gray	Howard Pease	James Playsted Wood

USING ENGLISH OUTSIDE SCHOOL

What hobbies interest you? The card catalogue can help you to find more and more pleasure in following them. Get the library habit!

4. Getting Acquainted with the Make-Up of a Book

Once you have found a book that looks as though it may contain needed information, you can save time by knowing how to use the various parts of the book.

The body of a book is the most important part, of course, but six other parts will help you to use the book efficiently. The first four come at the front; the other two, at the back.

1. The *title page* tells (1) what the name of the book is, (2) who wrote it, (3) who published it, and (4) where it was published. You will need this information if for any reason you want to write to the publisher.

2. The *copyright page* tells when the book was published. The date of publication is important, especially in fields such as science, where new discoveries are always being made.

3. The *preface* (or *foreword*) is the introduction to the book. It usually explains the purpose and tells in general what is covered.

4. The *table of contents* lists in order the chapter titles, usually with subtopics that are covered in them.

5. An *appendix* may follow the main text. It contains such things as explanatory notes, tables, lists of books, or other useful information.

6. The *index* comes last. It lists alphabetically all topics contained in the book and names the pages on which each topic is discussed. It also lists helpful cross references (*See . . .* or *See also . . .*) to other entries.

LEARNING ACTIVITY IN EXAMINING THE PARTS OF A BOOK

(1) Examine this book to find the six parts mentioned above; then use them to find answers to the following questions. (2) Write the answers in complete sentences. (3) *Proofread for careless errors.* (4) Exchange papers for checking. Tell where you found the answers.

1. How many chapters deal with grammar? What are their numbers?
2. On what page are homonyms defined?
3. Which chapter deals with improving reading skills?
4. What is in the appendix?
5. What is the newest date of publication?
6. How are the pages before the body of the book numbered?
7. How many authors has this book? What are their names? Who published it?

In English class, look through the textbooks used in your other classes. Do all have the six parts named on page 132? Do any have additional sections, such as lists of maps or of illustrations? Examine each part carefully; perhaps it has information that you were not aware of before.

5. Making Reports

"I DID BETTER THAN THAT. I JUST COPIED WHAT THE BOOK SAID."

"DID YOU TAKE NOTES ABOUT WHAT YOU READ?"

READ AND THINK ABOUT

You would not think of walking into a neighbor's or even a stranger's house and helping yourself to his money or property. Remember, then, that it is just as dishonest to steal the words someone else has written. To do so is to commit a crime called *plagiarism,* punishable by law.

PART ONE: MAKING A SHORT REPORT

When you are asked to report what is contained in a certain article (in an encyclopedia, a magazine, or a special book), you may make use of several skills: using reference books, the card catalogue, the *Readers' Guide;* taking notes of key words; and outlining. If you need to review any of these skills, use the Index of this English book to guide you to the right places for help.

GUIDES FOR MAKING A SHORT, ONE-SOURCE REPORT

1. Read the article through once to get the general idea.

2. Write, in your own words, a sentence that tells clearly what the article as a whole is about.

3. Go over the article again and jot down the words or groups of words that are key words. (Review the guides on page 89.)

4. Use those key words to make a topic outline. (See page 99.)

5. Decide definitely on an interesting opening sentence and a strong closing sentence.

6. In making your report, tell where you found the article.

7. For an oral report, practice at home. Probably you will say things differently each time, but if you put the important key words into your outline, the *ideas* will be the same.

LEARNING ACTIVITIES IN MAKING SHORT REPORTS

A. For your first practice, choose an article about a half column long in an encyclopedia. Leaf through the book until you find something that looks interesting. Then follow the Guides for Making a Short, One-Source Report. In preparing the report, check your Speech Chart.

After each report is given in class, jot down a note or two about the speaker. Use the Speech Chart, page 61, for points on which to comment. When all reports have been given, take time for each of you to mark his Speech Chart on the basis of the notes from classmates.

B. Repeat *A,* only this time write the report, using one of the topics listed below. Check each paragraph by the guides on page 214.

1. armor	7. geysers	13. scorpions	19. Eskimo dogs
2. honey	8. locusts	14. pheasants	20. battleships
3. rabies	9. marbles	15. parakeets	21. Death Valley
4. tulips	10. pelicans	16. kangaroos	22. Secret Service
5. stilts	11. rainbows	17. Robin Hood	23. watermelons
6. deserts	12. locoweed	18. sunstroke	24. Yankee Doodle

PART TWO: REPORTING ON MATERIAL FROM SEVERAL SOURCES

Often, in preparing a report, you are expected to gather material from several sources. In such cases, a different plan from that above should be followed. Study the plan suggested on page 135.

1. Decide what main points—no more than three or four—you want to cover. Write each main point on a separate sheet of paper and label each with a Roman numeral, I, II, and so on. For a report on *earthquakes,* for example, the first page might be labeled thus:

I. The causes of earthquakes

Page 2 might have this label:

II. The effects of earthquakes

Page 3 might be labeled thus:

III. Famous earthquakes

2. Find the material. In addition to encyclopedias, consult other books. Use the card catalogue to find them. (See page 128.) Remember that indexes and tables of contents will save you time. Use the *Readers' Guide* to find magazine articles.

3. Go through these references one by one.
   a) Select only facts that tell about one of your main points.
   b) Jot each fact down on a separate card, with the name of the source, the name of the author, and the page numbers.
   c) As a rule, put the information into your own words. If you do copy a sentence, use quotation marks and give credit.

4. Select the cards with the most important or most interesting facts.

5. Separate the cards into piles, one for each main idea.

6. Arrange each pile in what seems to you the best order.

7. Under each main point, copy from the cards the points that fit it. Write them in regular outline form. (See page 99.)

8. Make a bibliography, or list, of all the sources that you used. This should be put at the end of your report. Arrange the sources alphabetically in the style shown here.

   Hilton, W. F. *Manned Satellites,* pp. 3–45.
   Shatalov, Vladimir. "A Man on a Long Space Flight." *Space World,* October 1972, pp. 30–31.
   "Space Travel," *World Book Encyclopedia* (1967 edition), pp. 560–73.

9. Write the report.
   a) Write it quickly first, without stopping to go back over it.
   b) Go over each sentence and paragraph critically. (See page 453.)
   c) Check spelling, punctuation, and capitalization.
   d) Copy the report; then proofread it carefully.
   e) Make a cover sheet containing your name, the date, and the title of the report.

LEARNING ACTIVITY IN WRITING A REPORT FROM SEVERAL SOURCES

Choose a topic for a report; if possible, one assigned in some other class. If not, you may want to choose one of those listed here.

1. Radar	9. Carrier Pigeons	17. Skin Diving
2. Tornadoes	10. Diamond Mining	18. Hybrid Corn
3. Meteors	11. Flying Saucers	19. Miracle Drugs
4. Whaling	12. Poisonous Snakes	20. Helicopters
5. Comets	13. The Pony Express	21. Indian Houses
6. Archery	14. Peaceful Uses of the Atom	22. Hurricanes
7. Mummies	15. Atomic Submarines	23. Fingerprinting
8. Volcanoes	16. Jet Transports	24. Color Television

ENRICHMENT

From the list of topics in the Learning Activity above, select two and prepare a short bibliography for each one. Consult the card catalog (see page 128), the *Readers' Guide to Periodical Literature* (see page 123), and other reference books (see page 124) for possible sources. For the proper form for your bibliography, see guide 8 on page 135.

SECTION III

Writing

WRITING SKILLS

1. Checking the Form of Your Papers

"DID YOU EVER NOTICE HOW MUCH A PERSON'S WORK TELLS YOU ABOUT HIM?"

READ AND THINK ABOUT

Suppose that by some chance you were asked to appear on television. What would concern you most, aside from whatever you were to do on the program? You probably would answer, "How I'd look—that's what!"

In other words, like any sensible person, you would want to look your very best, knowing that you must face the inspection of many thousands of pairs of eyes.

Something that may never have occurred to you, however, is that whenever you hand in a school paper, you are also up for inspection. What does the appearance of your papers tell the world about *you?*

GUIDES TO PROPER MANUSCRIPT FORM

1. Leave even margins on the sides and at the top and bottom. Your paper should look like a picture set in a frame. See the example on the next page.

2. Unless a different form is used in your school, put the name of the subject on the top line at the left, and your name at the right, with the date below it. The heading should have the same margins as the rest of the paper.

3. Skip a line; then center the title on the next line. Skip another line before you begin your theme.

4. Indent all paragraphs the same distance, at least a half inch.

5. Write as plainly as you can. Avoid both large, scrawling handwriting and the tiny, cramped-looking kind. (See page 479.)

6. Avoid blots, smudges, and messy cross-outs. If your papers are written in ink, use a good ink eraser.

7. Use a hyphen if you must divide a word at the end of a line. Be sure to put the hyphen at the end of the line, never at the beginning of the following line.

> RIGHT: The candidates of both political parties were con
> fident of victory.
> WRONG: The candidates of both political parties were con
> fident of victory.

   a) Divide only between syllables. **(DEFINITION)** A syllable is a part of a word pronounced as one sound; it must always have a vowel (*a, e, i, o, u,* or *y*) and may have one or more consonants (all the other letters of the alphabet). When in doubt about the syllables in a word, use your dictionary.

> ath lete   hol i day

   b) Never carry over a syllable that has in it only one letter. For example, do not divide *copy* (cop′y), since the second syllable has only one letter.

   c) Never leave only the first letter of a word at the end of a line. For example, do not divide *about* (a bout′), since the first syllable has only one letter.

   d) Never divide words of one syllable.

> strength   broil   dealt

Elaine Daniels
October 12, 19—

The Hit of the Play

Several summers ago, some friends and I decided to give a play, using our garage as a theater. We did a lot of practicing, but since we had no written play, we just made up our lines as we went along.

On the day that we were to give our performance, we worked like beavers, cleaning our garage, putting up benches, and building a stage. Our curtain was a blanket. It was full of holes, more or less pinned together with large safety pins.

While we were still getting ready, our audience began to arrive. Someone had the bright idea of letting them help us. Soon these helpers were suggesting ideas for the play, and before we knew it, they were in the cast. By the time the play finally began, we had twenty actors—and three people in the audience!

About the middle of the play, my sister walked in and announced, "Elaine, you've got to go to the store."

Even though I explained that we were in the middle of a murder and that I was the victim, it did me no good.

I ran all the way to the store and back. On returning, I found the same act still going on. I rushed up to the stage—and fell flat on my face. It was not really time for my murder, but my fall was too good to waste.

The audience clapped and cheered my "murder." It was worth the price of admission by itself, they declared; and it probably was, for we had taken in exactly one penny—and six safety pins!

LEARNING ACTIVITIES IN MANUSCRIPT FORM

A. In class, find out whether the form that your teacher wants your papers to have is different in any ways from the form that is given in the guides. Take notes on what your teacher's answers are to the following questions:

1. What size of paper are we to use?
2. Are we to write with pen and ink?
3. What information are we to give in the heading? Should there be more than is shown in the example? Exactly where and in what order is the information to be given?
4. Are there to be equal margins on all sides of the paper? How wide are they to be?
5. Where is the title to be written? Shall there be a space below the title?
6. How far shall each paragraph be indented?
7. Are we to write on both sides of the paper?
8. Where do we begin writing on the back or on the second sheet?

B. (1) Copy the following words. (2) Put parentheses around the ones that you would not divide at the end of a line. (3) Mark the other words to show where you would divide them. If you are not sure, use your dictionary. (4) Exchange papers and go over the words in class, explaining the reason for dividing or not dividing each word.

EXAMPLES

(length)   mil|i|tary   care|ful|ness

1. waiting	6. hospital	11. yesterday	16. brought
2. borrow	7. beyond	12. busy	17. gasoline
3. communicate	8. health	13. waitress	18. locate
4. disappoint	9. breathe	14. honorable	19. wrench
5. stretch	10. grammar	15. dangerous	20. remember

FOLLOW-UP

Using the notes that you took in *A,* make a model of the form that all your English papers will be expected to have. See that your model is as neat as the one on page 141. Perhaps your teacher may also want you to make a check list from the notes that you took in *A.* If so, state the points in complete sentences. (See page 166 for what a complete sentence contains.) Hand in your model and your check list for your teacher's approval; or, if he prefers, compare your models and check lists in class to be sure that all of you agree. Then check with the model every paper that you write.

Find out what form your papers in all your classes are supposed to have—in science, history, arithmetic. If these are different from the form to be used in English class, make a model for each one. Keep the models in your notebook; then be sure to check the form of each paper that you hand in. Always be 100 per cent correct in the form of your papers.

2. Using Capital Letters Correctly*

"THE COACH SAID, 'WHEN WE FUMBLED ON THE FIVE-YARD LINE, THE BRUINS CAPITALIZED ON OUR MISTAKE!'"

TALK IT OVER...

What did the coach mean by "capitalized"? What more common meaning do you know for the word "capital"? What connection can you see between the two meanings?

How sure of yourself are you in your use of capital letters?

After Pretest 1 has been scored, go over it carefully to see how to correct your mistakes. Make a record of the kinds of errors that you had. If you made any errors on the capitalization part of the test, study carefully the rules and exercises that follow.

If you had a perfect score and your teacher excuses you from the instruction and practice that follow, you may enjoy doing the activities in the "Just For Fun" section on pages 175–77.

---

* Pretest 1 should be taken at this point. All tests called for in the text are contained in a test booklet that may be purchased for each student. The tests also appear in the *Teacher's Guide.* Schools not wishing to buy the booklets may mimeograph the tests.

PART ONE: CAPITALIZING PROPER NOUNS

● THESE ARE FACTS

1. (DEFINITION) A noun is a name word.

2. (DEFINITION) A *common noun* names any member of a *general group:* boy, day, city, holiday.

3. (DEFINITION) A *proper noun* names a *specific* member of any general group: John, Friday, Boston, Christmas.

| GENERAL: | boy | day | city | holiday |
| SPECIFIC: | John | Friday | Boston | Christmas |

RULES FOR USING CAPITAL LETTERS

RULE 1. Capitalize every proper noun.

COMMON NOUN	PROPER NOUN	COMMON NOUN	PROPER NOUN
boy	John	country	Norway
girl	Mary	nationality	Spanish
day	Friday	holiday	Christmas
month	January	newspaper	*Chicago Tribune*
city	Omaha	organization	American Legion
state	Nebraska	magazine	*Junior Scholastic*

RULE 2. Capitalize common nouns such as *street, lake, river, mountain, school* when used as part of a proper noun to name a particular place or thing.

I swam in the lake. (*The name of the lake is not given.*)
I swam in Lake Michigan. (*The name of the lake is told.*)
We have a new junior high school. (*The name is not given.*)
I attend Irving Junior High School. (*The name is told.*)

COMMON NOUN	PROPER NOUN	COMMON NOUN	PROPER NOUN
river	Missouri River	city	Sioux City
ocean	Atlantic Ocean	avenue	Forest Avenue
day	Labor Day	mountain	Mount Whitney

RULE 3. Do not capitalize prepositions (see the list on page 43b), the conjunction *and,* or the articles *a, an,* or *the* when used as part of a proper noun.

J. C. Smith *and* Company   Cape *of* Good Hope
"Home *on the* Range"

"LISTEN. I'VE WRITTEN A POEM:
"FOR ALL PROPER NOUNS, IT'S TRUE INDEED
THAT CAPITAL LETTERS ARE WHAT YOU NEED!"

LEARNING ACTIVITIES IN CAPITALIZATION

A. Copy the following list of common nouns. After each one write a proper noun that it suggests to you. EXAMPLE: *person—Bob Mehlen.* Read your lists aloud to see how many different proper nouns the class named. Be sure that each word on your list is capitalized correctly.

1. state	5. film star	9. theater	13. store
2. city	6. restaurant	10. month	14. business firm
3. explorer	7. airplane	11. holiday	15. baseball player
4. author	8. man	12. nation	16. automobile

B. Think of a proper noun to use with each common noun in the following list. EXAMPLE: *river—Hudson River.* Write the words in sentences; then read your sentences in class, telling which words you have capitalized. Be sure to apply guides 4 and 7 in the Guides for Reading Aloud, page 57. If you made errors in capitalization, study the rules again so that you understand your mistakes; then correct them.

1. street	4. railroad	7. junior high school
2. county	5. club	8. creek
3. mountains	6. canal	9. boulevard

C. (1) Write five sentences with geographical proper nouns of at least three words, one of which should not be capitalized (Rule 3, page 144). Use a map of the world to help you find names to use.

EXAMPLE: The *Strait of Gibraltar* separates Spain and Africa.

(2) *Proofread your sentences for careless mistakes.* (3) Read your sentences in class. Have someone list on the board the different proper nouns used.

D. Copy Rules 1, 2, and 3 into your notebook, leaving space below each rule for examples. Clip from magazines three examples of each rule and paste them under the rule that applies.

Page 144 gives rules for the capitalization of proper nouns. You should make sure that you know certain other uses of capital letters. Study the following rules and examples carefully.

RULES FOR USING CAPITAL LETTERS—Continued

RULE 4. Capitalize the first word of a sentence.

> Everyone wanted to go to the game.
> Are they coming with us?

RULE 5. Capitalize the first word of a quotation.

> Don complained, "No one asked me to go."
> "No one," complained Don, "asked me to go."

RULE 6. Capitalize titles used with names of people. Many times these titles are abbreviations. Capitalize initials that stand for names of people.

Mr. and Mrs. R. O. Lowry	Aunt Susan
Dr. Herbert A. Crandall	Professor P. K. Mull
Lieutenant S. M. Naylor	Superintendent J. B. Bell

RULE 7. Capitalize the word *I* and contractions formed with it. (See page 163 if you do not know what contractions are.)

> Yes, I plan to go, but I'll have to walk.

LEARNING ACTIVITIES IN CAPITALIZATION

A. (1) Copy the following sentences, placing capital letters where they belong. (2) *Be sure to proofread.* (3) Exchange papers with a partner and check your work.

1. the first thing that mr. rogers said was, "where have you been?"
2. When captain john r. dagen gives a command, things happen.
3. What i saw, i'll never forget.
4. we have an appointment to see superintendent baynes.
5. Marjorie asked, "are you sure that was professor jones?"
6. yes, aunt dorothy and i met the train.
7. The speaker was to be dr. w. l. hanlon of atlanta, georgia.
8. "you should," mrs. ellsworth reminded, "be in your seats."
9. If mr. franklin calls, say that i've left for school.
10. Sitting there, i heard a voice yell, "help!"

B. (1) Write sentences of your own as examples of the seven rules for capitalizing that you have studied. (2) *Be sure to proofread your sentences.* (3) In class, take turns at putting a sentence on the board, writing all the words with small letters. Call on a classmate to supply the needed capitals.

C. Copy Rules 4–7 into your notebook with Rules 1–3. Clip from old magazines three examples of each of the four added rules and paste them under the rule that applies.

RULES FOR USING CAPITAL LETTERS—Continued

RULE 8. Capitalize the words *Mother, Father, Grandmother,* and *Grandfather* when they are used instead of that person's name. Do not capitalize them when a word such as *my, your, his, her, our,* or *their* is used before them.

I think that Mother can come.   I think that my mother can come.

RULE 9. Capitalize the first word and all important words in the titles of *books, articles, themes, musical works, poems,* and *plays.* Capitalize a word such as *a, an, the, and, or, but, of, to, in, on, by* only if it comes first or last.

On to Oregon   "The Flag Goes By"   *The Prince and the Pauper*

RULE 10. Capitalize the name of a school subject when it comes from the name of a country, as *English, French, Spanish, Latin.* (*Latin* comes from *Latium,* a region of central Italy; therefore it needs a capital.)

Do not capitalize names of such subjects as *geography, science, history* except when used as headings or titles for papers that you hand in.

My brother studies history, science, English,
and industrial arts.

RULE 11. Capitalize *East, West, North, South,* and such words as *Northwest* when they indicate a section of the country. Do not capitalize such words when they simply indicate a direction.

Henry spent last summer in the West and in the Southwest.
Don lives south of the school, but we live northeast of it.

RULE 12. Capitalize references to *religions* and *denominations,* the *Bible and its parts,* and the *Deity.*

The Bible story of God's creation of the earth is found
in Genesis, in the Old Testament.

Learn about words!

The following words, taken from *A* of the Learning Activities, have interesting histories. Use your dictionary to find the story behind each word. With which word is the drawing connected?

piano   psalm   plastics   theme

LEARNING ACTIVITIES

A. Copy the following sentences, placing capital letters where they belong. In class go over the sentences orally, telling why you used each capital letter.

1. I told mother that the bible was on the piano.
2. "where men are men" is an article about the west.
3. The lutheran pastor's sermon was titled "trust in god."
4. My father knows all about plastics, but he has forgotten most of what he once knew about latin.
5. I read *the last of the mohicans* for a history report.
6. The title of her english theme is "where cinnamon comes from."
7. The action in that book takes place in the south.
8. My father walked east five blocks too far.
9. The responsive reading is taken from psalms, in the old testament.
10. Is the play *the king and i* based on a book?

B. Write two sentences to illustrate each usage that you missed in *A*. Ask a classmate to check your work.

C. Add Rules 8–12 to those in your notebook. Clip from magazines three examples of each rule and paste them under the right rule.

ENRICHMENT

To illustrate your knowledge of capital letters and to provide extra practice, use the following words in *two* sentences. In the first sentence, use it as it is; in the second, use it where it needs to be capitalized.

EXAMPLE: *lake*   1. Behind our farm is a small *lake*.
                 2. I spent my last vacation at *Lake* Towanda.

uncle	history	mountain
southeast	church	doctor
band	captain	building

USING ENGLISH IN ALL CLASSES

Bring to English class any papers that you are preparing for your other classes. Check carefully to be sure that you have followed all the rules for using capital letters.

USING ENGLISH OUTSIDE SCHOOL

The next time that you write a letter, check your use of capital letters by the rules copied in your notebook.

3. Punctuating Sentences Correctly

TALK IT OVER...

Understanding the purpose of punctuation is half the battle. Suppose that in a story you came to this last line on a page:

When at last it was time to eat my little brother

You would be surprised and shocked at the idea suggested. Upon turning the page to get the details, however, you would be relieved to find the rest of the sentence: "... was the first one at the table."

Where could you put a comma in that sentence to make the meaning clear even before you turned the page?

What is confusing about the following sentences? What marks of punctuation could you insert to make plain the meaning? (Show two different meanings for each sentence.)

The girls plans are a secret. (How many girls?)
Dick my brother needs help. (Are *Dick* and *brother* two people?)

Punctuation marks, rightly used, do two things: (1) they help make meaning clear, and (2) they help the reader to get the meaning quickly.

If you made any errors on the punctuation part of Pretest 1, you will want to study the rules and exercises that follow.

If you had a perfect score and your teacher excuses you from the work that follows, you may enjoy the "Just for Fun" section on pages 175–77.

RULES FOR END PUNCTUATION

RULE 1. Use a period to close a *declarative* sentence; that is, one that makes a statement.

Ice is cold.

When the Pan-American Exposition opened in Dallas, Texas, a $75,000 jeweled lock at the main gate, symbolic of international friendship, was opened by twenty-one girls.

RULE 2. Use a period to close an *imperative* sentence; that is, one that expresses a command or a request.

Do as I say.   Please bring me that book.

RULE 3. Use a question mark to close an *interrogative* sentence; that is, one that asks a question.

Where did John go?   Have you any questions?

RULE 4. Use an exclamation point after an *exclamation;* that is, words that express strong feeling. Sometimes an exclamation is a sentence, and sometimes it is not.

How excited I was! (*a sentence*)   Hurrah! (*not a sentence*)

LEARNING ACTIVITIES

A. Copy the following sentences, supplying the correct end punctuation. Exchange papers for checking.

1. Did you see the football game last Saturday
2. Jack Donalds, our speedy back, ran forty yards for a touchdown
3. What a runner he is
4. His run came in the second quarter
5. Late in the game, Don Beech threw a twenty-yard pass
6. Did you notice that his toss was a perfect spiral
7. Bud Foster caught the pass and crossed the goal line
8. He had to avoid three tacklers
9. It was a beautiful run
10. The final score was Wildcats 7–Tigers 6

B. (1) Write nine sentences about your family or friends, using periods, question marks, and exclamation points each three times. (2) *Proofread carefully for careless errors.* (3) Take turns in class at putting sentences on the board, omitting the end punctuation. Call on a classmate to provide the correct mark for each sentence.

C. Copy in your notebook the four rules for end punctuation, leaving space below each rule for examples. Clip from magazines three examples of each rule. Paste them in your notebook under the rule that applies.

RULES FOR OTHER USES OF THE PERIOD

RULE 1. **Use periods to show abbreviations.** As a rule, avoid abbreviations except for *Mr., Mrs., Dr.,* or *St.* (when it means *Saint*) before a name and *Jr.* or *Sr.* after one.

Mr. and Mrs. Beall met Dr. Hites in St. Paul.

Mich.	doz.	Ave.	etc.	Jr.	Mr.
N. Y.	bu.	St.	No.	Sr.	Dr.
Ill.	lb.	Tues.	Co.	Oct.	Mrs.

a) The title *Miss* is not an abbreviation and has no period.

My teacher is Miss [*not* Miss.] April Meade.

b) The two abbreviations used to indicate time, A.M. (*ante meridiem*—before noon) and P.M. (*post meridiem*—after noon), should be set off by periods: Be here at 1:30 P.M.

Use a period after an initial that stands for a name.

H. C. Bond   P. Anderson   T. Edward Wilson

RULE 3. **Use a period with figures to show** (1) **decimals and** (2) **dollars and cents.** (Note that in reading such a number, "and" shows where the decimal point belongs.)

3.6 (*three* and *six tenths*) $9.40 (*nine dollars* and *forty cents*)

LEARNING ACTIVITIES

A. Copy the following sentences, supplying periods where they are needed. Go over the sentences in class.

1. Dr and Mrs J R Griffith bought a painting for $76075 (seven hundred sixty dollars and seventy-five cents).
2. The 5:30 P M train for St Petersburg is late.
3. Among the guests were Mr John M Clark and Miss Marie Lane.
4. Two and a half can be written 25.
5. "830 Surrey Ave, Glenview, Ill 60025" was written on the card.

B. (1) Write six advertising signs that you might see in shop windows or along the highway. In them, illustrate the use of periods in abbreviations, initials, decimals, or dollars and cents. (2) *Be sure to proofread* *carefully.* (3) In class, read your work aloud. Call on someone to write on the board the abbreviations, initials, and figures that need periods. You may need to say how many periods are to be used.

C. Copy in your notebook Rules 1, 2, and 3. Clip three examples of each rule from magazines. Paste them in your notebook under the rule that applies in each case.

PART TWO: USING COMMAS

"I KNOW, MISS HALL. A COMMA IS A PAUSE WRITTEN DOWN."

READ AND DO

Is the boy right? How much do you know about using commas in written work? When you speak, your voice unconsciously puts in comma punctuation. When you read aloud, also, your voice usually points out to listeners where commas are.

Take turns reading aloud one of the following sentences. Call on someone to tell which sentence in each pair you have read.

1. Dick put the dishes away. 2. Dick, put the dishes away.

1. Mr. Jones, the lawyer is here. 2. Mr. Jones, the lawyer, is here.

Take two or three minutes to write a sentence pair similar to the examples. Read them aloud and call for a show of hands as to where the commas are.

The rules in the next two lessons will help you to use commas accurately*

---

* The use of commas in the parts of a letter is taught on page 253.
The use of commas in compound sentences is taught on page 450.

RULES FOR USING COMMAS

RULE 1. Use commas after the various parts of an address. (House number and street form *one* part, as do state and zip number.)

John moved to 115 Oak Street, Dayton, Ohio 45400 last year.

Sometimes an address ends a sentence. In that case, use only the period (or question mark or exclamation point) at the end.

Were you born in Tampa, Florida?
Write me at 915 Cedar Street, Yankton, South Dakota 57078.

RULE 2. Use commas after the parts of a date. (Month and day form a single part.) Use no comma after a part that ends a sentence.

That game was played on October 12, 1963.
That game was played on October 12, 1963, in a heavy rain.
They visited Florida in January, 1964.

RULE 3. Use a comma or commas to set off a noun in direct address. **(DEFINITION) A noun used in speaking directly to a person is called a** *noun in direct address.* (This construction is also known as a *nominative of address.*)
Use two commas when other words come both before and after it.

John, where did you put that ball of twine?
Where did you put that ball of twine, John?
Where, John, did you put that ball of twine?

RULE 4. Use a comma or commas to set off words used as appositives. **(DEFINITION) An** *appositive* **is a noun or pronoun that stands next to another noun and means the same person or thing.**

The assembly was conducted by our principal, Mr. James.
Our principal, Mr. James, spoke to the students.

If the appositive is one of a group of words, set off the entire group.

The Husky, an Eskimo **dog** used to pull sledges, looks much like a wolf.

LEARNING ACTIVITIES IN USING COMMAS

A. Copy the following sentences, inserting commas where they are needed. Above each comma, write the number of the rule that applies. Exchange papers and read the sentences in class. When you read a sentence, be sure that your voice shows where the commas are.

1. Fred tell Sally that I'll see her in Syracuse New York.
2. Today I saw Mr. Reed our old milkman. He left here in May 1964.
3. From Richmond Virginia we went to Greensboro North Carolina.
4. At noon on April 25 1957 the new Harbor Freeway was opened.

5. I wonder Mrs. Burt whether you know my aunt Mrs. Stone.
6. Where were you on this particular day June 20 1963?
7. Dr. Riggs the only dentist in town has his office at 112 Elm Street.

B. Write sentences using the following expressions as indicated:

1. the owner of the car (appositive)
2. our next-door neighbor (appositive)
3. Mother (direct address)
4. Miss Benton (direct address)
5. 229 Mill Street Salem Ohio 44460
6. Plymouth Indiana
7. July 4 1776
8. *your own birthday*

Proofread carefully. Take turns at writing sentences on the board, without the commas. Call on classmates to tell where commas are needed.

RULES FOR USING COMMAS—Continued

RULE 5. Use commas to separate three or more items in a series.

> Joan, Mary, Lou, and Hazel went to the movies.
> Dick plays football, runs the quarter mile, and is captain of the basketball team.

Note that a comma is used before the *and* that joins the last two items. (Some authorities approve omitting this comma.)
Use no commas when all items in a series are joined by *and* or *or*.

> We shall move to Georgia *or* Maryland *or* Texas.

RULE 6. Use a comma when, in reading a sentence aloud, you hear a pause. The pause may indicate (*a*) words out of their natural order or (*b*) the insertion of words not really needed.

a) When the test was over, everyone sighed with relief.

In its natural order, the above sentence needs no comma:
Everyone sighed with relief when the test was over.

b) There are, of course, several reasons for the action.

RULE 7. Use a comma after an introductory *yes, no, well, oh.*

> Yes, I plan to go.   Well, I'll think about it.

RULE 8. Use a comma or commas to separate the exact words of a speaker from the rest of the sentence.

> Jack said, "You may use this pencil."
> "I already have one," replied Bill.
> "Yes," said Jack, "but you need a spare."

Sometimes the sense of the sentence requires some other mark.

> "May I borrow a pencil?" asked Fred.
> "What a pretty color!" remarked Alice.

Learn about words!

The following words, taken from *A* of the Learning Activities, have interesting histories. Use your dictionary to find the story behind each word. With which word is the drawing connected?

hash   chop suey   spaghetti   game

LEARNING ACTIVITIES IN USING COMMAS

A. Copy these sentences, inserting needed commas. Above each comma, write the number of the rule that applies. Exchange papers for checking.

1. As soon as you are ready we'll go.
2. Well I am not sure that Bob is going.
3. "Yes" said Al "I like chop suey spaghetti and hash."
4. After the game was over we walked home.
5. Oh we'll have ice cream cake and cookies.
6. Mother said "When you reach home call Mrs. Finger."
7. I have friends living in Wisconsin in Kansas and in Oklahoma.
8. "No that man cannot float," said Bob.
9. While you were parking the car I saw Nancy.
10. As soon as I wash dress and eat I'll be ready.
11. "For dessert" said Pam "let's have cake or lemon pie or ice cream. If we have the last I'd like it of course with hot fudge."

B. (1) Write eight sentences, applying each of comma rules 5, 6, 7, and 8 twice. The illustrations on pages 47–53 may suggest ideas. (2) *Be sure to proofread for careless mistakes.* (3) Read the sentences in class and call on classmates to tell where the commas are. Use guides 1 and 4 of the Guides to Good Listening, page 26, and guides 4, 6, and 7 of the Guides for Reading Aloud, page 57.

C. Copy in your notebook all eight rules for using commas, leaving space for examples below each rule. Find in magazines and clip three examples of each rule. Paste each example under the proper rule.

USING ENGLISH IN ALL CLASSES

Look over papers that you are preparing for another class. (1) Check to see that you have used correct end punctuation and that you have placed correctly any other needed periods. (2) Check each comma use by the rules on pages 153 and 154. Insert any other needed commas.

Find and read to the class or to your small group, a paragraph containing eight or more commas. Your audience will listen closely to see how many commas they think are in the paragraph. In preparing to read, apply the Guides for Reading Aloud, page 57.

PART THREE: USING QUOTATION MARKS

"I'D LIKE TO GET A BOOK FILLED WITH DIRECT QUOTATIONS."

THINK IT OVER...

What is the student really asking for?

Why does a storybook with much conversation in it seem more interesting than one without it?

In your writing, how often do you use direct quotations? When you do use them, are you sure of where to place the quotation marks?

What is the difference between direct and indirect quotations?

One good way to make a story lively and interesting is to use *direct quotations;* that is, *conversation,* the actual words of the people in the story. An *indirect quotation* tells what the speaker said but does not use the speaker's exact words.

DIRECT QUOTATION: Mother said, "Jack, come with me."
INDIRECT QUOTATION: Mother said that Jack should come with her.

RULES FOR USING QUOTATION MARKS

RULE 1. Place quotation marks before and after a direct quotation. (Remember, every direct quotation begins with a capital letter.)

> Dan said, "I think that he went home."
> Joe asked, "Are you coming with me?"
> "I think that he went home," said Dan.
> "Come with me!" exclaimed Joe.

Note the commas and other marks used with the quotation marks.

RULE 2. When the explanatory words come in the middle, put quotation marks around each part of the speaker's words.

> "I think," said Dan, "that he went home."

Notice that the second part begins with a small letter, because it is part of the whole sentence *I think that he went home.*

> "I think that he went home," said Dan. "He was in a hurry."

Here Dan speaks two different sentences; therefore a period follows *Dan,* and *He* has a capital letter.

RULE 3. In writing conversation, begin a new paragraph for each change of speaker.

> "Bud, who played tonight?" yelled Ben.
> "The sophomores played the freshmen," answered Bud. "It was a good game. Slim Haas scored twenty points."
> "Who won?" asked Ben.
> "The freshmen won, 60–56!" shouted Bud. "Yippee!"

RULE 4. Use no quotation marks with an indirect quotation.

> Dan said that Bob had gone home.

RULE 5. Use quotation marks around the titles of *short stories, one-act plays, articles, songs, poems,* **and** *themes.*

> Betty's theme is called "On the Way Home."
> The poem "Trees" is one of my favorites.

LEARNING ACTIVITIES

A. Copy these sentences, inserting quotation marks. Make new paragraphs for a change of speaker. In class, explain your placement of the marks.

1. Clarence declared that he had seen a face at the window.
2. Wait for me! shouted Buck.
3. My favorite story is The Ransom of Red Chief.
4. Have you seen Doris? asked Clara.

5. There were only twenty passengers on that plane, remarked Ted. Yes, replied Bob, and five got off at the first stop.
6. Were all the fellows on time? asked Tom. No, I think all except one were on time, said Frank.
7. Coach Harkness yelled, Show some speed, men!
8. As the band played The Star-spangled Banner, we raised the flag.

B. (1) Copy the following sentences, supplying capital letters, quotation marks, and any other punctuation marks needed. (2) Exchange papers for checking. (3) Go over the sentences in class.

1. Some planes said Alex are still built of wood
2. This play, A Fight to the Finish, is very short but exciting
3. My father Harry announced will furnish a car for the Oakmont trip
4. The game has begun said Henry both teams are playing hard
5. What is your name the policeman asked
6. The conductor said we have been delayed because of a heavy snow
7. I plan to call my theme Baby-sitting in Reverse
8. Jack shouted here comes the parade

C. Change the following indirect quotations to direct quotations. Make this a class activity, in which one person dictates the direct quotation for another student to write correctly on the board.

1. Mother announced that I might go.
2. What he said was that he might be able to help us.
3. The nurse insisted that the doctor had just left.
4. Father exclaimed that I was being unreasonable.
5. Robert asked that he be excused early on Tuesday.
6. One man complained that the work was too hard.
7. Elaine said that in her opinion Bill should be our chairman.
8. Timmy boasted that he was not afraid in the dark.

D. (1) Write four sentences to show that you can apply the rules for using quotation marks. The drawing on this page may suggest ideas to write about. (2) Copy the sentences, omitting all quotation marks. (3) Exchange sentences with a partner and supply the needed marks. (4) Return the sentences for checking.

"HOW DO YOU INDICATE A BOOK TITLE?"

"YOU WRITE IT IN ITALICS."

THINK IT OVER...

How do you "write" something in italics?

Here are rules that you should know about using three additional marks of punctuation—the colon, underlining, and the hyphen.

THE RULES

RULE 1. Use a colon when you write the *time* in figures.

2:30 P.M.   10:30 A.M.   Mother calls me at 6:30 A.M.

NOTE: The use of the colon in business letters is taught on page 265.

RULE 2. When you write or typewrite, underline titles of *books* and the names of *magazines* and *newspapers*. In print, these appear in italic type. (*This is italic type.*)

(*handwritten*)   I read *King of the Wind* twice.
(*typewritten*)   I read King of the Wind twice.
(*printed*)   I read *King of the Wind* twice.

RULE 3. Use a hyphen in spelling out *numbers* from twenty-one to ninety-nine: I have visited thirty-two states.

RULE 4. Use a hyphen when you combine two or more words to put before a noun to describe it.

I like his never-say-die attitude.
Do you like this navy-blue suit?
A well-built man stood near the half-open door.

NOTE: The use of the hyphen in dividing a word at the end of a line is covered in guide 7, page 140.

The following words, taken from *A* of the Learning Activities, have interesting histories. Use your dictionary to find the story behind each word. With which word is the drawing connected?

elbow pupils pain cousins

LEARNING ACTIVITIES

A. Copy these sentences, supplying colons, underlining, and hyphens where needed. Go over your work in class.

1. We got up at 5 15 A.M. in that cold as an iceberg house.
2. My six year old sister has dark blue eyes and a volcano like temper.
3. One good to the last page book that we read in the sixth grade is Runaway Home.
4. Forty two of these men performed in old time minstrel shows.
5. We had two hours to get there, from 11 30 A.M. to 1 30 P.M.
6. At least twenty five people sent in some well written advice.
7. This hair raising story in the latest issue of Scholastic is true.
8. A sharp as a bayonet pain shot through my elbow.
9. The panic stricken pupils could not easily be quieted.
10. May I borrow your month before last *National Geographic* for forty five minutes this afternoon?
11. A large picture of my twenty seven cousins covered almost a whole page in last night's Daily News.

B. (1) Write sentences in which you tell something about five books that you have read or about magazines or newspapers that you read regularly. (2) *Proofread your sentences for careless mistakes.* (3) Read your sentences aloud, asking classmates to tell what words should be underlined and what words in the titles should be capitalized. Use the Guides for Reading Aloud, page 57, and the Guides to Good Listening, page 26.

C. Make a chart showing how your school day is divided. Express the time in each case in figures. Have several charts put on the board for class discussion. If you have a criticism, be courteous in expressing it. (See guides 3 and 4 on page 33.)

D. Copy in your notebook the rules for using quotation marks, colons, underlining, and hyphens. Clip examples from magazines and paste each of them under the appropriate rule. Remember that book titles are printed in italics, not underlined.

Examine papers that you are preparing or have completed for other classes. Proofread each one to be sure that you have followed the rules for proper use of quotation marks, colons, underlining, and hyphens. Make any needed corrections.

PART FIVE: USING APOSTROPHES

THINK IT OVER . . .

How do you make a noun possessive? What do you need to know in order to place the apostrophes (') in the right place in the sentence above?

Where would you put the apostrophe if there were just one cousin? two cousins? if there were one friend? two friends?

USING APOSTROPHES TO SHOW OWNERSHIP

Often in your writing, you need to show that something belongs to one or more persons. **(DEFINITION)** The noun form in which an apostrophe is used to show ownership is called a *possessive noun*. (If you are not sure what a noun is, see page 309.)

Here is the *boy's* cap.   Find *Ann's* book.

If you learn to apply two simple rules, you will never find it hard to write possessive nouns correctly.

RULES FOR USING APOSTROPHES TO SHOW OWNERSHIP

RULE 1. Form the possessive of any singular noun in this way:

a) **Write the noun. Do not change any letters. Do not drop any.**

b) **Add *'s* to the word.** Notice these examples:

SINGULAR NOUNS:	Lois	son-in-law
POSSESSIVES:	Lois's ring	my son-in-law's job

Remember that a possessive form shows *whose* something is. Do not make the mistake of using it as a plural.

RIGHT: I saw the *boy's* father. [The possessive tells *whose* father.]
WRONG: Both *boy's* helped me. ["Boy's" does not tell *whose* anything is.]

RULE 2. To form the possessive of a plural noun, follow this plan:

a) **Write the plural noun.** (For help with plurals, see the rules on pages 186–88.) **Do not change any letters; do not drop any.**

b) **If the plural does not end in *s*, add *'s*, just as you would in forming singular possessives.**

PLURAL NOUNS:	children	seamen
POSSESSIVES:	children's voices	seamen's travels

c) **If the plural does end in *s*, add only an apostrophe.**

PLURAL NOUNS:	boys	uncles
POSSESSIVES:	both boys' bicycles	my uncles' noses

LEARNING ACTIVITIES IN FORMING POSSESSIVE NOUNS

A. Give oral sentences using the possessive form of each of the following nouns. Spell the possessive. If you like, make this a team contest.

1. baby	4. Lincoln	7. Dr. Bruce	10. ladies	13. deer
2. kings	5. artists	8. Harris	11. crow	14. men
3. pupil	6. Charles	9. mice	12. hobo	15. girl

B. (1) Rewrite the following sentences, changing each italicized group of words to the possessive form of the noun. *Be careful of your spelling and penmanship.* (2) Exchange papers for checking. (3) Go over the sentences in class, spelling orally each possessive used.

EXAMPLE: The name *of the boy* is Don.   The *boy's* name is Don.

1. The pictures *of the boys* are interesting.
2. The costumes *of the Indians* seem strange to us.
3. The sense of smell *of the dog* is remarkable.
4. The ears *of the horse* pricked up at the strange sound.

5. Have you met the father-in-law *of Chris?*
6. The books *of Dickens* are still popular.
7. The uniforms *of the policemen* are new.
8. The plans *of the teacher* were definite.
9. Do you celebrate the birthday of *Washington?*
10. The playground *for the girls* is being repaired.

USING APOSTROPHES TO FORM CONTRACTIONS

When you are in a hurry, you usually are glad if you can find a short cut that will save you time.

Language has its short cuts, too. One short cut in speaking and writing that you use every day is the *contraction*.

● THESE ARE FACTS ABOUT CONTRACTIONS *

1. **(DEFINITION) A contraction is a shortened form in which two or more words are combined by dropping some letters and inserting an apostrophe to take their place.**

    you ha̶v̶e = you've   we a̶re = we're   of̶ t̶h̶e̶ clock = o'clock
    is no̶t = isn't   I a̶m = I'm   let u̶s = let's

2. **Two contractions change form more than most others.**

    shall not = shan't   will not = won't

3. **Some contractions have more than one meaning.** For example, *it's* is the contraction for *it is* as well as for *it has; I'll* is the contraction both for *I shall* and for *I will; I'd* is the contraction for *I had, I should,* or *I would.*

4. **Here are the contractions that you probably use oftenest. The ones that do double duty are underlined in red.**

1. aren't	10. he'd	19. let's	28. there's	37. weren't
2. can't	11. he'll	20. mightn't	29. they'd	38. we've
3. couldn't	12. he's	21. mustn't	30. they'll	39. who's
4. didn't	13. I'd	22. o'clock	31. they're	40. won't
5. doesn't	14. I'll	23. shan't	32. they've	41. wouldn't
6. don't	15. I'm	24. she'd	33. wasn't	42. you'd
7. hadn't	16. isn't	25. she'll	34. we'd	43. you'll
8. hasn't	17. it's	26. she's	35. we'll	44. you're
9. haven't	18. I've	27. that's	36. we're	45. you've

Instruction and practice on possessive pronouns confused with contractions will be found on pages 375–76.

A. (1) Write the *words* for which the forty-five contractions in the preceding list stand. Write at least two sets of words for each of the contractions underlined in red. *Do not copy the contractions.* (2) Then, with your book closed, strike out the letter or letters that are omitted when you form a contraction of the words. Watch out for the two exceptions, No. 23 and No. 40. (3) Write each contraction, putting in the apostrophe correctly. (4) Go over your work in class.

B. (1) Number your paper from 1 to 12. (2) Beside the numbers, write the contractions of the words in italics in each of the following sentences. (3) Exchange papers for checking.

1. I *cannot* read the name.
2. *Are* you *not* going with us?
3. We *have not* finished yet.
4. There *is not* time for a nap.
5. *We shall* do our best.
6. *It is* cold in this room.
7. We *were not* sure of the way.
8. I *do not* have my ticket.
9. He *does not* look like you.
10. *You are* needed at home.
11. *Who is* going with you?
12. Ted *will not* leave today.

C. (1) Copy the following sentences neatly, putting apostrophes where they belong. (2) After each sentence, write the words for which the contractions stand. *Do not write in this book.* (3) Exchange papers. (4) In class, put the contractions on the board as you go over the sentences.

EXAMPLE: I don't know why they're late. (do not, they are)

1. Theres someone at the door.
2. Its raining harder now.
3. Havent you forgotten something?
4. Youre too late to catch that train.
5. Dont you know whos been taking Joe's place?
6. Whos planning to help you?
7. Youve done very well.
8. If were going, we mustnt wait any longer.
9. Doesnt Mary think its been a pleasant place in which to live?
10. Im sure that shes been happy here.
11. I havent read that book, but Ive read other books by the author.
12. Frank says that he cant come now. He wont be late.

D. (1) Write two paragraphs that you might include in a letter to a friend. Use as your topic something that you have done during the past week. Use the Guides for Writing a Paragraph on page 214. In the paragraphs, use at least ten different contractions. (2) Below the paragraphs, list the contractions and, opposite each one, write the words for which it stands. (3) As paragraphs are read in class, jot down any contractions that you hear. Apply 1 and 4 of the Guides to Good Listening on page 26; and 4, 6, and 7 of the Guides for Reading Aloud, page 57.

Bring to English class papers for other classes. Check each one for errors in spelling (1) possessive nouns or (2) contractions.

USING APOSTROPHES TO FORM PLURALS

The sentence underscored in red on page 162 points out that possessive nouns should never be used for simple plurals.

RIGHT: My *mother's* name is Alice.   WRONG: Several *mother'*𝕩 came.

Some plurals—but never of nouns—do contain an apostrophe.

THE RULE FOR FORMING PLURALS WITH AN APOSTROPHE

RULE: **Use an apostrophe and *s* to form plurals of these expressions:**

   a) **Figures:** There are two *5*'s in our telephone number.

   b) **Signs:** How many *+*'s did you have on your paper?

   c) **Letters of the alphabet:** I can't tell your *a*'s and *o*'s apart.

   d) **Words referred to as words:** Avoid using those *and*'s and *uh*'s.

NOTE: In your own writing, to make clear that those four kinds of expressions are not nouns, underline them before adding the *'s*. In printed matter, they are set in italics, as shown in the examples above.

LEARNING ACTIVITIES IN USING APOSTROPHES TO FORM PLURALS

A. (1) Copy the following sentences, inserting apostrophes where needed. (2) Underline words and expressions that should be italicized. (3) Go over the sentences in class and explain each apostrophe.

   1. Do you spell "stopped" with two *ps*?
   2. Your plan contains too many *ifs*.
   3. Were those *6s*, or *9s*?
   4. Jack's *ls* look too much like *es*.
   5. Anyway, I have more *+s* than *—s*.

B. (1) Write sentences containing the plurals of *and, 7, m, +*. Remember to underline. (2) Read sentences in class, and write the plurals on the board. Comment on good sentences.

4. Speaking and Writing in Sentences

PART ONE: AVOIDING SENTENCE FRAGMENTS

READ AND THINK ABOUT

The listener probably wants to ask, "What about it? What happens at the sound of your voice?"

"At the sound of my voice," you see, is only *part* of an idea—an idea that might express many things, all different:

> The pigs come running *at the sound of my voice.*
> *At the sound of my voice,* the neighbors complain.
> The crowd cheers *at the sound of my voice.*
> *At the sound of my voice,* start running.

"At the sound of my voice" is an incomplete idea; that is, it is not a *sentence*. A complete thought, or sentence, may make a statement; it may ask a question; it may state a request or a command; or it may make an exclamation. "At the sound of my voice" does none of those things.

In speaking, as in a conversation, you need not always express yourself in complete sentences. You will be *thinking* a complete sentence, but in what you say, part may be understood.

> "When do you plan to rake the leaves, John?"
> "In the morning." [*I plan to rake them* in the morning.]

The words "In the morning" do not express a complete thought. How do you know, though, what words are missing? You know *because the question that goes before makes them clear.*

1. **(DEFINITION)** A *fragment* is only a piece of a sentence.

2. Sometimes a fragment fails to tell *who* or *what* is doing something; that is, it may lack a subject. (See page 313 if you are not sure what a *subject* is.)

   > Jumped through the fence. (*fragment*)

   Who jumped through the fence? *a man? a rabbit? a hog? a dog?* The fragment does not tell you. A sentence does:

   > **A man** jumped through the fence. (*sentence*)
   > **A rabbit** jumped through the fence. (*sentence*)

3. Sometimes a fragment has a subject in it but fails to say what that subject *does;* that is, it may lack a verb. (If necessary, see page 280 for an explanation of *verb.*)

   > Martin and his whole flock of sheep. (*fragment*)

   What about them? *Did they disappear? Did they go to the fair? Were they struck by lightning? Were they drowned?* The fragment keeps you guessing. A sentence tells what happened:

   Martin and his whole flock of sheep **disappeared.** (*sentence*)

4. Sometimes a fragment lacks both a subject and a verb.

   > Through the window. (*fragment*)

   Was someone looking through the window? If so, who? Did someone climb through the window—or throw something through it? "Through the window" *tells none of those things.*
   Can you make a complete thought by putting in one word?

   > **Bill** through the window. (*fragment*)

   No; the full meaning is still a mystery. The fragment does not say that Bill *is* or *was* looking through the window. But the following groups of words make sense:
   Bill *looked* through the window. (*sentence*)
   Bill *should have been looking* through the window. (*sentence*)

5. Sometimes a fragment in written work is simply a matter of incorrect punctuation and capitalization.

   > Wrong: I like to watch television. In the evening.
   > Right: I like to watch television in the evening.

6. Sometimes a fragment has in it the *to* form or the *ing* form of a verb.

   > Lou *to wash* the dishes. (*fragment*)
   > **Mother asked** Lou to wash the dishes. (*sentence*)
   > Father *driving* all day. (*fragment*)
   > Father **had been** driving all day. (*sentence*)

LEARNING ACTIVITIES IN CORRECTING FRAGMENTS

A. Here is a sentence fragment: "Almost every afternoon." Write a sentence, using the fragment. Let each one in the class read his sentence aloud so that you can see the many different ideas that people may get from a fragment.

B. (1) Number your paper from 1 to 16. (2) Read each group of words carefully; if it is a sentence, write *S* after the corresponding number. If it is a fragment, write *F*. (3) Make a good sentence from every fragment. (4) Write *2, 3,* or *4* to indicate which point on page 167 you used to change the fragment to a sentence. (5) Go over your papers in class, comparing your completed sentences.

EXAMPLE: Doing my homework. I *was* doing my homework. (4)

1. Raking leaves in the fall is fun.
2. In large piles about three feet high.
3. Burning them after dark.
4. Tim, Jack, Harry, my father, and I work as a team.
5. Sometimes Dick and Phil, too.
6. I like to light the leaves at the bottom of the pile.
7. Figuring the direction of the wind is important.
8. Careful to light it at the right end.
9. Huge, billowy clouds of smoke pour up.
10. Running through the smoke.
11. Hot flames on our cheeks.
12. Finally the pile seems all burnt out.
13. Suddenly there is a spurt of flame.
14. At last only a flicker.
15. Nothing but a narrow, low, dark pile about a block long.
16. Our fun is over for tonight.

C. The following paragraph contains some sentences and some sentence fragments. (1) Rewrite the paragraph, using only good sentences. Sometimes you may be able to add a fragment to a sentence that comes before it. In some cases you may have to add new words to change a fragment into a sentence. Work carefully. Be sure that every sentence makes sense. (2) *Proofread to catch careless mistakes in capitalization and punctuation.* (3) Go over the rewritten paragraphs in class, putting some of the best ones on the board.

I like to go into the woods to look for persimmons. In the fall. Have you ever seen one of them? Is a small, orange-red fruit. Having from six to eight seeds. It is from a half-inch to an inch in diameter. The tree is sometimes fifty feet high. The persimmon has a harsh taste. Before a frost. After a frost it is sweet and tastes good. According to some people, a persimmon would ripen anyway. Even without a frost. Persimmon trees mostly in the South.

D. A sentence fragment is an incomplete expression or idea. If you were to picture a fragment, part of the picture would be missing. Notice that the illustrations above are not complete. For each illustration write a complete sentence that shows what else you think the artist might have drawn to finish the picture. Compare your sentences in class.

USING ENGLISH IN ALL CLASSES

Examine papers or reports that you are preparing or have prepared for other classes. Check carefully to make sure that you have no sentence fragments. If you do find any, correct them.

Learn about words!

The following words, taken from *B* of the Learning Activities, page 168, have interesting histories. Use your dictionary to find the story behind each word.

important   pile   direction   finally

PART TWO: AVOIDING RUN-ON SENTENCES

THINK IT OVER . . .

Why do *you* think that some people run together a long string of sentences? Why is it a poor idea to do so?

How careful are you to speak and write in separate sentences?

Some people run sentences together when they are in a hurry or excited about something. In conversation this is not a big problem, but in written work it can lead to misunderstanding on the part of the reader. It can also be very tiring to follow.

1. **(DEFINITION)** A run-on sentence is made up of two or more sentences expressed incorrectly as one sentence.

   a) The run-together sentences may come from overuse of *and*'s, *and-so*'s, or *but*'s.

   > Last Friday's football game didn't get started until almost four-thirty *and* soon it began to get dark *and so* the other team wanted to quit playing *but* being six points behind we wanted to keep on *and so* finally after arguing about it we agreed to play ten more minutes *and* in a little while we made a touchdown *and* kicked the point practically in the dark *and so* we won by one point.

   This paragraph would be easier to read and to understand if it were broken up into separate sentences.

   > Last Friday's football game didn't get started until almost four-thirty. Soon it began to get dark. The other team wanted to quit playing. Being six points behind, we wanted to keep on. Finally, after arguing about it, we agreed to play ten more minutes. In a little while we made a touchdown and kicked the point practically in the dark. We won by one point.

   b) **A written run-on sentence may use a comma where there should be a period.**

   > WRONG: John came early, the others were late.
   > RIGHT: John came early. The others were late.

   c) **A written run-on sentence may be strung together without any joining words or punctuation at all between sentences.**

   > WRONG: The sky kept getting darker and darker soon snow began to fall.
   > RIGHT: The sky kept getting darker and darker. Soon snow began to fall.

LEARNING ACTIVITIES

A. Some of the following groups of words are run-on sentences. Others are correct. (1) Copy each run-on sentence and add correct end punctuation and capitalization. (2) For a correct sentence, simply copy the number and write "Correct" after it. (3) Compare sentences in class. Read the sentences aloud so that you can show by your voice where a sentence ends.

1. Don't go now, please wait for me, we have plenty of time.
2. All of us wanted to go to the zoo we had never seen a koala bear.
3. Bill tried three free throws and didn't miss one.
4. Hazel, come here I want to show you something.
5. The hickory nuts are ripe, we gathered a big supply in Hummel Park last Saturday and so Mother used some of them to make a batch of hickory-nut fudge for us.
6. Buck climbed the tree and slowly he crawled far out on one limb and so at last he dropped down into the yard on the other side of the high fence.
7. Betty can't go, she has to help her mother.
8. The sensible student does little whining and complaining.
9. Bud watches every plane he sees his brother is a pilot.
10. I rarely go to movies, they usually give me a headache.

B. Study the following paragraph carefully; then decide how you would get rid of the run-on sentences in it. Go over the paragraph in class.

Bathing in the ocean is real sport there's a trick in plunging into the waves, though. The waves are likely to knock you down they are powerful. The best thing to do is to go out about chest deep and watch the waves come in and then wait for a smallish one, you can jump up and ride it and so in that way you can avoid being knocked down. Sometimes a very large wave may come along, in that case you should dive right through it and you will come up beyond it.

C. The following paragraph has both run-on sentences and sentence fragments. (1) Rewrite the paragraph, using only correct sentences. You may need to add words to change some of the fragments into sentences. (2) *Be sure to proofread your paragraph for careless mistakes.* (3) Read the paragraph aloud, letting your voice show where each sentence ends.

One day while bathing in the surf. I had a rough experience. I tried to ride a high wave. Taking a deep breath, I jumped high, a second later I was dragging the ocean floor. Knocked down by the wave. Finally I came up, blowing and sputtering and my back was to the ocean and so I couldn't see anything coming. Crack! Down I went again this time the wave carried me along and pitched me onto the beach. There I lay. With my hands and knees scratched and bleeding.

USING ENGLISH IN ALL CLASSES

Check papers and reports that you have written or are writing for other classes. Make sure that they have no run-on sentences in them. Watch especially for errors of the comma type.

Writing Chart

Name *Harold Jinks* Date	¹⁰/₁₄	¹⁰/₁₆				
Theme Number	1	2				
Subject	Eng.	Sci.				
Grade	C	B				
	Errors	Errors				
A. Manuscript form	0	0				
B. Capitalization	3	3				
C. Punctuation						
1. Period	1	0				
2. Question mark	0	0				
3. Exclamation point	0	0				
4. Comma	3	2				
5. Quotation marks	2	2				
6. Colon	1	0				
7. Underlining	0	1				
8. Hyphen	2	1				
9. Apostrophe	4	2				
D. Sentence sense						
1. Fragment	1	0				
2. Run-on	2	0				
E. Spelling	1	1				
F. Paragraphing						
G. Usage						
H. Vocabulary						
I. Quality of content						

5. Making and Using a Writing Chart

This chapter (pages 139–177) is a review of manuscript form, capitalization, punctuation, and sentence sense. If you can use these skills well, whatever you write will be easy to read and to understand. One practical way to check your ability is to make and use a Writing Chart such as the one on page 172.

The preceding chart shows the number and kinds of errors made in (1) an English paper written on October 14 and (2) a science paper written on October 16.

Make a Writing Chart like this one. After you have made it, use it regularly in two ways.

(1) Refer to it whenever you write a paper for any class. See what kinds of errors you made last time. Check to see that you avoid such errors in the paper you are about to hand in.

(2) Use the Writing Chart as a permanent, continuous record of your improvement.

NOTE: If you have not yet studied Chapter 11 and Chapter 12, skip items F, H, and I for the time being.

Chapter Review*

A. Copy these sentences, capitalizing them correctly.

1. tomorrow father and judge r. o. nicolls have an appointment with principal brown to talk over plans for a new course in history here at logan junior high school.
2. John asked, "did you hear any foreign language in the south?"
3. Henry and i take english, geography, arithmetic, and social studies. In addition, i take music, because my mother wants me to.
4. when i was in the northwest, i always arose early; but j. b., my friend, slept late every morning.
5. Bill added, "be sure to bring your uncle oscar to our christmas party. he can speak swedish with my uncle."
6. my mother studied latin and danish in college, but father avoided languages in favor of mathematics and science.

---

* Check Test 1 should be taken at this point. If the results show need for further study, students should do this review practice. They should then take Mastery Test 1.

7. All dad's teachers were men, but mother's danish teacher was a woman, mrs. mary a. hamsum.
8. Clark Gable, who played the part of r. butler in the famous film *gone with the wind,* became a captain in the united states army during World War II.
9. Bill's theme, which he called "rampaging river," told a true story of a flood in the middle west.
10. ever since Frank spent a summer in the southwest, his themes have had such titles as "life in the desert." he even wrote a poem with the title "the song of the coyote."
11. Finally mrs. jones asked, "have you ever read *lassie come home?* i saw the film years ago, and i've never seen a better one."
12. All local doctors except dr. a. j. pollard have offices downtown.
13. The minister's sermon was titled "where the bible came from."

B. Copy these sentences, supplying needed punctuation. The number after each sentence or group of sentences tells how many punctuation marks you should insert. A pair of quotation marks counts as one mark. Underlining a title counts as one mark.

1. Bill here is a strange story about an island that almost disappeared said Captain J R Betts Have you read it As he spoke he pointed to the title of the story An Island That Blew Itself Up (12)
2. He and Mrs Betts, of Batavia Java were visiting Mr and Mrs Sanders Bills parents (8)
3. No I havent Captain Betts Bill replied Ive heard of magicians making rabbits coins and even people disappear In fact, this weeks Life has an article on that subject (14)
4. Captain Betts laughed and said Well Bill the magician behind this act wasnt a person Heres the story Krakatoa a little island lies near the western end of Java On August 26 1883 the island blew itself up A series of terrific explosions began at 1030 A M and lasted thirty six hours Dust cinders and bits of rock shot miles into the air High waves walls of water swept along all the neighboring coasts The great waves destroyed 300 villages killed 35,000 people and caused untold damage When the explosions finally ended half the island was gone (30)
5. That sounds like a good book Bill declared I see its called The Earths Changing Surface Do you have any more like it sir (10)
6. Captain Betts answered Yes I have a complete set of books similar to this one (4) *

---

*Adapted from *The Earth's Changing Surface* by Bertha Morris Parker; copyright © 1958, 1952, 1947, 1942 by Harper & Row, Publishers, Incorporated, Evanston, Illinois.

C. (1) Number your paper from 1 to 12. (2) Read each group of words below. (3) If it is a sentence, write *S* after the corresponding number. If it is a fragment, write *F*. If it is a run-on sentence, write *RO*. (4) Change the fragments and run-on sentences to make good sentences.

1. The trees in the park have lost almost all their leaves.
2. The oaks an exception.
3. Some trees keep their leaves all winter, others lose theirs early in the fall.
4. When the middle of October comes along.
5. Bud is usually the first to go into the woods to look for walnuts.
6. Shelling the walnuts and getting brown stains all over my hands.
7. Mother likes walnuts she puts them into cakes.
8. Red sumac standing beside the railroad track about a mile south of town.
9. Saw it early Friday morning.
10. I like pear trees the leaves turn a deep red.
11. Mother and Father like evergreens better than any other kinds of trees.
12. Some people do not like fall it makes them sad.

Word Games to Test Your Thinking

Here is the first of several sets of spare-time activities that you will find in this book. Each such section contains puzzles and exercises for your enjoyment if you are excused from some of the regular work in English.

You must be a good sport in using these pages. <u>Being a good sport means that you will not write anything in the book</u>; for if you do, you will spoil things for the next person who uses the book. Using a ruler, draw such items as crossword puzzles and checkerboards on your own paper before you try to figure them out.

SCRAMBLED CAPITAL CITIES

If you were traveling in the United States and came upon these scrambled city signs, could you figure out in which state capital you were?

EXAMPLE: GROOM MY NET would be Montgomery.

1. LEG HAIR
2. SAFE TAN
3. O MY PAIL
4. TAPE OK
5. NET TORN

6. HEN ALE
7. SALT UP
8. DOC CORN
9. SOB NOT
10. ANY LAB

11. LET RIM OPEN
12. SCARE TO MAN
13. JIFFY NO SECRET
14. DIG FERN SLIP
15. TICKET ROLL

HIDDEN BOWLING TERMS

Each of the following sentences has hidden in it a bowling term. Can you find them? EXAMPLE: He again looked at *the ad pin*ing to go on such a cruise. (*head pin*)

1. His parents are great bowling fans.
2. A wasp lit on my hand.
3. The Turk eyed me carefully.
4. The baby fell asleep ere I knew it.
5. If illegal methods are used, I shall withdraw.
6. He seemed to be making ping-pong his hobby.

A WORD SQUARE

The words defined below are four-letter words. Placed one under another, they will spell the same down as across.

1. Something on which to sit
2. Makes mistakes

3. Amount of surface
4. Another spelling of *czar*

WOULD YOU LIKE TO KNOW—?

You may be surprised at the answers that the encyclopedia gives to some of the following questions.

1. What kind of light do *fireflies* produce?
2. What is a *flycatcher*?
3. How do the swimming habits of the *flatfish* differ from those of other fish?
4. What special subjects must a man have studied before he can become a member of the FBI (*Federal Bureau of Investigation*)?
5. Can a *flea* fly?

VALENTINE CROSSWORD PUZZLE

Copy the crossword puzzle on page 177. *Do not write in this book.* (A HELPFUL HINT: 1, 4, and 29 across make a message that is found on many valentines.)

Across

1. To exist.
2. Will ...... be my valentine?
4. Possessive pronoun.
6. Cry of a cow.
9. Past form of *be*.
12. Very little.
14. A wading bird.
16. To perform.
17. Garden tool.
19. To fasten.
20. Roman numeral for *nine*.
21. A closed automobile.
23. Right (*abbr.*).
24. An organ of the body.
26. ...... are red;
Violets are blue.
29. Sweetheart.
32. Associated Press (*abbr.*).
34. Trade-last (*abbr.*).
35. Southwest (*abbr.*).
36. Longfellow's first two initials.
37. A girl's name.
39. Bristles.
42. Pass (*in playing bridge*).
43. Cornhusker state (*abbr.*).
45. Plural of *man*.
46. City in Italy (*place where St. Valentine was put to death*).
47. A piece of furniture.
49. ...... Valentine.
50. Therefore.
51. Georgia (*abbr.*).
53. Preposition.
54. South America (*abbr.*).
55. Nickname for *Elizabeth*.
56. February ...... is Valentine's Day (*Roman numerals*).
57. Ding Dong ....

Down

1. Preposition meaning near.
3. Conjunction.
5. Biblical form of *you*.
6. 1214 (*Roman numerals*).
7. A cereal grass.
8. A preposition.
9. First person pronoun.
10. Skill.
11. An evening party.
12. Move along on water.
13. Opposite of *here*.
14. A valentine is ...... -shaped.
15. Fish may be caught in these.
18. Officer of the Day (*abbr.*).
21. She ...... sea shells.
22. Sound.
25. A large vessel for liquids.
27. Jumbled New South Wales (*abbr.*).
28. Used by artist.
30. Short messages.
31. Sugar is ......,
and so are you.
33. Polite people say, "......"
36. A book of hymns.
38. Father superior of an abbey.
40. Printer's measure.
41. Indefinite article.
42. Capital of Idaho.
44. First two initials of the author of *Treasure Island*.
46. Egyptian sun-god.
48. For example (*abbr.*).
49. Same as 50 across.
52. Instrument for chopping.
53. Television (*abbr.*).

Chapter
9

LEARNING TO SPELL WELL

"ARE ALL THESE WORDS MISSPELLED, OR ARE YOU WRITING IN SOME OTHER LANGUAGE?"

SPELLING PRETESTS

Before you study this chapter on spelling, it is a good idea to test your present ability to spell certain important words.

(1) Write "Test One" at the top of a sheet of paper; then number from 1 to 50. (2) On another sheet of paper, write "Test Two"; then number it from 1 to 100. Your teacher will then dictate the words for the two tests. All the words in the first test are spelled according to certain spelling rules. The words in the second test are tricky, because they are not spelled according to rules.

After it has been returned, study your test paper carefully. How well did you do? Each word in that test is a common word that every person is likely to use in even the simplest kind of writing—a note to the milkman, a travel post card, a thank-you note.

Since the test words are ones that you cannot very well get along without, your own common sense will tell you that you will be wise to master their spelling. Remember, all through life you will be judged by how you spell. If you can spell well, poor spellers will look up to you. Even more important, good spellers will not underrate your intelligence, as they are likely to do if you cannot spell.

FOLLOW-UP

Begin now to keep in your notebook a special section on spelling. (1) Put into it first of all any words that you missed on the tests. Arrange them alphabetically, leaving room to insert other words. (2) When a paper is returned, note any spelling errors. Check to see whether the words are already on your list. If so, star them, and then work on them, using the following guides. (3) Add any new words. (4) Before handing in any paper, check carefully to see whether you have used any of your starred words. If you have, make sure that they are spelled correctly.

GUIDES FOR LEARNING TO SPELL TROUBLESOME WORDS

1. Look at the word carefully as you say each syllable distinctly. Note any double letters, silent letters, confusing endings, or other hard spots.

2. Use the word in a sentence. Let the dictionary help you.

3. Repeat each syllable slowly; then close your eyes and recall how the word looks.

4. Compare your picture of the word with the printed word.

5. Write the word without looking at the printed word.

6. Check to see that you are correct.

7. Repeat steps 1–6 three times.

1. Watch Out for Silent Letters!

READ AND DISCUSS

Here is a note found stuck up on the corner lamppost the other day.

Dear Archie,
   I waited an our, but I coud not stay any longer. Don't you no that on Wensday we begin corus at to o'clock? You'd better husl!
                George

How many words has George misspelled? What is wrong with them? (Every one has the same kind of error.)
What letters must you insert to correct the misspelled words?

There probably is no foolproof way to make sure that you never leave out any of the silent letters in a word. Here, however, are some pointers that will help you to remember and some activities to give you practice.*

● THESE ARE FACTS ABOUT SILENT LETTERS

1. **Silent *k*, *g*, and *w***

   a) Only a few common words have a silent *k*, and they have an *n* after the *k*, as in *knock*.†

   b) Not many common words have a silent *g*; they have an *n* after the *g*, as *gnaw*, *sign*, or *reign*. (Words with silent *gh* are taught on page 109.)

   c) Silent *w* usually comes only before *r*, as in *write*.‡ In a few exceptions, the *w* comes before *h*, as in *who, whose, whole*. Still another exception is the word *answer*.

LEARNING ACTIVITIES IN SPELLING WITH SILENT K, G, AND W

A. (1) Write the following words on your paper in two columns, leaving two inches of space between the columns. (2) Beside each word, write a word that rhymes with it and begins with *kn*, *gn*, *wh* (with the *w* silent), or *wr*.§ (3) Exchange papers for checking as the words are pronounced, spelled aloud, and written on the blackboard.

1. few	7. map	13. what	19. track	25. clawed
2. list	8. feel	14. pole	20. bench	26. sitting
3. sing	9. life	15. teeth	21. thawing	27. college
4. flat	10. long	16. stone	22. lockout	28. smashing
5. rob	11. deck	17. bright	23. mitten	29. going
6. me	12. clock	18. room	24. chuckle	30. twinkle

B. The following paragraphs contain twenty incomplete words. To help you, the first letters of the word are given and the number of letters that must be added. (1) Copy the paragraphs, completing and underlining the words that you think are needed. (2) Exchange papers. (3) Check the papers as various students read aloud the sentences in the

---

* Silent *e*, which gives spelling trouble, as a rule, only in connection with adding suffixes, is covered in the rules on page 192.

† Most "kn-" words are short, simple words from Anglo-Saxon.

‡ Most words with a silent *w* come from Anglo-Saxon.

§ For example, if the word "tree" were on the list, you would write "knee" beside it.

paragraphs, spelling the words used to fill the blanks. (4) After the papers have been returned, write a sentence using correctly and *underlining* each word that you missed. (5) When your sentences have been checked, file your paper for easy reference.

The day after I had wr (5) a letter re (7) from my job with an auto-wr (6) company, I got up and ate a quick breakfast. Then I strapped an old kn (6) on my back and set out for the country, where I planned to spend the wh (3) day.

I had to walk slowly, having hurt one kn (5) recently. When I felt the gn (5) of hunger, I looked at the watch on my wr (3). Since it showed noon, I unwr (5) my lunch and ate it under a gn (5) old oak outside a high board fence.

Afterwards I looked through a large kn (6) in the fence and saw a neat little farmhouse. Since there was no s (3) saying to keep out, I climbed over the fence and walked up to the house. As I drew near, a large dog, chained to a post, growled and gn (5) his teeth at me. Since there was no kn (5) on the door, I rapped hard on it with my kn (6). There was no an (4). I kn (3) down on my good kn (2) to look through the keyhole. This was the wr (3) move, for just then the dog wr (6) out of his collar. He headed straight for me. Forgetting my bad leg, I dashed for the fence and scrambled over it—but I left part of one trouser leg behind me!

● THESE ARE FACTS ABOUT SILENT LETTERS—Continued

2. Silent *t* and *d*

 a) Most words containing a silent *t* fall into one of these two classes:

 (1) Those that have an *s* before the *t*, as in *castle*.
 (2) Those that rhyme with *match, sketch, pitch, Scotch,* or *Dutch*. The most important exceptions that contain no silent *t* are *rich, which, much, such, touch, sandwich, attach, detach,* and words made from them.

 b) Silent *d* is usually followed by *g*.* Most of the words containing it rhyme with *badge, edge, bridge, dodge,* or *fudge,* or are made from such words.

* Exceptions include certain words that begin with *ad*, such as *adjust* and *adjective*.

LEARNING ACTIVITIES IN SPELLING WITH SILENT *T* AND *D*

A. (1) See how long a list you can make of words that rhyme with *match, sketch, pitch, Scotch, Dutch, nestle, whistle,* and *rustle,* and contain a silent *t.* (You should find more than twenty.) (2) In class, make a combined list on the board. Arrange the words in columns under the key words *match, sketch,* and so on. (3) Copy the list and file it in your notebook for easy reference.

B. (1) Write a paragraph in which you use the eight important exceptions that have no silent *t* before *ch.* The guides on page 214 will help you to write a good paragraph. (2) *Proofread your paper to catch careless errors in spelling and in capitalization and punctuation.* (3) Read the paragraphs in your small groups; then choose one of them to be read to the entire class. As the paragraphs are read, rate the readers by the Guides for Reading Aloud, page 57.

C. Repeat *A,* only this time use rhymes for *edge* and *fudge.* (You should find at least ten.)

● THESE ARE FACTS ABOUT SILENT LETTERS—Continued

3. **Silent** *p, b, l,* **and** *u*

   a) Silent *p* occurs only before *n, s,* or *t,* as in *pneumonia, psalm,* and *ptomaine.* All such words come from the Greek, and most of them are words that you are not likely to use often.

   b) A silent *b* usually has an *m* before it, as in *dumb.* There are only a few such words that you are likely to need. Exceptions are *debt, doubt,* and words made from them.

   c) Few words contain a silent *l.* The ones that you are most likely to use are the following, or words made from them.

balk	balm	could	half
chalk	calm	should	halves
stalk	palm	would	calf
talk	psalm		calves
walk	qualm		
folk	almond		
yolk			

   d) A silent *u* in most cases follows only the letter *g,* as in *guide.* (The purpose of the *u* is, as a rule, to indicate that the word should not be pronounced with a soft *g* [j] sound.)

LEARNING ACTIVITIES IN SPELLING WITH SILENT *P, B, L,* AND *U*

A. (1) In your dictionary, check the words that begin with *pn, ps,* or *pt*. (2) Make a list of ones with which you are familiar. (3) With a partner, practice both oral and written spelling of the words. (4) Put into the spelling section of your notebook those that you need to practice further.

B. (1) On your paper, rule four columns. (2) Over the first column, write *dumb;* over the second, *talk;* over the third, *calm;* over the fourth, *could*. (3) Under the right headings, write words that have the same two ending letters and that the following explanations describe. (4) Exchange papers for checking as the explanations are read and the words spelled orally. (5) For each word that you miss, write a good sentence using and underlining the word. (6) File these sentences in the spelling section of your notebook.

1. Tree that bears dates
2. Atom ?
3. "Ought to"
4. What a mule may do
5. Tiny bit of bread
6. Part of a mitten
7. Found inside an egg
8. Large branch of a tree
9. *Shall, should; will,* ?
10. Lotion (rhymes with No. 1)
11. A base on balls
12. A Bible song (silent *p* and *l*)
13. The stem of a plant
14. What you do on a ladder
15. Used on the hair
16. Used on a blackboard

C. (1) In an oral or a written drill, spell the words that begin with *gu* and rhyme with the following: *scarred, yes, dressed* [two words], *tried, filled, die, wilt*. (2) Write the words, correctly spelled, in the spelling section of your notebook. (3) With the aid of the dictionary, add to the list any other *gu* words that you think will be useful to you.

● **THESE ARE FACTS ABOUT SILENT LETTERS—Continued**

4. Silent *h* and *gh*

a) Silent *h* usually follows *c,* as in *ache, chorus, scheme; r,* as in *rhyme, rheumatism;* or *g,* as in *ghost*. (Almost all such words come from the Greek.)

b) Most words having silent *gh* rhyme with *fight* or *ought*. Other common words containing silent *gh* are these groups:

sleigh	dough	weight	high
weigh	though	freight	sigh
neigh	thorough	straight	thigh

Neighbor and *through* are two other words to remember.

LEARNING ACTIVITIES IN SPELLING WITH SILENT *H* AND *GH*

A. (1) With the aid of the dictionary, make three lists of words that you think are or will be useful to you. In one list, put words beginning with *ch* (with the *h* silent); in another, those beginning with *rh;* and in the third, those beginning with *gh*. (2) Compare lists in class; then in pairs practice the words on your own lists. (3) File your list in the spelling section of your notebook.

B. (1) Divide the class into two groups. (2) Let one person from each group go to the board and write the words "fight" and "ought." (3) In turn, each will pronounce a word that rhymes with either of those two words and contains "gh." He will then write it under the proper word. (4) Proceed in the same manner with the other members of the teams. A word correctly spelled by one team cannot be used by the other team. (5) Copy and file any words that are hard for you to remember.

ENRICHMENT

A. With the help of the unabridged dictionary, make a list of words beginning with *kn* or *wr*. Include only words now in your vocabulary or ones that you would like to add to it. After your teacher checks the list, make a "word tree" or some other kind of design in which you group all the related words. (A "group" would be *knit, knitting, knitted, knitter,* for example.) Perhaps your work can be exhibited on the bulletin board.

B. Write a nonsense poem using the twelve words in the rhyming groups in (*b*) of "These Are the Facts," page 183. If your teacher approves your work, you may be permitted to read the poem to the class. Practice beforehand, applying guides 4–7 of the Guides for Reading Aloud, page 57.

REVIEW ACTIVITY IN SPELLING WITH SILENT LETTERS

(1) With the help of the points on pages 180, 181, 182, and 183, and of the lists that you have filed in your notebook, make a list of what you think are the hardest or trickiest silent-letter words. (2) Divide the class into two teams. (3) Choose one person from each team to keep score at the board. (4) Let the first person on one team pronounce a word from his list. (5) The first person on the other team must then spell it orally. If he is right, his team scores a point. If not, the one who gave the word spells it correctly. (He does not score a point, of course, since he can look at the word on his paper.) The other side then has a turn at pronouncing a word, and so on. Each word spelled correctly by a team member should be written on the board by the scorer for that team. At the end of the game, the team with the longer list is the winner.

2. Learn to Apply Spelling Rules

"I'LL NEVER LEARN TO SPELL THESE WORDS!"

"THEY USED TO BOTHER ME, BUT NOW I KNOW THE RULES!"

writting ✓
recieve ✓
stoped ✓

writing
receive
stopped

THINK IT OVER . . .

How many of those words give *you* trouble?
How many spelling rules do you really know and use?

Being able to apply certain rules will not make you a perfect speller, because the English language has many words not spelled by rules. Rules can, however, keep you from ever making again the kinds of errors shown in the cartoon. Then you will be free to concentrate on mastering tricky words not spelled by the rules.

Learn about words!

The following words, taken from *A* of the Learning Activities, pages 186–87, have interesting histories. Use your dictionary to find the story behind each word.

quart   perfect   criminal   circus

PART ONE: SPELLING PLURAL FORMS

Occasionally the irregularity of some plural forms of nouns may disturb you. Luckily, however, only a few nouns have "odd" plurals. The others form their plurals by rules. Before you study those rules, make sure that you know certain things.

● THESE ARE FACTS ABOUT NUMBER

1. **(DEFINITION)** *Number* is the difference in the form of nouns or pronouns that shows whether they mean *one*, or *more than one*.

2. **(DEFINITION)** *Singular* number indicates *one*.

3. **(DEFINITION)** *Plural* number indicates *more than one*.

SINGULAR: a boy   an ax   a calf   a goose
PLURAL: six boys   two axes   ten calves   five geese

4. Most plurals not formed by adding *s* or *es* to the singular are given in the dictionary after the singular form, as *calf*, pl. *calves;* or *lady*, pl. *ladies*. If in doubt, see the dictionary.

Read the following rules and study the examples. Then do the practice that follows, using these rules.

THE RULES FOR SPELLING PLURALS: I

RULE 1. Add *s* to the singular to form the plural of most nouns.

SINGULAR: dog   parent   grandmother
PLURAL: dogs   parents   grandmothers

RULE 2. Add *es* to most nouns ending in *sh, ch, s, x,* or *z*. When you pronounce the plurals of words with those endings, you cannot help adding a syllable. That added syllable tells you that you need *es,* not just *s*. For example, try saying the plural of *wish*. It comes out as *wishes;* that is, in two syllables.

dish, dishes   dress, dresses   buzz, buzzes
church, churches   box, boxes

RULE 3. Add *s* to form the plural of nouns ending in *ay, ey,* or *oy.*

valley, valleys   delay, delays   boy, boys

RULE 4. For other nouns ending in *y,* change the *y* to *i* and add *es.*

baby babïes babies   lady ladïes ladies

LEARNING ACTIVITIES IN FORMING PLURALS

A. (1) Number your paper from 1 to 20. (2) Copy each of the following nouns and beside it write its plural. (3) Exchange papers and go over the words in class. As they are spelled aloud, have the words written

186

plainly on the board. (4) File in your notebook any words that you missed. (See the Follow-up activity on page 179.)

1. onion	6. branch	11. glass	16. ditch
2. mouth	7. gallon	12. envelope	17. towel
3. brush	8. quart	13. radiator	18. waltz
4. perch	9. table	14. criminal	19. banana
5. ax	10. wish	15. circus	20. pearl

B. (1) Write a short paragraph in which you use and underline the plural of each of the following nouns. (2) Compare paragraphs by reading them aloud in your small groups. (3) Ask a classmate to spell each plural that you have used. (4) Choose the best paragraph to read to the entire class. (Make sure that you follow guides 1, 3, and 4 of the Guides to Good Listening, page 26.)

1. sky	3. key	5. library	7. tray	9. alley
2. penny	4. party	6. monkey	8. fly	10. puppy

THE RULES FOR SPELLING PLURALS: II

RULE 5. Add *s* to form the plural of most nouns ending in *f*, *ff*, or *fe*.

chief, chiefs   cuff, cuffs   safe, safes

RULE 6. For some words ending in *f* or *fe*, change the ending; drop the *f* or *fe* and add *ves*.

calf, calves   loaf, loaves   wife, wives

If in doubt, say the plural of the word. If you hear the sound of *v*, follow Rule 6. If you hear the sound of *f*, follow Rule 5.

For example, say the plurals of the following words: *gulf, leaf, puff, knife*. Which plurals end in *ves*?

RULE 7. Add *s* to form the plural of most nouns ending in *o*.

solo, solos   radio, radios   studio, studios

Here are some important exceptions.

echo, echoes   tomato, tomatoes   torpedo, torpedoes
hero, heroes   potato, potatoes   mosquito, mosquitoes
veto, vetoes   Negro, Negroes

LEARNING ACTIVITIES IN FORMING PLURALS

A. (1) Number your paper from 1 to 15. Copy each of the following nouns and beside it write its plural. (2) Exchange papers. (3) Your teacher will then pronounce the plurals, and you will spell them orally in unison while he writes them on the board. Check the paper that you have received. (4) Use the Follow-up activity on page 179 if you miss any words.

1. handkerchief	4. wolf	7. proof	10. belief	13. roof
2. handcuff	5. gulf	8. life	11. leaf	14. safe
3. sheriff	6. knife	9. bluff	12. cliff	15. thief

B. In carrying out this activity, follow the same plan as in *A*.

1. alto	5. silo	9. rodeo	13. mosquito	17. echo
2. potato	6. hero	10. cello	14. torpedo	18. Negro
3. trio	7. tomato	11. bolero	15. kangaroo	19. veto
4. piano	8. tattoo	12. photo	16. soprano	20. auto

THE RULES FOR SPELLING PLURALS: III

RULE 8. **Spell the plurals of certain words irregularly.**

SINGULAR:	man	woman	goose	tooth
PLURAL:	men	women	geese	teeth
SINGULAR:	mouse	foot	child	ox
PLURAL:	mice	feet	children	oxen

RULE 9. **Add *s* to all proper nouns except those that end in *s, sh, ch, x,* or *z.* To those exceptions, add *es.* Never use an apostrophe.**

Brown, the Browns   Perkins, the Perkinses
Mary, both Marys   Walsh, the Walshes
Molloy, the Molloys   Burch, the Burches

RULE 10. **For some words, mostly names of certain animals, write the plural just as you do the singular.**

one *deer,* many *deer*   one *trout,* many *trout*
one *sheep,* many *sheep*   one *elk,* many *elk*

NOTE: Some words have only a plural form: *tweezers, trousers, scissors, pliers, shears, clothes, slacks, hose.* (Why, do you think?)

RULE 11. **For compound nouns** (made up of two or more words), **add *s* to the important name part.**

son-in-law, sons-in-law   car-dealer, car-dealers
drum major, drum majors   major general, major generals

NOTE: Compounds made with *ful* add *s* at the end: *cupfuls.*

LEARNING ACTIVITIES IN FORMING PLURALS

Directions: Activity A on page 189 concerns plurals covered in rules 8–11. Activity B covers all the rules for plurals. File any words that you miss, as explained in the Follow-up activity on page 179.

A. (1) Number your paper from 1 to 20. (2) Write the plurals of the words given below. (3) Exchange papers for checking. (4) Take turns at putting the plurals on the board and giving the rule.

1. Sally	6. fish	11. foot	16. father-in-law
2. Harris	7. fisherman	12. suds	17. man-of-war
3. ox	8. salmon	13. trout	18. teaspoonful
4. mouse	9. Riley	14. handful	19. commander in chief
5. Bess	10. sheep	15. Charles	20. saleswoman

B. (1) Make a list of ten plural nouns, each one of them illustrating a different rule. (2) On another paper, write these plurals, but mix up the letters in each; for example, for *ponies,* you might write *noisep.* (3) Exchange papers. (4) Figure out what each word is and write it beside the mixed-up form. (5) Write the singular form of each word. (6) Go over the papers with your partner.

USING ENGLISH IN ALL CLASSES

Bring into English class any papers that you are preparing for your other classes. Exchange papers with a partner and examine the papers that you receive for mistakes in spelling plural forms. If you are not absolutely sure of a word, check it by the dictionary. Return papers and list in your notebook any words that you misspelled. (See the Follow-up activity on page 179.)

PART TWO: ADDING SUFFIXES

"A SUFFIX IS SOMETHING THAT IS ADDED AT THE END."

"LIKE A POSTSCRIPT?"

A postscript is, of course, something added to the end of a letter, but it is *not* an example of a suffix. To explain clearly, he should have said, "A suffix is one letter or more added to a word to make a new word."

Some of the rules for forming plurals, pages 186–88, can be applied to the addition of other suffixes. Study the following rules and then do the practice exercises. After doing these activities, proceed as suggested in the Follow-up activity, page 179.

ADDING SUFFIXES TO WORDS THAT END IN Y

THE RULES

RULE 1. Make no other changes when you add *s, ed,* **or** *ing* **to a verb that ends in** *ay, ey,* **or** *oy.**

   stay, stays, stayed, staying   obey, obeys, obeyed, obeying

Important exceptions are the past of *say* (*said*), *lay* (*laid*), and *pay* (*paid*), and words based upon them, such as *mislaid, repaid,* and so on.

RULE 2. When you add a suffix to a word that ends in *y* **preceded by a consonant** (any letter except *a, e, i, o,* or *u*), **change the** *y* **to** *i.*†
The kinds of words below are typical of the many that can be made.

   a) **Verbs**
      (1) In making other verb forms: try, tries, tried; apply, applies, applied
      (2) In making adjectives: pity, pitiful, pitiless; rely, reliant, reliable
      (3) In making nouns: supply, supplier; deny, denial

   b) **Adjectives**
      (1) In making comparisons: happy, happier, happiest; icy, icier, iciest
      (2) In making adverbs: happy, happily; icy, icily
      (3) In making nouns: happy, happiness; icy, iciness

   c) **Nouns**
      (1) In forming plurals (covered in Rule 4, page 186)
      (2) In forming adjectives: duty, dutiful; penny, penniless

LEARNING ACTIVITIES IN ADDING SUFFIXES

A. (1) Number your paper from 1 to 20. (2) Copy the following items. (3) Beside each of them, write the word suggested, which must end in *y*. The first letters are given for you. (4) Beside the word write other words

---

* The idea here is like that of Rule 3 for forming plurals, page 186.
† The rule does not apply when adding a suffix beginning with *i*, such as *ing* or *ic*.

made by adding suffixes. You should find at least three other words. (5) Go over your work in class, putting the words on the board.

EXAMPLE: dangerous: ri—*risky, riskier, riskiest, riskily*

1. not hard: ea	11. not generous: st
2. misty: fo	12. vacant: em
3. beautiful: lo	13. oily: gr
4. rich: we	14. fast: sp
5. awkward: cl	15. loud: no
6. not steady: sh	16. fortunate: lu
7. not on time: ta	17. amusing: fu
8. powerful: mi	18. tired: we
9. not ambitious: la	19. foolish: si
10. not fat: sk	20. piggish: gr

B. (1) Copy the following paragraphs, filling in and underlining the incomplete words. Check the work by the Suggestions for Good Handwriting, page 479. (2) Exchange papers and correct them as the paragraphs are read aloud, with each incomplete word written on the board.

Once I knew a boy who ob.......... orders most of the time. Now and then, however, he pa.......... no attention, though he de.......... that he did so on purpose. One day his father sa.......... to him, "Son, I don't want to speak ang.........., but your conduct really ann.......... me. I hope it is only mental laz.......... that makes you act as you do. If I could see the tin.......... bit of improvement, I'd be sat.........., but it seems that you're stea.......... getting worse. Have you really tr.......... to do better?"

The boy rep.........., "Dad, ordi.......... I do listen, but sometimes my mind just str.......... away."

"Well," his father told him, "I think I can cure that trouble eas.......... From now on, every time you forget, I'll deduct a quarter from your allowance."

It worked!

C. Here are forty words that are likely to be misspelled if the writer does not know the rules for words ending in *y*. Practice spelling these words orally with a partner; then dictate them to each other.

1. business	11. muddier	21. employer	31. colonial
2. noisily	12. dustiness	22. paid	32. geographical
3. dried	13. notified	23. cries	33. spied
4. empties	14. married	24. buried	34. identifies
5. luckily	15. journeyed	25. satisfied	35. pries
6. thirstier	16. oilier	26. destroyed	36. dignified
7. mysterious	17. huskily	27. beautiful	37. carrier
8. victorious	18. hurried	28. glorious	38. trial
9. enjoyed	19. cloudiness	29. funniest	39. plentiful
10. sleepier	20. worrier	30. obeyed	40. clumsiness

THE RULES

RULE 1. In most cases, drop a final *e* before a suffix beginning with *a, e, i, o, u,* **or** *y.*

> write, writing   rose, rosy   salute, salutation

Two important exceptions are (1) *dyeing* (coloring), in which the *e* is kept so that the word will not be confused with *dying* (ceasing to live), and (2) *mileage.*

RULE 2. Keep the final *e* if the word ends in *ce* or *ge* and the suffix begins with *a* or *o*.*

> notice, noticeable   courage, courageous

RULE 3. Keep a silent *e* in most cases if the suffix begins with a consonant; that is, with any letter except *a, e, i, o, u,* or *y*.

> tame, tamely   hope, hopeful   trouble, troublesome
> pale, paleness   love, lovely   snake, snakelike

Exceptions include *true, truly; argue, argument.*

LEARNING ACTIVITIES IN ADDING SUFFIXES

A. (1) Copy the following words in a column. (2) Beside each of them, make new words ending with as many of these suffixes as you can: *y, ly, ing, ness, able, ation,* or *ition.* For one word, only one suffix will fit. (3) Have a combined list made on the board. (4) Check your own paper.

1. stone	6. curve	11. change	16. wire
2. explore	7. pure	12. large	17. pose
3. move	8. tune	13. true	18. service
4. peace	9. compose	14. lace	19. combine
5. excuse	10. lame	15. ripe	20. strange

B. (1) Have an oral drill in which you add *ing* to each of the following verbs. (2) Write the words as your teacher dictates them, and beside each, put the word formed by adding *ing.* (3) Exchange papers for checking.

1. divide	6. come	11. like	16. close	21. make
2. scrape	7. vote	12. smile	17. place	22. have
3. take	8. save	13. line	18. give	23. shake
4. note	9. prove	14. care	19. behave	24. date
5. blame	10. trace	15. store	20. price	25. serve

The *e* is kept to show that the *c* has the sound of *s,* and that the *g* has the sound of *j.*

THE RULES

RULE 1. In adding a suffix beginning with a vowel (*a, e, i, o, u,* or *y*), double a final consonant (except *h* or *x*) if the word has only one syllable and the consonant has a single vowel before it: bat, batter. The rule is most useful in spelling the following:

a) *Verb forms:* stop, stopped, stopping
b) *Comparisons of adjectives:* thin, thinner, thinnest
c) *Nouns made from verbs:* swim, swimmer; run, runner
d) *Adjectives made from verbs or nouns:* skin, skinny; fog, foggy

RULE 2. Follow Rule 1 for words of more than one syllable if they are accented on the last syllable.

refer (re fer′), referred, referring
permit (per mit′), permitted, permitting

Note that the words fit the pattern given in Rule 1: (1) the suffixes begin with a vowel (*ed, ing*) and (2) there is only one vowel (*e, i*) before the final consonant of the base word.

RULE 3. For most other words, do not double a final consonant when adding a suffix beginning with a vowel.

look, looked, looking (The *k* has *two* vowels before it.)
o′pen, o′pened, o′pening (The accent is on the *first* syllable.)

LEARNING ACTIVITIES IN ADDING SUFFIXES

A. (1) Copy the following sentences, putting in the needed form of each word in parentheses. (2) Exchange papers for checking. (3) Tell why each final consonant has or has not been doubled.

1. Are you (plan) to do your (shop) before (meet) Helen?
2. As I (step) inside, the lights (flicker) and grew still (dim).
3. You are (forget) that we haven't (unwrap) the (big) gift of all.
4. The (win) of the contest probably will be Tom. He's no (quit).
5. I'm (begin) to think that I (omit) one line of that poem.
6. He is always (brag) that he is a better (hit) than I am.
7. (Enter) that (swim) race was not my idea. I'm not very (speed).
8. Bill was (sit) on the porch when I (slip) up behind him.
9. I was really (stun) when I saw how much (fat) he is now.
10. After the rain had (stop), the day grew (sun).

B. (1) Add the indicated suffix to each of the following words, doubling the end consonant if necessary. (2) Use the new words in written sentences. Do your best to use vivid verbs and adjectives. (See pages 292 and 398.) (3) *Be sure to proofread for careless errors in spelling, punctuation, and capitalization.* (4) Exchange papers for checking. Using the Guides for Improving Expression, page 453, comment on good sentences.

1. war (ior)	3. equip (ment)	5. snob (ish)	7. drug (ist)
2. bit (en)	4. forbid (en)	6. fool (ing)	8. open (ed)

PART THREE: APPLYING THE PREFIXES DIS AND MIS AND THE SUFFIX FUL

In making words with the prefixes *mis* and *dis* and with the suffix *ful*, apply the following rules.

THE RULES

RULE 1. Never double the *s* of the prefix *dis* or *mis*.

dis + appear = disappear   mis + lead = mislead

RULE 2. Keep both *s*'s if the base word begins with *s*.

dis + satisfied = dissatisfied   mis + step = misstep

RULE 3. Never add any extra *l* to the suffix *ful*.

a cup, a cupful   care, careful

LEARNING ACTIVITIES IN SPELLING WITH *MIS, DIS,* AND *-FUL*

A. (1) As your teacher pronounces the words, write on your paper the new words made by using the prefix *dis* or *mis*. (2) Exchange papers for checking as words are spelled aloud and put on the board.

1. obey (dis)	6. miss (dis)	11. state (mis)
2. spell (mis)	7. use (mis)	12. place (mis)
3. approve (dis)	8. spent (mis)	13. lay (mis)
4. take (mis)	9. agree (dis)	14. own (dis)
5. appoint (dis)	10. solve (dis)	15. sent (mis)

B. (1) Add the suffix *ful* to the following words; then use them in sentences. Apply Rule 2, page 190, if necessary. Use a variety of sentence beginnings. (2) *Be sure to proofread.* (3) Exchange papers for criticism. (4) Put a star before especially good sentences.

1. hand	3. car	5. pity	7. spoon	9. mouth
2. room	4. cheer	6. peace	8. plenty	10. pocket

The old rhyme for remembering when to write *ie* and when to write *ei* probably is the best rule for helping you to avoid errors.

THE RULE

Use *i* before *e* except after *c*
Or when sounded as *ā*
As in *neighbor* and *weigh*.

Here are some examples:

field (Use *ie* because the letters follow *f*, not *c*.)
receive (Use *ei* because the letters follow *c*.)
eight (The letters sound like *ā*.)

Some common exceptions that you need to know are these:

their (Remember that *he* and *I* are in it.)
foreign (Remember that it has *ore* in it.)
either and neither (Remember that they have *it* in them.)
height (Remember that *he* and *I* are in it.)

LEARNING ACTIVITIES IN SPELLING WITH *IE* AND *EI*

A. Here are sentences containing one or more scrambled words. Some of them when written correctly contain *ei;* the others, *ie*. (1) Make two columns on your paper, one headed *ei* and the other, *ie*. (2) Figure out the words and write each of them under the right heading. (3) Check your own paper as the words are spelled orally and written on the board.

1. Did you (ceevire) a letter from your new (redfin)?
2. The storm brought some (efiler) from the heat, I (vilebee).
3. I paid cash for both books, but in (tenhire) case did I get a (petrice).
4. Write a (firbe) theme about a (firenog) land that interests you.
5. I've gained an inch in (hitheg), but I think I've lost (hegwit).
6. The son of our next-door (grobhine) often gets into (semifich).
7. The (hifet) who stole those (higet) cars is now in prison.
8. This (hildes) is so strong that no arrow can (erepic) it.
9. The (ivel) on that hat is its (hicef) trimming.
10. After (reefic) fighting, we made the enemy (edyil).

B. (1) Using the lists made in *A*, see how many other words related to them you can make. (2) Have a combined list put on the board.

You may prefer to make this a team contest in which you take turns in putting a word on the board and then adding words related to it. Score a point only if each new word is spelled correctly.

Before handing in your next paper for any class, go over it carefully to correct any errors in your spelling of (1) words beginning with *dis* or *mis* and (2) words containing *ie* or *ei*. Check it also by the Suggestions for Good Handwriting, page 479.

3. Watch Out for Tricky Spellings!

READ AND TALK ABOUT

> Wirdley's spelling is certainly queer,
> For he spells entirely by eer:
> "Boats dock at a peer;
> A globe is a spheer;
> And anything far is not neer."

What does this little poem show about the spelling of words in the English language?

If each letter had only one sound, spelling would be easy. Unfortunately, however, the same letters or combinations of letters have different sounds. Note the red letters in the examples below.

tap	city	grow	bead	boot	fill
tape	camp	germ	instead	foot	file
fall			great		machine
far					

How many sounds can you think of for *e?* for *o?* for *u?* for *s?*

Another problem is that the same sounds may be spelled in different ways. Note the red letters in these words:

> tape, great, wait, weigh, stay, they
> be, bead, field, seem, gasoline, seize

How many ways can you think of to spell the sound of *i* as pronounced in the word *fine?* of *o,* as in the word *go?*

Luckily, most words follow certain patterns, as you learned in studying the spelling of words with silent letters (pages 179–84) and in applying the spelling rules on pages 186, 187, 188, 190, 192, 193, 194, and 195. In your study of vocabulary, pages 104–19, you will learn more about word patterns.

HELPFUL HINTS FOR SPELLING TRICKY WORDS

1. Find words within the tricky words. For example, "heard" has an "ear" in it.

2. Pair tricky words with ones that you know how to spell. The words need not be rhymes, though they may be.

   r*ain*—ag*ain,* capt*ain,* cert*ain,* mount*ain,* vill*ain*
   s*ong*—am*ong,* wr*ong*   h*ide*—dec*ide*

3. Make a sentence giving a clue; underline the troublesome word and the clue or clues that will help you to spell that word.

   I feel all right, but my work seems to be all wrong.
   Divide the divers into two classes.

4. Keep a special list of tricky words. Write the trouble spots in red. Practice the words over and over.

   excellent   children   minute   answer   early

After doing the following activities, handle any misspellings as suggested in the Follow-up activity on page 179.

LEARNING ACTIVITIES IN MASTERING TRICKY SPELLINGS

A. In each of the following words, you can find one or more words that will help you to remember how to spell the tricky part. (1) Copy the words on your paper. (2) In each word, find another word and circle it. Be sure to circle only a word that you think will be helpful to you; then write it beside the word containing it. (3) Compare work in class. (4) Change your own list if necessary before putting it into the spelling section of your notebook.

EXAMPLES: soldier old   doctor or   sleeve eve

1. ache	13. expense	25. meant	37. safety
2. across	14. forty	26. motor	38. search
3. afraid	15. fourth	27. ninety	39. secretary
4. against	16. friend	28. notice	40. sensitive
5. before	17. grammar	29. often	41. separate
6. business	18. holiday	30. only	42. something
7. busy	19. ignorant	31. patient	43. temperature
8. college	20. instant	32. pleasant	44. thrown
9. color	21. invitation	33. ready	45. together
10. country	22. label	34. really	46. toward
11. definite	23. leather	35. recent	47. vacation
12. every	24. many	36. recognize	48. vegetable

B. In the following words, trouble spots are shown in red. In a class discussion, figure out ways of mastering the spelling of these words. Remember to be courteous. (See guide 4, page 33.)

1. absence	6. corner	11. February	16. Saturday
2. almost	7. describe	12. necessary	17. surely
3. always	8. doctor	13. nervous	18. through
4. built	9. doesn't	14. reason	19. until
5. committee	10. exercise	15. remember	20. Wednesday

ENRICHMENT

(*One or two students may volunteer to do this activity.*) (1) Examine in the large dictionary all the words that begin with *ph*. What do you find about their source? (2) Examine the words that begin with *ch* pronounced like *sh*. What do you learn about their source? (3) Make a list of the commonest *ph* and *ch* (sh) words. (4) Make a report to the class. Be sure to use the Speech Chart, page 61, and the Guides for Making a Short, One-Source Report, page 134.

4. Watch the Pronunciation!

"HE'S GOING TO THE LIBERY TO GIT A BOOK UH POMES."

THINK IT OVER . . .

What words is the boy mispronouncing?
Is mispronunciation part of *your* spelling trouble?

Many common words are misspelled simply because the user pronounces them carelessly or wrongly. For example, unless you are careful to say *escape,* you are likely to write *excape.*

A. What pronunciation faults in the following words are likely to lead to misspelling? (1) In a class discussion have the words listed on the board and the faults underlined. (2) Practice pronouncing the words and then spelling them aloud.

1. apologize	6. chocolate	11. hundred	16. perhaps
2. athlete	7. divide	12. Indian	17. permanent
3. athletics	8. government	13. library	18. sentence
4. children	9. congratulate	14. partner	19. surprise
5. chimney	10. history	15. perform	20. strictly

B. (1) As your teacher dictates them, write the words in *A* on your paper. (2) Exchange papers for checking. (3) Write a helpful sentence for each word that you miss. (4) Circle the misspelled part of each word.

5. Watch Out for Homonyms and Similar Words!

My favorite cake is an angle food.

READ AND TALK ABOUT

What wrong mental pictures do the italicized words in the following sentences suggest?

As they crossed the *planes*, the pioneers saw many buffaloes.
I write in this *dairy* every night.
I ate too much *desert*.

As those sentences suggest, certain words are likely to be confused with other words. Sometimes the confused words sound alike (as in *plains, planes*). Sometimes they just look much alike (as in *dairy, diary*).

1. **(DEFINITION)** Homonyms are words that have the same pronunciation but that differ in spelling and meaning.

> May I have a **piece** of pie?
> **Peace** is better than war.

2. **Here are some sentences that show how certain confusing homonyms should be used.**

   a) How much is the bus **fare?** I believe in **fair** play.

   b) Of **course** I know you. This thread is too **coarse.**

   c) **Steel** is made from iron. A good man will not **steal.**

   d) One **pane** of glass is cracked. See a doctor about that **pain.**

   e) **It's** [It is] time for lunch. The tree lost **its** leaves.

   f) **Your** car is ready. **You're** [You are] late.

   g) I know **their** names. **There** they go! **They're** [They are] here.

   h) **Here** comes the team! Can you **hear** me?

   i) Our ship will **sail** today. These coats are on **sale.**

   j) I lost a **pair** of gloves. Will you **pare** this **pear** for me?

   k) Who **led** the parade? My feet feel as heavy as **lead.**

   l) **Whose** book is this? **Who's** [Who is] going with you?

LEARNING ACTIVITIES

A. In class, go over the preceding sentences to make sure that the differences in meaning between the homonyms are clear. Give oral sentences of your own to show that you can tell the words apart. What other meanings can you illustrate for *fare?* for *fair?* for *course?*

B. Here is a list of common words that have homonyms. (1) Write each word and its homonym or homonyms. (2) Have the homonyms listed on the board to help you check your paper. (3) Have a team contest in which a member of one team pronounces and spells one of the homonyms. A member of the other team must then use that word in a sentence. Score a point for each correct sentence given.

1. beat	5. wait	9. great	13. peak	17. grown
2. bare	6. road	10. lane	14. break	18. toad
3. see	7. sole	11. heel	15. hole	19. vain
4. die	8. pail	12. seem	16. passed	20. seen

● THESE ARE FACTS ABOUT OTHER CONFUSING PAIRS

1. **Certain words are confused because they sound somewhat alike. If you pronounce them right, you will not confuse them.**

   a) Don't **lose** your ticket. Tighten that **loose** bolt.
   b) We have lived here **since** 1950. Use your own good **sense**
   c) I like cold **weather.** I don't know **whether** I can help.
   d) He is older **than** I. First John came and **then** Bill.
   e) Are you **quite** sure? The room was very **quiet**

2. **Some words are confused simply because they look much alike, even though they sound entirely different.**

   a) She behaved like an **angel.** Measure this **angle**
   b) We sell milk to that **dairy.** I should write in my **diary**
   c) Walk **through** that door. He gave us a **thorough** test.
   d) Hang your **clothes** in this closet. The tables had new **cloths** on them.
   e) Take a deep **breath.** It is hard to **breathe** in a stuffy room.

LEARNING ACTIVITIES

A. (1) Study carefully the sentences given as examples. (2) Close your book. (3) Number a sheet of paper from 1 to 20. As your teacher reads the sentences, one by one, write the correct words on your paper. (4) Exchange papers for checking as your teacher reads the sentences again and writes the words on the board.

B. (1) For each error that you made in *A*, write the word correctly in a sentence. Use the Suggestions for Good Handwriting, page 479. (2) Check your work and file the paper in your notebook.

ENRICHMENT

Begin a collection of errors that you find in the use of homonyms or other words that are confused. Look for them in advertising signs, circulars, newspapers, letters, and similar places. Copy or clip these examples, circling the wrong word and writing above it the word that should have been used. When you have a good collection, report to the class. The sign below has two mistakes. What are they?

WE MAKE YOU'RE OLD CLOTHS LOOK LIKE *NEW*

WHIZ CLEANERS

CHECK TESTS IN SPELLING

At the beginning of this chapter, you took two Pretests in spelling. You will now take those tests again. Follow the plan for the Pretests, page 178.

Follow the plan for the Pretests, page 178.

★ **Cumulative Review**

CAPITALIZATION

Copy these sentences, placing capital letters where they are needed.

1. The rev. o. d. post read from the old testament of the bible.
2. Then mother asked, "who else is in your english class?"
3. the story that betty wrote is called "the best of the bunch."
4. My grandfather and i went over to madison street to visit the new y.m.c.a.
5. The browns have just returned from the west. there they visited mr. and mrs. l. t. jackson in sacramento, california.

PUNCTUATION

Copy the sentences, supplying needed punctuation marks, including underlining.

1. Yes said the teacher Ive seen a big improvement in your spelling
2. When you do not use so many ands and uhs you sound better
3. Mother have you seen my book The Life of Daniel Boone
4. Dr and Mrs John J Rogers of Atlanta Georgia want us to visit them this week next week or Christmas week
5. Girls coats are priced at $4295 (forty-two dollars and ninety-five cents).

SENTENCE SENSE

Number your paper from 1 to 10. Read each of the following groups of words. If a group of words is a sentence, write *S* after its number. If it is a fragment, write *F*. If it is a run-on sentence, write *RO*. Change fragments and run-on sentences to make good sentences.

1. Leaves all over the yard.
2. Raking the leaves.
3. The wind blew the leaves to the ground.
4. Beautiful red, orange, and yellow leaves.
5. We rode into the country then we got out of the car and walked through the woods.
6. Going to the store to buy groceries.
7. Val, Marilyn, Fred, and Sally were on the entertainment committee.
8. Stood there waiting for the train to pass.
9. We went last night why didn't you go?
10. All the people on our street.

WRITING IN EVERYDAY SITUATIONS

1. Writing Clear Explanations

"MAYBE I SHOULD USE HIEROGLYPHICS TO EXPLAIN THAT NEW GAME."

READ AND THINK ABOUT

How well can you explain in writing how to do something?
Can you always follow written directions for tests?
Are you able to write directions that others can follow easily?

Chapter 4, you will remember, gave special instructions and practice in learning to make clear oral explanations and directions. This chapter is designed to make writing directions—and following them—and making explanations in writing easier for you.

Many suggestions given in Chapter 4 will apply here as well, but when you write, as you already know, some special helps are always welcome.

GUIDES FOR WRITING CLEAR EXPLANATIONS

1. Be sure you have all the facts and details clear in your own mind.
2. Arrange the facts and details in a step-by-step order. (An outline may be helpful. See page 99.)
3. As you write, follow your step-by-step order exactly.
4. Use simple language. Define any terms your readers may not know.
5. Include any drawings that will aid the reader.

LEARNING ACTIVITIES IN WRITING CLEAR EXPLANATIONS

A. (1) Write an explanation to fit one of the following situations, or one suggested to you by them. Use the Guides for Writing a Paragraph, page 214. (2) Exchange papers when you have finished. (3) If the person who reads your explanation does not understand any part of it, he should jot down questions on your paper so that you may reword it more clearly. (4) Read the explanations to the class; then discuss them on the basis of the Guides for Giving Clear Explanations.

1. Suppose that you must miss a day or more of school. Send a note to class by your brother. In the note ask a friend to give your brother certain things for you. Explain in the note just which books and other materials you want. Tell exactly where each one can be found. Ask also for any assignments that you need.
2. You have come down with measles just before a committee of which you are chairman is to have an important meeting. Send a note to the committee explaining several matters that must be settled at the meeting and the order in which they should be taken up.
3. You are leaving for a week's camping trip. Write clear, exact instructions for taking care of your rabbits or other pets while you are away. Make these explanations simple enough so that your little brother or sister can understand and follow them.
4. Your scoutmaster or club leader is well pleased with a project that you have just completed. He asks you to write a step-by-step account of your work so that other members may use your explanation as a guide in carrying out a similar project.

B. Write an explanation of one of the pictographs on the next page. Make it a one-paragraph summary. Use the Guides to Making a Summary, page 93, to help you include the important information in your explanation. Compare the explanations in class. Decide whether you think the charts or the written explanations present the ideas more vividly and clearly.

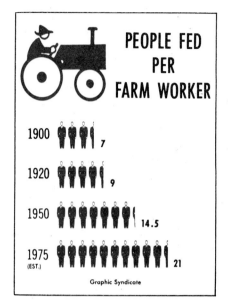

PEOPLE FED PER FARM WORKER

1900 7

1920 9

1950 14.5

1975 (EST.) 21

Graphic Syndicate

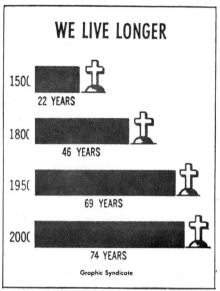

WE LIVE LONGER

1500 22 YEARS

1800 46 YEARS

1950 69 YEARS

2000 74 YEARS

Graphic Syndicate

2. Writing Directions

In writing directions you may follow the same general guides as you did for giving good oral directions. (See page 67.) Keep in mind that in writing directions you cannot "back up" and begin again to correct any error, so it is even more important to be completely accurate.

LEARNING ACTIVITY IN WRITING DIRECTIONS

Write clear directions to fit one of the following situations, or one suggested to you by one of them. *Proofread your paper carefully, using the Writing Chart, page 172.* When you have finished, be ready to read your paper to the class. Before anyone's directions are read, review in class the Guides to Speaking Clearly and Correctly, page 43. After reading your directions, ask someone to repeat them. To do so calls for careful listening.

1. Your parents are coming for the first time to visit you at camp. Write them exactly how to find the camp and your tent or cabin.

2. You have moved from your old home to a new house in another part of town. Your grandparents are coming by automobile for their first visit since you have moved. Give them careful instructions for finding your house.

3. You are to have work on display in the 4-H Club exhibit at your county fair. You will be on duty there at the time your favorite aunt from the city plans to arrive to visit the exhibit. Write careful directions for getting (1) to the fairgrounds, (2) to the 4-H building, and (3) to the booth where you will be.

3. Following Written Instructions

In these days of prepackaged foods, hobby kits, and other "do-it-yourself" projects, being able to follow written directions is very important. These guides will provide some help.

GUIDES FOR FOLLOWING WRITTEN INSTRUCTIONS

1. Read the instructions all the way through, perhaps several times, before you begin to work.

2. Ask questions if you do not understand.

3. When you are absolutely sure you know precisely what to do and how you are to do it, follow the directions step by step.

4. Check every step to be sure you have completed each one.

LEARNING ACTIVITIES

A. Work out the following exercise. Do this alone. Pay no attention to your neighbors and ask your teacher no questions. After you have finished, exchange papers for checking.

Using a ruler, draw on your paper a square, 4 x 4 inches. Divide this square into half-inch squares. Beginning with the upper left-hand square, number the squares across, 1, 2, 3, 4, 5, 6, 7, and so on, but skip every third square. In the first of the skipped squares, print the letter *a;* in the second, *b;* and so on through the alphabet until you have filled every blank square. You may use pencil in making the squares, but fill in the numbers and letters with ink.

In checking, be sure to go over every point in the instructions.

B. Copy the following words in one column on your paper, leaving three blank lines below each word. Then find each word where it appears *first* in your dictionary. Write the page number after the word on your paper. On the first blank line under each word, show how the word can be divided and where the chief accent falls. (You may want to look over the dictionary sample on page 113.) On the second blank line (and the third, if you need it), under each word, put down the *first* meaning that you find listed for that word. Use pen and ink and number each word.

If you finish before your teacher tells you to stop, take another sheet of paper and try your hand at writing an original sentence with each word. Underline the word and number the sentence to correspond with the number of the word on your first paper.

1. discriminate
2. bonanza
3. singular
4. testimony
5. inconsiderate
6. gratitude
7. octogenarian

4. Following Directions in Tests

READ AND DISCUSS

Most tests have directions. Some boys and girls just glance at such directions. Other students never even bother to read them at all, because they are sure that they know what is in the directions.

Here are the directions that one teacher gave for one part of a test. Read the directions and the answers that one boy wrote.

Directions: Copy the sentences in the test. Each sentence contains one wrong answer, which you are to cross out.

[*This is the boy's paper.*]

1. George Washington was (a) our first President; (b) a great inventor; (c) the husband of Martha Custis.
2. The Battle of Saratoga was (a) fought in Massachusetts; (b) the turning point of the Revolutionary War; (c) fought in 1777.
3. Nathan Hale was (a) hanged by the British; (b) a schoolteacher; (c) a sea captain.

What has the boy done that the directions did not say to do?
What has he *not* done that he should have done?

The boy who wrote that paper was a bright boy; he failed that test, however, simply because he did not study the directions.

It is very easy to do what he did unless you form the habit of giving careful attention to all test directions.

GUIDES FOR TAKING TESTS

1. Before you begin to write, read the instructions carefully; go over them more than once, if necessary.

2. Ask questions about anything that you do not understand.

3. Answer every question completely, in the form required.

4. Write or print clearly.

5. Go back over the directions, the questions, and your answers to see whether you have left anything out.

6. Proofread for careless mistakes.

LEARNING ACTIVITIES IN ANALYZING TEST DIRECTIONS

A. Here are some sample test assignments. Study them carefully. Then answer the following questions about each assignment.

How many different things must the student do?

What errors might he make in carrying out the various parts of the test?

1. Here are remarks made by certain characters in the stories that you have been reading. Below each remark are four names. Circle the name of the character who made the remark. In the blank at the left, write the name of the selection. Below, write a sentence identifying one of the other three characters named.

2. Here are some incomplete sentences, each of them followed by four possible endings. Copy the sentences and complete them with true endings. If more endings than one are true, copy those also.

3. Here is a list of characters in the stories you have been reading, followed by several quotations from the stories. Choose the name of the person who made each statement, and write it in the first blank after the quotation. In the second blank, name the person to whom the quotation was said. You may use any name more than once. You need not use all the names.

B. Bring to class any set of test questions that you can find. For example, you might bring tests from other subjects, from *Junior Scholastic* or *Read,* or "intelligence" quizzes from other magazines or from newspapers. Try taking some of the tests in class. Check afterwards to see how many people really followed the directions.

CAPITALIZATION

Copy these sentences, placing capital letters where they are needed.

1. our school, jefferson junior high school, will sponsor a food sale on st. patrick's day, march 17.
2. grandfather and uncle tobias grew up in grand rapids, michigan.
3. One of my favorite science fiction books is arthur c. clarke's search for tomorrow.
4. each student is required to take courses in english and physical education as well as science and mathematics.

PUNCTUATION

Copy these sentences, supplying needed punctuation.

1. I think remarked Mrs Edwards that you should follow Janes advice and go to the concert.
2. Mothers favorite short story is The Gift of the Magi by O Henry.
3. I am preparing a book report on Hot Rod a book of fiction by Gregor Felsen
4. His new address is 2543 Old Mill Road Fort Collins Colorado 80521

SENTENCE SENSE

Number your paper from 1 to 10. Read each of the following groups of words. If the group of words is a sentence, write *S* after its number. If it is a fragment, write *F*.

1. Everyone can bring one guest to the party.
2. Hanging on to the football with all his strength.
3. After Tom, Jerry, and Jane go home.
4. Walked and ran and whistled a tune.
5. There were cake crumbs all over the counter top.

SPELLING

Write on your paper the new words made by using the prefix *mis* or *dis* or the suffix *ful,* as indicated.

1. mind (ful)
2. (mis) lay
3. (dis) bar
4. (mis) name
5. can (ful)
6. (dis) arm
7. (mis) manage
8. bowl (ful)
9. (dis) appear

Chapter
11

PUTTING IDEAS INTO PARAGRAPHS

1. Understanding Paragraph Construction

"THIS PAGE LOOKS HARD. I'D BETTER MAKE FOUR OR FIVE PARAGRAPHS OUT OF IT."

THINK IT OVER...

A page with only one paragraph looks hard to read, but is there a better reason for making paragraphs? In other words, is the important aim of paragraphing to make reading look easy—or is it to set off ideas?

Exactly what is a paragraph?

How do you go about writing a paragraph?

Do you know what a topic sentence is?

In this chapter you will study and practice writing paragraphs that are built around a topic sentence. You will not be concerned with paragraphs in conversation or narration.

● THESE ARE FACTS ABOUT PARAGRAPHS

1. (DEFINITION) A *paragraph* is a group of sentences all about one main idea.

2. (DEFINITION) A *topic sentence* (or *topic statement*) is a sentence that states the main idea of a paragraph. It is oftenest the first sentence, but it may come at the end or (though not often) in the middle. If there is no topic sentence, the good reader puts the main idea into his own words.

3. All sentences in the paragraph should deal with the main idea.

4. Not all paragraphs need topic sentences. Many paragraphs, in stories, for example, have none.

5. In writing conversation, one should make a new paragraph for each change of speaker. (See Rule 3, page 157.)

Notice the location of the topic sentence (italicized) in each of the following three paragraphs. (The first two paragraphs are student-written.)

1. *Mistakes are worthwhile if you can learn from them.* One day, when I was in my first year of Junior League baseball, our team needed a catcher. I foolishly volunteered to catch, although I had never caught before in my life and did not know a thing about catching. The one important rule that I did not follow was to keep my right hand doubled up in a fist when the ball came into my glove. A ball came speeding in and hit the tip of the middle finger of my right hand. It felt as if the first knuckle had been shoved into the palm of my hand, although it turned out to be only jammed. Now I always close my fist when catching.

2. As I practice cheers and lead cheers at games, I have many opportunities to improve myself in getting along with others. Although it is very hard work, cheerleading helps keep me in good physical condition. It also helps me to become better coordinated. I have learned many new types of cheers and jumps. The activity causes me to be extra careful of my grooming. Finally, I have learned all the rules about cheerleading. *Cheerleading is really proving to be a good experience for me.*

3. He was smallish in stature, but well set and as nimble as a goat; his face was of a good open expression, but sunburnt very dark, and heavily freckled and pitted with the smallpox; his eyes were unusually light and had a kind of dancing madness in them, that was both engaging and alarming; and when he took off his greatcoat, he laid a pair of fine silver-mounted pistols on the table, and I saw that he was belted with a great sword. His manners, besides, were elegant, and he pledged the captain handsomely. *Altogether I thought of him, at the first sight, that here was a man I would rather call my friend than my enemy.**

LEARNING ACTIVITY IN FINDING TOPIC SENTENCES

Decide what the main idea is in each of the following paragraphs. Write the topic sentence on a piece of paper.

1. There was nothing small about Tom Evans. He had a huge beak of a nose, a cavern of a mouth, and ears that fairly flapped in the breeze. His feet were the size of snowshoes. A lion-like head covered by a great mane of wiry hair was set on the thick neck that rose from his barrel-like chest. Enormous hands dangled far out of the sleeves that were strained tightly over Tom's bulging muscles. Yes, even his *voice* was big.

2. The only television programs that Jack Lewis enjoys must have airplanes in them somewhere. His sister Mabel concentrates on dance bands. Their father turns to a news broadcast every time he sits down to watch. Their mother, on the other hand, really enjoys television plays. Little Billy, whenever he gets his way, tunes in on cowboy programs. Since the Lewis family owns but one TV set, the question of what to watch sometimes leads to arguments.

3. You might think that since there are so many kinds of insects in the world, there must be only a few of each kind. No idea could be more mistaken. There are tremendous numbers of the different kinds of insects. A single tree may have twenty million plant lice on it. A swarm of gnats may have in it hundreds of thousands of gnats. And so it goes. In the world as a whole, there are thought to be about twenty-five million insects for every square mile of land.†

---

*From *Kidnapped* by Robert Louis Stevenson; copyright 1880, 1917 by Charles Scribner's Sons; copyright 1908, 1922 by Mary Day Lanier. Charles Scribner's Sons, New York.

†Adapted from *Insect Friends and Enemies* by Bertha Morris Parker and Robert E. Gregg; copyright © 1959, 1952, 1947, 1941 by Harper & Row, Publishers, Incorporated, Evanston, Illinois.

A. *(Based upon the three example paragraphs, pages 211–12)*
1. Explain why the two words in the middle of the second sentence of paragraph 1 are capitalized.
2. Why is *opportunities* spelled as it is *(paragraph 2)*?
3. Explain the hyphen toward the end of the first sentence of paragraph 3.

B. *(Based upon the Learning Activity in Finding Topic Sentences)*
1. Explain the commas in the second sentence of paragraph 1.
2. Why are *mother* and *father* not capitalized in paragraph 2?
3. Spell the plural of the name of the family in paragraph 2.
4. Explain the hyphen in the last sentence of paragraph 3.

ENRICHMENT

Search through newspapers and magazines for good examples of paragraphs that have well-defined topic sentences. Underline the topic sentences. Bring the paragraphs to class and use them as the basis for group discussion. Post the best examples on the bulletin board. (Try to find paragraphs in which the topic sentence occurs (1) at the beginning (2) in the middle, and (3) at the end.

USING ENGLISH IN ALL CLASSES

A. From one of your other books, bring to class an example of a paragraph that you think does a good job of developing its topic sentence. Read that topic sentence to the class, and tell how the other sentences develop it.

B. Go over a theme or other paper that you have written this year in any class. Is the main idea in each paragraph easy to locate, or have you run together several ideas? Does every sentence add to the main idea? Could you have expressed any topic sentences better? Could you have put any topic sentence in a better location? If so, it will be good practice for you to rewrite the paper.

2. Building Good Paragraphs

The purpose of writing in paragraphs is to make it easy for readers to follow your ideas. Each new paragraph indicates a new idea, or another slant on an idea expressed in an earlier paragraph.

GUIDES FOR WRITING A PARAGRAPH

1. Plan your paragraph. Think first; then write.

2. Tell in a topic sentence exactly what the paragraph is about.

3. Develop (expand) the main idea expressed in the topic sentence. You may want to do so in one of these ways:
   a) Give reasons to support the topic sentence.
   b) Give examples to support it.
   c) Write a brief amusing or interesting or curious incident (happening) to illustrate it.
   d) Give facts or details to support it.

4. Stick to the point expressed in the topic sentence. Include in the paragraph only ideas that support the main idea.

5. After having written a paragraph, check it by these guides; then proofread it, using the points in the Writing Chart, page 172.

6. Whenever you are tempted to use "and" or "so" to tie ideas together, try using some other word or word group instead, such as *also, after all, besides, as a result, then, therefore.* If you make skillful use of these words, your sentences will show a better relationship to each other, and you will avoid writing run-on sentences (see page 170).

Following are four paragraphs illustrating the four methods of development mentioned in point 3 of the guides. Notice that in each of the example paragraphs the first sentence is the topic sentence.

1. REASONS

The horseshoe is considered good luck for several reasons. Because it is made of iron and because iron is thought to be a powerful force against witchcraft, a horseshoe nailed over the door protects the household from witches and devils. The crescent shape has long been symbolic of sacred things, and therefore it is doubly potent. In some parts of the world the horse is considered man's best friend, and anything associated with the horse brings good fortune. Fastened over the door, near the cash register, on a tree in the field, or on the mast of a ship, the horseshoe brings luck, particularly if the curve is down and the points are up. In this way it catches the good luck and holds it without letting it spill out.*

* From *Lore of Our Land: A Book of American Folklore* by Hector H. Lee and Donald Roberson; copyright © 1963 by Harper & Row, Publishers, Incorporated, Evanston, Illinois.

In the preceding paragraph, three definite *reasons* are given to explain why the horseshoe is considered good luck: (1) it works against witchcraft; (2) it is a symbol of sacred things; (3) it is associated with the horse, often considered "man's best friend." A fourth reason might be that the shape of the horseshoe enables it to hold good luck.

2. EXAMPLES

> There are a number of simple motors which a young electrician can make. The "whirling cork" motor is extremely simple and can be assembled with bits and parts which can be found around the house. The "Simple Simon" motor is great for high speed and will last for years, but it is not much for power. "Little Speedy," as the boys who made the original called it, is a remarkable motor. It is capable of a speed of 2,000 revolutions per minute and is always ready and willing to supply power for toys. In the little "roofing nail motor" the magnetism generated by the electromagnet applies itself to the attraction of four roofing nails driven into an ordinary thread spool which serves as the armature for the little machine. Any boy who is at all clever with his hands should be able to construct any of these motors in a short time.*

In the preceding paragraph of *examples,* four easy-to-make motors are pointed out: (1) the "whirling cork," (2) the "Simple Simon," (3) the "Little Speedy," and (4) the "roofing nail."

3. INCIDENT

> It is not easy for a very young child to learn how to be a barber. When I was three years old, I was sure I wanted to cut hair. I thought of my mother as a possible customer, but I knew she didn't need a haircut. Then I thought of my cat. I found her, took her to the porch, and began to cut away. I spent about five minutes giving her what I thought was a fine-looking pixie-do. The cat became terrified when I decided to finish off with a shampoo. Her yowling brought my mother, who immediately put an end to my barbering.

Notice how well the *incident* approach of the preceding paragraph lends itself to development of the topic sentence; it is natural and adds interest at the same time.

*Adapted from *A Boy and a Motor* by Raymond F. Yates; copyright 1944 by Raymond F. Yates; copyright © renewed 1972 by Marguerite W. Yates. Harper & Brothers, New York.

4. DETAILS

One cold November night that year [1887] a big fire destroyed the Bridgeport, Connecticut, winter headquarters of the Barnum & Bailey circus. Leaping flames were visible for miles. All the wild animals except thirty elephants and a lion named Nimrod perished in the disaster. Nimrod was found in a barn, eating a calf. A farmer's wife, thinking he was a huge yellow dog, belabored the beast with a broom and nearly fainted when she learned the truth. One elephant survived by swimming in the dark, chilly waters of Long Island Sound.*

Observe how the *details* in the above paragraph support the opening sentence. The description gains added vividness from the accounts of the elephant that swam to safety and of Nimrod's encounter with a farmer's wife.

LEARNING ACTIVITIES IN WAYS OF DEVELOPING PARAGRAPHS

A. In each of the following paragraphs, find the topic sentence. Explain in class how each paragraph is developed (see guide 3, page 214). Discuss each paragraph in the light of the preceding guides.

1. Although De Soto's expedition seemed to end sadly, it was an important one in the history of North America. He had discovered a great river. He had made the first definite exploration of Florida, Alabama, Georgia, South Carolina, Mississippi, and Arkansas. This beautiful region had riches more important than gold. It had rich soil and a mild climate, which one day would attract thousands of settlers.†

2. There had been many stormy times for Columbus. There had been quarrels with the natives in some places. His first settlement at La Navidad had been burned to the ground, and all the settlers had been killed. There had been quarrels with enemies among his own men. Once they had succeeded in having him sent back to Spain as a prisoner.‡

---

*Adapted from *Great Days of the Circus* by the Editors of *American Heritage;* copyright © 1962 by American Heritage Publishing Company, Inc., New York.

†Adapted from *Hernando de Soto* by Vesta E. Condon; copyright © 1950 by Row, Peterson and Company, Evanston, Illinois.

‡Adapted from *Christopher Columbus* by Ruth Cromer Weir; copyright © 1950 by Harper & Row, Publishers, Incorporated, Evanston, Illinois.

3. Time brought the Emperor Augustus expressions of the love his people felt for him. One day at the arena, for example, he received a thrilling surprise. When he entered, the whole audience rose. Everyone wore a wreath of the sacred laurel, the tree of honor and victory. The crowd shouted, "Hail, Father of the Country!" This was the noblest title that could be awarded to a benefactor of Rome.*

4. Dinner, which came at the end of the day, was an important event to the wealthy people of ancient Rome. The Romans did not sit on straight chairs at a dining table but reclined on couches. The couches were arranged on three sides of an open table on which the food was placed. Slaves walked in the open space and passed the food. The Romans helped themselves with their fingers to chicken, fish, sliced eggs, lettuce, onions, beans, or other food. Usually there was entertainment for the guests. Sometimes a slave read aloud. Sometimes a juggler did his tricks, or a musician played his flute.†

B. Following are the topic sentence and the first words of the other sentences of a paragraph. Complete the sentences with details that support the main idea. Compare the paragraphs in class.

All the members of our family enjoy outdoor sports. My father .... Mother .... Both John and I .... My sisters, Meg and Ann, ... We all ....

C. Write a topic sentence for each of the following ten topics. A *topic* is a subject that people write, think, or talk about. It could be the title for a paragraph. Before writing your topic sentences, notice these examples of topics and topic sentences developed from them:

TOPIC: Picnic Weather
TOPIC SENTENCE: The weather was perfect for our picnic last Sunday.

TOPIC: Birthday Surprises
TOPIC SENTENCE: Since my mother is an expert in planning surprise birthday parties, my twelfth birthday was a "wow."

1. Planning
2. Buying a New ....
3. My First Cake
4. Naming Our Dog
5. Homesickness
6. Home Responsibilities
7. Getting Up
8. Cleaning My Room
9. Escalators
10. Baby-sitting

*Adapted from *Caesar Augustus* by Jay Williams; copyright © 1951 by Harper & Row, Publishers, Incorporated, Evanston, Illinois.
†Adapted from *The Old World* by Mabel Rockwood Grimm and Matilda Hughes; copyright © 1955, 1953, 1948 by Row, Peterson and Company, Evanston, Illinois.

D. Choose one of the following topic sentences, or one suggested to you by them. Write a paragraph about your topic sentence, using the guides on page 214 to help you. Check to see that you have no sentence fragments or run-on sentences (see pages 337 and 341). When you have finished, read your paragraphs to the class. Review the Guides for Reading Aloud, page 57. Take time to discuss each paragraph to see how well it meets the requirements of a good paragraph.

1. I have a good idea for an invention.
2. We have telephone problems at our house.
3. My favorite television program is ....
4. Speaking without thinking often gets me into trouble.
5. Little brothers (or sisters) can be a nuisance.
6. Ours is a great family for pets.
7. I always dread a visit to the dentist.
8. It is easy to tell airplanes apart.
9. Our dog knows some clever tricks.
10. Carelessness can be expensive.
11. My fight against a fear of .... was a hard one.
12. I harmed myself by my stubbornness.
13. I tried to find out something that was none of my business.
14. I can't stand to touch a ....
15. Fog makes me feel ....

E. Match the following five topic sentences with the five lettered paragraphs on the next page; that is, decide which topic sentences belong with which paragraphs. (When their topic sentences are supplied, the five paragraphs together make a complete composition entitled "Bronc-busting As It Really Was in the Old West."*)

1. The bronc-buster who really knew his business was one who played the part of a teacher, not a bully.
2. After a group of three- or four-year-old geldings was separated from the rest of the stock horses, the first step was to get a halter on each.
3. The next steps all consisted of teaching the horse not to be afraid.
4. There is a good deal of misunderstanding about the process of bronc-busting.
5. Western horses raised on the range practically wild from birth, with little or no contact with human beings, had two sets of fears to overcome.

*Adapted from *Pardner of the Wind* by N. Howard (Jack) Thorp in collaboration with Neil M. Clark; copyright 1945 by The Caxton Printers, Ltd.; copyright © renewed 1972 by Neil M. Clark. Reprinted by permission of The Caxton Printers, Ltd., Caldwell, Idaho.

a. Sometimes it is pictured as a battle of wills between an unbeatable bronc and an unthrowable cowboy. As a matter of fact, bronc-busting was really a case of a man and horse getting better acquainted and making friends, and learning not to be afraid of each other.

b. He wasn't supposed to break the bronc's will, but to gentle it, overcome its fears, so it would be willing to carry a rider. With teeth, heels, muscle, speed, and sufficient dynamite in their dispositions, cow ponies could be more than a match for any man. A spoiled horse knows this and will take advantage of it.

c. They had the natural fear of wild creatures for men, and the fear of those disquieting things, the saddle and the bridle.

d. A roper stood in the middle of the corral. As the broncs circled around him, he would catch the forefeet of one, causing the horse to turn a somersault. A helper immediately piled onto the horse's head, so it couldn't get up. Then the roper could tie all four feet and slip a rope halter on the horse's head. Into the noseband of the halter he tied a heavy thirty-foot rope. The animal's feet were then untied and it was allowed to get up.

e. First, the bronc was tied to a heavy log in the pasture. It soon learned not to run too hard against the rope because if it did there would be pull on the sensitive brain area just behind the ears. Next, the trainer would put a blinder on the horse. Then he would gently stroke the horse with his hands, then with a saddle blanket. Eventually he would leave the blanket in place. Gradually he would ease the saddle onto the horse. When the horse became used to the saddle, the rider eased himself into it. The first day's ride was usually not over three or four miles. All of these steps together might take a number of days. Remember, the horse probably never had had anything bigger than a cottonwood leaf on its back before.

F. In "Bronc-busting As It Really Was in the Old West" (Activity E), list the words and word groups that tie ideas together. (See guide 6 on page 214.)

3. Getting Rid of Unrelated Sentences

READ AND THINK ABOUT

A paragraph should develop one thought, and only one. Therefore, of course, all the sentences in the paragraph should be about that one thought. A good paragraph (1) states an idea, or topic, in a topic sentence and (2) develops the topic sentence by means of supporting sentences.

In these paragraphs, the sentences in italics do not belong:

1. The Indians were experts at sending messages with smoke. They would build a fire and then heap damp leaves and grass on it. The fire would be almost smothered and would be very smoky. *Smoke from bonfires sometimes makes people cough and wipe their eyes.* Then the signalers would hold a blanket down close to the fire. Whenever they moved the blanket aside, a puff of smoke would rise. The number of puffs gave the message.*

2. The cowboy we see on movie and television screens usually bears little if any resemblance to the working cowboy of yesteryear. Except in the very early days, a range rider did not habitually wear a six-shooter strapped around his waist wherever he went. When he did wear one, he did not expect to shoot at another human being. He might strap it on as a kind of ornament when he went calling on a girl on Sunday. When he and other hands who worked for the same outfit rode into the nearest town on a Saturday night, he might wear it as a sort of mark of distinction. If he did, he usually had to check it at the livery stable or at the first bar, for most western towns prohibited the carrying of guns within town limits. *My uncle grew up in one of those towns.*†

3. Thunderbirds were important to the Indians of the Northwest, the Plains, and the Eastern Woodlands. They were powerful supernatural creatures who not only produced thunder but also befriended man in many magic ways. They produced thunder by opening and closing their eyes. The thunderbird is frequently mentioned in Indian myths and appears on totem poles in the North Pacific coast area. *Rain and hail then sleet and snow often come down on the coast area. Sometimes rain drips from the thunderbird's massive wooden wings.* Carved with animal heads, the totem stood beside graves or near houses to indicate the family's mythical ancestors or kinfolk or supernatural helpers. Thus the totem stood as a kind of coat-of-arms, and a thunderbird was pretty strong medicine if he appeared there.‡

*Adapted from *Light* by Bertha Morris Parker; copyright © 1959, 1952, 1949, 1941 by Row, Peterson and Company, Evanston, Illinois.

†Adapted from *Cowboys and Cattle Country* by the Editors of *American Heritage;* copyright © 1961 by American Heritage Publishing Co., Inc., New York.

‡Adapted from *Lore of Our Land: A Book of American Folklore* by Hector H. Lee and Donald Roberson; copyright © 1963 by Harper & Row, Publishers, Incorporated, Evanston, Illinois.

LEARNING ACTIVITIES IN REMOVING UNRELATED SENTENCES

A. Two of the following paragraphs have unrelated sentences. In class, explain specifically why the unrelated sentences do not belong in the paragraphs.

1. A great deal of air is caught between the snowflakes in any layer of newly fallen snow. Some snow is much fluffier than other snow; but even in a layer of dry, powdery snow, there is a great deal of air space. Farmers are glad to have snow on their winter wheatfields because it makes a good blanket for young plants. There is so much air in snow that on the average ten inches of snow has only about as much water in it as one inch of rain.*

2. Solid particles of any kind, unless they are very, very tiny, can be filtered out of water with filter paper. There are tiny spaces between the fibers of which filter paper is made. Water can go through these tiny spaces, but the particles of chalk and sand are too large to go through them. Those particles are left on the filter paper.*

3. A magnet will attract practically nothing except iron and steel. Magnets have many different shapes. Magnets attract paper clips, thumbtacks, and nails because these objects are made of either iron or steel. Paper fasteners are made of brass, not iron or steel. Magnets will not attract them. Toothpicks and rubber bands have no metal in them, and, therefore, are not attracted.*

B. The following paragraph really *is* unified—but not the way it reads now. Sentences are out of order; two sentences do not even belong. Copy the paragraph, (1) arranging the sentences in proper order and (2) omitting the two sentences that do not belong.

I can't watch television tonight; I have to study for a biology test. Another time, he gave the impression that the "Mohawks" involved in the Boston Tea Party were actually Indians, not disguised patriots. Every student of history knows that it was Whistling River that Mr. Bunyan straightened out, not Whistling Road! For instance, once he said that Columbus was *trying* to discover America. Our class visited the local newspaper plant the other day. But perhaps his most glaring "boo-boo" was the time he told the class that Paul Bunyan straightened out Whistling Road. Thomas gives interesting class reports, but he often overlooks important facts or twists the truth a bit.

*Adapted from *Science Experiences: Elementary School* by Bertha Morris Parker; copyright © 1958, 1952 by Row, Peterson and Company, Evanston, Illinois.

4. Putting Ideas in Proper Order

The order in which you give the supporting sentences in a paragraph is important. To explain something or to give directions clearly, you must not jump around. In other words, you must start at the beginning and go step by step to the end.

Notice the step-by-step order in this paragraph.

A medicine dropper would not work if it were not for air pressure. When the bulb is squeezed, some of the air is squeezed out of it. After you have put the end of the tube in a liquid, you stop squeezing the bulb. The air pushing down on the liquid outside the tube pushes some of the liquid into the tube to take the place of the air that was squeezed out.*

Learn about words!

The following words, taken from *A* of the Learning Activities, have interesting histories. Use your dictionary to find the story behind each word. With which word is the drawing connected?

capital   article   idea   magazine

LEARNING ACTIVITIES IN IMPROVING SENTENCE ORDER IN PARAGRAPHS

A. Read the following paragraph and decide how it can be improved. Copy the paragraph, arranging the ideas in a better order. Read your paragraphs in class. Let the Guides for Reading Aloud, page 57, help you.

A person must read a magazine article carefully in order to outline it. The subpoints in the outline will be the ideas that support the main ideas. Each of the main points in the outline will be a main idea in the article. These points will be labeled with capital letters. These points will be labeled with Roman numerals.

*Adapted from *Science Experiences: Elementary School* by Bertha Morris Parker; copyright © 1958, 1952 by Row, Peterson and Company, Evanston, Illinois.

B. Copy the following paragraph, completing the sentences. Compare paragraphs in class, checking to be sure that the steps are in their proper order.

> It is not far from here to the station, but it is a little tricky to get there. You go .... When you ...., turn .... and go .... Take the .... and go .... until .... Turn ...., and you .... Good luck!

C. (1) Choose a topic for a paragraph. (2) Write your paragraph, being sure to put the ideas in their proper order. (3) *Proofread, using the Writing Chart, page 172.* (4) Take turns reading the paragraphs in your small groups. Listen for any sentences that are out of order or that do not really concern the main idea.

5. Writing a Unified Book Report

"YOU'RE SUPPOSED TO REPORT ON THE BOOK, NOT ON WHAT IT REMINDED YOU OF IN YOUR OWN LIFE!"

READ AND THINK ABOUT

You have learned that a paragraph is a group of sentences all about one main idea. Often you will want to put together two or more paragraphs *about a larger idea*—such as a book report.

Making an outline helps you to *write* clearly, just as it helps you to *understand* material that you read (see page 99). If you first outline your book report, the main points will be the topic sentences of your paragraphs. The subpoints in the outline will be sentences that support the main ideas.

GUIDES FOR WRITING A BOOK REPORT

1. Plan carefully what you will cover in the report.
   a) Tell the kind of book: *fiction, biography, travel, science, . . .*
   b) Give the exact title and the name of the author.
   c) For *fiction,* do not try to tell the complete story.
      (1) Tell one or two important, amusing, or exciting incidents.
      (2) Tell briefly about the main character or characters.
   d) For *biography, travel, history,* or *adventure* books, tell an event or two.
   e) Give reasons for recommending the book to your classmates. Do not just call it *interesting* or *exciting;* tell why.

2. Arrange in an outline (either sentence or topic) the items called for above. Use that outline in writing the report.

3. Proceed as follows for your report:
   a) Write quickly. Do not go back or stop to check anything.
   b) Write an introductory paragraph.
   c) Write a concluding paragraph that summarizes your report or gives your final feeling about the book.
   d) Check your report by the guides on pages 232 and 453.
   e) Check all spelling, capitalization, and punctuation.
   f) Copy the report in your best handwriting.

As you write and revise your paragraphs (see Correcting and Revising What You Write, pages 472–73), strive to tie them together. Here are two good ways to tie paragraphs together:

1. Make the first sentence of a paragraph connect with the preceding paragraph.

   LAST SENTENCE OF A PARAGRAPH: Jase's wallet with just barely enough money for his summer's expenses was stolen.

   FIRST SENTENCE OF NEXT PARAGRAPH: *About three weeks later,* Jase came across the thief.

   (See also point 6 of the paragraph guides, page 214.)

2. Occasionally make the first sentence of two succeeding paragraphs similar by repeating some parts.

   FIRST SENTENCE OF ONE PARAGRAPH: Jim Kjelgaard, author of *Wildlife Cameraman,* studied nature in his boyhood.

   FIRST SENTENCE OF NEXT PARAGRAPH: Mr. Kjelgaard shows in *Wildlife Cameraman* how man, depending upon his attitude toward conservation, can help or tear down the balance of nature.

Knowing about an author's life and his purpose in writing a book often helps the reader to understand and appreciate the book. If possible, then, learn something of the author and his purpose in writing the book. As cautioned in guide 1c, page 224, do not try to tell everything; tell just enough to stir interest.

In your report, see whether you can capture the *spirit* of the book. The spirit, or intent, of a book may be one or more of the following.

1. To entertain
   a) with something amusing
   b) with excitement
   c) with suspense
   d) with something sad (many people prefer sad books)
2. To instruct
3. To inspire (a biography, for example)
4. To inform
5. To shock into action

LEARNING ACTIVITIES IN WRITING A UNIFIED BOOK REPORT

A. Read the student book report that follows. Then discuss it in class; among other points, consider the questions that follow the report.

The Light in the Forest

The Light in the Forest, by Conrad Richter, is about the problems of 15-year-old True Son, who has been unwillingly returned to his White parents by the Lenni Lenape Indians, who had captured him when he was four years old. True Son, or John, felt that he had reason for discontent. First, he believed he really was an Indian. Next, he could not stand the confining clothing which his White mother told him to wear. Finally, his feelings were hurt because his relatives made fun of his language.

When he went to bed, True Son felt as if he were sealed in a grave. He just could not understand why the White people imprisoned themselves in houses and barns when the life-giving forest stood all around. In fact, all the customs and heavy ways of the White race were hateful and joyless to him.

At length True Son ran away and rejoined his Indian friends, the Lenni Lenapes, even though he knew that to return now was to face possible death. True Son's adopted Indian father, however, was overjoyed to have his "son" back and caused his life to be spared.

True Son much preferred the ways of the Indians. No matter how serious they could be sometimes, the Lenni Lenapes had fun. Warriors and hunters enjoyed going from house to house visiting and eating. The men shook bowls of painted plum stones for dice. They twanged on crude musical instruments and played hollowed cane flutes which made a high, whistling sound. Most of all, the Indians enjoyed hunting. True Son felt "at home" with his adopted tribe.

For True Son, the forest meant freedom and happiness. His sisters, the birds, sang for him. His brother, the black squirrel, coughed at him. His mother, the Earth, held him on her breast. There were no prison fields, no unjust fences, no clocks to watch, and no imprisoning houses.

In contrast, the White man purposely protected himself from the out-of-doors. True Son thought that the walls and ceiling of the White man's house were closed up with some kind of white mud. He thought the dwellers covered this mud with paper to make it air-tight. He could not understand why the only holes in the walls were blocked up with wood and glass.

Finally, however, True Son was sent back to his White parents in disgrace. Even though he preferred to live with the Indians, he did have sympathy for the Whites; therefore, when the Lenni Lenapes were about to attack some settlers, he warned them to turn back. Of course, the Indians were furious at this act of "treachery" and treated him with contempt and abuse. It was True Son's adopted Indian father who was responsible for saving his life by sending him back to live with his real family.

The reader of this book is left with a new understanding that can help him do a better job of getting along with people whose ideas and ways of life differ from his. First, he realizes better how hard it is for people really to understand a way of life entirely different from their own. Second, he sees how easy it is for people to have their feelings hurt when others make fun of their beliefs, language, or customs. Finally, the reader is inclined to watch his own actions toward others more carefully.

Conrad Richter used western Pennsylvania as the setting for *The Light in the Forest;* some of the places mentioned are of interest to us today. Once True Son was overtaken by his White father at Kittatinny Mountain; today the Pennsylvania Turnpike goes through a tunnel cut in this mountain. True Son loved the forests of Blue Mountain; another one of the Turnpike's seven tunnels goes through Blue Mountain. Fort Pitt, which is Pittsburgh today, is mentioned a number of times. Most of the action takes place in the forests; today there are still fifteen million acres of forest in Pennsylvania.

Mr. Richter spent much time in reading old accounts. He also spent many hours talking with oldtimers in order to learn the many details of early America that have gone into this book. The author even lived in certain places that he uses in the book.

The title *The Light in the Forest* was suggested to the author by this passage from a poem by William Wordsworth:

> Shades of the prison-house begin to close
> Upon the growing boy,
> But he beholds the light, and whence it flows.
> He sees it in his joy. . . .

1. What types of information are covered in the above book report?
2. Is each paragraph unified?
3. Are the paragraphs tied to each other logically? What are some of the unifying devices used?
4. What is the *spirit* of the book?
5. What reading other than *The Light in the Forest* did the student do before writing his report? How do you know?

B. Make an outline of the *The Light in the Forest* book report. Observe the Guides for Outlining, page 99.

C. Write a unified book report of your own. First, outline the report. Be sure that you select a book that is up to your age level or grade level.

ENRICHMENT

(1) Select a good book and read it carefully. (2) Then select five of the following paragraphs to write, based upon the book that you have read; select your paragraph ideas carefully and arrange them in logical book-report order. (3) Write your paragraphs and combine them into a book report. Observe the Guides for Outlining (page 99), the Guides for Writing a Paragraph (page 214), and the Guides for writing a Book Report (page 224). (NOTE: Some of the following paragraph suggestions are suited to a particular kind of book—*biography, travel, history, adventure, fiction,* etc.)

1. Write a paragraph about the author.
2. Write a paragraph explaining the author's purpose in writing the book.
3. Write a paragraph telling briefly what the book is about.
4. Write a paragraph in which you tell about a belief, attitude, or custom of a person or a people.
5. Write a paragraph telling what a person or a people do for fun.
6. Write a paragraph about the title of the book.

7. Write a paragraph explaining the "exactness" of the title.
8. Write a paragraph about the book's setting, or some part of it.
9. Write a paragraph explaining a strong feeling or impression that you have gained from reading the book.
10. Write a paragraph in which you relate an incident.
11. Write a paragraph in which you describe a character.
12. Write a paragraph in which you describe a place or a thing.
13. Write a paragraph telling what ....'s contribution was to mankind. (*for a biography*)
14. Write a paragraph telling what caused .... to make a contribution to mankind. (*for a biography*)
15. Write a paragraph telling how mankind has recognized, or paid tribute to, ... for his contribution.
16. Write a paragraph telling why you think the book is unusual.
17. Write a paragraph telling why you did or did not like the book. Give exact reasons.

★ **Cumulative Review**

CAPITALIZATION

Copy these sentences, supplying needed capital letters.

1. On saturday, november 10, sam grant and i saw on television an old movie, *mr. lucky.*
2. The coach announced, "all members of the football team from brown junior high school are invited to principal jones's house after the game."
3. dr. james and superintendent banner were in plymouth, indiana, on labor day to visit mr. and mrs. r. c. kline.
4. at nine o'clock dan and i go to history class; and the rest of the day i have classes in arithmetic, english, and science.
5. Did grandfather say that the bible stories originated in the part of the world known as the near east?
6. when i was a small child, my favorite book was the five little peppers and how they grew.
7. Everett's aunt lucy visits europe regularly; she is a buyer for a large department store, the emporium.

PUNCTUATION

Copy these sentences, supplying needed punctuation.

1. Yes on January 12 1962 Robert K Brooks of Evanston Illinois passed the tests for a drivers license
2. Was it hard for him to shift gears steer properly and read all the road signs

3. Bobs father had always said Keep your eyes on the road and dont get excited
4. After he had practiced for a week under both parents guidance Bob could drive fairly well
5. Whee exclaimed John as he swept down the slope on his new skiis.
6. She ordered bacon and eggs cereal whole wheat toast and orange juice for breakfast.

SENTENCE SENSE

(1) Number your paper from 1 to 5. (2) Read each of the following groups of words. (3) If it is a correct sentence, write *S* on your paper. If it is a sentence fragment, write *F*. If it is a run-on sentence, write *RO*. (4) Make sentences of the fragments and run-ons.

1. Four teachers and most of the parents.
2. During intermission Mother, Father, Bud, and I remained in our seats.
3. The game was over we all went home.
4. Many of the people in the store.
5. Standing there day after day.

SPELLING

Here are sentences containing one or more scrambled words. Some of them when written correctly contain *ei;* the others, *ie*. Make two columns on your paper, one headed *ei* and the other, *ie*. Figure out the words and write each of them under the right heading.

1. Did the sharp metal (preeci) the (ceeip) of paper?
2. He said that (thenier) of those railroad (reghift) cars is full.
3. The rain brought (fliere) from the hot weather.
4. The boys stretched themselves to (rethi) full (thighe).
5. How many bushels of corn did the forty acres (dilye)?

Write the plural of each of these nouns.

1. life	5. woman	9. reef	13. Ferris
2. bunch	6. 9	10. hero	14. *r*
3. son-in-law	7. Mahoney	11. jelly	15. foot
4. mouse	8. alley	12. wolf	16. calf

MAKING STORIES AND POEMS

1. Describing Vividly and Exactly

"WRONG SIZE — WRONG COLOR —
WRONG STYLE! I MUST HAVE
DESCRIBED IT WRONG!"

TALK IT OVER...

The boy ordered that sweater over the telephone.

What information must he have given incorrectly or what must he have failed to include?

You have probably seen a customer outside a shop window pointing out some article to a clerk. Perhaps you yourself have had that experience. When you cannot describe what you want, you have to point to it. Sometimes it is impossible to point, however, because the article is not within reach. In that case, you must depend on your ability to describe what you want.

Being able to give an exact picture of something has another value: it helps to make stories interesting. The following two paragraphs tell about the same thing, but only one of them gives a real description.

1. When I visited the museum, I went through a room that had prehistoric animals in it. These animals were all big. The ones I remember best were a dinosaur, an elephant, a saber-toothed tiger, and a black bat.

2. Of the many places I visited during my first trip to the museum, one that I'll always remember is the room with prehistoric animals in it. I shall never forget that dinosaur! It breathed and blinked its eyes and roared frighteningly. Not far away was a huge elephant, much larger than any living today, with shaggy, buffalo-like hair and fierce-looking tusks. He flapped his ears, stamped his feet, and winked his little pig eyes sharply, right at me. Farther on a saber-toothed tiger, huge and scary looking, was devouring a smaller animal that had blood flowing out of its side. The tiger's yellow eyes glittered greedily. I remember, too, a horrible black bat with wings that I am sure measured at least two feet across. It flapped these wings slowly and gruesomely, like some evil spirit hovering over the earth. I saw many animals in that room, but these were the ones that haunted my dreams for months afterwards.

Both paragraphs tell of seeing prehistoric animals in a museum. Why does only one of them give you a clear and interesting picture of those animals? The answer is easy. (1) The second paragraph gives *details* and *comparisons*. (2) It uses *exact, vivid* words.

Often you are asked to describe a *place*. Notice what a good picture the following paragraph gives of the East African bush.

The East African bush is unique. It is doubtful if similar country occurs in any other part of the world. The bush is neither forest nor open plains. There are few tall trees. The growth is mainly low thorn trees growing ten or fifteen feet high. Sometimes these thorn trees, or "thorn bushes," grow in great clumps of an acre or more. More often, they are scattered about and a man can walk easily between them. The soil is mixed sand and reddish earth. Generally this soil takes impressions easily and makes tracking fairly simple. But there are many patches of tough elephant grass where tracks do not show. In some places the grass grows in tufts, leaving open stretches of sandy soil between. But often the hunter comes upon stretches of bush where the grass grows knee high, making a heavy carpet under the thorn trees. Here the hunter is really put to it to follow a spoor, which is a track or trail of a wild animal.*

GUIDES FOR DESCRIBING

1. Observe carefully; notice details. You cannot give a good picture of something that is blurred in your own mind.

2. Make details exact. Do not be satisfied with general words.

   WEAK: We live in a *white house* with a *fence* around it.
   BETTER: We live in a *little white cottage* with a *low green picket fence* around it.

   GENERAL: She was wearing a *red* scarf.
   EXACT: She was wearing a scarf *of fire-engine red.*

   GENERAL: Joe *looked* at me.
   EXACT: Joe *stared* at me.

3. Use vivid picture words that make appeals to the senses; that is, to (*a*) sight, (*b*) hearing, (*c*) taste, (*d*) smell, or (*e*) feeling.

4. Use comparisons.

   a) If you are describing only to identify or to give an actual picture, use real comparisons.

   The buttons on the coat are *the size of a quarter.*
   She is about *as tall as I am.*

   b) To give a vivid picture, include imaginative comparisons.

   He has a voice *like a squeaky door.*
   A soft *breeze whispered* in my ear.

*Adapted from *African Hunter: Young Readers' Edition of 'Hunter'* by J. A. Hunter with an Introductory Note by Captain A. T. A. Ritchie, O.B.E., M.C.; copyright 1952, 1954 by J. A. Hunter. Harper & Brothers Publishers, New York.

LEARNING ACTIVITIES

A. Have someone read aloud the second paragraph about prehistoric animals. On the board make two lists, one of exact and vivid words in the paragraph, and one of the comparisons in it.

B. (1) Rewrite the following sentences, changing the underscored words or expressions to more exact or vivid ones. Add other words if you like. In some cases, you may want to use comparisons. (2) Go over your work orally. (3) Suggest changes to make sentences even better. Let the Guides for Improving Expression, page 453, help you.

1. A large man in a brown suit walked up to me and said, "Stop!"
2. A cold rain was falling as we left the house.
3. I like to be outside on a dark night when a wind is blowing.
4. We saw some large red flowers along the road.
5. An old automobile with two people in it came down the street.

C. The following sentences contain imaginative comparisons that Stevenson used in *Treasure Island*. Name these comparisons and talk them over in class. Decide what idea or impression the author wanted to give by using the comparison.

EXAMPLE: Then followed *a battle of looks* between them; ... [*anger*]

1. The stranger kept hanging about just inside the inn door, peering round the corner like a cat waiting for a mouse.
2. I could hear from far before me ... the continuous thunder of the surf, ...
3. Mutiny, it was plain, hung over us like a thundercloud.
4. I observed the doctor sniffing and sniffing, like someone tasting a bad egg.
5. He stood where he was, ... like a snake about to spring.
6. The boarders swarmed over the fence like monkeys.
7. My own accidental cut across the knuckles was a flea bite.
8. I was dead tired, as you may fancy; and when I got to sleep, ... I slept like a log of wood.
9. The blind man clung close to me, holding me in one iron fist, and leaning almost more of his weight on me than I could carry.
10. I stood straight up against the wall, my heart still going like a sledge hammer, ...
11. The dirk, where it had pinned my shoulder to the mast, seemed to burn like a hot iron.
12. "Back we will go, the way we came, and small thanks to you big, hulking, chicken-hearted men "

D. In your literature book, in a library book, or in a magazine, find a paragraph that does a good job of describing. Read your paragraph in class and point out the words that help to make a clear picture.

E. Here are some nouns modified by imaginative *compound adjectives* (adjectives made up of more than one word, and usually hyphenated). In class, discuss the idea that each described noun brings to mind. (Watch for this kind of adjective as you read; you will be surprised at how many you will find. Make use of this kind of adjective in your writing.)

1. *soul-stirring* speech
2. *moth-eaten* jokes
3. *saucer-eyed* look
4. *jewel-sprinkled* sky
5. *light-fingered* man
6. *tempest-tossed* feelings
7. *silver-voiced* singer
8. *swan's-down* clouds

9. *flame-colored* hair
10. *white-feather* behavior
11. *cast-iron* opinions
12. kid-glove treatment
13. *half-baked* ideas
14. *pitch-dark* thoughts
15. *stiff-necked* attitude
16. *true-blue* friend

F. (1) Write one of the following descriptions. Plan and check your paragraph by the guides on page 214. (2) *Proofread for careless errors in spelling.* (3) Exchange the paragraphs in your small groups. (4) Examine critically the paragraph that you receive. (5) Read it to the group, telling what is good about it as well as how you think it might be improved.

1. Pretend that you have lost some article. Write the description that you would place upon the bulletin board at school, telling exactly what the article looks like.
2. You want a certain pair of gloves, a tie, a jacket, or some other article for your birthday. Write a paragraph, describing the article so well that your mother will be sure to buy the right one for you.

G. Have someone bring an object to class, such as a china or cloth dog. Place it where everyone can see it. Then write a short description of it. Read your paragraphs in class. Notice how differently people see things. Decide who used exact words and comparisons.

Use your Writing Chart, page 172, and the Suggestions for Good Handwriting, page 479. Concentrate on the points that cause you most trouble.

USING ENGLISH IN ALL CLASSES

From time to time in your other classes, you are called on to describe something. When next you must do so, let the Guides for Describing help you to make the description clear and vivid.

ENRICHMENT

Begin a collection of vivid descriptive words that you find in your magazine or book reading. Poems contain many such words. Classify your collection under such heads as *colors, sounds, smells,* and so on.

2. Describing People

"OH, HE'S AVERAGE IN SIZE AND HAS BROWN HAIR."

"BUT WHAT IS HE LIKE?"

THINK IT OVER . . .

Which is really more important—what a person looks like, or what kind of person he is?

In describing things, one gives outside appearances only. In describing persons, *what they are like* is more important than what they *look* like. Sometimes, of course, describing outward appearances can help to indicate the kind of person a man is.

A person's character, or what he is really like, can be shown in different ways. Here are some of them:

1. *By his appearance:* He was a thin, stoop-shouldered fellow with a sharp, narrow face.
2. *By his actions:* He is the kind who pats you on the back with one hand while he steals your last cent with the other.
3. *By what he says:* "I know it," said Lee. "I know I shouldn't say things like that, but they pop out."
4. *By what someone says about him:* "Well," said Dan, "if I were in a really tough spot, Frank is the fellow I'd like to have there with me!"

From these examples you can see that it is not necessary to go into a great many details to show what kind of person someone is. If you give a good hint or two, the reader can fill in the rest of the picture. Sometimes you may use only one of the four ways that you have just examined, and sometimes you will combine them.

The following description shows a girl through her mother's eyes. It reveals much about Barbara, as well as about her mother.

Mrs. Perry's glance strayed back to Barbara, who looked pretty and indignant. She really is all eyes, thought her mother. And she has such sense about her appearance. This way of wearing practically no lipstick, so that her eyes show up even more. Barbara knows how to achieve effects. Yes, she was a very pretty girl, who seemed to be in a constant state of discontent, and Mrs. Perry didn't see what there was to do about it. From time to time, during the past couple of years, both she and her husband had tried having talks with Barbara. Talks had gotten them nowhere, gotten Barbara nowhere. She seemed almost unreachable by either love or logic, and probably the only thing to do was wait. And hope.*

Now read this vivid description of a hermit, from *The Prince and the Pauper,* by Mark Twain.

The old man glided away, stooping, stealthily, cat-like, and brought the low bench. He seated himself upon it, half his body in the dim and flickering light, and the other half in shadow; and so, with his craving eyes bent upon the slumbering boy, he kept his patient vigil there, heedless of the drift of time, and softly whetted his knife and mumbled and chuckled; and in aspect and attitude, he resembled nothing so much as a grizzly, monstrous spider, gloating over some hapless insect that lay bound and helpless in his web.

Learn about words!

The following words, taken from *A* of the Learning Activities, have strange histories. Use your dictionary to find the story behind each word. With which word is the drawing connected?

rascal   purse   gentle   villain

LEARNING ACTIVITIES

A. What sort of person would you say each of the following probably is? Make this an oral discussion. Which methods of describing are used?

1. "Aw, what if we do help ourselves to some cash? Nobody will ever know the difference."

*Adapted from *Good-By My Shadow* by Mary Stolz; copyright © 1957 by Mary Stolz. Reprinted by permission of Harper & Row, Publishers, Inc., New York.

2. Mrs. Barry was likely to have good ideas about things—and she was always sure that she knew what people ought to do about them.
3. Mr. Evans could see some good in even the meanest man in town.
4. "You'll never get that rascal to look you in the eye!"
5. You couldn't change his mind with a charge of dynamite.
6. "Let's see. Where *did* I put my purse? Maybe it's in this drawer—or, no, it might be in that book, or mixed in with those old newspapers. Well, it *must* be around here somewhere!"
7. "When my gentle old great-grandmother smiles, it is just like having the sun come out on a cloudy day," said the young man.
8. To him every referee is a villain.

B. How could you show in a short description, like one of the descriptions in *A,* that a person has one of the following kinds of dispositions? Choose four of the words and then write descriptions that will give the impression without using the words from the list. Try to use each of the four methods on page 235. Compare work in your small groups.

1. hot-tempered	4. sarcastic	7. brave	10. careless
2. lazy	5. reckless	8. frank	11. timid
3. easygoing	6. stingy	9. loyal	12. friendly

C. Study the following description of a character in *Treasure Island.* Make two lists of words: (1) those that describe the squire's appearance and (2) those that suggest his character. Compare lists in class.

I had never seen the squire so near at hand. He was a tall man, over six feet high, and broad in proportion, and he had a bluff, rough-and-ready face, all roughened and reddened and lined in his long travels. His eyebrows were very black, and moved readily, and this gave him a look of some temper, not bad, you would say, but quick and high.

"Come in, Mr. Dance," said he, very stately and condescending.

D. Write a paragraph that will picture the appearance of someone whom you know and that will suggest something about his character. Try to get all four methods into your description. If you use quotation marks, be sure to do so correctly. See the rules on page 157. Read and discuss your descriptions in class. The best ones may be mounted upon the bulletin board, or you may wish to keep yours for possible use in a story.

Spot Review ★

(Based upon the sentences in A *of the preceding activities)*
1. How would you spell the plural of the name in number 2? in 3?
2. What is the reason for the apostrophe in number 4?
3. Why is a comma used after *Well* in number 6?
4. What is the verb in number 8? What kind of verb is it?

3. Telling a Short Story

Which do you think is the most interesting of the following stories? Why?

Which is the least interesting? Why?

Which gives away the ending in its title?

Which one makes no use of conversation?

Which one has a weak ending?

GUNPOWDER!

Sitting on a barrel of gunpowder wouldn't be very easy on the nerves of most people. Well, when my great-great-grandmother was a girl in Wilmington, Delaware, one hundred years ago and more, she did practically that very thing all the time.

That remark sounds strange, I know; but you see, Wilmington is the home of the Du Ponts, and even in those long-ago days, the Du Ponts manufactured gunpowder. They had a whole train of wagons in which they hauled the gunpowder out of the city.

The road that these wagons traveled ran right past my great-great-grandmother's house. Since the road was rough and the wagon wheels were heavy, the gunpowder jounced up and down a good deal. For that reason it was not uncommon for a wagon-load to explode. Because the wagons were in a train, one following the other, if one exploded, the others were likely to do the same thing.

One sunny day as Granny was sitting out in her own front yard entertaining a visitor, all of a sudden a horse's head flew through the air and landed right near them. Granny just looked up for a moment and then explained, very matter-of-factly, "One of those Du Pont wagons exploded again, I expect," and went right on with her knitting.

—BETTY PETERS

I Was Bitten by a Mouse

I have had some funny things happen to me, and one of them was when a mouse bit me.

It was washday, and my mother told me to change into a different pair of jeans, because she wanted to wash the ones I was wearing.

I changed into the other jeans and went outside. Pretty soon I put my hand into my pocket, and something bit me. I pulled it out. It was a mouse, which was about enough to knock me off my feet.

This all took place when I was nine years old and was living on a farm three miles east and four miles south of town.

—Harry Winkler

Teacher's Pet

I've never thought of myself as teacher's pet, but some of the boys once suspected me of trying to be one.

One Saturday afternoon several of us were hurrying home from a football game in the vacant lot across the street from the school. Suddenly just ahead of us I saw Miss Scott, our English teacher.

"Slow down!" I said to the others. "Let's not pass Miss Scott."

"Aw, come on, I'll be late for dinner," Dick answered, as he turned on more speed.

"No," I said, grabbing him by the arm. "You fellows stay back here, and I'll go up and walk with her."

"It's almost six o'clock. What's the idea, Sam?" Bill asked.

"Never mind. You just walk behind us."

I caught up with Miss Scott and walked along with her for a while, saying the things you usually say to a teacher. She was slightly puzzled by the escort behind us. Several times she turned around when Bill whispered something to Dick, and Dick snickered. Finally her curiosity couldn't stand it any longer.

"What are you doing, Sam? Is this your good deed for the day?" she asked me.

"No, I just thought I'd like to walk with you," I told her.

"Well, then, what's all the snickering about?"

"Oh, those fellows are hungry and want to get home fast, but I didn't want to walk in front of you.—I tore my pants in the last scrimmage we had."

—Sam Baird

The second storyteller could have made his story really interesting had he studied and applied the guides that follow on page 240.

GUIDES FOR TELLING A STORY

1. Choose a title that will make people want to hear your story. **For** example, "Chicken-Thief Trap" sounds more exciting than does "My Visit to a Farm."
   Make certain that the title does not tell too much so that it gives away the ending. "I Was Bitten by a Mouse" tells what happened; "The Wrong Move" has a better chance to arouse interest.

2. Choose a beginning sentence that will catch the interest of the audience so that they will wonder what is coming next.
   a) Begin, for example, with an unusual or exciting remark, as Betty did in her story.
   b) Use a question, if you like, to get the audience's attention: "Have you ever known . . . ?"
   c) Never begin like this: "I couldn't think of anything else, so I'm going to tell you about something that happened to my grandmother." That beginning is a good way to put an audience to sleep. It indicates that you do not think much of the story yourself; if that is the case, it certainly is not very likely that your audience will feel like listening!

3. As soon as possible, tell *who* is concerned, *what* the story is about, *where* and *when* it happened.

4. Keep the audience guessing; that is, do not give away the ending.

5. Tell things in the order in which they happened. An outline will help you. (See the Guides for Outlining, page 99.) Every sentence should build up gradually to the *climax,* which is the most interesting or most exciting part in the story.

6. Leave out details that have no direct connection with the story.

7. Use vivid words and comparisons to give life to your story. Include conversation if you can. An audience likes to hear the characters speak.

8. Stop very soon after the climax. It should not be necessary, for example, to end by saying that everyone laughed or was surprised or was shocked.

LEARNING ACTIVITIES

A. In your small groups, discuss the stories on pages 238–39. Decide how well the tellers applied the guides. To help you with the discussion, review guides 3 and 4, page 33.

B. Here are ten story titles. Some of them are good; some tell too much; others sound uninteresting. (1) On your paper, make a list of the titles that you think could be improved. (2) Beside them, write titles that you think would be better. (3) Go over your lists in class.

An Experience	An Incident in My Life
My First Cake Was a Failure	The Meanest Thing I Ever Did
Locked Out	A Half Hour with the Baby
Was It a Dream?	A Spanking for Showing Off
A Trick That Failed	Look Pleasant, Please

Put into your notebook for future use any titles that remind you of experiences that you or persons in your family have had.

C. Choose a title from the list in your notebook and plan to tell the story that it suggests. The easiest stories to tell probably will be about yourself or your family; for example, something that happened to Dad or Grandfather as a boy. Be sure to use the Guides for Telling a Story. Practice at home; get your mother or someone else to listen to you. Time yourself so that the story will not run over two or three minutes. Before telling the story in class, review the Guides to Speaking Clearly and Correctly, page 43.

D. Have a "storytelling bee" in class. This time choose a long joke or a true-life experience that you find in a magazine. (Try to find a magazine old enough so that your hearers are not likely to remember the story.) Stay within a three-hundred-word limit if possible. In carrying out the storytelling, follow this plan:

1. Choose two people to alternate as announcers of the story titles. Each should have beforehand a list of the stories he is to announce, and should have them arranged in the order in which he will announce them.
2. As you listen, have your Speech Chart before you so that you can jot down notes on the way that the speakers tell their stories. If your class is large, the stories may take more than one period.
3. After all the stories for one day have been told, take time to discuss them. Point out any features that you liked especially; suggest ways to improve weaknesses in certain stories.
4. Then give to each the notes that you took on his story.
5. Be sure to check your Speech Chart (page 61) by the notes on your story. Decide (*a*) where you are making progress and (*b*) what you need to do better.

FOLLOW-UP

On your Speech Chart, begin marking all the items, instead of only the first seven. Always check content by asking, "Does this make sense? Does it fit the topic? Is it well organized? Is it interesting?"

4. Writing a Longer Story

You have had experience in telling very short stories, but it is interesting to write longer stories, too. Here is a story that one girl wrote about her grandmother. Read it and then talk over the following questions:

What vivid descriptive verbs and other words make the story interesting?

What details help you to see Gammy and the Indian woman?

Was the ending a disappointment? Why or why not?

Skaw Skaw

Grandmother Hoyt has always insisted that Indian squaws can be as dangerous as Indian braves. She should know, because when she was a little girl, she lived at the Santee Indian Agency in northeast Nebraska. Her mother worked in the government school there. Gammy played and went to school with the Indian children, and she learned to speak the language of their tribe almost as well as they did.

It was the custom for the government employees to gather up all the little Indian children so that they could learn English and have some schooling. At the school they were given English names. One little boy was named William, but everyone at the agency called him "Baby William" because he cried so much.

Usually the parents did not object very strongly to having their children taken to the school, but sometimes there was trouble. That was the case with Baby William. It all began when one of the agency workers tried to give him a bath, the first thing always done with the new youngsters. As with many of the others, it was the little boy's first bath. Probably he thought that this was the white man's way of torturing him. At any rate, he yelled and screamed so wildly that his mother grabbed him in her long, thin arms and started for the door. He was taken from her, anyway, though she put up a fierce struggle before she gave up and went back to her home.

One wintry day a few weeks later, Baby William's mother came back. She wanted her boy. She stalked into the main building muttering, "Skaw skaw," meaning *white*. At the time, Gammy and three Indian girls were alone in the building. Since she was the only white person there, Gammy was sure that the Indian

woman was after her. Gammy was practically paralyzed with fear, and it seemed to be catching, for the Indian girls suddenly turned two shades lighter, as Gammy tells the story. The next minute the four girls turned and dashed upstairs into the sewing room. Gammy, her short legs working and her pigtails flying, led them all.

With wildly beating hearts—and you can imagine whose was beating hardest—they piled boxes against the door. Then they heard the old Indian plodding up the stairs, still muttering and muttering "Skaw skaw!"

Stiff with fright, they held their breath until at last her voice seemed to die away. Just as they were beginning to hope that she had really gone, they heard a snarling "Skaw skaw" that seemed to come from above. There was her haglike old face glaring at them through the transom! Gammy's red hair stood on end. She thought her time to be scalped had come!

At this thrilling moment, some of the agency men arrived. They dashed up the stairs, grabbed the old woman, and put her out, though she was almost a match for them all.

For a long time after that, whenever Gammy ventured on those shadowy stairs at dusk, all anyone had to do was to yell "Skaw skaw!" and she would scoot up those stairs like a frightened rabbit.

—BETTY PETERS

The steps to follow in writing a story are the same as those in telling a short story orally. (See the Guides for Telling a Story, page 240.) However, you will want to give more details, making use of what you have learned about describing things and people.

GUIDES FOR WRITING A STORY

1. Jot down notes of what you want to tell. Then arrange the notes in the order in which things happened. Guides 2–7 on page 99 will help you to arrange the notes in an outline.

   Here, as an example, is Betty's outline for writing "Skaw Skaw."

       I. Introduction
           A. Gammy's opinion of Indian women
           B. Reason for her being in an Indian school
       II. The school
      III. Little William
           A. Reason for name
           B. Reaction to bath
           C. Mother's reaction and the result
       IV. The mother's return
        V. The escape upstairs
       VI. The rescue
     VII. Conclusion

2. Write your story in pencil first. Then check it with the Guides for Telling a Story, page 240. Be sure it follows all the guides.
3. Read the story critically and revise it. Do not be afraid to scratch out certain words or sentences if you can think of better ones. Apply the Guides for Improving Expression, page 453.
4. Check your paper by all the items on the Writing Chart, page 172. Make any changes that you think are necessary.
5. Copy the story in ink, being sure to follow the Guides to Proper Manuscript Form, page 140.
6. Proofread for careless mistakes in capitalization, punctuation, spelling, and sentence sense.

LEARNING ACTIVITIES IN WRITING A STORY

A. In your small groups, judge the story "Skaw Skaw" by each of the Guides for Telling a Story, page 240. Point out some examples of guide 7. To get the most from your discussion, apply guides 3 and 4, page 33.

B. Using the guides on pages 240 and 244, write a true story of your own. Tell about something that really happened, either to you or to someone you know. The titles below may suggest a story. Read your stories in class, letting the Guides for Reading Aloud, page 57, help you.

Trapped!	Fire! Fire!	Admission, One Cent
More Luck than Sense	A Narrow Escape	Thin Ice
Runaway	Who's Afraid?	Look before You Leap
Learning the Hard Way	Fare, Please	One Dreadful Night

A. Ask your parents or grandparents to tell you some interesting experiences of their childhood. Write a story about one of the most interesting ones.

B. Write a story, using one of the following lines as the beginning.

1. I used to think the strangest thing.
2. Once I heard the funniest thing.
3. I used to believe that . . .
4. I was sure I could do everything my big brother (sister) did.
5. Once I was very close to danger.
6. Someone could have said to me, "I told you so!"

FOLLOW-UP

After all the stories in activity B have been heard, take a written vote to see which ones were best liked. Try to arrange to have these stories read to another class, in an assembly program, or at a P.T.A. meeting.

5. Writing Poems

"I WONDER WHETHER EVEN SHAKESPEARE COULD HAVE FOUND A RHYME FOR ORANGE!"

READ AND TALK ABOUT

Examine the three short pieces of writing below and at the top of page 246. Would you call any of them poetry?

Tall and strong stands the pitcher, his eyes on his battery mate. Calmly and coolly he nods as the catcher tips him the sign. Now comes the smooth, sure roll of the arm—and a hot white bullet streaks through the air. "Strike three!"—and the game is over.

During my vacation one of my favorite places for spending lots of time is down on the beach, which is not very far away from our summer cottage. I never seem to get tired of being there.

Ben Battle was a soldier bold, and used to war's alarms. But a cannon-ball took off his legs, so he laid down his arms.

Now listen as your teacher reads aloud each of those three selections. What are your conclusions? Perhaps you will say, "The third one must be a poem, because I can hear the rhyme."

True, the third one *is* a poem, but it would still be one if "war's alarms" were changed to "combat fierce." Why, do you think?

One of the other two selections is poetry, too. Which one is it, and how do you know?

What does the remaining selection lack that the others have?

● THESE ARE FACTS ABOUT POETRY

1. **Poetry has rhythm.** Reading aloud is a good test. If a piece of writing is poetry, the ear is sure to hear the rhythm; that is, *a fairly regular beat.*

2. **Poetry may rhyme, but rhyming is not necessary.**

3. **Poetry, more than any other kind of writing, uses vivid words and imaginative comparisons—words that make the reader** *see, hear, smell, taste,* **and** *feel* **with the author.**

4. **Poetry may deal with any subject.** Famous poems have been written about a rainbow, a telephone wire, a purple cow—and a louse crawling on the hat of a woman in church!

Poetry can be the most *serious* kind of writing, or it can be the most *carefree*—or it can be anything in between; the subject matter and the author's purpose are the determining factors. It is fun to experiment with different kinds of poetry and different rhyme schemes.

You may wish your own early poetic efforts to be in the form of *verse,* or "light" poetry, since verse usually rhymes and has no serious, or "deep" underlying thought. Many radio and television commercials are written in verse. Because they are catchy and very rhythmical, short verses are often called "jingles"; read the following "advertising" jingles.

1. Get Drippy, the hair spray that's different;
      It will keep your hair in trim;
    But if your husband is getting bald,
      Please, lady, DON'T use it on him!

   Get Drippy, the hair spray that's different;
      Then throw away your comb.
   One can of Drippy—and brother, you'll have
      A completely hairless dome!

2. Your dog will howl for Tweetsies,
      But he'll yelp with pleasure when
   You take the stuff away and give
      His old food back again.

   Your dog will howl for Tweetsies,
      But one swallow will be enough,
   And unless you want it wasted,
      You'll have to eat the stuff!

3. Your very first taste of Glubglub,
      And you'll smack your lips in delight;
   There's just one thing—don't be surprised
      If they fall off during the night!

   Your very first taste of Glubglub
      Will be a real taste sensation.
   As down it goes, you'll be convinced
      You'd much prefer starvation!

LEARNING ACTIVITIES

A. Try making up a two- or four-line jingle that pokes a little fun at some product, as in the examples above. If you wish, you may use this line as a start: "Wash your face with Scrubby—."

B. (1) To save class time, prepare the following exercises at home. In carrying them out, you need write only a line or two in each case. As you write, keep in mind especially point 3, above. (2) Exchange papers in class. (3) Have the lines read aloud. (4) Talk them over, being careful to apply guide 4 of the Guides for Holding Discussions, page 33.

1. Here is how one poet has described a cold wind:
      "The wind has teeth, the wind has claws."
   How would *you* describe a cold wind? a rainy wind? a hot wind? a strong wind? a loud wind?

2. Here is how one poet has described a sunset:
      "Large and smoky red the sun's cold disk drops, . . ."
   How would you describe a sunset? a sunrise? moonlight?

3. Here is how one poet has described some flying birds:

"Far flickers the flight of the swallows, . . ."

If you have ever watched swallows, you know that "flickers" is the perfect word to describe their flying. How would you describe the flight of a hawk? a humming bird? a crow? a parakeet?

4. Here is how poets have described various sounds:

"The ring of hoofs, galloping hoofs, trembling over the ground—"

"The hard snow underfoot squeaks like a mouse."

"He tinkledy-binkledy-winkled a bell, . . ."

"Then the huntsman's horn rang yap, yap, yap, . . ."

How would you describe the sound of a saxophone? a referee's whistle? an outboard motor? a jet plane? a drum? a lawnmower? a fire siren? a violin?

C. One dark fall day, a girl about your age was on her way to school. She saw the last brown leaves falling from an elm tree, and a poem began to stir in her head. Here is Barbara's poem, as it finally turned out.

GOOD-BY TO AUTUMN

Gray is the autumn sky;
The elm tree croons a last good-by
To the dry leaves, fluttering to the ground
And whispering with a frightened sound,

"Is this our home? Where is the tree
That mothered and rocked us tenderly?"
"This is where you come to rest;
To sleep through winter is always best."

Soon the snow comes sifting down
And blankets the leaves and the meadows brown.
Now the tree stands bare and forlorn,
But when spring comes, new buds will be born.

—BARBARA FARLEY

Talk over the poem. What good picture words has Barbara used? What feeling does the poem give you? Who do you think says lines 7 and 8?

D. Add at least one line to each of the following lines so that you make a little poem. Keep the rhythm, of course, but use rhyme only if it really fits. Read your work in class. Your classmates will listen to decide how good your ideas are and how well you have expressed them.

1. Poised to dive, I stare down at the lake
2. If I could have a magic wish, here's what that wish would be
3. I like my parents, but I'm sure I'd like them even more
4. The smell of food that I like best
5. Over and over, my dad has said,
6. Sharp black trees on a sunset sky,

E. Now try writing a poem all by yourself. Use any topic you like, but be sure that it is a topic about which you really feel something—*excitement, pleasure, anger, unhappiness, pain, . . .*

(1) Review the points about poetry on page 246.

(2) Write quickly first, just to get your ideas on paper.

(3) Read aloud what you have written; your ear will tell you whether the lines have rhythm.

(4) Rewrite, making improvements in the wording and putting in whatever commas or other punctuation will help the reader.

(5) Copy your poem as neatly as you can, centering it on the page.

(6) Hand the poem in.

Your teacher may choose some of the poems to read to the class, without telling who wrote them.

FOLLOW-UP

In your magazine reading, keep your eye out for poems that you think your classmates might enjoy. With your teacher's permission, read a poem to the class or mount it on the bulletin board. If you read a poem, use the Guides for Reading Aloud, page 57, in your preparation.

ENRICHMENT

A. In discarded magazines, find pictures that you think illustrate any of the lines of poetry that you wrote for activities B, D, and E. Mount each picture on harmonizing construction paper and below write the lines.

B. Use Barbara's poem, page 248, for an exercise in choral reading. Choose a committee to plan and read it with you. Practice outside school; then ask your teacher to let you read the poem to the class. The Guides to Choral Reading, page 46, will help you to give a good performance.

Cumulative Review

CAPITALIZATION

Copy these sentences, supplying needed capital letters.

1. Last friday, september 20, sue and i gave a report at franklin junior high school on the book *nose for news* by edwin arnold.
2. on labor day mr. and mrs. j. m. landis visited dr. putter and superintendent burg in higginsville, missouri.
3. Yes, i took tests in english, history, science, and arithmetic.
4. both bill and i attended the meeting of our club, the shutter bugs.
5. Then Ed said, "to get to the high school, walk west on elm road."

PUNCTUATION

Copy these sentences, supplying needed punctuation.

1. On January 12 1957 R J Bruces aviation training began at Glenview Illinois northwest of Chicago
2. Did you know that three requirements for becoming a flying cadet are a good education sound health and keen spirits
3. After a cadet has trained ten weeks he can do loops snap rolls and Immelmann turns
4. One time an army doctor a major asked a cadet If Id give you a thousand dollars Bruce what would be the first thing you would do
5. Im afraid Id be speechless sir said Bruce

SENTENCE SENSE

(1) Number your paper from 1 to 5. (2) Read each of the following groups of words. If the words are a correct sentence, write an *S* on your paper. If they are a sentence fragment, write *F*. If they are a run-on sentence, write *RO*. (3) Make sentences out of the fragments and run-ons.

1. The telegram came at four o'clock my brother signed for it.
2. We packed our bags and left as soon as possible.
3. Everyone waiting at the station for us.
4. The women and all the small children.
5. Walking up and down nervously.

SPELLING

Copy the following words in a column on a sheet of paper. Beside each word write another word made from it by adding a suffix.

1. report	5. object	9. change	13. crude
2. wave	6. multiply	10. copy	14. place
3. play	7. finish	11. fool	15. wrap
4. follow	8. cheer	12. funny	16. bounce

WRITING LETTERS

Since I don't have anything interesting to do, I'll drop you a line.

THINK IT OVER . . .

How would you feel if you were the receiver of the above letter?
How often do you write something that is just as uncomplimentary?

1. Learning Correct Letter Forms

READ AND THINK ABOUT

The heading of this section tells that you are to study letter writing. Do not feel that too much fuss is made about learning correct letter forms. It is true that *what you say* is the most important part of any letter, but if you want your letters to "amount to something," interesting content is not enough. You need to begin by learning correct letter form; then you can concentrate on making the content of your letter interesting.

This chapter on letter writing observes the ZIP code numbering system for *all* addresses, on both the letter and the envelope. The

ZIP coding system, developed for speedier, more efficient postal service, does away with zone numbers.

If you do not know the ZIP code number for a certain address, ask at your local post office. All ZIP numbers are contained in the *Directory of Post Offices* supplied to each office by the Post Office Department.

The ZIP code number goes on the same line as the city and state. (If the line is too long, the ZIP code may be placed on a separate line, below the name of the city.)

Mr. Richard Wilcox
612 Charles Avenue
Ogden, Utah 84401

PART ONE: THE FORM OF A FRIENDLY LETTER

A friendly letter has five parts. When handwritten, it usually is written in indented, or *slant,* style, as shown here.

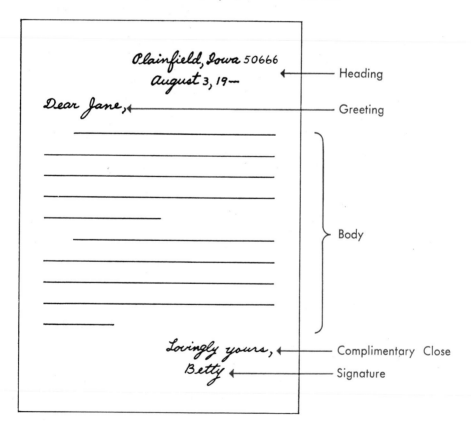

GUIDES TO CORRECT LETTER FORM

1. Tell in the *heading* where and when the letter is being written.

   a) Use this style if you live on a farm:

   > Rural Route 4
   > Alma, Missouri 64001
   > December 12, 19–

   b) Use this style if you live in a small town:

   > Bloomfield, Nebraska 68718
   > January 12, 19–

   c) Use this style if you live in a city:

   > 617 East Oak Street
   > Chicago, Illinois 60622
   > February 2, 19–

   d) Use a comma in these ways:

   (1) Between the name of the town or city and that of the state. Remember: do not insert a comma between the state and ZIP code number.

   (2) Between the day of the month and the year.

   Use no other punctuation.

   e) Capitalize all words in the heading.

   f) Avoid abbreviations.

2. In the *greeting* (or salutation) give the name of the person.

   RIGHT: Dear Harry,   Dear Mother,
   POOR: Dear Friend,   Dear old Pal,

   a) Capitalize the first word and the name of the person.

   Dear Phil and George,   My dear Mary,

   b) Use a comma after the greeting.

   Dear Mother,   Dear Uncle Tom,

3. Divide the *body* of the letter into paragraphs. Begin a new paragraph for each new idea.

4. Capitalize only the first word of the *complimentary close*. Follow the closing with a comma.

   Your loving sister,   Lovingly yours,
   Gratefully yours,   Yours sincerely,

5. Use no punctuation after the *signature*. Sign the name by which the person to whom you are writing calls you.

LEARNING ACTIVITIES IN USING CORRECT LETTER FORM

A. Arrange and punctuate the various parts of each letter indicated below. For the body, draw lines across the paper to indicate paragraphs, as in the model on page 252. Exchange papers for checking as the forms are put on the board and explained.

1. 115 north elm street boston massachusetts 02116 june 16 19— dear uncle frank (*body of letter*) your loving nephew jim
2. rural route 3 blissfield ohio 43805 september 5 19— dear mother and dad (*body of letter*) your affectionate daughter mary
3. pinecliffe colorado 80471 august 4 19— my dear alice (*body of letter*) your loving cousin louise
4. 1627 scott boulevard austin texas 78710 may 10 19— my dear oscar (*body of letter*) sincerely yours tom
5. rural route 5 clayton kansas 67629 april 4 19— dear bob (*body of letter*) your friend ted

B. Write three letter models of your own, one for a letter written from a rural address, one from a small town, and one from a large city. Have these put on the board for criticism and any needed corrections.

PART TWO: THE ENVELOPE ADDRESS

GUIDES FOR ADDRESSING THE ENVELOPE

1. Indent as shown in the model on page 255.

2. Capitalize all words.

3. Do not use abbreviations for names of streets, cities, or states. Abbreviations are hard to read and may cause the letter to be delivered to the wrong address.

4. Put the main address in the lower part of the right-hand half of the envelope. In this location it will not be blotted out when the post office cancels the stamp, and it is well away from the return address.

5. Put the ZIP code number after the name of the state if there is room; if not, put it below the name of the city.

6. Use a comma between the name of the city and that of the state. Use no other punctuation except for the period after the abbreviation of a title such as *Mr., Mrs., Dr.*

Here is a model to follow in addressing an envelope.

LEARNING ACTIVITIES IN ADDRESSING ENVELOPES

A. Draw rectangles to represent envelopes and write the main address and the return address for each of the following:

1. A letter to Miss Carol Elaine Wedemeyer, Rural Route 2, Eugene, Oregon 97401, from Miss Karen Cohee, 2853 Ocean Drive, San Diego, California 92110
2. A letter from Alan Scheer, 7232 Thirtieth Street, Cincinnati, Ohio 45208, to Daniel Bannister, 121 Anne Street, McMinnville, Oregon 97128

B. Draw rectangles on your paper to represent envelopes for the letters in *A,* page 254. Address them, following the form in the model above. Make up the last name of each writer and the address and full name of the person who is to receive each letter. Exchange papers for checking.

C. For further practice in addressing letters correctly, take names and addresses from your daily newspaper. Draw envelope forms and address them. Use your own return address. Go over your work in class.

FOLLOW-UP

Put in your notebook examples of correct letter form and envelope form. Be sure that your teacher has approved them. In the future when you need to write friendly letters, use these forms as guides.

PART THREE: GOOD APPEARANCE IN LETTERS

Using correct letter forms and addressing letters properly are important, but so is the general appearance of the letters. The guides on page 256 will help you to write attractive letters.

GUIDES FOR MAKING LETTERS LOOK ATTRACTIVE

1. As a rule, use only black or blue ink and white (or lightly tinted) stationery.

2. Avoid blots and messy scratch-outs or erasures.

3. Keep neat, even margins. Allow at least a half-inch at sides and top; allow a somewhat wider space at the foot of the page.

4. Write plainly, forming all letters carefully. Avoid writing that is either large and scrawly or tiny and crowded. (See page 479.)

5. Keep lines straight and paragraph indentions even.

LEARNING ACTIVITIES IN LETTER FORMS AND APPEARANCE

A. The following letter has many faults, both in form and in appearance. Go over it in class to find those faults. List them on the blackboard.

643 W. 5th St.
Portland, Me., 04106
July 8 19—

Dear mother

It doesn't seem possible that I have been here at Uncle Edward's for two weeks. There are so many interesting things to do that the days just sail by. I've had a good time every minute. This afternoon we are: ~~driving~~ driving to the seashore for a picnic. According to Uncle Edward we are having it at the same old spot where you and he had so many good times when you were children. ~~Tom~~ Tomorrow I'll write you a long letter ~~till~~ all about the picnic.

your loving son
Jack

B. Rewrite this letter. Arrange it in correct form and include all necessary punctuation and capitalization. The letter contains two paragraphs. *Be sure to proofread carefully.*

2516 north tenth street mobile alabama 36609 september 7 19— dear mother Your letter telling us that Aunt Helen is better and that you probably will be home next week is good news for all of us. We miss you very much, but you mustn't worry about things here at home. Visit with Aunt Helen an extra day or so if you like. After all, you don't get away from home very often. There was some big excitement in the neighborhood yesterday. Little Billy Rogers disappeared for several hours, and everyone up and down the street was out looking for him. Just when his mother was about to call the police, Billy crawled out of their doghouse. No fooling! He'd been asleep in there all the time. Your loving daughter Ellen

C. Draw a rectangle about the size of an envelope. Address the envelope to Ellen's mother, mrs. george adams 1928 east williams street birmingham alabama 35211. Put Ellen's return address upon the envelope.

2. Making Letters Interesting

"I CAN'T THINK OF A THING TO TELL HER!"

"JUST PRETEND YOU'RE TALKING."

READ AND THINK ABOUT

How can it be that a person who never runs out of something to say in a conversation feels that he has nothing to say in letters?

If you feel as Richard's sister does, the trouble may be that you think too much about yourself and not enough about the one to whom you are writing. What would that person like to hear?

Well, Grandfather and Grandmother and your aunts and uncles probably are most interested in hearing about *you* and what you have been doing. When you write to someone near your own age, though, you should write mostly about things that show your interest in *him* and his activities. That is to say, the word "you" should appear in your letters oftener than "I."

If you know the person well, there are many things that you can ask about: pets, hobbies, Scouting or 4-H work, books, sports, television, people that you both know, plans for visiting each other, memories of visits that you have had in the past. Remember, this is the body of the letter, the most important part. It is *you*. Make your reader know that you are glad to write.

If you are writing to a new friend, ask about some of those same things and tell a little about yourself in connection with them.

GUIDES FOR GOOD LETTER WRITING

1. Bring the other person into the things that you write about. Ask him questions about himself and his activities; ask for his opinions or for his advice about ideas that you have.

2. Write as you would talk; that is, avoid stiff, formal language.

3. Make him feel that you enjoy his friendship.

4. Keep your letter cheerful.

5. Be sure that each sentence has a subject. (See the discussion of sentence fragments on page 337.) Do not say, "Hope that you are enjoying your vacation." Say instead, "*I* hope that you are enjoying your vacation."

6. Do not spoil your letter with such worn-out expressions as these:
    How are you? I am fine and hope you are the same.
    Since I have nothing to do, I'll write you a letter.
    Excuse mistakes.
    Well, I guess I'd better close now.
    Hoping to hear from you soon.

Read the following letter that one boy wrote to a friend.

Plainfield, Iowa 50666
November 1, 19—

Dear Phil,

Your letter came yesterday. How I wish I could be in your shoes at that football game Saturday! Last Saturday our Scout troop went on an overnight hike to Oakview Park. That's the place where we had our Fourth of July picnic. Remember? The weather was frosty, but that didn't bother us, except that it gave us big appetites. You never saw bacon and eggs disappear so fast!

How are you getting along with your stamp collection? I've been writing to a boy in Venezuela, and he has promised to send me some South American stamps. If there are any special ones you've been wanting, I may be able to get them for you from him.

Are you to have a Thanksgiving vacation? If so, you're invited to spend it here. I hope you can come.

Your old pal,
Tom

LEARNING ACTIVITIES

A. Discuss the letter that Tom wrote. Why do you think Phil was glad to get it? Check it by the guides on page 258.

B. If you have received an interesting (and not too personal) letter lately, read it to the class. Explain why you think that it is a good letter. Use the Speech Chart, page 61, to help you prepare your talk.

C. Write the letter that you think Phil might have sent in replying to Tom. If you prefer, write the one from Phil that Tom was answering. Check your letter by each point on your Writing Chart. The Guides for Good Letter Writing on page 258 will help you to make good scores in *content.* Check the letter also for sentence fragments and run-on sentences (see pages 337 and 341). Read these letters in class. Before reading, look over the Guides to a Pleasing, Effective Voice, page 41. Perhaps you will want to vote on the best letters.

D. Write a real letter now to some friend or relative. Check through it to see whether you have followed the guides on page 258. The second guide is, "Write as you would talk." Think of all the things that you tell the family about your school day. Think of what you do after school and on Saturdays and Sundays. Tell about those things in detail. Pages 292, 343, 398, and 420 will help you to use vivid words to make your descriptions interesting. Do not forget good paragraphing. (See the Guides for Writing a Paragraph, page 214.)

Ask a friend to give his opinion of the letter, or ask your teacher.

Check the form of the letter and its envelope before mailing. Be sure that both are correct.

ENRICHMENT

Using the card catalogue (see page 128), find in the library a letter written by some famous author to a boy or a girl. Look either under the subject heading *Letters* or under the name of an author. Using the Guides to Reading Aloud, page 57, prepare and read to the class a letter that you like.

USING ENGLISH OUTSIDE SCHOOL

A. Probably your school subscribes to magazines that contain letters from boys and girls your age, or perhaps you have seen such letters in a Sunday-school or church paper. Try writing a letter to one of those magazines. Tell your age and grade in school; describe your appearance, if you like; discuss your pets and hobbies; ask others who read the magazine to write to you. Your letter may lead to some interesting friendships. Be sure that your letter form is correct; check it by the guides on page 253. *Proofread the letter carefully before sealing the envelope.*

B. Instead of writing to the magazine itself, you may prefer to write to someone whose letter appears in one of the magazines. It will be especially interesting to write to someone who lives in a different part of the country or in some foreign land. Be sure to check form and appearance before you mail the letter.

FOLLOW-UP

Check your Writing Chart. In what ways are you improving? What are your weakest points?

3. Writing Invitations and Replies

Invitations and replies to invitations are special letters that you will need to write from time to time.

GUIDES FOR WRITING AND ANSWERING INVITATIONS

1. Tell exactly what the invitation is for. Include helpful details, such as naming any special clothes or other items that may come in handy.
2. Make the time and the place definite.
3. Send invitations as early as possible.
4. Make the person feel that you really want him to come.
5. Answer any invitation promptly.
6. Show your appreciation, even when you cannot accept.
7. If you refuse an invitation, give a good reason.
8. Keep both invitations and replies short.

Here is an example of a letter of invitation.

250 Pearl Street
Yankton, South Dakota 57078
July 16, 19—

Dear Ted,

We shall be driving to Sioux City on Friday, July 25, to see the Air Circus. Would you like to go with us?

We plan to leave at eight in the morning. If you are able to go, we'll stop for you. Tell your mother that we'll be back by ten in the evening.

I surely hope that you can go with us, for that will make it all the more fun for me. Please let me know at once.

Your friend,
Ralph

A. In your small groups, discuss Ralph's letter. Use the Guides for Holding Discussions, page 33, to help you have a good discussion. Decide how well the letter follows guides 1, 2, 3, 4, and 8 on page 261.

B. Write Ted's reply accepting or declining the invitation. Be sure to keep in mind guides 5, 6, 7, and 8 as you write. Follow also the Guides to Correct Letter Form, page 253. Take turns at reading the replies in class. As letters are read, have them checked both on content and on the reading. For example, when a boy reads his letter, have the boys check it for what he says; have the girls check it by the Guides to Speaking Clearly and Correctly, page 43. When a girl reads, check the other way round.

C. Write a letter inviting a friend to go on a camping trip with you. *Be sure to proofread for careless mistakes.* Exchange letters with a partner. Using the Guides to Correct Letter Form, page 253, and 1, 2, 3, 4, and 8 of the Guides for Writing and Answering Invitations, check the letter that you receive. Correct any mistakes on your own paper.

D. Write an invitation for some other occasion, and exchange papers with a partner. Write a reply to the invitation that you receive. Read letters in class, using the same plan of checking as in *B.*

4. Writing Thank-You Letters

Most thank-you letters are of two kinds: (1) letters thanking someone for a gift or for a special favor, and (2) letters written after a visit, called "bread-and-butter" letters.

GUIDES FOR WRITING THANK-YOU LETTERS

1. Write thank-you letters promptly.

2. Give some particular reason for appreciating the gift or favor.

3. After a visit, write a "bread-and-butter" letter to your hostess. Usually she will be the mother of the friend whom you visited. Write also to that friend.

4. Keep the letter short.

958 Pine Street
Wilson, North Carolina 27893
June 16, 19—

Dear Aunt Laura,

How did you know that I've been wishing hard for an overnight case all my own? Well, I have — and now, thanks to my thoughtful aunt, my wish has come true.

I had an exciting birthday, with far more gifts than I deserve, I am sure. The gift that is tops, though, is the one from you. I like everything about it — the color, the size, the fittings, and the material. It is perfect!

Thank you again, Aunt Laura.

Your loving niece,
Carol

A BREAD-AND-BUTTER LETTER

Andover, Kansas 67002
September 10, 19—

Dear Mrs. Mason,

New Mexico is now my favorite state, and the people there are the best. I shall never forget all the things that you and Mr. Mason did to make my visit enjoyable. The trip into the Red River country was the high spot. I'm still singing that song!

As soon as I get some of these bothersome school assignments out of the way, I'll write Bob a long letter.

Sincerely yours,
Perry Lewis

LEARNING ACTIVITIES IN WRITING THANK-YOU LETTERS

A. Check the two sample letters by the guides on page 262.

B. Here are some sentences from thank-you letters. What criticisms would you make of them? Discuss the sentences in class.

1. I don't feel much like writing, but Mother says I have to get my birthday thank-you letters sent today.
2. Thank you for the billfold. Three other people gave me one, too.

3. I'm sorry that I did not write to you a week ago to thank you for the birthday gift. I forgot all about it.
4. Tell your mother thanks for me. I really enjoyed my visit.
5. Thank you for the sweater. I guess you just forgot that I don't like brown very well.

C. Write a letter of thanks for a birthday gift or a Christmas gift. Check the letter by the Guides to Correct Letter Form, page 253, and by the Writing Chart, page 172. Read letters in class and discuss them.

D. Write a "bread-and-butter" letter. *Proofread for careless mistakes in capitalization, punctuation, and spelling.* Check also to see that you have not used any sentence fragments or run-on sentences (see pages 337 and 341). Go over letters, naming good points and suggesting improvements.

E. Write a letter of appreciation for favors done for you while you were in the hospital. Review the Guides to a Pleasing, Effective Voice, page 41, before reading the letters in class.

USING ENGLISH OUTSIDE SCHOOL

Think of someone to whom you actually owe a letter of thanks for a favor or a gift. Write the letter, following the Guides for Writing Thank-You Letters, page 262, and the Guides to Correct Letter Form, page 253. Proofread the letter carefully, using the Writing Chart, page 172. Address the envelope and mail the letter.

5. Writing Business Letters

"WELL, MISS BROOKS SAID TO USE A COLON INSTEAD OF A COMMA IN A BUSINESS LETTER."

THINK IT OVER . . .

Where is a colon correctly used in a business letter?
In what other ways is a business letter different from a friendly letter?

Here are the differences between the form of a friendly letter and that of a business letter:

1. The business letter usually is not written in slant style. The example here is in semiblock style; that is, only the paragraphs are indented. Most typewritten letters follow this style.
2. There is an added part, the *inside address*.
3. The salutation is followed by a colon, not a comma.

FORM FOR BUSINESS LETTERS

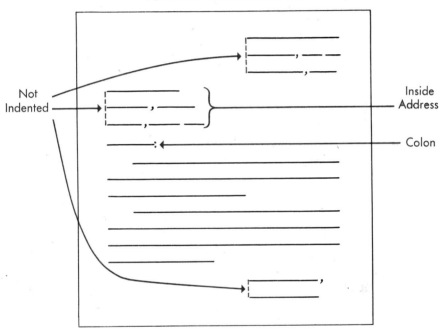

FORM FOR ENVELOPE ADDRESS

The envelope for a business letter should be addressed in block form, as shown here.

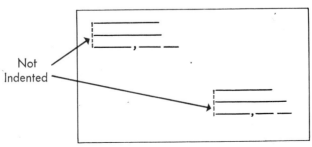

In business letters, the aim should be to present facts clearly, neatly, and briefly. The following guides will be helpful.

GUIDES FOR WRITING BUSINESS LETTERS

1. Get to the point immediately.
2. If the letter is handwritten, use your most careful penmanship.
3. Be polite.
4. Give exact information; do not make it necessary for the receiver to write you for missing facts.
5. If you ask a favor, enclose a stamped, self-addressed envelope.
6. If you enclose money, tell the amount and the form (check, money order, draft).
7. Sign your full name. If you are writing as a club or class officer, put your title below your signature.

Business letters that you might need to write include letters of subscription and letters of request.

SUBSCRIPTION LETTER

432 South Drive
Buffalo, New York 14216
March 3, 19—

Brown Publishing Company
2 North Apple Avenue
Kansas City, Missouri 64104

Gentlemen:

Please send Good Manners magazine to me for one year, beginning with the April issue. This is a new subscription.

I am enclosing a money order for $3.50, your advertised rate for a one-year subscription.

Yours truly,
Mary Ann Myers

2427 Maple Street
York, Nebraska 68467
April 12, 19—

Eastman Kodak Company
45 North State Street
Rochester, New York 14604

Gentlemen:

Please send me your latest catalogue describing flash-bulb cameras. I should appreciate receiving also a price list and an order blank.

Sincerely yours,
John R. Scott

LEARNING ACTIVITIES IN WRITING BUSINESS LETTERS

A. Check the two sample letters by the guides on page 266. How well do they follow the guides?

B. Write to a magazine publisher a letter ordering a magazine. *Proofread the letter, using the Writing Chart, page 172.* Exchange letters with a partner; check form, spelling, capitalization, punctuation, and content. Perhaps you can make this a real letter.

C. Write a letter to a magazine, giving a change of address. Give both the old and the new address. Most publishers request that you enclose the address label from a copy of the magazine.) *Proofread carefully for any mistakes.* Be sure that you have no sentence fragments or run-on sentences. (See pages 337 and 341.) In your small groups, take turns at reading and judging the letters.

USING ENGLISH OUTSIDE SCHOOL

Write a letter to a company asking for information or for a catalogue or a sample of some product. The advertising pages of a magazine will suggest a letter that you might like to write. Check the letter by the Writing Chart, page 172; by the letter form on page 265; and by the guides on page 266. Have it approved by your teacher before you mail it.

CAPITALIZATION

Copy these sentences, supplying needed capital letters.

1. "well," mother asked, "isn't jacksonville in the south?"
2. Last saturday the flying aces, our new club, held a model-plane contest in the large field on the west bank of davis creek.
3. In geography class yesterday, we learned that the source of the arkansas river is in the rocky mountains.
4. just before the thanksgiving holidays, judge r. t. mahoney, who was a great athlete at center college, spoke to the boys of field junior high school on the subject "the thrills of the game."

PUNCTUATION

Copy these sentences, supplying needed punctuation.

1. Father added that on December 15 1962 the city of Chicago Illinois opened the Dan Ryan Expressway to the public
2. Sue asked Didnt you see any horses cattle or pigs on your uncles farm Warner
3. Well if you should ever be in that town be sure to look up Dr J R Byers a good friend of mine Ive known him for twenty five years.
4. Mens and womens coats arent on this floor said the floorwalker.

SENTENCE SENSE

(1) Number your paper from 1 through 6. (2) Read each of the following groups of words. (3) If a group is a sentence, write *S* on your paper after the corresponding number. If it is a sentence fragment, write *F*. If it is a run-on sentence, write *RO*. (4) Make sentences out of the fragments and run-ons.

1. It is fun to pick wild berries in the woods.
2. Black and red berries on green vines.
3. Some people don't like to pick berries, they're afraid of snakes.
4. When Bob saw a small snake on a vine.
5. Gooseberry and blackberry bushes have sharp thorns.
6. Picking berries and hearing them drop into a pail.

SPELLING

Write on your paper the plural of each of the following nouns. These words are spelled by rules.

1. monkey	4. man-of-war	7. child	10. lady
2. sheep	5. handful	8. church	11. Sandy
3. James	6. piccolo	9. loaf	12. stray

Building Sentences

GRAMMAR: THE CODE OF LANGUAGE

This chapter will introduce you to some interesting facts and ideas about the English language. They are the results of discoveries made by researchers who have traced English all the way back to its very beginnings, long ago. The name given to their work is "linguistics"; it means "the scientific study of language."

In later grammar chapters, you will learn more about the facts and ideas presented here in Chapter 14.

1. Language *vs.* Communication

"ALL RIGHT, FRISKY ——— I'LL THROW IT FOR YOU ONCE MORE!"

TALK IT OVER

Frisky has not actually *said* anything; that is, he has not used *words.* Has he communicated an idea, however? How can you tell?

Richard speaks to Frisky, but is it really what he *says,* or what he *does,* that answers the dog?

Do you agree that "language" and "communication" are not necessarily the same? Which one includes the other?

As the drawing suggests, language is purely a human activity. Words and the way in which they are arranged form a code. That code gives human beings the power to express meanings and shades of meanings that mere sounds or gestures could never communicate.

The English language is one code; so is the French language; so is the German; so is each one of the many other languages in the world. Certain codes are alike in some ways, but no two are exactly the same. As an example, you say, "Thank you," but if you were French, you would say, "Merci"; if Spanish, "Gracias"; if German, "Danke"; if Italian, "Grazie"; and so on.

LEARNING ACTIVITIES IN LANGUAGE *VS.* COMMUNICATION

A. What different things may a dog be trying to express when he barks? when he growls? when he whines? Is he using language?

B. You have heard the expression "as helpless as a baby." How does it apply to communication of the baby's feelings? Are the sounds that the baby makes (before it learns words) language?

C. Suppose you had a parrot or a mynah bird that you had taught to say, "Hello; how are you?" when someone came into the room. Would the bird be communicating? Justify your opinion.

2. English: A Changing Language

"HAST CONNED THY LESSON FOR TODAY?"

"COME ON, BILL! TALK ENGLISH!"

Strange as his remark may sound, Bill *is* speaking English—but not in its present-day forms. Certainly you can figure out what he means. How would that sentence be worded today?

What word have you substituted for "Hast"? What word must you insert after it? What word would you use instead of "conned"? What has happened to "thy"?

A sentence such as "Hast conned thy lesson for today?" is a good example of how language changes as the years go by. When the greatest English writer, Shakespeare, was a boy, four hundred years ago, "hast" and "conned" were as much a part of everyday speech as "have" and "studied" are today.

LEARNING ACTIVITIES

A. Find the word "hast" in your dictionary. On the basis of what you discover, decide why Shakespeare would not have been likely to say, "*He* hast conned his lesson."

Now look up "con." Does it, like "hast," have the label *Archaic*? (That word means "no longer in common use.") Examine the definition. Do you agree that "con" is more specific than "study"? Why?

B. Here are other English sentences as Shakespeare might have expressed them. On your paper, "translate" them into modern English.
1. Be thou thyself mine enemy?
2. Methinks the clock hath strucken thrice.
3. I wot not whereof thou dost speak.
4. Mayhap he doth but wish to fright thee.
5. Whence cometh this man? Wast thou who brought him?

C. Many of the changes in the English language down through the years have been in spelling. A great number of words today are the very same words that Chaucer, the first great English poet, used six hundred years ago. The words simply are spelled differently now.

Here are sentences in which the italicized words are spelled as Chaucer would have written them. With the help of the other words in the sentences, figure out the italicized ones. (Reading aloud will help.) Rewrite the sentences, using today's spelling.
1. *Thenne I bigan to thinke* that I *sholde retourne hoom.*
2. He *seyde,* "I *hidde* the *tresor* in a *litel feeld nat ferre fro heer.*"
3. *Oon* of *thise* men *wol helpe yow peynte* the *dores.*
4. *Laste somer* Ed and I *toke a journee togidre thurgh* that *contree.*
5. A *longe whyle* ago my *fader yaf* me *som goode avys:* "*Alwey* do your *duetee.*"

D. Many words that Chaucer and Shakespeare used are in your own vocabulary, but they no longer mean what they did. The word "girl," for example, once was a name used for *any* young person, girl or boy; "cattle" was *any* kind of property; an "ally" was a *relative;* "take" often meant *give;* "let" meant *prevent.*

To test how meanings have changed, do the following activity.

1. Write these words in a column on your paper: *arrive, borrow, crop, danger, depart, dress, forfeit, repair, quick, sky.*
2. By checking in the dictionary the derivation of those words, decide which original meaning of the following fits each word: *pledge, alive, do wrong, reach the shore, master, cloud, go back to one's own country, divide, top, arrange.* Write each original meaning beside the word it fits.

3. English: A Patterned Language

"TOMMY WANTS A DRINK OF WATER."

READ AND THINK ABOUT

Tommy has not yet learned to use "I" instead of "Tommy" in that sentence, but he *has* learned to say, "Tommy wants a drink of water," and not "Of water a drink wants Tommy," or "Wants of water a drink Tommy."

Though he does not realize the fact, Tommy has already learned an important truth about English: it is a "patterned" language.

In English sentences, you see, words and groups of words tend to fall naturally into a certain order; that is, into *patterns*. Sentence meaning depends upon the pattern. Notice this sentence, for example: *The boy chased the dog.*

You know that the boy is the one who is doing the chasing; *boy* is, in other words, the "subject" of the sentence. You know that the dog is what is being chased; *dog* is, you know, the "object" in the sentence. The pattern, then, looks like this:

subject + *verb* + *object*

boy + chased + dog

What happens if you change the position of the two nouns?

The dog chased the boy.

The pattern (*subject* + *verb* + *object*) is the same, but the meaning has changed.

LEARNING ACTIVITY IN WORD ORDER

The pairs of sentences in this activity have exactly the same words. In class explain what difference in meaning the word order causes.

1. Everybody likes John. John likes everybody.
2. Fred, change your mind. Fred, mind your change!
3. He supplies ships for the navy. He ships supplies for the navy.
4. Did Harry vote? Harry did vote.
5. He rakes leaves. He leaves rakes.
6. Everyone here works. Everyone works here.
7. Those boys are workers! Those workers are boys.
8. The men with him are partners. The men are partners with him.
9. Did you check the date? Did you date the check?
10. He will plan the attack. He will attack the plan.

ENRICHMENT

READ THIS

Many sentences that Shakespeare wrote differ from the English of today not only in sentence order but in their use or omission of *do, does,* or *did.* Note the following sentences from one of Shakespeare's plays. (Today's wording is shown in parentheses.)

Why blame you me? (*Why* do *you blame me?*)
I know him not. (*I* do *not know him.*)
Twice did he turn his back. (*He* turned *his back twice.*)

DO THIS

A. Make all changes needed to turn into today's English these quotations from Shakespeare's *Julius Caesar.*

1. Why stare you so?
2. 'Tis Cinna; I do know him by his gait.
3. Horses did neigh, and dying men did groan.
4. Why, know'st thou any harm's intended towards him?
5. How died my master, Strato?

B. The following sentences are "translated" from *Julius Caesar.* Write them as you think Shakespeare did.

1. What do you mean by that?
2. Didn't you know Pompey?
3. He did not come back.
4. You do not know what you are doing.
5. Do I know these men that have come along with you?

4. English: Spoken Language *vs.* Written

Is the meaning clear both of the remark made in the first drawing (page 276) and of the statement given in the second one? Why are they worded differently?

What advantages has the speaker in the first drawing over the person who wrote the instructions in the second? Which person, in other words, has the harder job? Why?

As those drawings illustrate, written English and spoken English often differ. The meaning of what you *say* can be brought out not only by your words but by the tone of your voice, by gestures, by pauses, by the expression on your face, . . . You use those things naturally; that is, you do not really have to *learn* them.

When you write, however, you must get along without those aids to meaning. You must study how to choose words carefully and then put them together as clearly as you can. You must learn how to use the signals of punctuation to take the place of voice, pause, gesture, and facial expression.

Written language does have its disadvantages, you see, but it also has some important advantages. It is permanent; a person can read it over and over again, and it will stay the same each time. To carry its message, speaking needs at least two persons: the speaker and the listener. Writing needs only a reader. Writing keeps the great thoughts of the past alive.

Though you may never have thought about it before, you can see now that writing is *not* "just speaking written down." If you are to write well, you must *learn* how to do so.

LEARNING ACTIVITIES IN WRITTEN *VS.* SPOKEN LANGUAGE

A. Look at this sentence: "He has visited here lately." You could suggest five different meanings by saying it five times, emphasizing a different word each time. Try it; explain the changes in meaning.

If you write the sentence, how can you show which meaning you want the reader to get?

Here is another sentence: *I don't like that blue coat.* In an oral class activity, take turns at reading it aloud, emphasizing one word. After you read the sentence, call on someone to tell the meaning that your emphasis seems to suggest.

B. Which sentences in the following pairs are more likely to occur in ordinary spoken language than in written?

1. They're going to have to change their plans.
   They will be obliged to change their plans.

2. I have an uneasy feeling about much of this material.
   I've got a funny feeling about a lot of this stuff.

3. We're getting pretty worried about all this rain we keep on having.
   The amount of rain we continue to have is beginning to worry us seriously.

4. If you're going to succeed, you have to keep on trying.
   The secret of success is persistence.

5. He who gives up something certain for that which is unsure shows little wisdom.
   Anyone who gives up a sure thing for a gamble isn't likely to be using his head.

ENRICHMENT

Here are quotations from the writings of famous authors. Reword them in everyday conversational speech.

EXAMPLE: They fail, and they alone, who have not striven.—ALDRICH
        The only failures are the people who haven't really tried.

1. Not every man is so great a coward as he thinks he is.—STEVENSON
2. Ignorance never settles a question.—DISRAELI
3. He who sleeps in continual noise is wakened by silence.—HOWELLS
4. Fame is the thirst of youth.—BYRON
5. There is no good in arguing with the inevitable.—LOWELL
6. The greatest of faults, I should say, is to be conscious of none.—CARLYLE
7. Nothing great was ever achieved without enthusiasm.—EMERSON
8. Go forth to meet the shadowy future, without fear, and with a manly heart.—LONGFELLOW
9. If you once forfeit the confidence of your fellow citizens, you can never regain their respect and esteem.—LINCOLN
10. I have no talent for making new friends, but oh, such a genius for fidelity to old ones!—DU MAURIER

USING VERBS IN BUILDING SENTENCES*

I certainly —— you.

TALK IT OVER ...

How important is the missing word in that sentence?

Why is there no real sentence idea without it?

Which of these words will "make sense" in the blank: *admire, truth, rich, like, believe, about, trust?*

1. Recognizing Doing (Action) Verbs

When a runner hears the signal "Go!" what does he *do?* What does a football team *do* when the signal "Hike!" is called? What *action* takes place when these commands are given: "Halt!" "Aim!" "Fire!" "March!" Such a word as those calls for doing something and, therefore, might be called a "doing" word. The grammatical name is *verb*.

* Pretest 2 should be taken at this point.

1. **(DEFINITION)** A *verb* is a word that will fit at least one of the blanks, or slots, in these sentences:

> He ....   We ....

A verb fits in those slots by showing (*a*) what something does or (*b*) that something exists. Use those "slot sentences" as *test frames* for identifying verbs.

EXAMPLES: He **works.**   We **are.**

2. **Verbs can change form or take endings as needed.**

> You **look** well.   He **looks** well.   She **looked** well.
> We often **go.**   He often **goes.**   They often **went.**

3. **(DEFINITION)** Verbs that express action are "doing" verbs.

4. **Verbs are one of the two most important of the parts of speech.*** **Every sentence must have a verb.**

> The boy *hit* the ball.

Take out the doing word (*hit*) and you have no idea what the boy did, except that it concerned a ball.

> The boy ___?___ the ball.

Did he *throw it, bat it, drop it, kick it,* . . . ? You must have that word *hit* before you can know what is happening. *Hit,* in other words, is the verb, the most important word.

The boy hit the ball.

To get a "picture" idea of what happens as you add various sentence parts to the verb, look at the above drawing and then at the drawings on pages 313, 329, 390, 415, 438, 439, and 449.

---

* *Parts of speech* are the different classes of words out of which sentences are built. The *noun* is the other one of the two most important parts of speech.

Learn about words!

The following words, taken from *B* of the Learning Activities, have interesting histories. Use your dictionary to find the story behind each word. With which word is the drawing connected?

immense   nasturtiums   tent   luggage

LEARNING ACTIVITIES

A. Many words suggest action, but only verbs show that it actually takes place, has taken place, or will do so. By using the test frames on page 280, find which of the following words can be verbs.

1. hike	3. runner	5. song	7. yell	9. bought
2. sits	4. rapidly	6. jump	8. argues	10. explosion

B. The following groups of words will not mean much until the blanks are filled with verbs. Copy the sentences, putting a good "doing" word of your own choice in each blank. *Do not write in this book.*

When you have finished, each group of words will be a sentence. In other words, it *will make sense.* Read your sentences in class to see how many different meanings were given by the use of different verbs.

1. Irene ....
2. Ted .... his mother.
3. Sally .... loudly.
4. Phil .... into the house.
5. The audience .... the program.
6. The wind .... through the trees.
7. The old man .... slowly.
8. Jack .... down the road.

C. (1) Copy the following sentences, underlining twice the verb in each sentence. (2) *Proofread for careless errors in copying.* (3) Exchange papers for checking.

1. An airplane flew over the city.
2. Father reads many books.
3. Many bright nasturtiums grow in Aunt Sue's garden.
4. Yes, my uncle whittled this cowboy for me.
5. The cat raced to the top of the tent.
6. Mr. Johnson shipped his luggage to Oregon.
7. Jean brought some milk to the kitten.
8. The Ohio River runs into the Mississippi.
9. The fire engine dashed noisily down the street.
10. The rain soaked quickly into the dry earth.
11. Tom climbed to the top of the old maple tree.
12. The baby upset his bowl of cereal.
13. The travelers saw an immense black bear.
14. Harry swam across the pool.
15. Jim missed the football game.

D. Try substituting other verbs for the ones used in the following sentences. List on the board the different verbs suggested for each sentence.

1. The child fed the birds.
2. Alice bought a new coat yesterday.
3. Harry sent the message.
4. The class learns many poems.
5. Mary wrote a long letter.
6. Henry builds model planes.
7. The boys walked home today.
8. Gene sings well.

★ **Spot Review**

Notice the above title, for you will see it often. Each time it will be the heading for a short check-up to see whether you are remembering and using what you study.

(*Based upon the sentences in* C *of the preceding activities*)

1. Why is *Aunt* capitalized in sentence 3?
2. Why is *uncle* not capitalized in sentence 4?
3. Explain the comma in sentence 4.
4. Why is *River* capitalized in sentence 8?

2. Recognizing Auxiliary Verbs

What is missing in the sentences?

THINK IT OVER ...

What does each of those sentences need?

Which of the following words will fit in the first blank? in the second? in the third? Here are the words: *is, was, has, had, does, did, shall, will, should, would, may, might, must, can, could.*

5. **(DEFINITION)** An "auxiliary" verb is one that helps a doing verb express an idea. (*Auxiliary* is from the Latin *auxilium,* meaning "aid" or "help.") The auxiliary signals that another verb is coming.

> The sun has *broken* through the clouds.

In that sentence, the verb is *has broken,* made up of the helping verb *has* and the doing verb *broken.*

6. **(DEFINITION)** A doing verb with its auxiliaries is a *verb phrase.* In a verb phrase, the auxiliaries are sometimes called "verb markers."

7. **The auxiliaries are so few in number that you can memorize them.** Here they are, grouped in families to help you learn them easily.

I		II	III	IV	V
is	were	has	do	shall	may
am	be	have	does	will	might
are	being	had	did	should	must
was	been			would	can
					could

8. **Changing the helping verb changes the meaning of a sentence.**

> I *shall* walk. I *could* walk. I *must* walk.
> I *may* walk. I *did* walk. I *should* walk.
> I *can* walk. I *do* walk. I *might* walk.

9. **A doing verb may have one, two, or even three helping verbs.** In verb phrases all but the last verb will be auxiliaries.

> Don will *go* tomorrow. (*one auxiliary*)
> Don should have *gone* today. (*two auxiliaries*)
> Soon Don will have been *gone* a week. (*three auxiliaries*)

LEARNING ACTIVITIES IN VERB PHRASES

A. Auxiliaries keep a definite order when two or more of them are parts of a verb phrase. You would never say, for example, "Roy *have should* helped you"; the right order is "should have."

In class, go over the five groups of auxiliaries. See how many two- or three-word combinations you can make from them. Which group cannot be used as auxiliaries with words in any of the other groups?

B. (1) Number your paper from 1 to 20. (2) Find the verb phrase in each sentence and write it after the corresponding number on your paper.

1. The settlers had brought their families with them.
2. Our neighbors are planning a long trip.
3. Joe might agree with you.
4. My brother could have come sooner.
5. The letter may have arrived early.
6. Those poor people do need our help.
7. Your brother must be told about our plans.
8. The new plans should have been explained to us.
9. James was polishing the car.
10. The men were working in the garden.
11. The work is being completed rapidly.
12. Yes, Helen does make her own clothes.
13. Father will be leaving very early.
14. Our house can be seen from this corner.
15. Tim has changed his mind again.
16. George did go to the game after all.
17. Jane is planning a trip for next summer.
18. No mail will be delivered tomorrow.
19. Most boys would like my Uncle Jack.
20. These men shall be instructed carefully.

C. Go back to the sentences in *B.* Find those with two or more auxiliaries. Can you arrange those auxiliaries in any other sensible order?

● **THESE ARE FACTS ABOUT VERBS: III**

10. *Has, have, had, do, does,* and *did* are not always auxiliary verbs; that is, they can stand alone as the verb in a sentence.
   Sue has the tickets.   We had a heavy snow.
   Joe does his best.   Ellen did well.

11. (DEFINITION) A verb that shows only existence or condition is a *verb of being,* or a *being verb. Is, am, are, was, were, be, being,* and *been* sometimes are verbs of being.
   The boys are cousins. The book was open. Tom may be late.
   Being verbs may have auxiliaries. Note the "may," just above.

LEARNING ACTIVITIES IN FINDING AND USING VERBS

A. In an oral activity, see how quickly you can pick out the verbs in the following sentences. They may look like helping verbs, but here they are used alone. Tell which ones are verbs of being.

1. The book was on the table.
2. The owners of the farm are away.

3. Jerry is my friend.
4. May has a new watch.
5. The boys did their best.
6. Those two days were holidays.
7. A good soldier does his duty.
8. The patient had a good doctor.
9. The nights have been colder lately.
10. Angry words often do great harm.

B. (1) Write two sentences for each of the following verbs or verb phrases: *has been, might have, should be, were, could have been.* Use them (*a*) as auxiliary verbs and (*b*) by themselves; that is, without doing verbs. (2) *Proofread your sentences for careless mistakes in capitalizing, punctuating, spelling, or sentence sense.* (3) Exchange papers in class and underline twice each verb or verb phrase in the sentences that you receive. (4) Return papers and check to see that all the verbs are correctly underlined.

The illustration on this page may suggest things to write about.

FOLLOW-UP

Keep a list of the helping verbs in your notebook or in some other convenient place. If you will read them over aloud several times a day, you will soon have the verbs memorized. Practice to see how quickly you can say them. Test yourself from time to time to see how well you can write them from memory. When you really know these verbs, you should be able to write the entire list in less than a minute.

3. Recognizing Verbs with Separated Parts

Look at this sentence: *The book could not be found.*

What is the verb? At first glance you might say it is *could not be found.* Which word in "could not be," however, is not an auxiliary? (See point 7, page 283.) What, then, is the verb phrase?

● **THESE ARE FACTS ABOUT VERBS: IV**

12. **Often the parts of a verb will be separated by other words.**

    The road is already being repaired.
    Don can almost always help us.

13. **In a question, the parts of the verb are often separated.**

    Has John bought a ticket?

    Turning a question into a statement helps to locate the verb.

    QUESTION: Has John bought a ticket?
    STATEMENT: John has bought a ticket.

14. **To turn a statement into a question, you must make certain changes in the sentence.**

    a) If the statement has (1) a verb phrase or (2) a being verb, you need to change only the sentence order.
       (1) Lou is waiting.   Is Lou waiting?
       (2) Those boys are cousins.   Are those boys cousins?

    b) If the statement has a doing verb with no auxiliaries, you
       (1) will need to insert the auxiliary *do, does,* or *did* and
       (2) may need to change the form of the doing verb.
       (1) The boys work here.   Do the boys work here?
       (2) Alice lives here.   Does Alice live here?
       Dean left today.   Did Dean leave today?
    Note that the auxiliary inserted will be *do, does,* or *did.*

15. **Sometimes part of the verb is within a contraction.** (See page 163 for a discussion of contractions.)

    Jack hasn't gone yet.   Why wasn't the bell rung?

Learn about words!

The following words, taken from *A* of the Learning Activities, have interesting histories. Use your dictionary to find the story behind each word. With which word is the drawing connected?

soldier   muscle   bonfire   ventriloquism

LEARNING ACTIVITIES

A. In an oral activity, find the verb phrase in each sentence. The number of auxiliary verbs is indicated in parentheses.
1. The sun has not shone all day. (1)
2. The boys have surely watched that bonfire carefully. (1)
3. That soldier may soon see his home again. (1)
4. A visit to the mill can probably be arranged. (2)
5. Harry is just beginning a new book. (1)
6. Joe must always have been reading about ventriloquism. (3)
7. The bell had already rung. (1)
8. The curtain will then be lowered. (2)
9. Jane isn't really living here now. (1)
10. This muscle has evidently been strained before. (2)
11. The speaker's voice is not being heard clearly. (2)
12. Our plans are almost always made at the last minute. (1)

B. (1) Copy the questions below and underline twice the verbs. If it will help you, think of the question in the form of a statement. *Do not write in this book.* (2) Exchange papers for checking.

1. Why has Joe come with you?
2. What is Father bringing tonight?
3. In what year did Texas become a state?
4. By what nickname was Andrew Jackson known?
5. Could Jean have come with us?
6. Where was Lincoln born?
7. When will the game begin?
8. Will your brother tell Sally of the change in plans?
9. Have any letters come for me?
10. How can Frank plan the party?

C. Turn the following ten statements into questions. As you go over them in class, explain the changes that you needed to make.

1. Alvin has always lived in Florida.
2. Jean found her lost gloves.
3. The books will be delivered tomorrow.
4. Ed's uncle still pitches for the Dodgers.

5. Mr. Burns came here from Canada.
6. The names of the winners were announced last night.
7. The wind blew the roof off that house.
8. Both boys made the basketball team.
9. Everyone except John left early.
10. That plant needs more sunlight.

D. Write five questions of your own, underlining the verbs. You may want to write questions about a hobby, about sports, or about a book that you have read. Read your questions in your small group and ask a member of the group to name the verb in each sentence.

ENRICHMENT

Compose a paragraph of five or more sentences about a motion picture that you have seen recently. For help, refer to guides 2–4 of the Guides for Writing a Paragraph, page 214. In two or more sentences, use verbs with their parts separated by other words.

Read your paragraph in class. Let guides 4, 6, and 7 of the Guides for Reading Aloud, page 57, help you. Ask classmates to jot down each verb that they hear. (This activity will require careful listening. Review guides 1 and 4 of the Guides to Good Listening on page 26.)

4. Telling Time with Verbs

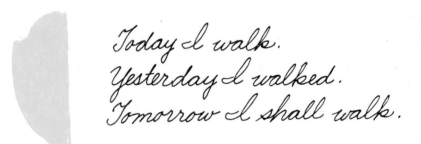

Today I walk.
Yesterday I walked.
Tomorrow I shall walk.

THINK IT OVER . . .

What happens to the verb "walk" in the second and third sentences in the drawing?

The verb form used in a sentence tells the time when an action takes place. It tells (1) whether something is happening in the *present,* (2) whether it happened in the *past,* or (3) whether it will happen in the *future.*

16. **(DEFINITION)** *Tense* is the grammatical term for the form of a verb that shows the time of the action or state of being that the verb expresses.

(*Tense* comes from the Latin word *tempus*, which means *time*.) The tense that is used will show when something *is*, *was*, or *will be* happening.

PRESENT TENSE: Today I *play*.
PAST TENSE: Yesterday I *played*.
FUTURE TENSE: Tomorrow I *shall* (or *will*) *play*.
PRESENT PERFECT TENSE: Today I *have played*.
PAST PERFECT TENSE: Yesterday I *had played*.
FUTURE PERFECT TENSE: Tomorrow I *shall* (or *will*) *have played*.

Note that only the present *play* and the past *played* show time by themselves. In the other tenses, the time is shown by using auxiliaries with the present form *play* or the past form *played*.

LEARNING ACTIVITIES IN VERB TENSES

A. In an oral activity, name the verbs in the following sentences and tell their tense.

1. An old man answered the door.
2. The bus will leave early in the morning.
3. Several birthday cards had arrived late.
4. By next June our family probably will have moved to Florida.
5. My father likes pie for breakfast.
6. Will some kind friend help me with this problem?
7. Jack has always lived on Maple Street.
8. Susan found her tennis shoe.
9. Father will have arrived in New York by now.
10. Their radio plays all day.
11. Has the mail come?
12. Next week Bob will go to St. Louis.
13. Mary had washed the dishes every night of that week.
14. The team has lost only one game all season.
15. The hunter found no game in the woods.
16. Ralph had never seen the man before.
17. Perhaps the snow will have ended by morning.
18. Every year Aunt Sally bakes a cake for my birthday.
19. Our vacation has gone too fast.
20. This road certainly needs repairs.

B. (1) Copy the following sentences, putting in the verb tense called for in the parentheses. Write carefully, applying the Suggestions for Good Handwriting, page 479. (2) Exchange papers for checking.

1. Which man (*past of* lock) this door?
2. By tonight Tom (*future perfect of* finish) his trip.
3. No guard (*past perfect of* close) his eyes that night.
4. The price (*future of* go) up tomorrow.
5. On Saturdays Bill (*present of* help) his father in the drugstore.
6. The children (*present perfect of* decide) on a name for their dog.
7. The butler usually (*present of* open) the door.
8. The snow (*past perfect of* pile) up in huge drifts.
9. Which boy (*future of* do) that errand for you?
10. The color in this dress certainly (*present perfect of* fade).

Learn about words!

The following words, taken from Activity A, page 289, have interesting histories. Use your dictionary to find the story behind each word.

| tennis | season | bus | radio |

5. Understanding Verbs and Their Principal Parts

TALK IT OVER . . .

How good is *your* knowledge of principal parts? For example, which word in each of the following groups has principal parts that do not match those of the other verbs in the group?

1. grow	2. fall	3. reach	4. drink
glow	call	bleach	sink
know	stall	teach	shrink
blow	wall	preach	wink

What you need to know, in other words, is that some verbs have "regular" principal parts but that others have "irregular" ones.

17. Verbs have three main parts, called their *principal parts:* the *present* form, the *past* form, and the *past participle.**

Present	Past	Past Participle
dare	dared	dared
play	played	played
go	went	gone

a) **(DEFINITION)** Verbs like *dare* and *play* are called *regular verbs* because they form the past and the past participle simply by adding *d* or *ed* to the present.

dare + d = dared play + ed = played

b) **(DEFINITION)** Some verbs, like *go* in the example, change their spelling to form the past and the past participle, and are therefore called *irregular verbs.*

c) The dictionary gives the principal parts of all irregular verbs. If the parts are not given, a verb is regular.

18. **(DEFINITION)** A *conjugation* is the orderly arrangement of the principal parts and the tenses of a verb. For examples, see the conjugations of *to draw* and *to be* on pages 477–78.

LEARNING ACTIVITIES IN USING PRINCIPAL PARTS

A. (1) As your teacher dictates the following regular verbs, write on your paper their principal parts. (2) Exchange papers for checking.

1. rake	4. warm	7. need	10. harm
2. clean	5. form	8. land	11. scout
3. blame	6. pretend	9. excuse	12. test

B. The following verbs are irregular only in that a spelling change takes place as *ed* is added to form the past and the past participle. (1) Write a sentence, at least six words long, using the past of each of the verbs. (Rule 2 on page 190 and Rules 1 and 2 on page 193 will help you to spell the words correctly.) (2) Take turns reading your sentences in class or in your small groups, spelling the verb orally. (3) Exchange papers for criticism of spelling, punctuation, and neatness. *Note good things as well as bad.*

1. carry	3. stop	5. refer	7. hop	9. study
2. bat	4. hurry	6. marry	8. omit	10. cry

* The *present participle* is sometimes included with the principal parts. It is made by adding *ing* to the present: *walk, walking.*

6. Using Vivid Verbs

TALK IT OVER ...

What verbs would express the movement of the above pictures better than the word *walked?* In which picture is Relmond *strolling* down the street? In which picture is he *strutting?* In which picture is he *limping* down the street. How else might he *walk* down the street?

GUIDES FOR USING VIVID VERBS

1. Use strong verbs. "The car *screeched* around the corner," for example, gives a clearer picture than "The car *turned* the corner."

2. Use exact, vivid substitutes for the verb *said.* "She *screamed* at him," for example, gives a more vivid impression than "She *said* to him." (The guide does not mean that you should never use *said.* What it does mean is that many times other words will express your meaning better.)

3. Avoid "big" verbs when simple ones give the meaning that you want to express. "*Chew* your food well," for example, is usually better than *"Masticate* your food well."

LEARNING ACTIVITIES IN VIVID VERBS

A. *Run, say,* and *look* are general verbs. (1) Make a list on your paper of exact, vivid words that you might substitute for them. For example, in thinking about *run,* picture to yourself the various ways in which people run and then find the exact word to describe each way: *gallop, scurry, scoot,* and so on. (2) In class, make a combined list on the board. (3) Copy into your notebook vivid, exact verbs for future use.

B. One reason that good writers are good writers is that they use vivid verbs. Here are examples from the work of famous poets. Read them together and then discuss the verb choices. Use the Guides for Choral Reading, page 46. (Be sure to follow discussion guides 3 and 4, page 33.)

1. . . . the wind on the warm sea dozes, . . .—SWINBURNE
2. . . . the door upon its hinges groans.—KEATS
3. The high masts flickered . . .—TENNYSON
4. The light white cloud swam over us.—TENNYSON
5. The last red leaf is whirled away.—TENNYSON
6. Cows flap a slow tail knee-deep in the river, . . .—MEREDITH
7. The white foam spun behind us.—KIPLING
8. How the sleet whips the pane!—ARNOLD
9. Where the grey seas glitter, . . .—CHESTERTON
10. A late lark twitters from the quiet skies . . .—HENLEY
11. And the rain poured down from one black cloud; . . .—COLERIDGE
12. All day the wind breathes low . . .—TENNYSON
13. So all night long the storm roared on: . . .—WHITTIER
14. The spotted hawk swoops by . . .—WHITMAN
15. The night wind wailed round the empty room . . .—ROSSETTI
16. The hot sun bit the garden beds, . . .—MORRIS

C. In class or in your small groups, make a list on the board of vivid verbs that tell different ways in which you might describe the following:

1. The blowing of the wind
2. The running of a stream
3. The flying of birds
4. The shining of sun, stars, moon
5. The sounds made by birds
6. The falling of snow, rain, hail
7. The noises made by automobiles, trucks, planes, motorboats
8. The sight and sound of a fire

D. Replace the "big" verbs in these sentences with ones better suited to ordinary conversational speech.

1. Have you perused that copy of *Seventeen* yet?
2. You should cerebrate at least an hour before deciding.
3. Unexpected company always discomposes Mom.
4. I prognosticate a win for our team in Friday's game.
5. Why don't you manifest a little interest in our plans?

FOLLOW-UP

From the lists made in *C*, copy words that appeal to you. File them in your notebook for use in your themes, letters, or other writing.

7. Using Standard English

"DAD, WHY SHOULDN'T I SAY, 'I DONE MY BEST'? IT MEANS THE SAME AS 'I DID MY BEST.'"

TALK IT OVER...

Is the boy right in saying that "I *done* my best" and "I *did* my best" mean the same thing?

If so, what difference does it make which one he uses?

Is there more to language than simply expressing meaning?

What the boy's father probably would have explained to him is that there are two main levels of English usage: *standard* and *nonstandard*. Standard English is the kind of language used naturally by well-educated speakers. Nonstandard English is language that such speakers would not normally use. "I *did* my best" is standard English; "I *done* my best," nonstandard.

The boy's father, you see, wants his son to make a habit of using standard English, because he knows that using nonstandard expression can handicap his son when he grows up—and even before then.

PART ONE: USING TROUBLESOME VERBS

Nonstandard use of irregular verbs is a common problem. From time to time in this book practice is provided in the proper use of the principal parts of irregular verbs. Each time, before doing the practice, learn the standard forms. <u>Notice that the third form, the past participle, always has an auxiliary with it.</u> (You may want to review the auxiliary verbs; see point 7 on page 283.)

USING IRREGULAR VERBS

RULE 1.   (*Do* and its forms)
Always use an auxiliary (helping) verb with *done*. *Did* **is a strong verb and stands alone.**

Today I **do.**   Yesterday I **did.**   Often I *have* **done.**

LEARNING ACTIVITIES IN USING *DID* AND *DONE*

A. Go over the following sentences orally in class, choosing the standard forms from the parentheses. Repeat the activity several times. If you use the past participle, tell what the auxiliary verb is. You might want to make this a contest (boys against girls, for example) in which you score a point for each proper choice.

1. Have you (did, done) the assignment yet?
2. Jack should have (did, done) his homework.
3. Frank (did, done) extremely well on the test.
4. We (did, done) all the puzzles correctly.
5. What has television (did, done) for people?
6. I (did, done) all the reading except the last chapter.
7. Has anything been (did, done) about the mistake?
8. Who (did, done) most of the planning?
9. The hardest job was (did, done) early in the morning.
10. This work must be (done, did) over.

B. (1) Write these sentences, filling each blank with the standard form of *do*. (2) Underline twice both the form of *do* that you use and any auxiliary verbs. (3) Exchange papers for checking as the sentences are read aloud. Go over them more than once. *Do not write in this book.*

1. Your work should always be .... neatly.
2. Yes, Jim .... his best in the last contest.
3. Who .... this?
4. Terry has .... very well this time.
5. We .... this assignment yesterday.
6. Has Father ever .... this kind of work before?
7. These papers must not be .... hastily.
8. I have .... these exercises every morning for a month.
9. Yesterday I .... something very foolish.
10. I've never .... this trick successfully.

C. Write five sentences of six or more words, using *did* or *done* in each of them. Write about something that you have done in connection with your schoolwork, with your clubs, or with any other activity.

Have the sentences read aloud in your small groups. Listen carefully and be ready to say why a sentence is or is not standard English.

D. Do this drill with a partner. (1) Ask a question using *done* properly. (2) Your partner must answer the question using *did*. (3) He must then ask you a question using *done,* which you must answer using *did.* (4) Continue until each has asked and answered five questions.

★ **Spot Review**

(Based upon the sentences in B *of the preceding activities)*
  1. Account for the comma in sentence 2.
  2. How would you spell the plural of the proper noun in sentence 4?
  3. Why is *Father* capitalized in sentence 6?
  4. Account for the apostrophe in sentence 10.

USING IRREGULAR VERBS—*Continued*

RULE 2. (*Know* and its forms)
Always use an auxiliary verb with *known;* **never, with** *knew.* **Remember that** *knowed* **is not standard English.**
  Today I **know.**   Yesterday I **knew.**   Often I *have* **known.**

LEARNING ACTIVITIES IN USING *KNEW* AND *KNOWN*

A. (1) Write these sentences, filling each blank with the standard form of *know.* (2) Underline twice the form of *know* that you use. Underline in the same way any helping verbs. (3) Read the sentences aloud; read them more than once if you have time. *Do not write in this book.*
  1. Years ago Mother .... this city from one end to the other.
  2. Mr. Smith is not very well .... here.
  3. You should have .... better!
  4. We all .... the speaker a long time ago.
  5. Father .... nothing of the accident until today.
  6. Have you .... those people long?
  7. The results of the contest should be .... soon.
  8. Mary has always been .... as a good student.
  9. The news might not yet be .... to our friends.

B. Write five original sentences, using *knew* and *known* properly. You may want to write about friends at school or in your neighborhood.

In your small groups, read your sentences aloud. Call on classmates to name the helping verbs used with *known*. Listen carefully to teach your ears to recognize the standard forms.

C. Write sentences on the board, leaving blanks to be filled with *knew* or *known*. Have classmates read the sentences, using the proper forms.

D. Do this activity in pairs. (1) Say a sentence using *knew*. (2) Your partner must change it to use *known* properly. (3) Then he will say a sentence using *knew*, which you must change to use *known*.

EXAMPLE: I *knew* the right answer.
I *should have known* the right answer.

Practice until the proper forms sound right to you.

USING IRREGULAR VERBS—Continued

RULE 3. (*Speak* and its forms)
Always use an auxiliary verb with *spoken;* never, with *spoke.*

Today I **speak**. Yesterday I **spoke**. Often I *have* **spoken**.

LEARNING ACTIVITIES IN USING *SPOKE* AND *SPOKEN*

A. (1) Write these sentences, filling the blanks with the proper form of *speak*. (2) Underline twice the form that you use and any helping verbs. (3) Read the sentences aloud as many times as needed to make the right forms sound natural. *Do not write in this book.*

1. Have you .... to Mother about our trip?
2. You should certainly have .... first to my mother.
3. In giving that report, Charles .... clearly.
4. Mary has already .... to me about the picnic.
5. Not many of Anne's sentences are .... above a whisper.
6. The last words were .... very loudly.
7. Is English, Italian, or French .... in that country?
8. I had already .... to Alice about the change in plans.
9. Who .... just then?
10. You might have .... up sooner.

B. (1) See how many combinations of helping verbs and *spoken* your class can name. Have these written on the board. (2) Practice reading them aloud together so that you can hear the proper forms. Here are a few combinations to start you off: *was spoken, may have spoken, can be spoken, had been spoken.*

C. (1) Write five original sentences, using *spoke* and *spoken* properly. To get ideas for your sentences, think about conversations that you have had recently with friends or members of your family. (2) Read your sentences aloud in your small groups. (3) Call on classmates to identify any auxiliary verbs. Listen to hear the standard forms.

★ **Spot Review**

(*Based upon the sentences in* A *of the preceding activities*)
1. Why is *Mother* capitalized in sentence 1 and not in sentence 2?
2. How would you write the plural of the name in sentence 3? in sentence 4?
3. Account for the apostrophe in sentence 5.
4. Account for the capitals and the commas in sentence 7.

USING IRREGULAR VERBS—Continued

RULE 4. (*Begin* and its forms)
Always use an auxiliary verb with *begun;* never, with *began.*

Today I **begin.**   Yesterday I **began.**   Often I *have* **begun.**

LEARNING ACTIVITIES IN USING *BEGAN* AND *BEGUN*

A. Write these sentences, filling the blanks with the proper form of *begin.* Underline twice (1) the form that you use and (2) any helping verbs. Read the sentences aloud as often as needed to make the proper forms sound natural. *Do not write in this book.*

1. Work has finally .... on the new building.
2. We .... the long trip back to the ranch at 9:30 A.M.
3. Both men's vacations .... yesterday.
4. Who .... this argument?
5. The program must not have .... on time.
6. The Joneses .... their trip last week.
7. Our club was .... as a class activity.
8. Early last Easter morning a heavy rain ....
9. Has the new schedule .... yet?
10. Wars are usually .... for selfish reasons.

B. Here is oral practice in using *began* and *begun.* (1) Go around the class, saying and completing this sentence: "Yesterday I began . . ." Each ending must be different and must make sense. Any person who cannot think of an ending or who repeats one already given must write down and hand in five sentences given after his turn. If fewer than five are given then, he must add original ones to make that number. (2) Repeat the process, only this time complete the following question: "Have you begun . . . ?"

C. Write five sentences similar to those in *A.* Perhaps your hobbies, your pastimes, or your school activities will give you ideas for your sentences. Exchange papers and read the sentences orally, supplying *began* or *begun.* Listen closely to hear whether the standard forms are chosen.

D. Practice the following activity in pairs. (1) Say a sentence using *began.* (2) Your partner must change the sentence to use *begun.* (3) Then he will say a sentence using *began,* which you must change to use *begun.* (4) Continue this activity until the proper forms sound right to you.

Spot Review

(*Based upon the sentences in* A *of the preceding activities*)
1. Account for the colon and the periods in sentence 2.
2. Explain the location of the apostrophe in sentence 3.
3. Explain the spelling of the proper noun in sentence 6.
4. In sentence 8, why is *Easter* capitalized?

USING IRREGULAR VERBS—Continued

RULE 5. (*See* and its forms)
Always use an auxiliary verb with *seen;* **never, with** *saw.*

Today I **see.**   Yesterday I **saw.**   Often I *have* **seen.**

LEARNING ACTIVITIES IN USING SAW AND SEEN

A. (1) Write these sentences, filling the blanks with the proper form of *see.* (2) Underline twice the form that you use and any helping verbs. (3) *Proofread for careless mistakes in copying.* (4) Read the sentences aloud to get used to hearing the standard forms.

1. Yesterday I .... a good new television program.
2. Haven't you .... that man before?
3. You must have .... my little brother Donny.
4. On his way to school this morning, James .... two gray squirrels.
5. Who .... you at last night's game?

6. We've never .... most of these out-of-the-way places before.
7. My neighbor, Mr. Black, ... a strange sight last week.
8. Hasn't Randy ever .... a circus?
9. Last Thanksgiving Day I .... an exciting parade.
10. The votes were not .... by any of us candidates.

B. In an oral activity, complete the following sentences. (1) Use *saw* if no helping verbs are given; otherwise use *seen*. (2) Add at least three other words to make a good sentence. (3) Repeat the activity until everyone has given at least two proper sentences. Speak distinctly; be sure, for example, that you say "must *have*," not "must *of*" or "must *uh*."

1. Somebody in that crowd must have . . .
2. As a matter of fact, nobody . . .
3. Have you ever . . .
4. On our trip through Texas, we . . .
5. According to the police report, only one man . . .
6. Even a careless driver surely would have . . .
7. During his visit to Chicago, Paul had . . .
8. In my opinion, no one could have . . .

C. (1) Take turns telling about something that you saw this morning on the way to school. To give your sentences variety, tell *where*.

EXAMPLE: "I saw a sports car parked by the bank."

(2) See how many combinations of helping verbs and *seen* you can name. Have these written on the board. Remember to include combinations containing *be, being,* or *been;* for example, *can be seen, are being seen, had been seen.*

D. Write five sentences using *saw* and *seen* properly. Write about things that you saw once and about things that you have seen often. Make your sentences interesting. Use the Guides for Improving Expression, page 453. Read sentences aloud in your small groups. Listen carefully to hear the standard forms.

E. Do this activity with a partner. Ask a question using *seen*. Your partner must answer, using *saw*. Then he will ask you a question using *seen*, which you must answer using *saw*. Practice until the proper forms really sound natural to you.

★ **Spot Review**

(*Based upon the sentences in* A *of the preceding activities*)

1. How would you write the plural of the proper noun in sentence 4?
2. Explain the use of the hyphens in sentence 6.
3. What is the reason for the commas in sentence 7?
4. Which sentences contain contractions? What do they stand for?

RULE 6. (*Choose* and its forms)
Always use an auxiliary verb with *chosen;* **never, with** *chose.*

Today I choose. Yesterday I chose. Often I *have* chosen.

LEARNING ACTIVITIES IN USING *CHOSE* AND *CHOSEN*

A. (1) Copy these sentences, supplying either *chose* or *chosen* and adding at least three other words to make interesting sentences. (2) Underline the verb twice, including any auxiliary verbs. (3) *Proofread to catch careless errors.* (4) Read the sentences aloud in class.

1. New officers for our club will not be . . .
2. A new president was . . .
3. For the first time in my life, I . . .
4. The members of the picnic committee have not yet . . .
5. Last night the team . . .
6. According to that traffic sign, we should have . . .
7. The poster winners will be . . .
8. On the spur of the moment, Jerry . . .
9. You could not have . . .
10. At that moment new members were being . . .

B. Write five sentences, using *chose* three times and *chosen* twice. Read the sentences aloud in your small groups. As you read, the other members of the group should listen and then jot down *Standard* or *Nonstandard* for each sentence. Afterwards, compare notes to see how well you agreed. Have doubtful sentences read again to see who was right.

C. Do this activity with a partner. Say a sentence using the past form of *choose.* Your partner must change the sentence to use the past participle. Then he will say a sentence using the past, which you must change to use the past participle.

PART TWO: STUDYING CONFUSING PAIRS

The verbs on pages 295–301 are troublesome mostly because the past form is used when the past participle form really should be used, and the other way round. The pairs of verbs in this lesson are troublesome because they are confused with each other, even though they have different *meanings*.

TELLING CONFUSING PAIRS APART

RULE 1. (*Learn, teach*)
Use *learn* when you mean "to get knowledge"; use *teach* when you mean "to give instruction." You *learn* for yourself, but someone else *teaches* you. You learn *something*, not *somebody*.

My teacher *teaches* me.

I *learn* a new word every day.

RULE 2. (*Sit, set*)
Use *sit* when you mean "to rest in an upright position"; use *set* when you mean "to place or put something." *Sit* never takes an object; *set* always needs one. ("Object" is explained on page 329.)

Phil *sat* on the bench.

He *set* the **glass** on the table.

For *sit* and *set*, you need to know not only the *present*, the *past*, and the *past participle*, but also the *present participle*.

Present	Present Participle	Past	Past Participle
sit	sitting	sat	sat
set	setting	set	set

RULE 3. (*Lend, borrow*)
Use *borrow* when you mean "to *get* the use of something"; use *lend* when you mean "to *give* the use of something."

May I *borrow* your pencil?

I'll *lend* you my pen.

NEVER say, "Will you *borrow* me some notebook paper?"

LEARNING ACTIVITIES IN TELLING CONFUSING PAIRS APART

A. (1) Copy these sentences, choosing the proper verb from each parentheses. (2) Before choosing the verbs in parentheses, be sure to *proofread for careless errors in copying.* (3) Exchange papers for checking as the sentences are read aloud.

1. (Lend, Borrow) me your pencil, please.
2. Jack (sat, set) the telephone down gently.
3. In which seat were you (sitting, setting)?
4. Who (learned, taught) you that song?
5. Will you (lend, borrow) me a dime?
6. Tom should have (set, sat) the box upon the desk.
7. A good teacher can (teach, learn) pupils to like school.
8. How long shall I (sit, set) here?
9. Our teacher (taught, learned) us a new poem today.
10. This pen was (borrowed, lent) to me by my cousin.

B. In your small groups, take turns giving sentences that use these confusing pairs of verbs. First each student should give a sentence using *learn* or *learned,* and then one using *teach* or *taught.* Continue with *sit, sat, sitting; set, setting; lend, lent;* and *borrow, borrowed.* Listen carefully to be sure that the proper form is used each time.

C. Answer in complete sentences the following questions, using the proper verb forms. Make this an oral activity.

1. Where did you set the books?
2. Why did the dog sit in the sun?
3. Have you ever sat all evening watching television?
4. Which room did Grandmother sit in?
5. When was the last time you set the table?
6. Where did you sit in the theater?
7. What did you set on the desk?
8. Why were the flowers set on the window sill?
9. Who sat behind you last year?
10. When did you set the chairs around the table?

D. With a partner, take turns giving sentences using the three pairs of confusing verbs. Continue to practice until you are sure of yourself.

Chapter Review*

A. Copy the following sentences, underlining twice each verb. Some of the verbs are one-word verbs; some of the verbs have two or more

---

* Check Test 2 should be taken at this point. If the results show need for further study, students should do this review practice. They should then take Mastery Test 2.

words. Some sentences have separated parts, and some are questions. Read carefully. *Do not write in this book.*

1. The organ grinder has a monkey.
2. Three planes have flown over our house today.
3. What is Joe building in the basement?
4. The actors had been studying their parts.
5. Has your brother ever been given a part in a play?
6. The rain must not have soaked into the ground.
7. Where did Mother send you for the groceries?
8. Jim's new fishing pole was almost lost in the pond.
9. Hasn't Betty told you the way to the library?
10. Father must not have been ready for dinner.
11. Mince pie couldn't have been his favorite dessert.
12. Does your bicycle have balloon tires?
13. The other car was a red convertible.
14. Where might the boys have gone for help?
15. Bob had not been studying in his usual corner.

B. Go over these sentences, choosing the proper forms from the parentheses. Read the sentences aloud in your small groups. Listen to hear the standard forms.

1. Have you (spoke, spoken) to Henry yet?
2. I (saw, seen) the accident happen.
3. We should have (begun, began) the meeting on time.
4. What have you (did, done) with the paper?
5. New officers will be (chose, chosen) today.
6. I (borrowed, lent) my pencil to Mary.
7. Did you (sit, set) near the front of the auditorium?
8. Have you (knew, known) Mr. White long?
9. Who (learned, taught) you that trick?
10. The show (began, begun) exactly on time.
11. The vase had been (sat, set) carefully on a shelf.
12. Spanish is (spoke, spoken) in Mexico.
13. Father would have (knew, known) the answer.
14. Maybe the game has not yet (began, begun).
15. Who (did, done) the work on this ship model?
16. Was Dean (setting, sitting) beside you?
17. Frank could have (spoke, spoken) more clearly.
18. You should have (did, done) something about this request.
19. Robert (knew, knowed) me a long time ago.
20. Has anyone (saw, seen) Fred this morning?
21. Susan was (chose, chosen) as class representative.
22. Will Marilyn (borrow, lend) me her bike?
23. That package has (set, sat) there for a week.
24. Mrs. Darrow (learned, taught) us that poem in one day.
25. The rain must have (began, begun) during the night.

CAPITALIZATION

Copy these sentences, supplying needed capital letters.

1. Is it true that lindblom high school of chicago, illinois, is the only high school in the middle west to play football in the south?
2. Whenever grandfather comes to our house, mother gets out his favorite book, *the adventures of huckleberry finn.* he likes to sit in the sun just south of the lilac bush and read.
3. Last august mr. i. r. smith, who teaches french and latin in our high school, and coach lambert took a trip to georgian bay.
4. That little store on garnett street is now owned by j. jones. He calls it jones's general store.
5. He spoke at great length about what god means to christians.

PUNCTUATION

Copy these sentences, supplying needed punctuation.

1. No the Los Angeles Dodgers didnt lose the World Series in 1963
2. Have you Dick ever heard of Dr David Livingstone What a man he was
3. Fred said that he saw a ship flying a blue yellow and white flag off Miami Florida on June 12 1964
4. When it looks like rain Mr P A Bailey always wears hip boots
5. This team exclaimed Al lacks pep makes errors and cant hit

SENTENCE SENSE

(1) Number your paper from 1 to 5; then read each of the following groups of words. (2) If a group is a sentence, write an *S* on your paper after the corresponding number. (3) If it is a sentence fragment, write *F*. (4) If it is a run-on sentence, write *RO*. (5) Make sentences out of the fragments and run-ons.

1. Ten of us boys will be busy tomorrow.
2. Going to the ball game in the afternoon and to the beach.
3. All the boys on the basketball team.
4. Most of the other boys in our class will be taking a field trip they probably won't be back until after nine o'clock.
5. After the game, we'll eat hamburgers and then go to the motion picture at the Tivoli.

SPELLING

Copy the following words in a column on a sheet of paper. Beside each word write another word made from it by adding a suffix. These words are spelled by rules.

1. beat	4. time	7. pity	10. cool	13. easy
2. carry	5. swat	8. bake	11. step	14. use
3. enter	6. healthy	9. warn	12. begin	15. fit

Word Games to Test Your Thinking

GET THE HINT

All the words defined below rhyme with *hint*.

1. The place money is coined
2. To spring or leap
3. To close the eyes partly
4. A thin strip of wood
5. To form letters
6. Flash or gleam
7. Fluff of any material
8. Any one of the Fisher five
9. Color
10. Stone used in arrowheads

A WORD SQUARE

Each of the four words defined below has four letters in it. Placed one under another, the words will spell the same down as across.

1. A sharp nail on the foot of an animal
2. Crippled
3. The close of a prayer
4. Past tense of *go*

BEHEADING PUZZLE

A CITY IN INDIANA

Behead the following, and the letters beheaded, when placed in order, will spell the name of a city in Indiana. *Example:* Behead *not happy* and leave *a public notice.* (*sad—ad;* the letter would be *s.*)

1. Behead *to run away with a lover* and leave *an easy stride.*
2. Behead *valleys* and leave *light-colored beers.*
3. Behead *nearly* and leave *a boxing match.*
4. Behead *at no time* and leave *at all times.*
5. Behead *a backless seat for one person* and leave *an instrument.*
6. Behead *sells* and leave *finishes.*
7. Behead *a standard of perfection* and leave *to distribute cards.*
8. Behead *a shelf-like projection* and leave *a border or margin.*
9. Behead *to gain knowledge* and leave *to gain by labor.*
10. Behead *a hard, heavy wood* and leave *consisting chiefly of bone.*

WOULD YOU LIKE TO KNOW—?

Find the answers the encyclopedia gives to the following questions.

1. What causes the humming that gives the *hummingbird* its name?
2. Is the *hawk* related to the eagle?
3. How did the *Hessian fly* get its name?
4. What is unusual about the legs of the *hyena*?

A "LUCKY" CROSSWORD PUZZLE

Copy the crossword puzzle. *Do not write in this book.*

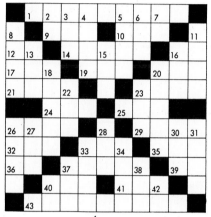

Across

1. A U-shaped lucky piece.
9. Fifteen ......'s for the team.
10. ......s grow from acorns.
12. Preposition.
14. A ...... in your shoe for luck.
16. Virginia (*abbr.*).
17. A bloodhound is ......-eared.
19. A ...... is man's best friend.
20. Nickname for *Mildred*.
21, 23. .... clover.
24. Furrow made by vehicles.
25. The wrong kind of luck.
26. Baking-part of a stove.
29. To go by something.
32. Atmosphere.
33. A ship's distress signal.
35. Allow.
36. Rhode Island (*abbr.*).
37. Opening in a fence (*plural*).
39. Preposition.
40. Girl's name—mixed up *Nan*.
41. At or near the middle.
43. Good-luck birds.

Down

2. Conjunction.
3. To knock.
4. A rude structure built for shelter, storage, etc.
5. That which is sung.
6. Cut and dried grass.
7. Okay (*abbr.*).
8. Offspring of a cow.
11. One of two equal parts.
13. Also.
15. Negative adverb.
16. By way of.
18. Comparative degree of *pure*.
20. A flat piece of metal given as an award.
22. Present tense of *ran*.
23. Take up liquid with the tongue.
26. Rowing implements.
27. Lucky number (*Roman numerals*).
28. A small bed.
30. To place.
31. Halt.
33. Of sound mind.
34. Prefix meaning *half*.
37. African antelope.
38. A title of respect used in addressing a man.
40. Man's nickname.
42. Doctor of Divinity (*abbr.*).

USING NOUNS IN BUILDING SENTENCES *

1. Recognizing Nouns

"CAN YOU THINK OF SOME NOUNS?"

"NOW'N' THEN I SWIM.
NOW'N' THEN I PLAY BALL.
NOW'N' THEN I WATCH
TELEVISION."

THINK IT OVER...

What do *you* know about nouns?

You have learned that a verb is one of the two most important words that you use. The other is the *noun*. It and the verb are two of what are known as the "parts of speech." You will learn other parts of speech as you study this book.

*Pretest 3 should be taken at this point.

1. **(DEFINITION)** *Nouns* are "name" words. They meet certain tests:

    a) **A noun fits into one or both of these "slot" sentences:**

        He wrote something about ....

        He wrote something about a (an) ....

    EXAMPLES: He wrote something about **money.**

                 He wrote something about a **friend.**

                 He wrote something about an **island.**

    b) **A noun can change its form so that it means more than one:** house, houses; box, boxes; man, men.

    c) **A noun can take special signal words (*markers*) before it:**

a book	**some** idea	**ten** cars	**my** luck
the news	**any** day	**that** face	**first** job

    Such "noun markers" are known as "determiners." You will study them in Chapter 17 and Chapter 18.

2. **The nouns easiest to recognize name** (1) PERSONS, **such as** *boy, soldier;* (2) PLACES, **such as** *school, church, town, farm;* **or** (3) THINGS, **such as** *book, dog, table, pie, tree.*

    NOTE: The part of speech of a word is determined by the way that it is used. For instance, *hit* is sometimes a verb:

        The boy *hit* the ball. [*Hit* shows action.]

    But in this sentence, *hit* is used as a noun:

        His *hit* was a double. [*Hit* is the name of something.]

LEARNING ACTIVITIES IN RECOGNIZING AND USING NOUNS

A. List all the nouns in this paragraph. Exchange papers for checking.

    Four playful dogs, followed by a crowd of laughing children, ran out of the yard. Each boy carried a box or a parcel, and each girl had an empty pail or a basket. These young people were going to the woods to gather walnuts. The boys were carrying the lunch. The merry party entered the woods, laughing and shouting. Even the dogs seemed excited, chasing squirrels and chipmunks through the trees.

B. In an oral activity, tell how you know that the italicized "nonsense" words in the following sentences are used as nouns.

    1. The *flibbider* gave us some *calooches.*

    2. *Rikbligs* usually like a *gruggle* on their *smirzes.*

    3. The first *prokle* made some *zilzies* out of a *bamgan.*

* For information about possessive nouns, see page 162.

C. (1) Go over these sentences in class, deciding what each italicized word is, a noun or a verb. (2) Write sentences using each of the following words, first as a verb and then as a noun: *work, ring, fight, train, change.* (3) Compare work in class or in your small groups.

1. The *park* is not open today.
2. Where did you *park* the car?
3. *Face* the class as you talk.
4. Jack's *face* was covered with mud.
5. Shall we *run* to school?
6. That *run* won the game for us.
7. The *match* burned my fingers.
8. Your shoes and mine *match*.
9. Do your parents *baby* you?
10. The *baby* soon went to sleep.

D. Copy the following paragraph, filling each blank with a noun. Read your paragraphs in class. Note how differently they turned out!

As soon as I knew that I was alone, I opened the .... Inside, I found some surprising things. One of the strangest was a...... with a ...... on one end. Near it were three shiny ...... decorated with little .... I was about to open one of them when I heard a ...... behind me. I turned around and saw two huge ...... with ...... in their .... They gave me a ......, took my ......, and then disappeared through the ....

LEARNING MORE ABOUT NOUNS

Most nouns are easy to recognize because they name things that you can see or touch. Other nouns are less easy to recognize.

● THESE ARE FACTS ABOUT NOUNS: II

3. **Some nouns name things that you cannot see or touch:** *honesty, happiness, beauty, courage, loyalty,* **for example.**

4. **Most nouns can be classed as "count" nouns; that is, they can be counted:** *one book, two books, many books.* **Some nouns, however, are "mass" nouns; they are not ordinarily countable.** *Spinach* is an example, for you are not likely to say *one spinach.*

   Use the marking words *a* (or *an*) and *many* to test whether a word is a mass noun. If those markers do not fit, you have a mass noun. Would you say, for example, "a spinach"? "many spinach (*or* spinaches)"? No; therefore *spinach* is a mass noun.

5. **Each noun covered by points 1 and 2, page 309, is called a** *common noun,* **because it refers to** *any* **member in its general group. Words that name** *special* **members of a general group are** *proper nouns.* (To review their capitalization, see page 144.)

Common Nouns	Proper Nouns
girl	Martha
organization	Boy Scouts
street	Magee Street
city	Jefferson City

Learn about words!

The following words, taken from *A* of the Learning Activities, have interesting histories. Use your dictionary to find the story behind each word. With which word is the drawing connected?

blanket　　　　barn　　　　chair　　　　yacht

LEARNING ACTIVITIES IN SPECIAL TYPES OF NOUNS

A. All words in the following list are nouns. Copy the ones naming things that you cannot see or touch. Exchange papers for checking.

1. apple	6. kindness	11. silence	16. blanket
2. strength	7. cowardice	12. radio	17. tool
3. wickedness	8. bravery	13. duty	18. chair
4. telephone	9. star	14. freedom	19. fun
5. barn	10. sunrise	15. snow	20. yacht

B. Make two columns on your paper. Label one column *Count Nouns;* the other, *Mass Nouns.* By applying the marker tests (*a, an, many*), put each noun in these sentences into the right column. Compare lists in class.

1. The music to that song was composed by my uncle.
2. Every farmer in our community harvested a large crop of wheat.
3. Lightning struck the building but did no damage to the machinery inside.
4. With the money the boy bought a new tire for his bicycle.
5. My sister would like celery on the table at every meal.
6. Scenery along this road gives a person a chance to use his camera.
7. Was this rice cooked in milk, or in water?
8. To that man, grass is always greener on the other side of the fence.
9. My cousin had little luck with his latest scientific experiment.
10. His favorite food was spaghetti but now is pizza.

C. Here are quotations from famous authors. (1) Take turns at reading the lines aloud. (2) Call upon someone to name the nouns in the lines read. (3) The listeners should be ready to comment on the reading.

1. The day is done, and the darkness
    Falls from the wings of Night,
   As a feather is wafted downward
    From an eagle in his flight.—Henry Wadsworth Longfellow
2. The brightest blade grows dim with rust,
    The fairest meadow white with snow.—Oliver Wendell Holmes
3. The winds were yelling, the waves were swelling,
    The sky was black and drear,
   When the crew with eyes of flame brought the ship without a name
    Alongside the last Buccaneer.—Thomas Babington Macaulay

4. Small feet were pattering, wooden shoes clattering,
   Little hands clapping and little tongues chattering,
   And, like fowls in a farmyard when barley is scattering,
   Out came the children running.—ROBERT BROWNING
5. Four gray walls, and four gray towers
   Overlook a space of flowers.—TENNYSON
6. All in a hot and copper sky,
      The bloody sun, at noon,
   Right up above the mast did stand,
      No bigger than the moon.—COLERIDGE
7. The key turns, and the door upon its hinges groans.—KEATS
8. And on the bay the moonlight lay,
   And the shadow of the moon.—COLERIDGE
9. Spanish sailors with bearded lips,
      And the beauty and mystery of the ships,
         And the magic of the sea.—LONGFELLOW

ENRICHMENT

Choose one of the nouns named as examples in point 3, page 310. Write a paragraph explaining what that particular word means to you. The Guides for Writing a Paragraph, page 214, will help you.

2. Using Nouns as Subjects

"OH NO! MARK, NOT LARRY, HIT A HOME RUN IN THAT GAME."

"THERE YOU GO—ALWAYS TRYING TO CHANGE THE SUBJECT!"

1. **(DEFINITION)** The *simple subject** in a sentence is the *main word* that tells *who* or *what* about the verb.

   The little white **dog** ran down the street.

2. **(DEFINITION)** The *complete subject* is *all* the words in the sentence that together tell *who* or *what* about the verb.

   The little white dog ran down the street.

   The little white dog **may be called a** "noun cluster."

3. **(DEFINITION)** The *simple predicate*† is the *verb*.

   The little white dog **ran** down the street.

4. **(DEFINITION)** The *complete predicate* is *all* the words in the sentence that together tell something that the subject *is* or *does*.

   The little white dog **ran down the street.**

   Ran down the street **may be called a** "verb cluster."

5. To find the subject, first find the verb. The word that answers *who* or *what* about the verb is the subject.

   The boy hit the ball. (The verb is *hit*.)
   Who or *what* hit? *boy* (*Boy* is the subject.)
   <u>boy</u> <u>hit</u>

The **boy** hit the ball.

---

* In this book the term *subject* when used alone refers to the *simple subject*.
† In this book the term *predicate* when used alone refers to the *simple predicate*; that is, the *verb*, sometimes called the *predicate verb*.

LEARNING ACTIVITIES IN VERBS AND THEIR SUBJECTS

A. Copy the following sentences, underlining with one line the *complete subject* and with two lines the *complete predicate*. Exchange papers for checking.

1. Tickets for the operetta will go on sale tomorrow.
2. Both boys build model trains.
3. My dog has very good manners.
4. The girls from our room walked slowly down the stairs.
5. Mrs. Baker bought two dozen oranges.
6. The horses climbed slowly to the top of the mountain.
7. Martha was playing shuffleboard with three friends.
8. Johnny took his little sister Patty to the basketball game.
9. That man is an electrician.
10. Sharon went with her mother to the grocery store.

B. (1) Write the headings *Subject* and *Verb* on the blackboard. (2) Go over the following sentences in class. Locate the verb first; write it under the verb heading. Then ask, *"Who or What ... ?"* to locate the subject (simple subject); write it under the subject heading.

EXAMPLE: The boy hit the ball.

Subject	Verb
boy	hit

1. My younger brother is a Cub Scout.
2. The heavy snow blocked the road past our farm.
3. My best friend moved away.
4. Our doctor hired a new nurse.
5. Irene helped with the plans for the Halloween party.
6. The wind howled around the corners of the house.
7. Most people like this town.
8. Beautiful flowers bloomed in the meadow.
9. My favorite uncle comes to our house often.
10. A terrible storm raged through the valley.
11. Mother went into the house.
12. This letter arrived before breakfast.

C. If you missed any of the verbs and subjects in *B*, use *C* and *D*, pages 281–82, for more practice. (1) Copy the sentences. (2) Underline each verb with two lines and each subject with one line. (3) Exchange papers for checking.

D. (1) Copy the sentences on page 315, supplying subjects to complete the meaning. Use *exact* nouns, not general ones such as *boy, man, animal*. (See the guides on page 343.) Write each sentence neatly. (2) When you have finished, read the sentences aloud. Notice how each sentence picture changes with the different subjects used by the class.

1. The little .... lay hidden in the forest.
2. Several .... whizzed past.
3. The .... fell to the floor with a crash.
4. A .... came softly into the room.
5. The .... tasted delicious.
6. The .... changed our plans.
7. This .... is new.
8. A huge .... flew overhead.
9. That .... looks expensive.
10. The .... belongs to my brother.

E. Write an original paragraph to show that you know how to use verbs and subjects in sentences. (1) Choose a topic from any that you have listed in your notebook, one suggested by the drawing on this page, or one from those listed under "Topics" in the Index. Use at least six sentences. The Guides for Writing a Paragraph, page 214, will help you. (2) Exchange papers with a partner. (3) In the paragraph that you receive, underline each verb with two lines and each subject with one line. (4) Go over your paper with the one who checked it. Call attention to errors in spelling, capitalization, and punctuation as well as in underlining.

MORE ABOUT VERBS AND SUBJECTS

As is explained in Chapter 14, page 275, the normal sentence order in the English language has the subject followed by the verb. Not all sentences, however, are so arranged. If they were, the English language would be far less interesting than it is. The following points will help you to find the subject in sentences that do not follow normal sentence order.

6. **Sometimes a sentence will be turned around. Such a sentence is said to be in "inverted order."**

   > Down the street ran the little white dog.

   The rule for finding the subject still holds.
   a) Find the verb. It is a doing word, *ran*.
   b) Ask, *"Who* or *What* ran?" *Dog* ran; so *dog* is the subject.

7. **Sometimes a sentence is a question.** (For help with finding the verb in a question, review point 13, page 286.)

   > Is Jane going with us?

   In this sentence the verb is *is going. Who* or *what* is going? *Jane* is going; so *Jane* is the subject.

8. **Sometimes a sentence begins with an introductory** *there.* Do not be fooled into thinking that it is the subject.

   > *There* has been a change in our plans.

   The verb is *has been. Who* or *what* has been? *Change* has been; so *change* is the subject.

9. **Sometimes a sentence that is not a question may have words separating the parts of a verb.** (For help with finding the verb when the parts are separated, see point 12 on page 286.)

   > The boys have not yet finished their work.

   The verb is *have finished. Who* or *what* have finished? *Boys* have finished; so *boys* is the subject.

10. **Sometimes words separate the subject and the verb.**

    > A box of Jonathan apples came today.

    The verb is *came. Who* or *what* came? At first you might say *apples.* If you stop to think about it, you will realize that what came is a *box,* although it is true that the box had apples in it. Therefore *box* is the subject. *

LEARNING ACTIVITIES IN FINDING VERBS AND THEIR SUBJECTS

A. The sentences in this activity are like those above. Remember that if the verb has two words, the first will be a helping verb. If it has three or more words, all but the last of them will be helping verbs. Any verb after the helping verbs will be a doing verb. The figure in parentheses tells how

---

*"Of Jonathan apples" is the kind of word group called a *prepositional phrase.* You will study such phrases on pages 435–43.

many words the verb has. (1) Copy the sentences, underlining each verb with two lines and each subject with one line. (2) *Proofread for careless errors in copying.* (3) Exchange papers for checking. (4) Go over the sentences orally.

1. Near the end of September came several bad storms. (1)
2. Has Alfred been doing good work? (3)
3. The boys were not expecting visitors. (2)
4. The man left a keg of nails on the doorstep. (1)
5. There may be a slight delay. (2)
6. The wind had just died down. (2)
7. In a little cabin on Bear Mountain lived two old women. (1)
8. How can the Boy Scouts raise money for their camp? (2)
9. A box of books was lying on the teacher's desk. (2)
10. The Browns have often visited Yellowstone Park. (2)
11. In *The Animal World* Fred found two chapters about snakes. (1)
12. A gift of flowers pleases most women. (1)
13. Does your school have a holiday before the end of the month? (2)
14. Which detective solved this case? (1)
15. The committee has set the time for the picnic at last. (2)
16. Hasn't the father of those boys bought a new car? (2)
17. On the table lay the tickets to the game. (1)
18. Did your uncle play football in college? (2)
19. Those three albums of records must have pleased Mrs. Scott. (3)
20. There might be a good reason for Joe's absence. (2)

B. If you need more practice in selecting verbs and subjects, use the sentences in *A* and *B*, page 287. Make this an oral activity.

Spot Review   ★

(*Based upon the sentences in A of the preceding activities*)
1. Why is *September* capitalized in sentence 1? Why is *Boy Scouts* capitalized in sentence 8?
2. Why is *The Animal World* italicized in sentence 11?
3. Account for the apostrophe in sentence 9; in sentence 16.

USING ENGLISH IN ALL CLASSES

Look over papers that you have written for other classes. Do all the sentences have the subject first and then the verb? If they have, change a few of them so that the verb will come before the subject. Then read your papers in your small groups to see whether in your classmates' opinion the changes are an improvement.

3. Recognizing a Sentence Pattern

As explained in Chapter 14, English is a patterned language. How many sentence patterns do you think it has?

Well, every day you speak many sentences. So do other people: in your school, your town, your state, and all over the country. If you stop to think of all those sentences, you might easily guess that there must be millions—or at least thousands—of sentence patterns. You would be wrong, for you can count on your fingers the number of basic sentence patterns in English—and you would have fingers left over!

In this lesson you will study Pattern 1 sentences.

● THESE ARE FACTS ABOUT SUBJECTS AND PREDICATES: III

1. Pattern 1 sentences need only a *subject* and a *verb*.
>   EXAMPLES: Plants grow.   Rain fell.   Fish swim.

2. Pattern 1 sentences fit this formula: N (*noun*) + V (*verb*).
>   **N + V   N + V   N   +   V**
>   Plants grow.   Rain fell.   Accidents happen.

3. A Pattern 1 sentence may have other words in it.
>   **N + V**
>   EXAMPLE: Many tall **plants grow** in our garden.

4. A Pattern 1 sentence will not have in it a noun that completes the action of the verb. Look at this sentence:
>   The boy hit the ball.

That cannot be a Pattern 1 sentence, for the noun *ball* completes the action of the verb *hit*. (The boy did not just *hit;* he hit *something*.)

5. A Pattern 1 sentence will not have in it a noun that completes the verb and renames the subject.
>   The boy is my cousin.

That cannot be a Pattern 1 sentence, for the noun *cousin* completes the verb *is* and renames *boy,* the subject.

LEARNING ACTIVITIES IN PATTERN 1 SENTENCES

A. In an oral class activity, find all the Pattern 1 sentences in *A* and *B,* page 314. Tell why the others do not fit Pattern 1.

B. Fill out the following Pattern 1 sentences with details about the subject, the verb, or both. Keep the **N + V** pattern, however. Compare sentences in class or in your small groups.

EXAMPLE: Rain fell.
A soaking rain fell *here just after midnight.*

1. Birds sang.
2. Visitors arrived.
3. Days passed.
4. Thunder boomed.
5. Men work.

DIAGRAMMING VERBS AND SUBJECTS*

READ AND DISCUSS

A doctor analyzes a case of sickness; a detective analyzes a criminal case; a chemist analyzes drugs. If you want to feel sure about your speaking and writing, you should be able to analyze the sentences that you use. One way to analyze a sentence is to make a *diagram* of it.

As you go on with your study of grammar, you can learn how to diagram all the words in the sentences that you study. For the present, you need work only with the two necessary parts of any sentence: the *verb* and the *subject.*

STEPS IN DIAGRAMMING VERBS AND SUBJECTS

SENTENCE: "The boy hit the ball." *Hit* is the verb. *Boy* is the subject.

1. Draw a straight line, like this:
2. On the right-hand half, write the verb.
3. Draw a vertical line before the verb, extending the line through the horizontal line.
4. Write the subject in front of the vertical line.

*This section and all the following sections on diagramming can be used as a supplement to the teaching done earlier in the chapter. These sections on diagramming are so placed that they may be omitted without disturbing the sequence of instruction.

Look now at another sentence: "A new house will be built across the street." What is the verb? *will be built*. Put it into a diagram. *Who* or *what* will be built? *House* will be built; so *house* is the subject. Put it into the diagram.

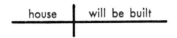

You have found and named the most important words in the sentence.

LEARNING ACTIVITIES IN DIAGRAMMING VERBS AND SUBJECTS

A. (1) Diagram the verb and the subject in the sentences that follow. Always find the verb *first*. (2) After you have diagrammed the verbs and subjects on paper, put the diagrams on the board. Explain the diagrams in some regular form: "The verb in this sentence is *hit,* and the subject is a noun, *boy.*" Form the habit of using a definite pattern for explaining diagrams. *Always go over diagrams orally.*

1. Then Father ran rapidly down the street.
2. The wind has been blowing hard.
3. The early settlers had many adventures.
4. The captives were taken to the bandit leader.
5. Four small boys were playing in the park on Elm Street.
6. My father has returned from Canada.
7. This team should win the pennant.
8. The roses were blooming in every garden.
9. Our club will meet in the new clubhouse.
10. Five pictures hung on the walls of the room.
11. The four children were waiting on the steps.
12. That first diver should win a medal.

B. For further practice in sentence analysis, diagram the verbs and subjects in the sentences in *B*, page 314.

DIAGRAMMING OTHER ARRANGEMENTS OF VERBS AND SUBJECTS

In the sentences that you have been diagramming, (1) the verb parts are not separated and (2) the verb comes immediately after the subject. On page 316 you saw five other arrangements of verbs and subjects. Whatever the arrangement of the verb and subject in a sentence may be, the pattern of the verb and the subject in a diagram always looks the same. Study the sentences and diagrams that follow.

Down the street ran Bob.

Bob	ran

Is Jane going with us?

Jane	Is going

There was silence in the room.

There | silence | was

(Since *there* is only an introductory word, it is diagrammed separately.)

The boys have not yet finished.

boys	have finished

The box of apples has come.

box	has come

LEARNING ACTIVITIES IN DIAGRAMMING VERBS AND SUBJECTS

A. (1) Diagram verbs and subjects in the sentences that follow. If you need help in locating subjects, review points 1–4 on page 316. (2) Have the diagrams put on the board. (3) Go over the diagrams orally, explaining in this way: "The verb in the sentence is *ran,* and the subject is a noun, *Bob.*"

1. Where was George going with that man?
2. Over the hill came the hunters.
3. There will be a short intermission.
4. This bushel of peaches should be canned at once.
5. A bucket of sand was put into the trunk of the car.
6. Will your father help with the plans for the rally?
7. Near the tree sat two gray squirrels.
8. The bark of both trees had been scarred by lightning.
9. Where did the girls go after school?
10. The plumbers have almost finished the repairs.
11. The days of the week pass rapidly.
12. Up the hill ran the boys.
13. Most members of our class listen carefully.
14. There has been a change in our plans.
15. Does Mary want that red coat?

B. (1) Diagram each verb and subject in *A,* page 317. Be sure to find the verb first. (2) Exchange papers. (3) Put the diagrams on the board. (4) Go over the diagrams orally.

4. Using Compound Verbs and Subjects

● THESE ARE FACTS ABOUT COMPOUND VERBS AND SUBJECTS

1. The subject of a sentence may have more than one verb.
   (DEFINITION) When the subject has two or more verbs, the sentence is said to have a *compound verb*.

   > The *boy* hit the ball and ran to first base.
   > The *boys* swam, fished, and rode their bicycles.

2. The verb in a sentence may have more than one subject.
   (DEFINITION) When the verb has two or more subjects, the sentence is said to have a *compound subject*.

   > Sally or Barbara *will do* the dishes.
   > The boys, their father, and their uncle *went* to the game.

3. A sentence may have both a compound verb and a compound subject.

   > Ann and Sue stopped and stared.

4. In a Pattern 1 sentence that has compound parts, the labels will be repeated.

   > **N   N   V   V**
   > Many days and nights came and went.

LEARNING ACTIVITIES IN COMPOUND VERBS AND SUBJECTS

A. (1) Copy the following paragraph. (2) Draw two lines under each part of a compound verb and one line under each part of a compound subject. (3) Exchange papers for checking. *Do not write in this book.*

The dog and the cat stood and glared at each other. Which enemy would strike first? Suddenly the cat raised its paw and swung. In a flash Spot turned and raced away. Now the cat crept up and teased Spot again. Spot seemingly paid no attention but suddenly sprang. Round went cat and dog in a fierce struggle. Finally the cat pulled away, dashed up the nearest tree, and was safe. Spot barked angrily for a time but then slunk off. Again, a cat had baffled him.

B. (1) Write ten sentences of your own in which you use compound subjects and compound verbs. (2) Exchange papers. (3) *Proofread first for careless errors the paper that you receive.* (4) Underline twice the compound verbs and once the compound subjects. (5) Correct any mistakes on your own paper when it has been returned.

ENRICHMENT

Here are quotations from Longfellow's long poem *Hiawatha*. Many of them have compound verbs or subjects; all are in inverted order. The poet has used it to give emphasis to a word or to achieve rhythm. Read the quotations aloud; then restate each one in normal sentence order. Note how different they sound, how much less rhythmical.

1. Round about the Indian village
   Spread the meadows and the cornfields.
2. On the air about him wildly
   Tossed and streamed his cloudy tresses.
3. Then up started Hiawatha,
   And with threatening look and gesture
   Laid his hand upon the black rock.
4. Like a ring of fire around him
   Blazed and fired the red horizon.
5. Down into that darksome cavern
   Plunged the headlong Hiawatha.
6. Weltering in the bloody water,
   Dead lay all the fiery serpents.
7. Winged with feathers, tipped with jasper,
   Swift flew Hiawatha's arrow.
8. At the feet of Hiawatha
   Lifeless lay the great Pearl-Feather.
9. In the Northland lived a hunter,
   With ten young and comely daughters.
10. On their pathway through the woodlands
    Lay an oak, by storms uprooted.
11. On the border of the forest,
    Underneath the fragrant pine trees,
    Sat the old men and the warriors
    Smoking in the pleasant shadow.
12. From the memory of the old men
    Pass away the great traditions,
    The achievements of the warriors,
    The adventures of the hunters.
13. Fearing not the Evil Spirits,
    Forth to hunt the deer with antlers
    All alone went Chibiabos.
14. Then in swift pursuit departed
    Hiawatha and the hunters
    On the trail of Pau-Puk-Keewis.
15. Through the forest, wide and wailing,
    Roamed the hunter on his snowshoes.
16. Homeward then went Hiawatha
    To the lodge of old Nokomis.

Diagramming Compound Subjects and Verbs

In diagramming compound subjects and verbs, each part of the compound should be put on a separate line. The conjunction should be written on the line joining the compound elements.

Compound Subject

Sally or *Barbara* will do the dishes.

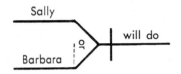

The *boys,* their *father,* and their *uncle* went to the game.

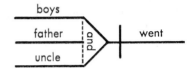

Compound Verb

The boy *hit* the ball and *ran* to first base.

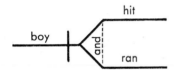

The boys *swam, fished,* and *rode* their bicycles.

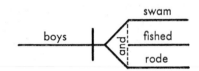

Compound Subject and Compound Verb

Ann and *Sue* **stopped** and **stared.**

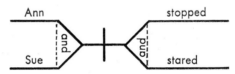

ACTIVITIES IN DIAGRAMMING COMPOUND VERBS AND SUBJECTS

A. (1) Diagram the subjects and the verbs in the following sentences. (2) After you have finished, put the diagrams on the board. (3) Explain each diagram orally in this way: "The verb is *will do;* the parts of the compound subject are the nouns *Sally* and *Barbara.*"

1. Jean hopped and skipped down the street.
2. Haven't Roy and Harry left for the game?
3. That private and his captain come from the same small town.
4. Jim or his brother cut the grass and trimmed the hedge.
5. Helen and Jack saw and heard the fire engine.
6. This car runs like a dream and doesn't use much gas.
7. Up the mountain climbed the cowboy and his horse.

8. The apples and the plums looked ripe and tasted delicious.
9. Hasn't Mother or Father seen your drawing?
10. The small boy and the dog ran outside.

B. On the blackboard, diagram the verbs and subjects in the sentences of the paragraph in *A*, page 322. Two of the sentences have neither compound subjects nor verbs. Go over each diagram orally.

(*Based upon the sentences in* A *of the preceding activities*)
1. Why are *captain* and *private* not capitalized in sentence 3?
2. Why are *Mother* and *Father* capitalized in sentence 9?
3. Explain the use of the apostrophes in sentences 2, 6, and 9.
4. How would you write the plurals of the subjects in sentence 2?

5. Using Nouns as Predicate Nominatives

THINK IT OVER . . .

How *is* the proper noun "Mary" used in the sentence?
What is the relationship between *girl* and *Mary*?

On pages 318–19, you studied Pattern 1 sentences (N+V). In this lesson you will learn to recognize Pattern 2 sentences, which are ones that have nouns used as *predicate nominatives*.

1. **People, animals, and things often have more than one name to explain or identify them, as in these examples.**

> Mr. Jones is a carpenter.
> Mr. Jones is a hard worker.
> Mr. Jones is my uncle.

Note that each of the nouns in red follows the verb and is another name word applied to the subject, *Mr. Jones.*

2. **(DEFINITION) A noun that follows the verb and renames the subject is a** *predicate nominative,* **or** *predicate noun.*

3. **The verb in a sentence having a predicate nominative can always be replaced by the word** *equals.*

> Mr. Jones *equals* a carpenter.
> Mr. Jones *equals* a hard worker.
> Mr. Jones *equals* my uncle.

4. **(DEFINITION) Verbs that join a subject and a predicate nominative are called** *linking verbs.* **They are verbs of** (*a*) *being,* (*b*) *seeming,* **or** (*c*) *condition.* **The commonest linking verbs are** *am, is, are, was, were, be, being, been, become, seem.*

> *George Washington* was our first *President.*
> *John F. Kennedy* became *President* in 1960.
> *Betty* seems a friendly *girl.*

5. **A sentence that has a predicate nominative is a** *Pattern 2* **sentence. The formula for it is N + LV + N.**

> **N + LV + N**
> Those two boys are cousins.

6. **Predicate nominatives may be compound.**

> My favorite desserts are pie, cake, and ice cream.

The formula for that sentence is **N + LV + N, N, N.**

ACTIVITIES IN FINDING AND USING PREDICATE NOMINATIVES

A. Go quickly around the room, having each person suggest a predicate nominative for one of the four following sentences. List on the board all the predicate nominatives suggested.

1. That dog is ....   3. That man must be ....
2. My father was once ....   4. My favorite flower is the ....

B. (1) Copy the following sentences. (2) Put parentheses around each predicate nominative. (3) Go over each sentence orally when you have finished, naming the verb and the subject and the predicate nominative.

1. Lewis Carroll is the author of *Alice's Adventures in Wonderland*.
2. Mr. Roberts has been our friend and neighbor for years.
3. Mark Brown may be our next principal.
4. Benedict Arnold became a traitor to his country.
5. Was the location of the mine a secret?
6. Ralph should have been the captain of the team.
7. The first arrivals at the party were Joe, Wayne, and Harry.
8. Usually Mr. Evans seems a happy man.
9. Abraham Lincoln became President in 1860.
10. The state flower of Texas is the bluebonnet.

C. (1) Look at the illustration on page 315. (2) Write six sentences, using as predicate nominatives persons or things that you see illustrated there. Make two of them fit the formula **N + LV + N, N.** (3) Exchange papers with a partner. (4) On his paper, draw two lines under verbs and one line under subjects. Put parentheses around predicate nominatives. (5) Go over your work in class.

DIAGRAMMING PREDICATE NOMINATIVES

You are ready now to learn where to put the predicate nominative in a diagram.

Mary is my *sister*.

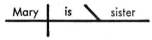

Notice that the predicate nominative is placed on the line with the subject and the verb. This line you will think of as the *back-bone* of any sentence, because it contains the really important words. Notice, too, that the line separating the predicate nominative from the verb is slanted. It points back to the subject to show that the predicate nominative means the same as the subject. The slanted line does not cross the base line.

Here are diagrams of *compound* predicate nominatives.

The winner will be *Joe* or *Fred*.

Fruits in season now are *pears, peaches,* and *plums.*

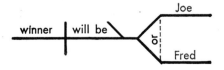 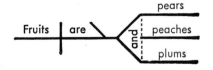

A. Diagram verbs, subjects, and predicate nominatives in the following sentences. Put them upon the board when you have finished. Go over the diagrams orally, giving each part its correct name.

1. That man is my uncle.
2. Our best players are Ollie and Gary.
3. Llamas are the sheep of the Andes.
4. The first prize was a trip to Hawaii.
5. Gold is a valuable mineral.
6. Paul has been my friend for a long time.
7. The signal will be one blast of the whistle.
8. Was Mr. Barnes ever a member of Congress?
9. My favorite sports are baseball, golf, and track.
10. Tom could have been president of his class.

B. For further practice, use the sentences in *B,* page 327. Explain the diagrams orally in your small groups.

6. Using Nouns as Direct Objects

The term "direct object" may be new to you. Nouns, you have learned, may be used as subjects of verbs and as predicate nominatives. Another common use of nouns is as objects of a verb, or *direct objects,* as they are also called. They are found in Pattern 3 sentences, which you will study in this lesson.

---

* The uses of nouns as objects of prepositions and as indirect objects are covered on pages 436 and 445.

1. **(DEFINITION)** A direct object names the person or thing to which the subject does something.

   The boy hit the **ball**.   The boys built a **clubhouse**.

2. To find the direct object in any sentence having an action verb, say the subject and the verb, followed by *whom* or *what*. The noun that answers the question is the direct object.

   Boy **hit** whom or what? ball   *Boys* **built** what? clubhouse

3. If no word answers the question *whom* or *what,* you know that the sentence does not have a direct object.

   The dog barked loudly.

   Did he bark anything? No; *loudly* tells only *how* he barked.

4. **(DEFINITION)** A verb that has a direct object is a *transitive** verb.

   The boy hit the *ball*.   The boys built a *clubhouse*.

   "Hit" and "built" are *transitive* verbs.

5. A sentence with a direct object is a *Pattern 3* sentence. The formula is **N + V + N.**

       N + V + N   **N + V + N**
       Jim saves his money.   My sister likes her new job.

6. Direct objects may be compound.

   Mother raises **ducks** and **geese**.
   Our team defeated **Wayne, Dixon, Laurel,** and **Tilden**.
   The formula for the second example is **N + V + N, N, N.**

The boy hit the **ball**.

---

* An advanced study of transitive and intransitive verbs is presented in later books of the Basic Language series.

Learn about words!

The following words, taken from *B* of the Learning Activities, have interesting histories. Use your dictionary to find the story behind each word.

athlete   waltzes   thimble   gas

LEARNING ACTIVITIES IN FINDING AND USING DIRECT OBJECTS

A. Copy the following sentences, supplying a direct object for each blank. *Do not write in this book.* In class, read your sentences orally. Note how the different direct objects change the sentence picture.

1. My little brother lost his ....
2. Yesterday Jack found a ....
3. Uncle Edward bought some ....
4. The package contained a ....
5. For his birthday Jim received some ....
6. On his farm Mr. Jackson raises ....

B. Locate the direct objects in the following sentences. Find the verb and the subject first. Then, so that you may be sure that you are selecting the right word, say the subject and the verb, followed by *whom* or *what*. Make this an oral exercise in your small groups.

1. Mother has lost her silver thimble.
2. Mary surely will help her sister.
3. Mr. Jones bought a new tractor and a secondhand hayrack.
4. The burglar stole my typewriter.
5. Robert Louis Stevenson wrote *Kidnapped* and *The Black Arrow.*
6. Mother baked beans, rolls, and a pie for dinner.
7. Johann Strauss composed many beautiful waltzes.
8. The athletes enjoyed their visit to Mexico.
9. Queen Victoria ruled England for sixty-four years.
10. Does this furnace burn gas?

C. (1) Write ten Pattern 3 sentences of your own. Use compound objects in at least two sentences; write their formula above them. You might write sentences having to do with your spare-time activities. The illustrations on page 331 may suggest ideas. (2) Exchange papers with a classmate and ask him to name each verb, subject, and direct object. (3) Go over your partner's paper with him.

D. For further drill in finding direct objects, use the sentences in *A,* page 317. Seven of them have no direct objects. What is the pattern of those seven sentences? Make this an oral activity.

(*Based upon the sentences in* B *of the preceding activities*)

1. Explain the abbreviation in sentence 3.
2. What is the reason for italics in sentence 5?
3. Give the rule for spelling the plural of *waltz* in sentence 7.
4. Explain the capital letters and the hyphen in sentence 9.

Diagramming Direct Objects

Direct objects are diagrammed similarly to the way that predicate nominatives are diagrammed. See whether you can tell the only difference.

The boy hit the *ball*.

| boy | hit | ball |

The direct object is placed on the line with the subject and the verb. So is a predicate nominative. Notice, though, that the line between the verb and the direct object is perpendicular, not slanted. This perpendicular line meets the base line but does not cross it.

Here are diagrams of *compound* direct objects.

Mother raises *ducks* and *geese*.   Our team defeated *Wayne, Dixon, Laurel,* and *Tilden*.

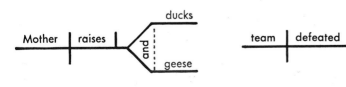

331

A. Diagram verbs, subjects, and any direct objects in the following sentences. Two sentences have predicate nominatives, not direct objects. Diagram them also. Go over the diagrams orally when you have finished.

1. Father has bought a tweed coat and a sleeveless sweater.
2. Have the boys finished their work?
3. My father was once the owner of a restaurant.
4. Our neighbors are building a house.
5. That child needs glasses.
6. One boy in our class has had measles, mumps, and chicken pox.
7. Rodney sold ten tickets in a very short time.
8. Your song will be the first number on the program.
9. The farmers are cutting their wheat, oats, rye, and barley now.
10. Little Bopeep has lost her sheep.

B. Diagram the verb, the subject, and the direct object in the sentences in *B,* page 330.

7. Using Nouns as Appositives

"WHAT'S AN APPOSITIVE?"

"TAKE A LOOK AT PAGE 153. THAT'LL TELL YOU!"

READ AND DISCUSS

Are *you* sure what an appositive is? If not, you, too, should turn back to Rule 4 on page 153.

What do appositives and predicate nouns have in common? How are they different? Which italicized word is which in the following sentence?

Our milkman, *Mr. Greer,* is a jolly *man.*

● THESE ARE FACTS ABOUT APPOSITIVES

1. **Appositives are set next to, or near, the words with which they are in apposition; that is, the words that they explain or identify.** In the example above, *Mr. Greer* (the appositive) comes right after *milkman* (the noun that it explains).

2. **Most appositives are set off by commas or a comma.**

    A new teacher **,John Dean ,**has been hired.
    This dish is my favorite dessert **,shortcake.**

    If the appositive is used in a group of words, the entire expression is set off.

    Jean's father **,a tall man with a friendly smile ,**met us.
    Don won the award **, a trip to Hawaii.**

3. **Appositives may be compound.**

    Mary received two gifts, a **ring** and a **watch.**

4. **Appositives should not be confused with predicate nominatives.** Remember, a predicate nominative completes a linking verb.

    John, my *brother,* came early. (*appositive*)
    John is my *brother.* (*predicate nominative*)

5. **Often an appositive helps to make one smooth sentence out of two short, choppy sentences.** (See also guide 4, page 453.)

    Glen is a careful driver. He does not take chances.
    Glen, a careful *driver,* does not take chances.

LEARNING ACTIVITIES IN FINDING AND USING APPOSITIVES

A. In the following sentences, find the appositives and tell where commas are needed to set them off, or to set off the group of words containing the appositives. Make this an oral activity.

1. Rome the capital of Italy is also its largest city.
2. A city on the equator is Quito the capital of Ecuador.
3. Paris the capital and largest city of France is on the Seine River.
4. Christiania is the former name of Oslo the capital of Norway.

5. Austin the capital of Texas was named for Stephen Austin founder of the first settlement in that region.
6. Denver the capital of Colorado is called "the mile-high city."
7. The most famous "twin cities" are St. Paul the capital of Minnesota and Minneapolis its largest city.
8. Bolivia actually has two capitals La Paz and Sucre.
9. The seaport for Tokyo the capital of Japan is Yokohama.
10. Mexico City the capital of Mexico has a fine climate.

B. (1) Rewrite the following sentences, combining each pair into one sentence by the use of an appositive. (2) *Proofread for careless errors in spelling, capitalization, or punctuation.* (3) Exchange papers. (4) Read the revised sentences aloud, telling where commas are needed.

1. Gilbert du Motier was the Marquis de Lafayette. He was born in a wild and rocky part of France.
2. During his childhood, he was left mostly in the care of three women. These women were his grandmother and two aunts.
3. At the age of fourteen, Gilbert began his military career in a famous regiment. This regiment was the Black Musketeers.
4. As a young man, he became interested in a new nation. It was the United States of America.
5. To take him to America, he bought a ship. The name of the ship was the *Victoire*.
6. Two opponents tried but failed to stop him from going. They were his father-in-law and the French government.
7. In America he fought bravely and helped to win the last battle of the Revolution. It was the Battle of Yorktown.
8. Later, during the French Revolution, Lafayette helped to save the rulers of France from an angry mob. These rulers were Louis XVI and Marie Antoinette.
9. When France became a republic, Lafayette refused its highest office. It was the presidency.
10. Declared a traitor, he was captured and imprisoned for five years in two different countries. These countries were Germany and Austria.
11. Lafayette's son, smuggled to America, was cared for by George Washington. That was the man for whom he had been named.
12. In 1824, Lafayette returned to visit the United States and to receive from Congress two gifts. These gifts were two hundred thousand dollars and a township of land.

USING ENGLISH IN ALL CLASSES

Bring into English class the next composition assignment (such as a report) for any class. Write your first draft quickly. Next, see whether you can improve it by using appositives to combine certain sentences.

Diagramming Appositives

Appositives are placed inside parentheses and are located next to the words with which they are in apposition.

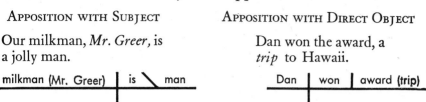

Apposition with Subject

Our milkman, *Mr. Greer,* is a jolly man.

milkman (Mr. Greer) | is \ man

Apposition with Direct Object

Dan won the award, a *trip* to Hawaii.

Dan | won | award (trip)

Apposition with Predicate Nominative

This dog is Prince, our family *pet.*

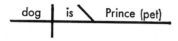

dog | is \ Prince (pet)

Compound Appositives

These gifts, a *ring* and a *watch,* were a real surprise.

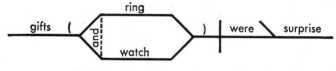

gifts ([ring and watch]) | were \ surprise

Sally has two sisters, *Jane* and *Sue.*

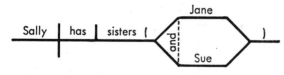

Sally | has | sisters ([Jane and Sue])

LEARNING ACTIVITY IN DIAGRAMMING APPOSITIVES

Diagram verbs, subjects, appositives, and any predicate nominatives or direct objects in these sentences. Exchange papers for checking as the diagrams are put on the board and explained orally.

1. Sunday, my birthday, was a rainy day.
2. The high scorer in every game has been Arnold, our center.
3. Both men, my father and my uncle, were born on a farm.
4. Laura plays two games well, checkers and chess.
5. Our neighbors, the Smiths and the Barrys, are also our friends.
6. Has your wife met our new leader, that tall man in the gray suit?
7. Mr. Lewis provided the entertainment, slides of his trip to Spain.
8. The speakers were two strangers, a Dane and a Swede.
9. These girls, Sheila and Karen, are new in school.
10. Sitting on the fence were two birds, a robin and a sparrow.

8. Speaking and Writing in Sentences

PART ONE: AVOIDING SENTENCE FRAGMENTS

"THESE FLOWERS CERTAINLY SMELL FRAGMENT!"

THINK IT OVER...

What word is he thinking of?

How would *you* use the word "fragment"?

You have learned that it takes a verb to make any sense of what you say. (See pages 279–80.) You might call the verb the *motor* of a sentence because it is what makes the sentence go. A group of words trying to be a sentence without a verb is as useless as an automobile without a motor. A motor, however, is not much good unless there is a guiding force, a driver, behind it. The guiding force behind a verb is its subject.

If either verb or subject is missing, a group of words is only a part of a sentence: that is, a *fragment*.

1. **Every complete sentence must have a** *subject* **and a** *verb* **(predicate).** Short as they are, each word group below has a subject and a verb. Each group *makes sense,* as a sentence must do.

   Birds sing.   Stars shine.   Time passes.   Darkness fell.

2. **(DEFINITION) A group of words that lacks a verb, a subject, or both a verb and a subject is a** *sentence fragment.*

   > The *boy* in the middle. (*A subject, but no verb.*)
   > *Waited* in the hall. (*A verb, but no subject.*)
   > For an hour or more. (*No verb or subject.*)

3. **Sometimes fragments can make sense.** For example, the italicized words below carry little meaning in themselves. However, if you hear them in a conversation, those words make sense, because they are answers to questions that have just been asked. The missing parts are understood.

   > QUESTION: What did John want from you?
   > ANSWER: *A dollar.* [He wanted a dollar.]
   > QUESTION: Where is he now?
   > ANSWER: *At the game.* [He is at the game.]

4. **In your written work and in your speaking when you need to make sure that your meaning is clear, you should use complete sentences.**

5. **(DEFINITION) A** *simple sentence* **is a group of words that together (***a***) make a statement, (***b***) ask a question, or (***c***) express a command or a request. It contains a verb and a subject, either of which may be compound.**

   a) The band played a march. (*statement*)

   b) When did Uncle Bill leave? (*question*)

   c) Take me to the owner. (*command*)   Help me. (*request*)

   In the last two examples above, no subject is named. Who is supposed to do the *taking* and the *helping?* It is the person to whom the speaker is talking; that is, *you.* When *you* is the subject, but not actually named, the subject is said to be "understood"; that is, taken for granted.

   A diagram of a sentence with an understood *you* as the subject looks like this:

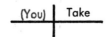

Learn about words!

The following words, taken from *B* of the Learning Activities, have interesting histories. Use your dictionary to find the story behind each word. With which word is the drawing connected?

cloud   parasol   terrier   tall

LEARNING ACTIVITIES

A. *Make this an oral activity.* (1) Take turns telling which of the following groups of words are sentences and which are only fragments. (2) Add words that will turn the fragments into sentences. (3) Tell whether you added a verb (or part of a verb), a subject, or both. Each member of the class should listen to see whether he agrees and should be ready to tell why or why not.

1. Looks like mine.
2. The dog jumped the fence easily.
3. Only two or three cows.
4. Always waits for me.
5. Running around the corner in a hurry.
6. Those two girls moved here from Akron.
7. Don't wait for me.
8. Walking along slowly on the muddy streets.
9. Harold and the other boys on the team.
10. Birds singing in the trees outside my window.

B. (1) Number your paper from 1 to 15. (2) If a group of words below is a sentence, write *S.* (3) If it is a fragment, write *F.* (4) Make the fragments into complete sentences. (5) Read the sentences in your small groups. (6) Explain what you did to make the fragments into sentences.

1. Sometimes Uncle Jim took all of us to the zoo.
2. The woman with the parasol is my aunt.
3. Singing at the top of his voice.
4. Opened the door carefully and peeked through.
5. That terrier has been barking for an hour.
6. Don't forget your gloves.
7. Everywhere, even in the tall grass beside the road.
8. Buzzed around in the morning sun.
9. At exactly ten o'clock every morning.
10. Through the cloud the sun was shining.
11. After a long wait in the station.
12. Always makes nine free throws out of ten.

13. Had the boys ever seen a deer before?
14. Early in the morning of every day but Saturday.
15. Stepping lightly over the stones.

C. Charles Dickens used sentence fragments effectively in his books, as the following conversation from *David Copperfield* illustrates. In class, students should read it aloud. Then other speakers should read the conversation again, putting in words to turn each fragment into a sentence. Note how stiff and unnatural the conversation now sounds.

The clerks were there, but nobody was doing anything. Old Tiffey, for the first time in his life, I should think, was sitting on somebody else's stool, and had not hung up his hat.

"This is a dreadful calamity, Mr. Copperfield," he said.
"What is?" I exclaimed.
"Don't you know?"
"No!" said I.
"Mr. Spenlow," said Tiffey.
"What about him?"
"Dead!"
"Dead?" said I.
"He dined in town yesterday, and drove down by himself."
"Well?"
"The horses stopped at the stable gate. The man went out with a lantern. Nobody in the carriage. They found Mr. Spenlow a mile off."
"More than a mile off, Mr. Tiffey," interposed a junior clerk.
"Was it? I believe you are right. More than a mile off—not far from the church. Lying partly on the roadside, and partly on the path, upon his face."

USING ENGLISH IN ALL CLASSES

Go over a paper that you have written for any subject. If you find any fragments, make complete sentences of them. Put on the board each fragment and the sentence made from it; then explain to the class what you added.

FOLLOW-UP

Each time that you must write a paper for any class, check carefully before handing in your work. Examine every group of words that you have punctuated as a sentence. Correct any fragments, except ones you have put purposely into a conversation. (1) Add words to turn each fragment into a sentence or (2) attach the fragment to another sentence.

ENRICHMENT

Natural-sounding conversation makes much use of sentence fragments. Here is a conversation as it would be expressed if it had only complete sentences. Rewrite it, turning some of the sentences into fragments.

The stranger tapped my uncle on the shoulder and snarled, "I have something to say to you!"

"You have something to say to me?" he asked. "Who are you?"

"I am someone who has followed you for the past week."

"Why have you followed me for the past week?"

"I have done so," the man said, shaking his fist, "because you are my enemy."

"I am your enemy? That is impossible! As sure as my name is Willard Effingham, I have never seen you before in my life!"

"You are Willard Effingham?" exclaimed the man. "You mean you are not Archibald Willoughby? I am sorry!" And off he ran, leaving my uncle bewildered but greatly relieved.

PART TWO: AVOIDING RUN-ON SENTENCES

The sentence fragment fails to give clear meaning because it does not express a complete thought. The run-on sentence fails to give clear meaning because it runs together too many separate thoughts. The following guides will help you to get rid of run-on sentences in your own writing. Before studying the guides, review the types of run-on sentences, page 170.

GUIDES FOR CORRECTING RUN-ON SENTENCES

1. Break run-on sentences into separate sentences, correctly capitalized and punctuated.

   RUN-ON: Our neighbors in the big white house across the street have a great many pets and so their house is very popular with all the boys and girls in the neighborhood, in fact, my little brother Tommy spends more time there than at home.

   IMPROVED: Our neighbors in the big white house across the street have a great many pets. Their house is very popular with all the boys and girls in the neighborhood. In fact, my little brother Tommy spends more time there than at home.

2. When you can, combine two or more parts by using compounds.

   RUN-ON: Eric was running fast and he did not notice the hole in the road and so suddenly down he went but luckily he did not break his leg.

   IMPROVED: Eric **was running** fast and **did** not **notice** the hole in the road. Suddenly down he **went** but luckily **did** not **break** his leg. (*compound verbs*)

   RUN-ON: Dick will go to camp this summer, so will Ted.

   IMPROVED: **Dick** and **Ted** will go to camp this summer. (*compound subject*)

   RUN-ON: Mr. Olson is the owner of this plane he is also the pilot.

   IMPROVED: Mr. Olson is the **owner** and **pilot** of this plane. (*compound predicate nominative*)

   RUN-ON: Larry collects stamps, he also collects pencils.

   IMPROVED: Larry collects **stamps** and **pencils**. (*compound direct object*)

3. Use appositives to combine parts of run-on sentences.

   RUN-ON: Joe Denny has won many golf medals, he is my cousin.

   IMPROVED: Joe Denny, **my cousin,** has won many golf medals.

LEARNING ACTIVITIES

A. (1) Number your paper from 1 to 15. (2) If a group of words below is a sentence, write *S* after the corresponding number. (3) Rewrite each run-on sentence by applying the preceding guides. Use end punctuation and capital letters correctly. (4) Read aloud the rewritten sentences. Let your voice show where each sentence ends.

1. John Flynn is a new member of our class he came here from Florida.
2. Follow me, the doctor can see you now.
3. Burt ran the distance in three minutes.
4. We didn't hear the bell and so we kept on playing but in a short while the teacher came out and he called us in and then he kept us after school.
5. Helen made Mother's birthday gift, it was a knitting bag.
6. Today Mother baked a chocolate cake she also baked some cookies.
7. Father takes his vacation in June we usually go to the mountains.
8. Judie is diagramming the sentences in her notebook and Lynn is diagramming them in his notebook also.
9. Bill rewrote his paper three times before the end of that tiresome day.
10. Ronnie paid attention to the coach's advice and so he practiced jumping over and over and he did knee-bending exercises every night and finally he could jump higher than anyone else on the team.
11. Come early, we must finish before nine o'clock.
12. Those two boys are good students, they are also fine athletes and excellent musicians.
13. He could not back the long car into the parking space.
14. The lights should be turned out, electricity costs money.
15. Please turn off the radio it bothers me.

B. (1) Rewrite the following paragraph, correcting it by applying any of the guides on page 341. Review the Suggestions for Good Handwriting, page 479. (2) *Be sure to proofread for careless errors.* (3) Compare the results in your small groups.

> The game was not yet over, it had been a very exciting one and so with the score tied 6–6, no one in the stands had left the stadium, now there were only seven or eight seconds left. Then the referee blew his whistle, and he called time out. Could the Bears still pull the game out of the fire only those last few speeding seconds would tell.

USING ENGLISH IN ALL CLASSES

Look for run-on sentences in papers that you have written for other classes. Bring these to class. Read them aloud and then explain how you would correct them.

9. Using Vivid, Exact Nouns

Here are three pairs of sentences. In each pair, pick out the sentence that you think gives the better picture. Tell why you think so.

1. Suddenly I heard a loud noise.
2. Suddenly I heard a loud crash.

1. I fell asleep to the drumming of rain on the roof.
2. I fell asleep to the sound of rain on the roof.

1. In the glass bowl were some lovely yellow tulips.
2. In the glass bowl were some lovely yellow flowers.

Only one word is different in each pair of those sentences. Name other words that might have been used for the "different" words. As you will see, the picture changes as you change those nouns.

One good way to widen your vocabulary is to learn to use vivid, exact nouns. The following guides suggest how to go about it.

GUIDES TO USING VIVID, EXACT NOUNS

1. Go over written work that you do, at home or at school. Think about each noun. Ask yourself, "Can I find a more exact, or definite, word? Can I find a word that makes a clearer picture?"

2. In your reading, learn to notice the author's choice of nouns. Being aware of what words good writers choose can help you in your own oral and written expression.

3. As a rule, avoid weak nouns like *sound, noise, light, motion*. Find, for example, a noun that names the *special kind* of sound: the *splash* of waves, the *trickling* of a stream, the *rattle* of hail.

4. Avoid a general noun when a specific (exact) one fits.

   GENERAL: Ann was wearing red *shoes*.
   SPECIFIC: Ann was wearing red *sandals*.

   GENERAL: A tall *tree* shades the front of our house.
   SPECIFIC: A tall *elm* shades the front of our house.

   Be as specific as you can. For example, *food* is general; *dessert* is more specific; *pie* is still more specific.

LEARNING ACTIVITIES IN USING VIVID, EXACT NOUNS

A. (1) Write these three headings on your paper: *General, More Specific, Most Specific.* (2) Write each word in the following groups under the right heading. (3) Go over your work in class. Study the example below, which classifies *carrot, plant, vegetable.*

General	More Specific	Most Specific
plant	vegetable	carrot

1. soldier, man, general
2. money, dime, coin
3. cabin, building, house
4. Nile, river, water
5. plant, grain, wheat
6. woman, nurse, person
7. entertainer, violinist, musician
8. shortstop, ballplayer, athlete
9. relative, uncle, man
10. cedar, tree, evergreen

B. Here are some lines from Mark Twain's *The Adventures of Tom Sawyer.* In each line one of the words in parentheses is the one that the author chose. (1) Copy the lines, putting in the words that you think he used. (2) Exchange papers, (3) *Proofread for careless errors in copying.* (4) Check the words chosen as the sentences are read aloud.

1. . . . a candle was casting a dull (glow, light) upon the curtain of a second-story window.
2. Then there was a wild (yelp, bark) of agony, and the poodle went sailing up the aisle; . . .
3. A tremendous (blow, whack) came down on Tom's shoulders, . . .
4. . . . no sound but the far-off (noise, hammering) of a woodpecker, . . .
5. The boys moved off and disappeared in the (gloom, darkness).
6. . . . a thin blue (breath, column) of smoke rose straight into the air.
7. A (touch, sweep) of chilly air passed by, . . .
8. He did not go skipping and prancing, but moved with a dignified (swagger, walk).
9. . . . the air was drowsy with the (sounds, hum) of study.
10. Then they crept to the door and took a trembling (look, peep).
11. Away off in the flaming sunshine, Cardiff Hill lifted its soft green sides through a shimmering (veil, layer) of heat, . . .
12. Just here the (blowing, blast) of a toy tin trumpet came faintly down the green (paths, aisles) of the forest.
13. The (calling, hooting) of a distant owl was all the sound that troubled the dead stillness.
14. . . . an old-fashioned tin lantern that freckled the ground with innumerable little (spots, spangles) of light.
15. Presently a great (jet, amount) of white smoke burst from the ferryboat's side, . . .

C. Write a paragraph describing a strange, exciting, or frightening experience or dream that you once had. If you cannot think of a real one, make one up. Write the paragraph quickly first; then improve it. To do so, (1) check it by the paragraph guides, page 214; (2) try writing some sentences in inverted order (see page 316); (3) replace any weak verbs or nouns with vivid, specific ones; (4) choose a good title (see page 240).

Copy the paragraph neatly and carefully. In your small groups, pass the paragraphs around. Choose ones that you would like the teacher (or someone else) to read to the entire class. Be ready to tell how these paragraphs might be made better.

USING ENGLISH OUTSIDE SCHOOL

Who would be glad to have a letter from you? Write it now while the Guides to Using Vivid, Exact Nouns are fresh in your mind. Before you write, check the form on page 253 and the guides on page 258. Check also the Suggestions for Good Handwriting, page 479.

10. Using Standard English

PART ONE: MAKING VERBS AGREE WITH NOUN SUBJECTS

THINK IT OVER . . .

Most nouns have two forms: *singular* (referring to *one* of anything, as *boy*) and *plural* (referring to *more than one* of anything, as *boys*). This difference in form is called *number*. (See page 186 if you wish to review singular and plural nouns.) Verbs, too, have number.

Many verbs, however, unlike nouns, have the same form in the plural as in the singular. Here are a few examples:

The girl *ran.*	A change *may come.*
The girls *ran.*	Changes *may come.*
John *had left.*	He *will go* later.
The boys *had left.*	They *will go* later.

Here are some rules about number that can help you to use verbs and subjects together properly.

RULES FOR AGREEMENT OF VERBS WITH NOUN SUBJECTS: I

RULE 1. Use a singular verb with a singular subject. (A present singular verb used with a noun subject will end in *s*.)

This *boy* **comes** every day.   *George* **works** hard.

RULE 2. Use a plural verb with a plural subject.

These *boys* **go** every day.

RULE 3. Use a plural verb with compound subjects joined by *and*.

Phil and *Lon* **live** here.   The *boys* and their *fathers* **help** us.

RULE 4. For compound subjects joined by *or, nor, either-or,* or *neither-nor,* follow these rules:

a) **Use a singular verb if both subjects are singular.**

Either *Sally* or *Frances* always **helps** us.

b) **Use a plural verb if both subjects are plural.**

Neither the *apples* nor the *pears* **look** ripe.

RULE 5. Use *is, was, has,* or *does* with a singular subject.

Tom **is** my cousin.   That *man* **has** left.
One *girl* **was** late.   *Myron* **does** careful work.

RULE 6. Use *are, were, have,* or *do* with a plural subject.

The *skies* **are** blue.   Our *teams* **have** won.
The *books* **were** mailed today.   Those *boys* **do** their part.

RULE 7. Use only plural verbs with such subjects as *slacks, shears, tweezers, trousers, pliers, clothes,* for they are always plural.

LEARNING ACTIVITIES IN VERB-SUBJECT AGREEMENT

A. Go over the following sentences orally, choosing the proper verbs. Listen carefully to get used to hearing the standard forms.

1. Pam and Karen (was, were) at Jean's house yesterday.
2. Mother's scissors (is, are) right here.
3. Neither Mother nor Father (is, are) at home.
4. My brothers-in-law (is, are) lawyers.
5. These papers (goes, go) on top.
6. The monkey's eyes (was, were) almost closed.
7. Both families (do, does) need larger houses.
8. These boys (has, have) never been in a subway before.
9. The man and his son (were, was) wearing boots.
10. Those men (come, comes) here often.

B. (1) Copy the following sentences, choosing the proper verbs. *Do not write in this book.* (2) Exchange papers for checking as the sentences are read aloud. (3) Go over the sentences more than once so that your ears will get used to the sound of the standard forms.

1. Both a drought and a flood (is, are) hard on crops.
2. Neither boys nor girls (is, are) going alone.
3. These books (go, goes) in the next room.
4. Neither the girls nor their parents (has, have) returned.
5. John and his brother (was, were) weeding the garden.
6. Jane and her sister (was, were) at the beach.
7. Your services (is, are) always appreciated.
8. Either George or his cousin (has, have) the key.
9. By the end of the day, the players (was, were) tired.
10. The carpenter and the plumber (does, do) good work.

C. (1) Write eight original sentences in which you use the verbs *is, was, has, does, are, were, have, do.* Use compound subjects in three of your sentences. (2) Take turns at reading the sentences aloud in your small groups. (3) Explain why you chose a singular or a plural subject in each case. (4) Call on a listener to judge whether you are right.

Spot Review ★

(*Based upon the sentences in A of the preceding activities*)
1. Why are the subjects in sentence 3 capitalized?
2. Explain the spelling of the plural subject in sentence 4.
3. Why does the apostrophe in sentence 6 come before the *s?*

RULES FOR AGREEMENT OF VERBS WITH NOUN SUBJECTS: II

RULE 8. Apply Rule 5 and Rule 6, page 346, to contractions formed with the verbs named in those rules.

a) Use *isn't, wasn't,* or *hasn't* with a singular subject.

b) Use *aren't, weren't,* or *haven't* with a plural subject.

c) Use *doesn't* with a singular subject.

> That *girl* doesn't remember me.

d) Use *don't* with a plural subject.

> Those *girls* don't remember me, either.

Warning! In standard usage, the contraction *ain't* should not be substituted for *isn't, hasn't, aren't, haven't.*

STANDARD: Joe isn't coming.   The boys haven't left.
NONSTANDARD: Joe ~~ain't~~ coming.   The boys ~~ain't~~ left.

LEARNING ACTIVITIES IN VERB-SUBJECT AGREEMENT

A. Listed below are twenty subjects. Go around the class, saying each subject four times, with (1) *isn't* or *aren't,* (2) *hasn't* or *haven't,* (3) *wasn't* or *weren't,* and (4) *doesn't* or *don't.* You may want to make this a team contest.

EXAMPLE: *money:* Money *isn't.* Money *hasn't.* Money *wasn't.* Money *doesn't.*

1. trees	5. cities	9. price	13. house	17. weeds
2. river	6. truck	10. expense	14. mice	18. children
3. game	7. crops	11. friends	15. tickets	19. radios
4. teams	8. stars	12. geese	16. parks	20. women

B. Copy the following sentences, using the proper contractions. Read the sentences orally when you have finished.

1. The editors (isn't, aren't) meeting today.
2. Aunt Laura (doesn't, don't) object to extra guests.
3. Last night the planes (wasn't, weren't) flying over our house.
4. That dog (doesn't, don't) look like a collie.
5. This road (don't, doesn't) run past the school.
6. My boots (hasn't, haven't) any holes in them.
7. The radiators (ain't, aren't) very hot.
8. The barber's scissors (wasn't, weren't) sharp enough.
9. From the air our farm (doesn't, don't) look large.
10. The neighbors (hasn't, haven't) moved yet.

C. Write original sentences in which you use the contractions from Rule 8. In your small groups, take turns reading your sentences aloud. Tell the rule for each contraction used.

★ **Spot Review**

(*Based upon the sentences in B of the preceding activities*)

1. Account for the apostrophes in sentence 8.
2. What rule regulates the spelling of the subject in sentence 10?
3. What is the *number* of the subject of sentence 8?

Learn about words!

The following words, taken from *A* of the Learning Activities, have interesting histories. Use your dictionary to find the story behind each word.

extra   road   scissors   neighbor

RULES FOR AGREEMENT OF VERBS WITH NOUN SUBJECTS: III

RULE 9. Use a singular verb with a singular subject and a plural verb with a plural subject. *Do so regardless of where they come in the sentence order.*

a) **Do not be fooled by questions in which the verb stands before the subject.**

Is your *hat* a new one?

To be sure that the verb and the subject agree, turn the question into a statement:

Your *hat* is a new one.

b) **Do not be fooled by the introductory word** *there.* **You should find the subject just as in any other sentence.**

There are some apples in the bowl.

What is the verb? *Are.* What are? *Apples* are; so *apples* is the subject. Since *apples* is plural, the plural verb *are* is needed.

c) **Use the contraction** *there's* (*there is* or *there has*), **only if the subject is singular.**

There's [There is] one green *apple* in the bowl. (*Apple* is.)

LEARNING ACTIVITIES IN VERB-SUBJECT AGREEMENT

A. Copy each of the following sentences, using the proper forms. *Do not write in this book.* Read the sentences orally when you have finished.

1. (There is, There are) twenty boys in my class.
2. (There has, There have) been many visitors at the exhibit.
3. (There's, There are) several parks in this state.
4. (Has, Have) your shoes ever been polished?
5. When (was, were) your friends coming?
6. (There was, There were) some letters for you.
7. (Is there, Are there) any eggs in that bowl?
8. (There has, There have) been a reduction in prices.
9. (There's, There are) not one boy here yet.
10. (Has, Have) the furniture been polished?

B. In your small groups, take turns giving sentences orally using *there* as an introductory word and *is, are, was, were, has,* or *have* as the verb. You might tell facts about the downtown part of your city or town. Continue the practice until you are sure of yourself and until the proper forms sound natural to you.

C. Let half of the class write upon the blackboard questions beginning with *is, are, was, were, has,* or *have,* followed by *there.* Let the other half write answers to the questions.

> EXAMPLE: *Are there* any apples in the basket?
> *There are* five apples in the basket.

RULES FOR AGREEMENT OF VERBS WITH NOUN SUBJECTS: IV

RULE 10. **Do not choose a verb that agrees with some word that comes between it and the subject.** (Review point 10, page 316.)

> The **superintendent** of both schools **is** Mr. Day.
> That **row** of trees **does**n't belong to me.
> Both **parents** of that boy **were** here early.
> The **rules** on that page **look** easy.
> This **box** of books **is**n't mine.

Learn about words!

The following words, taken from *A* of the Learning Activities, have interesting histories. Use your dictionary to find the story behind each word. With which word is the drawing connected?

pantry   pay   compliments   arrived

LEARNING ACTIVITIES IN VERB-SUBJECT AGREEMENT

A. *All ten sentences below show the proper verbs.* Check by locating the verb and the subject in each sentence. First find the verb; then say, "Who or what?" to locate the subject. In each case you will see that a singular subject is used with a singular verb, and that a plural subject is used with a plural verb. Read the sentences aloud. Listen carefully to get used to the standard forms.

1. My pay for these services is generous.
2. Have the parents of that child arrived yet?
3. One teacher of the lower grades lives near us.
4. A small heap of nuts was on the shelf in the pantry.
5. One page of the exercises was torn.
6. The father of those boys has built many monuments.
7. The location of the mines was a secret.
8. The work of your assistants has received many compliments.
9. Was the bundle of papers here?
10. The captains of the teams were chosen today.

B. (1) Copy the following sentences, supplying a proper verb for each of them. (2) Compare work orally in class or in your small groups. The verbs chosen may vary, but each singular subject should have a singular verb, and each plural subject should have a plural verb.

1. A truckload of bricks .... delivered at our house.
2. Both owners of the store .... on vacation.
3. The price of these tires .... been raised.
4. The answer to your questions .... me.
5. All houses in this block .... alike.
6. One copy of these instructions ....n't match the others.
7. Two buttons on his coat .... loose.
8. The father of the twins .... here often.
9. The opinions of this man .... reasonable to me.
10. A can of baked beans .... with us on every hike.

C. In an oral activity, go over the following groups of words, completing each of them properly with (1) one of these helping verbs: *is, are, was, were, has, have, do,* or *does* and (2) any other needed words. Explain each time why the verb should be singular or plural.

1. A quart of strawberries . . .
2. The bunch of bananas . . .
3. The train on the tracks . . .
4. The poorest people in the world . . .
5. The traffic lights on this corner . . .
6. The best road through the hills . . .
7. The longest pencils on the table . . .
8. The mother of those children . . .
9. The best players on the team . . .
10. The paper with the scribbles . . .

D. (1) Write five sentences of your own in which the subject is separated from the verb by other words. Use both singular subjects and plural subjects. (2) *Proofread carefully for errors in capitalization, punctuation, and spelling.* (3) Exchange papers and read the sentences aloud in class. The illustration below offers ideas for sentences.

Following is practice on the principal parts of five troublesome verbs—*give, go, take, bring,* and *write.* Remember that your aim is not just to be able to *write* the standard forms but to *put them into practice.*

USING IRREGULAR VERBS

RULE 1. (*Give* and its forms)
Always use at least one auxiliary verb with *given*. Never use one with *gave*.

    Today I **give**.   Yesterday I **gave**.   Often I *have* given.

LEARNING ACTIVITIES IN USING GAVE AND GIVEN

A. Copy these sentences, filling the blanks with the proper form of *give*. Underline (1) the form of *give* that you use and (2) any helping verbs. Read the sentences aloud in class. *Do not write in this book.*

1. John's mother .... a party for him yesterday.
2. The answer was .... correctly.
3. Careful attention should be .... to the appearance of your papers.
4. Who .... you those flowers?
5. On Monday a short play will be .... in the auditorium.
6. Father .... me a bicycle for Christmas.
7. Full directions are .... on the package.
8. The list of winners is .... in the morning paper.
9. He has .... his opinion on that subject already.
10. Mother was .... the prize for flower arranging.
11. Aunt Mary always .... me money for my birthday.
12. .... me some help!

B. Write sentences on the board, leaving blanks to be filled with *gave* or *given*. Call on a classmate to read the sentences, supplying the proper forms. When a past participle is used, tell what the helping verb is.

C. (1) Write five sentences, three using *gave* and two using *given* correctly. You might write about presents that you have given for birthdays or for Christmas. (2) In your small groups, take turns at reading sentences aloud. (3) Have classmates tell what helping verbs you used. Listen carefully to get used to hearing the proper forms.

D. Pretend that your class held an auction last week to raise money for a trip to some historic place. Each of you donated one item or more. Tell what you gave. One person may begin by saying, "I gave an elephant. What did *you* give, George?" George then tells what he gave. It must be something that begins with the letter before or the one after the first letter of the thing given by the person who called on him. In other words, George might say, "I gave a deer," or "I gave a flagpole." He then asks the question of anyone else he wishes, and so on. You will need to listen closely, for if your gift begins with a wrong letter, you are out of the game. You will be out, too, if you say, "I *give* . . ." instead of "I *gave.*"

Spot Review

(*Based upon the sentences in* A *of the preceding activities*)
1. Account for the apostrophe in sentence 1.
2. Why is *mother* not capitalized in sentence 1?
3. How do you spell the plural of the last word in sentence 6?
4. What is the subject of sentence 5?

USING IRREGULAR VERBS—Continued

RULE 2. (*Go* and its forms)
Always use at least one helping verb with *gone.* **Never use one with** *went.*

Today I **go.**   Yesterday I **went.**   Often I *have* **gone.**

LEARNING ACTIVITIES IN USING *WENT* AND *GONE*

A. (1) Copy these sentences, filling the blanks with the correct form of *go.* (2) Exchange papers. (3) Check the papers for careless errors in copying. Circle any that you find. (4) Read the sentences aloud in class. Each time that *gone* is used, name the helping verbs.

1. On Thanksgiving Day John should have .... to Boston.
2. George has .... away to college.
3. Until this year, Ed had always .... to Florida for a month.
4. Who .... with you yesterday?
5. The notes for your speech should be .... over carefully.
6. I'd never .... to that dentist until yesterday.

7. Everyone has .... except us.
8. The alarm must have .... off.
9. Had the Joneses .... to the station before five o'clock?
10. Where has Frank ....?
11. The Sunday newspapers were all ....
12. For our last vacation we .... to the beach.

B. Write five original sentences, three with *went* and two with *gone*. Use these helping verbs with the past participle: *has, have, had, should have, might have*. In your small groups, take turns at reading sentences aloud. Listen to hear whether helping verbs are used each time with the past participle, *gone*.

C. With a partner, take turns at saying sentences that use *gone* properly. For example, make them the answers to a question: "Has anyone in your family ever gone to Mexico?" Give a separate and complete answer for each member of your family. "My mother has gone to Mexico. My brother Fred has never gone to Mexico." Practice until the correct forms sound perfectly natural.

★ **Spot Review**

(Based upon the sentences in A of the preceding activities)

1. Name three proper nouns in sentence 1. What common noun would fit each of them?
2. How would you spell the words for which the contractions stand in sentences 6 and 9?
3. What is the subject in sentence 5?
4. What rule covers the spelling of the proper noun in sentence 9?

USING IRREGULAR VERBS—Continued

RULE 3. (*Take* and its forms)
Always use a helping verb with *taken*; never use one with *took*.
Today I take.   Yesterday I **took**.   Often I *have* taken.

LEARNING ACTIVITIES IN USING *TOOK* AND *TAKEN*

A. Copy these sentences, filling the blanks with the standard form of *take*. Underline that form and any helping verbs. Read the sentences aloud in class. Listen to be sure that the proper forms are given.

1. This picture of pine trees was .... on Mount McKinley.
2. Has your family ever .... a long vacation trip?
3. In 1664 the English .... possession of New Amsterdam.
4. Samuel Clemens .... the pen name "Mark Twain."
5. This name was .... from his experiences on the Mississippi River.
6. We should have .... defeat like good sports.
7. The story of this film is .... from a famous book.
8. In my opinion, the first speaker should not have .... so much time for questions from the audience.
9. The two boys had .... a short cut to the beach.
10. Who has .... your place on the committee?

B. For each error that you made in *A,* write two sentences using the correct form. Read these aloud to a partner, who will judge their correctness. If you and he disagree, ask your teacher to settle the problem.

C. Pretend that your class has just returned from the trip in activity D, page 353. Each of you forgot to take along something that would have come in handy. Go around the class, saying, "I wish that I had taken..." (or "I should have taken..."). You can have fun by naming some unusual items; for example, "I wish that I had taken a polar bear." (If anyone asks *why,* be ready with a good answer.)

Spot Review ★

(Based upon the sentences in A of the preceding activities)

1. Find and write the proper nouns in sentences 1, 3, and 5. Beside each write a common noun that it describes.
2. Name the subject, the verb, and the direct object in sentences 2 and 8.
3. How would you spell the plural of the subject in sentence 7?
4. Why are *Mount* (sentence 1) and *River* (sentence 5) capitalized?
5. Why is the verb in sentence 1 singular?

USING IRREGULAR VERBS—*Continued*

RULE 4. (*Bring* and its forms)
Brought is the only proper form both for the past tense and for the past participle. *Brang* and *brung* are nonstandard forms.

Today I **bring**   Yesterday I **brought.**   Often I *have* **brought.**

LEARNING ACTIVITIES IN USING *BROUGHT*

A. Go over the following sentences orally, supplying the standard form of *bring*. Listen to get used to hearing the proper form. *Do not write in this book.*

1. William .... his friend to the last party.
2. I should not have .... my camera.
3. Tobacco was first .... to England from America.
4. Mary has .... her share of the money.
5. John was .... up by his grandmother.
6. Irene .... back many souvenirs from Hawaii.
7. As usual, Tim and I .... our binoculars.
8. The dog must have .... the neighbors' paper.
9. Has each member .... a visitor?
10. The rain .... a little relief from the heat.

B. Take turns at writing sentences on the board, leaving blanks to be filled with the proper form of *bring*. Call on classmates to read the sentences, using the standard forms.

C. Pretend that your class has had a picnic. It was a great success because of the delicious food. Each person will tell what someone else brought. You must drop out of the game (1) if you use *brang* or *brung* or (2) if you name a food that someone else has already named. As you can see, you will need to listen closely. Stop at the end of five minutes. You may want to make this activity a team contest.

★ **Spot Review**

(*Based upon the sentences in* A *of the preceding activities*)

1. Rewrite sentence 2, using a contraction.
2. Write the plural of *party* (sentence 1). Give the rule.
3. Which sentences have direct objects? Name those objects.
4. Why is *grandmother* not capitalized in sentence 5?

USING IRREGULAR VERBS—*Continued*

RULE 5. (*Write* and its forms)
Always use a helping verb with *written;* **never use one with** *wrote.*
Writ **is a nonstandard form.**

Today I write.   Yesterday I wrote.   Often I *have* written.

LEARNING ACTIVITIES IN USING *WROTE* AND *WRITTEN*

A. Copy these sentences, filling the blanks with the standard form of *write*. Underline that form and any auxiliary verbs. Read the sentences aloud in class.

1. Most of the Declaration of Independence was .... by Thomas Jefferson.
2. Henry Wadsworth Longfellow .... the poem "The Children's Hour."
3. Louisa May Alcott .... many books for boys and girls.
4. *The Adventures of Huckleberry Finn* was .... by Mark Twain, a great author.
5. He .... that book after he had .... *The Adventures of Tom Sawyer.*
6. Have you .... to your Aunt Mary?
7. Your sentences should be .... carefully and neatly.
8. Every year many new books are .... for children.

B. Write five original sentences, using *wrote* in two and *written* in three of them. Think of books that you have read lately and letters or papers that you have written. Take turns at reading sentences aloud. Listen carefully to get used to hearing the standard forms.

C. (1) Jot down the names of at least five books or poems that you have read. (2) Take turns at asking who wrote your selections. For example, say, "Tom, who wrote *Treasure Island?*" (3) The one called upon will say, "*Treasure Island* was written by Robert Louis Stevenson." If he does not know, he should say, "I don't know by whom it was written." In that case, call upon someone who raises his hand. (4) Continue until everyone has asked at least one question and given one answer using *wrote* or *written* properly.

Chapter Review*

A. (1) Copy the following sentences. (2) Label each *verb* (v.), and each noun used as *subject* (subj.), *direct object* (d.o.), *predicate nominative* (p.n.), or *appositive* (app.). (3) Exchange papers for checking. (4) Identify the sentence patterns. *Be sure to proofread your work.*

1. The rain brought some relief from the heat.
2. Mark is the only boy in his family.
3. The detectives searched the house and the garage.
4. The man in the middle is Mr. Elson, our coach.
5. Suddenly the roar of an airplane broke the silence.

* Check Test 3 should be taken at this point. If the results show need for further study, students should do this review practice. They should then take Mastery Test 3.

6. Hamburgers and steaks are my favorite meats.
7. My father and Jack, my oldest brother, are very good drivers.
8. In the package were two footballs.
9. An honest man would have told the truth about the matter.
10. An angry elephant can be a very dangerous animal.

B. Read the following sentences aloud, choosing the standard forms.

1. The scissors on the table (is, are) sharp and pointed.
2. (Has, Have) your brothers-in-law left?
3. There (is, are) a pie and a cake in the refrigerator.
4. The woman with the two children (don't, doesn't) like streetcars.
5. The two little men at the end of the row (was, were) fast asleep.
6. (Is, Are) the potatoes in that sack from your garden?
7. The basket of roses (wasn't, weren't) on the piano.
8. There (has, have) been some lovely days this fall.
9. (Doesn't, Don't) Fred or Dick ever wait for you?
10. Five loads of coal (was, were) delivered this morning.
11. There (isn't, aren't) any oranges or lemons left in the refrigerator.
12. (Don't, Doesn't) your father remember that game?
13. A peck of apples (don't, doesn't) last long.
14. There (hasn't, haven't) been any storms for two weeks.
15. (Has, Have) the box of records and the table been moved?

C. Read these sentences aloud, supplying the proper form of each verb.

1. A program was (give) in our school last Friday.
2. We (bring) our books with us this morning.
3. Have you (write) to your Uncle Ned?
4. Ted (give) me the wrong address yesterday.
5. Lois might have (go) without me.
6. This picture was (take) in Florida.
7. Everyone had (bring) his share.
8. This letter was (write) last week.
9. Carl has always (take) his work seriously.
10. Phil has (go) to sleep again.

★ **Cumulative Review**

CAPITALIZATION

Copy these sentences, supplying needed capital letters.

1. according to gene's report in english class, many austrians, hungarians, poles, and russians came to america after 1850.
2. at last mother said, "we shouldn't go to kansas city on thanksgiving day. our friends from the west cannot be there then."

3. father added, "that settles it. we stay on maple avenue. perhaps uncle jim and aunt clara will spend the holiday with us."
4. jack and bob, who worked in a machine shop during july and august, saw the film *war and peace* as guests of colonel r. k. clark of the simplex radio company.
5. that quotation, i'm sure, is from the old testament, not from the new testament.

PUNCTUATION

Copy these sentences, supplying needed punctuation.

1. Ive won the contest shouted Don
2. I wonder said Henry whether its too late to call Harold
3. Yes Sam has won letters in baseball basketball and football
4. The childrens *ohs* and *ahs* showed their excitement
5. Have you read Flight to the Misty Planet by M E Patchett the author of Space Captives of the Golden Men

CONTRACTIONS

Write sentences using the correct contractions of the words below.

1. cannot	3. she will	5. will not	7. did not	9. I have
2. there is	4. it is	6. you are	8. who is	10. we are

SPELLING

Here are sentences containing one or more scrambled words. Some of them when written correctly contain *ei;* the others, *ie.* Make two columns on your paper, one headed *ei* and the other, *ie.* Figure out the words and write each of them under the right heading.

1. I don't (veelbie) I have met your (eenic).
2. There were (thige) men working in the (lidef).
3. Our (binehorgs) are painting (rheti) house.
4. Do you think that (ithree) of those boys has lost (twighe)?
5. The Indian (hifec) was a (recief) fighter.

TROUBLESOME VERBS

Go over these sentences orally, choosing the standard forms.

1. Helen (did, done) more than her share for last night's meeting.
2. Have you (knew, known) Mrs. Scott long?
3. The last contestant has not yet (spoke, spoken).
4. The game (began, begun) early. You should have (saw, seen) it.
5. Mr. Watts (learned, taught) us many things.
6. Mr. Vance (knew, knowed) Father in college long ago.
7. Nobody (saw, seen) us leave.

8. Everything had been (did, done) for the sick puppy.
9. Where did you (sit, set) during the program?
10. Two boys were (chose, chosen) to carry the flag.
11. Will you (borrow, lend) me your bicycle?
12. We had (began, begun) to worry about you.

Word Games to Test Your Thinking

DIAMOND PUZZLE

The middle letter is the same in each of the following words. Place the words one under the other so that the middle letters will form a straight row up and down. The number of letters in each word is shown in parentheses. (CLUE: Only four letters are used in these words.)

1. One of the three articles in grammar (1)
2. Past of *sit* (3)
3. One of the 50 divisions of the United States (5)
4. Property (plural) left by a person who has died (7)
5. Places on which to sit (5)
6. To chew and swallow (3)
7. *Same as No. 1*

ALPHABET TREE QUIZ

Can you figure out what trees the following are? EXAMPLE: *O* plus a stove = *orange.*

1. *O* plus a verb meaning *to have life*
2. *D* plus a word meaning *dined*
3. *P* plus a part of the body
4. *A* plus a sound used to tell someone to be quiet
5. *P* plus a word meaning *every*
6. Part of the body plus NUT
7. An insect plus CH
8. The lower edge of a dress plus LOCK
9. To attempt to throw a rider plus EYE
10. PA plus *animal foot*
11. PE plus a metal container
12. Nickname for *father* plus LAR

A "CROSS" CROSSWORD PUZZLE

Copy the puzzle. *Do not write in this book.*

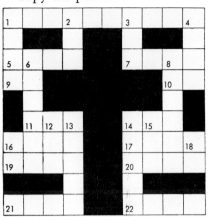

Across

1. Western state.
5. Small island.
7. Necessity for.
9. Thirteenth letter of the Greek alphabet.
10. Adverbial conjunction.
11. What you should put after an abbreviation.
14. A house pet.
16. Every Fourth of July should be safe and ....

17. Opposite of *shut.*
19. Past participle of *see.*
20. Comparative degree of *much* or *many.*
21. Opposite of *there.*
22. Opposite of *go.*

Down

1. Biblical character who slew his brother Abel.
2. President Eisenhower's nickname.
3. Past of *run.*
4. Helps.
6. Not a day for going to church, but something to eat.
8. The day on which the resurrection of Christ is celebrated.
12. A number.
13. In grammar, the word for *time.*
14. Kind of books read by many people, especially children.
15. Army Post Office (*abbr.*).
16. Sunday School (*abbr.*).
18. Northeast (*abbr.*).

WOULD YOU LIKE TO KNOW—?

You probably will be surprised at the answers the encyclopedia gives to some of the following questions.

1. What kind of disposition has the *camel?*
2. Where in North America did *chocolate* originate?
3. Is *coffee* native to Central and South America?
4. What causes the tail of a *comet?*
5. Where are a *cricket's* ears located?

USING PRONOUNS IN BUILDING SENTENCES *

1. Recognizing Personal Pronouns

READ AND DISCUSS

Read these sentences:

The boy swung at the ball. The *boy* hit the *ball*.

Now read these sentences:

The boy swung at the ball. *He* hit *it*.

Which pair of sentences sounds better? Why?

He hit it.

* Pretest 4 should be taken at this point.

1. **(DEFINITION)** *Pronouns* **are words that can substitute for nouns or for groups of words used as nouns.** (*Pro* is a prefix meaning *for;* therefore, *pronoun* means "for a noun.")

    The *boy* hit the *ball.*   *He* hit *it.*

    We saw the *Statue of Liberty.*   We saw *it.*

    (DEFINITION) The word for which a pronoun stands is its *antecedent. Boy* and *ball* are the antecedents of *he* and *it.*

2. **(DEFINITION) Pronouns that refer chiefly to persons are called** *personal pronouns.*

    a) **(DEFINITION) Personal pronouns have** *number;* **that is, they can be singular or plural.**

    b) **(DEFINITION) Personal pronouns have** *person;* **that is, they name the** *speaker,* **the** *person spoken to,* **or the** *person spoken of.* **(See the chart below.)**

3. **(DEFINITION)** *Compound personal pronouns* **are ones formed by adding** *self* **or** *selves* **to** *my, your, his, her, it, our, them.*

    Here is a chart of the personal pronouns.

    SINGULAR

FIRST PERSON:	I, me, my, mine	myself
SECOND PERSON:	you, your, yours	yourself
THIRD PERSON:	he, him, his	himself
	she, her, hers	herself
	it, its	itself

    PLURAL

FIRST PERSON:	we, us, our, ours	ourselves
SECOND PERSON:	you, your, yours	yourselves
THIRD PERSON:	they, them, their, theirs	themselves

    Notice that the second person pronouns are the same in the singular and in the plural, except for *yourself* and *yourselves.*

SINGULAR	PLURAL
You are my friend.	You are my friends.
Ted, close your eyes.	Don and Lee, close your eyes.
My boy, yours are good ideas.	Boys, yours are good ideas.
Tom, help yourself.	Boys, help yourselves.

4. *My, your, our,* and *their* **are always used as noun markers, or** *determiners: my* book, *your* car, ... *His, her,* and *its* **are sometimes determiners and sometimes simple pronouns.**

    I have her book. (*determiner*)   I saw her. (*pronoun*)

363

Learn about words!

The following words, taken from *A* of the Learning Activities, have interesting histories. Use your dictionary to find the story behind each word. With which word is the drawing connected?

table   squirrels   chimney   bicycle

LEARNING ACTIVITIES IN PERSONAL PRONOUNS

A. Go over these sentences. Locate each pronoun and tell (1) what its person is, (2) which it is, singular or plural, (3) whether it is used as a determiner in the sentence, and (4) what its antecedent is, if given. The figure in parentheses tells the number of pronouns in each sentence.

1. Tom found Mary with her mother. (1)
2. You must do it yourself. (3)
3. My brother gave me his pet squirrels. (3)
4. The bird carried a worm in its beak. (1)
5. Their house is near ours. (2)
6. He will repair the chimney himself. (2)
7. The clock on the table is mine. (1)
8. She herself gave them to us. (4)
9. Jim's plans are much like theirs. (1)
10. They can't help themselves now. (2)
11. I can repair your bicycle by myself. (3)
12. We ourselves saw him. (3)

B. Rewrite the following awkward-sounding paragraph. (1) In each blank use a first-person pronoun. (2) Change the italicized word groups to pronouns that stand for them.

Exchange papers. *Proofread for careless errors in copying;* then have the sentences read aloud to check the pronouns chosen.

One day before I was old enough to go to school, ... went there as a visitor. *The school* was a country school. On the playground the boys were making "parachutes" of *the boys'* handkerchiefs. *The boys* would tie each corner to a string and then tie the strings together around a stone. Then the boys would throw *the boys'* parachutes into the air, and the parachutes would sail away. Some lit in the treetops, and one of *the parachutes* landed on top of the flagpole. When the bell rang, I ran up to the teacher and shouted at the top of .... voice, "That big boy put *the boy's* handkerchief on top of that big post. *That boy* is naughty, isn't *that boy!*"

(Based upon the sentences in A *of the preceding activities)*

1. Why is *mother* not capitalized in sentence 1?
2. What are the direct objects in sentences 1, 4, 6? How would you spell the plural of the object in sentence 1? in sentence 6?
3. Explain the apostrophe in sentence 9; in sentence 10.

USING ENGLISH IN ALL CLASSES

Look over papers that you have written for any of your classes. Are there any places where you might better have used pronouns? Rewrite any such sentences. Be sure, however, that it is clear to what noun each pronoun refers.

2. Learning the Uses of Pronouns

This section is concerned with how pronouns are used in English sentences. It should not surprise you that, like nouns, they can function in numerous ways. The facts below summarize those functions.

● **THESE ARE FACTS ABOUT PRONOUNS: II**

5. **Pronouns may be used in the same ways as nouns.**

   a) **A pronoun may be a** *subject:* I saw Mary.

   b) **A pronoun may be a** *predicate nominative.*
   > The owner is she in the red dress.

   c) **A pronoun may be a** *direct object.*
   > Father met me at the station.   John found us in the park.

   d) **A pronoun may be an** *appositive.*
   > Only one boy, you, can help us.

   e) **Pronouns may be compound.**
   > She and I look alike. (*subjects*)
   > The losers were she and I. (*predicate nominatives*)
   > Mother called you and me. (*direct objects*)
   > He has chosen two boys, you and me. (*appositives*)

6. **In sentence patterns,** *N* **stands for** *pronoun,* **just as it stands for** *noun.*

N+V	N+V + N	N+LV+N
We left early.	I like them.	It was you!

LEARNING ACTIVITIES IN THE USES OF PRONOUNS

A. In an oral activity, tell how each italicized pronoun in the following sentences is used. Give the pattern for each sentence.

1. *He* never watches television.
2. *You* have met *him* before.
3. *It* is *he*.
4. *They* are not strangers.
5. *She* must be a good friend.
6. *He* invited *me* to the party.
7. *We* have sent the package.
8. *She* helped *us*, Tom and *me*.
9. *I* saw *them* at the movies.
10. The captains are *you* and *he*.

B. (1) Copy the following sentences. (2) Underscore verbs twice and subjects once. The subject may be a noun or a pronoun. (3) Enclose in parentheses and label each pronoun used as a direct object or a predicate nominative. (4) Go over the sentences in your small groups, explaining why each pronoun is a subject, direct object, or predicate nominative.

EXAMPLE: Will you and she help (me)?

1. Where were you and she?
2. Yes, it was we.
3. The author is she.
4. We were not expecting him.
5. Was it you or he at the door?
6. Did they choose her?
7. In the first game, Val was it.
8. Down the street they hurried.
9. She has visited us often.
10. How can I help you?
11. Surely the winners were John and he.
12. They saw us at the game.

C. (1) Write six original sentences about your family or your neighbors. In two of them, use pronouns as subjects; in two, as predicate nominatives; in two, as direct objects. (2) *Proofread for careless mistakes in capitalization, punctuation, and spelling.* (3) Exchange papers. (4) On the paper that you receive, mark each pronoun as you did in *B*.

★ **Spot Review**

(*Based upon the sentences in* B *of the preceding activities*)

1. What is the tense of the verb in sentence 2? 3? 8?
2. Which sentences are interrogative?
3. Account for the commas in sentence 7.
4. Which sentences contain regular verbs?

DIAGRAMMING PRONOUNS

Pronouns are diagrammed just as nouns are. You may want to review pages 319, 327, 331, and 335.

PRONOUN SUBJECT
He was skating at the rink.

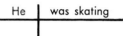

PRONOUN PREDICATE NOMINATIVE
The winner is *you.*

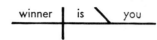

PRONOUN DIRECT OBJECT
Fred met *me* after lunch.

PRONOUN APPOSITIVE
The teacher wants one person, *you.*

COMPOUND SUBJECT AND DIRECT OBJECT
He and *I* saw *you* and *them* in the store.

LEARNING ACTIVITIES IN DIAGRAMMING PRONOUNS

A. Diagram verbs, subjects, and any predicate nominatives, direct objects, or appositives in the following sentences. Put the diagrams on the board and explain them orally.

1. It most certainly is she.
2. How can I answer her at this time?
3. I just saw them inside the gym.
4. It could have been they.
5. Did you hear it yesterday?
6. We saw them in the park.
7. They took us to lunch afterwards.
8. It surely must have been you.
9. She unexpectedly invited me to dinner.
10. I need one person, you.

B. For additional practice, use the sentences in *A,* page 290. Go over the diagrams orally in your small groups.

3. Using Standard English

INTRODUCTORY ACTIVITY

Draw three columns on your paper. Above the first column write *subject;* above the second, *predicate nominative;* and above the third, *direct object.* Go back over the sentences in *B,* page 366. Put each pronoun in the right column. Check your lists in class.

The preceding activity shows that pronouns are different from nouns in one important way. A noun stays the same in form whether it is used as subject, predicate nominative, or object.

> **Mary** went home. (*subject*)
> John saw **Mary.** (*direct object*)
> The speaker was **Mary.** (*predicate nominative*)

Personal pronouns, however, sometimes change their form, depending upon how they are used in the sentence.

> **She** went home. (*subject*)
> John saw **her.** (*direct object*)
> The speaker was **she.** (*predicate nominative*)

● **THESE ARE FACTS ABOUT PRONOUNS: III**

7. Pronouns (and nouns) **used as subjects or predicate nominatives are said to be in the** *nominative case.* **Therefore** *I, he, she, we,* **and** *they* are *nominative pronouns.*

8. Pronouns (and nouns) **used as objects are said to be in the** *objective case. Me, him, her, us,* **and** *them* are *objective pronouns.*

9. *It* and *you* are used both in the nominative case and in the objective case.

10. **You should memorize these two lists of pronouns that have different nominative and objective forms.**

NOMINATIVE:	I	he	she	we	they
OBJECTIVE:	me	him	her	us	them

RULES FOR USING PRONOUNS PROPERLY

RULE 1. Use the nominative pronouns *I, he, she, we,* and *they* only as subjects or predicate nominatives. (Remember that predicate nominatives complete *linking verbs*. To review linking verbs see point 4, page 326.)

> **They** played well. (*subject*)
> The players were **they**. (*predicate nominative*)

RULE 2. In a compound subject or predicate nominative made up of a noun and a pronoun, be sure to use a nominative pronoun.

STANDARD: John and I helped.   NONSTANDARD: John and ~~me~~ helped.

(You would not say, "*Me* helped." No more should you say, "John and *me* helped.")

> STANDARD: The altos are Jean and she.
> NONSTANDARD: The altos are Jean and ~~her~~.

RULE 3. Use the objective pronouns *me, her, him, us,* and *them* only as objects.

> A big dog chased me. (*direct object*)

RULE 4. In a compound direct object made up of a noun and a pronoun, be sure to use an objective pronoun.*

> STANDARD: The dog chased Bill and me.
> NONSTANDARD: The dog chased Bill and ~~I~~.

RULE 5. In speaking of yourself and others, name yourself last, as a matter of politeness.

> POLITE: John and I agree.   POORER: ~~I and John~~ agree.
> POLITE: The dog chased Bill and me.
> POORER: The dog chased ~~me and Bill~~.

ACTIVITIES IN USING NOMINATIVE AND OBJECTIVE PRONOUNS

A. The sentences that follow on page 370 need predicate nominative pronouns. (1) In an oral activity, go over the sentences, choosing the standard pronoun form in each case. (2) Let half the class read a sentence while the others listen for the proper choices; then they will read the next sentence for the first group to hear and check. Continue in this way for all ten sentences. *Do not mark in this book.*

The proper uses of pronouns in a compound object of a preposition and in a compound indirect object are taught on page 456.

1. I agree with Mother. It was (he, him).
2. It surely wasn't (they, them).
3. Was it (she, her)?
4. No, it was (I, me).
5. It was (we, us) who were chosen.
6. May I speak with May? Is this (she, her)?
7. Was that John calling? Yes, it was (he, him).
8. It must have been (she, her) at the door.
9. Could it have been (they, them) in the car?
10. It was not (I, me), but Jane.

B. Each of the following sentences contains compound subjects, predicate nominatives, or objects. Copy each sentence, choosing the proper form. To help you to decide, drop the other part of the compound.

> EXAMPLE: Ray chose Sue and (I, me).
> Ray chose (I, me).
> Ray chose *me*.

Read the sentences aloud and listen carefully to hear the proper forms.

1. The creaking of a door awakened Jack and (I, me).
2. Father and (he, him) made a huge kite.
3. Will you and (she, her) be ready at nine?
4. Five big geese chased Jerry and (we, us).
5. You and (they, them) were here early.
6. Jane met Ruth and (I, me) at the movie.
7. (She, Her) and (we, us) came too late.
8. That car missed the wagon and (they, them) by inches.
9. At the station (he, him) and (I, me) found the trunk.
10. My uncle and (he, him) once worked in the same office.

C. For each italicized noun or pair of nouns in the following sentences, substitute the proper pronoun. Where the italicized words are "your own name," use *I* or *me;* where they are "you and another person," use *we* or *us*. Decide first whether the pronoun is to be used as a subject, an object, or a predicate nominative. Then, if you cannot remember which are the nominative and which are the objective pronouns, refer to the lists on page 368. Make this an oral practice.

> EXAMPLE: Joe and (*your own name*) agree. Joe and *I* agree.

1. Alice and *Lois* will bring the salad.
2. John and *George* planned the program.
3. The tardy students were Louise and (*your own name*).
4. She needs only Jane and (*you and another person*).
5. Harold called Don and *Paul*.
6. Laura and (*your own name*) went early.
7. The owners are Mr. Black and *Dr. White*.
8. Miss Williams visited Carol and (*your own name*).

9. Tom always helps Bill and *Dick and Greg*.
10. The new officers are Fred and *Ann*.
11. You and *Dean and Doug* should come early.
12. The first visitors will be you and *Joyce and Audrey*.
13. Sally and (*you and another person*) should wait for Mother.
14. *Lon and Bob* and (*your own name*) went to the movies.

D. (1) Write sentences using the following combinations properly as *subjects, predicate nominatives,* or *direct objects.* (2) Exchange papers with a partner. (3) *Proofread for errors in spelling, capitalization, or punctuation.* (4) On the paper that you receive, underscore the compound and label it according to the way that it is used. (5) Call attention to any nonstandard uses. (6) Go over the marked sentences orally.

1. May and I	4. Leo and him	7. Allen and them
2. George and they	5. you and he	8. Jack and me
3. Helen and us	6. him and her	9. you and we

E. (1) Write four combinations similar to those in *D.* (2) Exchange papers with a classmate. (3) In class, take turns at giving sentences using correctly the combinations that you received. Remember, if you mention yourself, name the other person or persons *first*.

Spot Review ★

(*Based upon the sentences in* C *of the preceding activities*)
1. Write the plural of the italicized word in sentence 1.
2. Account for the periods in sentence 7.
3. Why is *Mother* capitalized in sentence 13?

ENRICHMENT

Draw a cartoon that suggests in an amusing way the fact that *you* and *it* do not have different nominative and objective forms. Here, as an example, is one showing the Nominative family and the Objective family starting out on a trip in their automobiles. The families are arguing over whose turn it is to take little You and It.

RULES FOR USING PRONOUNS PROPERLY—Continued

RULE 6. Before a noun, choose *we* if a *subject* or a *predicate nominative* is needed. Use *us* if an *object* is needed. As a help, say the sentence without the noun.

(We, Us) boys went.   (We, Us) went.
We went. [You would never say, *"Us* went."]

He helped (us, we) boys.
He helped (us, we).
He helped *us.* [You would never say, "He helped *we."*]

The cooks were (we, us) girls.
The cooks were (we, us).
The cooks were *we.* [*Us* is not a predicate nominative pronoun.]

Learn about words!

The following words, taken from *A* of the Learning Activities, have interesting histories. Use your dictionary to find the story behind each word. With which word is the drawing connected?

amateur   friend   janitor   faculty

LEARNING ACTIVITIES IN USING *WE* AND *US* BEFORE NOUNS

A. Copy the following sentences, filling the blanks with *we* or *us*. *Do not write in this book.* Go over the practice orally several times, alone and together, so that you get used to the sound of the standard forms.

1. Shall .... girls wait for you?
2. Have they chosen .... boys?
3. .... men cannot help your friend.
4. .... boys have an amateur baseball team.
5. The winners are .... three girls.
6. Our guide met .... tourists at the park gates.
7. The youngest players on the team were .... two boys.
8. The faculty entertained .... students at dinner.
9. .... members of the committee should be there.
10. .... boys often help the janitor at our church.

B. Divide the class into teams. Take turns at giving sentences using standard combinations of a noun and *we* or *us*, such as *us swimmers, we students.* Keep a record of the number of misuses by each team. The team with the fewer misses is the winner. You will need to listen carefully to catch any nonstandard uses.

PART THREE: USING POSSESSIVE PRONOUNS PROPERLY

RULES FOR USING PRONOUNS PROPERLY—Continued

RULE 7. *Never* **use an apostrophe in a** *possessive personal pronoun.* **These pronouns are** *my, mine, his, her, hers, its, our, ours, your, yours, their, theirs.*

> The dog wagged its tail.   That car is like ours.
> Is that book yours?   This ring is hers.
> Our house is gray; theirs is white.

WARNING: Do not confuse the possessive personal pronouns *its, your,* and *their* with the contractions *it's, you're,* and *they're.*

> It's time for dinner. (*It is* time for dinner.)
> You're late again. (*You are* late again.)
> They're coming now. (*They are* coming now.)

If you have trouble deciding between *it's* and *its, you're* and *your, they're* and *their,* substitute in the sentence the words of which the contraction is made.

> The dog wagged (its, it's) tail.

"The dog wagged *it is* tail" does not make sense; use *its.*

> (It's, Its) time for lunch.

"*It is* time for lunch" makes sense; use *It's.*

> (It's, Its) been raining all day.

"*It has* been raining all day" makes sense; use *It's.*

> Give me (you're, your) word.

"Give me *you are* word" does not make sense; use *your.*

> (You're, Your) just in time.

"*You are* just in time" makes sense; use *You're.*

> (They're, Their) team won.

"*They are* team won" does not make sense; use *Their.*

> (They're, Their) my friends.

"*They are* my friends" makes sense; use *They're.*

LEARNING ACTIVITIES IN USING POSSESSIVE PRONOUNS

A. Copy the following sentences, correcting any mistakes in spelling. *Do not write in this book*. Put the sentences on the board so that everyone can see what changes have been made.

1. Mary thinks that the box must be your's. It's not mine.
2. This is her's, but our's is not here.
3. Is that you're book or theirs?
4. It's their's, not ours.
5. Collect all toys that are your's, but do not touch hers.
6. Did the toy dog lose its eye?
7. Its their turn, not ours.
8. Their's are not here with his.
9. They're waiting for us.
10. You're wearing a new hat today. Its very pretty.

B. (1) Write sentences using properly *its, it's; their, they're; your, you're.* (2) Divide the class into two teams. (3) Send the first person of one team to the board. (4) The first member of the other team will read his sentences, one by one. (5) The person at the board must spell correctly the pronoun or contraction used.

PART FOUR: MAKING VERBS AGREE WITH PRONOUN SUBJECTS

THINK IT OVER...

Why is "don't" nonstandard here?

"It (or *He* or *She*) don't" is a serious fault in verb-subject agreement. If you have that habit, now is the time to get rid of it.

The important rules for making verbs agree with noun subjects apply also to agreement with pronoun subjects. Those rules are restated here, plus two (4 and 5) that deal only with pronouns.

RULES FOR AGREEMENT OF VERBS WITH PRONOUN SUBJECTS

RULE 1. Use a singular verb with the singular pronoun subjects *he, she,* and *it.* Use a plural verb with the plural pronoun subjects *we* and *they.*

He does live here.	*They* do live here.
He was at the game.	*We* were at the game.
She has blue eyes.	*They* have blue eyes.
It is late.	*We* are late.

RULE 2. Use *doesn't, isn't, wasn't,* and *hasn't* with the singular subjects *he, she, it.* Use *don't, aren't, weren't,* and *haven't* with the plural subjects *we* and *they.*

He doesn't live here.	*They* don't live here.
It isn't ready.	*They* aren't ready.
He wasn't sure.	*We* weren't sure.
She hasn't decided.	*We* haven't decided.

RULE 3. Never use *ain't* with any subject, singular or plural.

RULE 4. Always use a plural verb with the subject *you,* whether it means one or more than one.

You are the winner.	*You* are the winners.

RULE 5. Use *have* [not *has*], *don't* [not *doesn't*], and *am* [not *is*] with the pronoun subject *I.*

I have seen him.	*I* don't want it.	*I* am here.

LEARNING ACTIVITIES IN MAKING VERBS AGREE WITH PRONOUN SUBJECTS

A. In an oral activity, take turns at asking and answering the following questions. Make each answer a negative one, using a contraction. In sentences 4, 8, and 12, use *we* in your answer. *Do not mark in this book.* Your answer must be a complete sentence.

EXAMPLE: (Don't, Doesn't) he need help? He *doesn't* need help.

1. (Don't, Doesn't) it look like rain?
2. (Is, Are) she going with us?

3. (Was, Were) they born in this state?
4. (Wasn't, Weren't) you and your brother at the beach yesterday?
5. (Doesn't, Don't) he know your mother?
6. (Don't, Doesn't) it seem cold in this room?
7. (Was, Were) they angry about the delay?
8. (Wasn't, Weren't) you and Sally here for the party?
9. (Don't, Doesn't) he live near you?
10. (Wasn't, Weren't) we on time?
11. (Doesn't, Don't) she ever wear red?
12. (Was, Were) you and he at the game?

B. (1) Copy these sentences, choosing the proper forms from the parentheses. (2) *Proofread for careless errors in copying.* (3) In your small groups, check the verb choices as sentences are read aloud.

1. They (wasn't, weren't) looking for us.
2. (Ain't, Aren't) you going horseback riding?
3. (Doesn't, Don't) he like the milkman?
4. You (was, were) busy last night.
5. It (doesn't, don't) make sense to me.
6. We (wasn't, weren't) there at first.
7. (Was, Were) you busy?
8. She (don't, doesn't) want black shoes.
9. He (doesn't, don't) like them very much.
10. We (wasn't, weren't) planning any games.

C. (1) Write two sentences for each of these pronoun subjects: *he, it, she, you, we, they.* In one sentence of each pair, use *wasn't* or *weren't;* in the other, *doesn't* or *don't.* (2) Divide into two teams. (3) Take turns at reading sentences in class. (4) After reading a sentence, call upon a member of the other team to repeat it. If he has failed to listen and cannot say the sentence, his team will be charged with a miss. The team with the fewer misses is the winner.

USING ENGLISH IN ALL CLASSES

Bring to class papers that you have written for any of your classes. Examine them carefully for agreement of verbs with pronoun subjects. Look especially for any misuses of *don't* with the subjects *he, she,* or *it.*

ENRICHMENT

To the tune of some popular song, write a song of your own that will help your class to remember to say *he doesn't, she doesn't, it doesn't, we weren't,* and *they weren't.* If your teacher approves, put your song on the board for the class to copy and practice singing.

TALK IT OVER . . .

The next few pages contain practice in using the standard forms of *come, freeze, lie, break,* and *run,* five troublesome irregular verbs.

USING IRREGULAR VERBS

RULE 1. (*Come* and its forms)
  a) **Never use an auxiliary** (helping) **verb with** *came.*
  b) **Use** *come* **in two ways:** (1) **in present time without a helping verb, and** (2) **in past time with a helping verb.**

Today I **come.**   Yesterday I **came.**   Often I *have* **come.**

LEARNING ACTIVITIES IN USING *CAME* AND *COME*

A. (1) Write each of the following sentences, using the proper form of *come.* (2) Underline the form of *come* that you use. Underline also any helping verbs. (3) Read the sentences aloud when you have finished. Go over them more than once if you have time. *Do not write in this book.*

1. The Norsemen .... to the New World long before Columbus.
2. An idea has just .... to me.
3. Suddenly the moon .... out from behind a cloud.
4. The children's father had recently .... home.
5. That box of books has finally ....
6. The end of the war could have .... sooner.
7. Many interesting stories have .... down to us from Colonial days.
8. My father .... to this country at the age of three.
9. My mother had .... two years earlier.
10. We should have .... with you.
11. Mr. Adams .... home with a present for each of his children.
12. Grandmother .... to visit us last Easter.
13. Mr. Martinez .... up from the basement two steps at a time.
14. He will .... home as soon as possible after the game.
15. They .... early and stayed all day.

B. Write three sentences using *come* with helping verbs and three using *came*. The illustration on this page may give you ideas for sentences. In your small groups, take turns at reading sentences.

C. Pretend that your class had a costume party last Friday night. Take turns at telling how someone in the class was dressed. Use this sentence pattern: "Dick came as ..." To make sure that everyone really listens, decide beforehand on some penalty (1) for anyone who names someone already named and (2) for anyone who uses a type of costume already named. Have fun, but avoid hurting anyone's feelings.

★ **Spot Review**

(*Based upon the sentences in* A *of the preceding activities*)

1. Is *Norsemen* (sentence 1) singular or plural? How can you tell?
2. Why does the apostrophe in *children's* (sentence 4) come before the *s?*
3. Why must you use *has* instead of *have* in sentence 5?
4. How would you spell the plural of the second noun in sentence 8?

USING IRREGULAR VERBS—Continued

RULE 2. (*Freeze* and its forms)

a) **Always use an auxiliary verb with** *frozen;* **never use one with** *froze.*

b) **Never use the forms** *friz* **or** *freezed.*

Today water **freezes.**   Yesterday it **froze.**   Often it *has* **frozen.**

LEARNING ACTIVITIES IN USING *FROZE* AND *FROZEN*

A. Write these sentences, filling the blanks with the proper form of *freeze*. Underline the verb, including any helping verbs. Read the sentences aloud in class. *Do not write in this book.*

1. Early in the winter the little streams had ....
2. The icy wind .... the buds on the trees last night.
3. Commander Byrd's ships .... fast in the ice.
4. We boys almost .... at yesterday's game.
5. Ice cubes can be .... quickly in this electric refrigerator.
6. Yesterday Mother .... ice cream for our luncheon.
7. Luckily, I've never .... my ears.
8. Has the ice on the hockey field .... yet?
9. Wages and prices were .... during World War II.
10. Ice safe for skating must be .... to a certain thickness.
11. Edith really thought her big toe was ....
12. A lost mitten was .... into the ice of the pond.
13. The water in the pond is not yet ....
14. The rain .... on the windshield.

B. Write sentences using these helping verbs with the proper form of *freeze: has, was, might have been, is, will be.* In your small groups, take turns at reading your sentences. Listen carefully for the standard forms.

Spot Review ★

(Based upon the sentences in A *of the preceding activities)*

1. Rewrite sentence 7, replacing the contraction with the words for which it stands.
2. Why does the apostrophe come before the *s* in *Byrd's* in sentence 3?
3. Why is *we boys*, not *us boys*, the proper form in sentence 4?
4. Why is *Mother* capitalized in sentence 6?
5. What are the direct objects in sentences 2, 6, 7?
6. Which sentence has a compound subject?

Learn about words!

The following words, taken from *A* of the Learning Activities, have interesting histories. Use your dictionary to find the story behind each word. With which word is the drawing connected?

hockey   electric   mitten

RULE 3. (*Lie* and its forms)
 a) **Always use a helping verb with** *lain;* **never use one with** *lay.* **Remember that when you use the forms of** *lie,* **you are talking about** *resting* **or** *sleeping.*

Today I **lie** down.   Yesterday I **lay** down.   Often I *have* **lain** down.

 b) **Use the right present participle,** *lying.* (See the footnote on page 291.)

> STANDARD: My dog was **lying** on the porch.
> NONSTANDARD: My dog was ~~laying~~ on the porch.

LEARNING ACTIVITIES IN USING THE FORMS OF *LIE*

A. Write these sentences, filling the blanks with the proper form of *lie.* Underline each verb, including any helping verbs. In class, read the sentences aloud, more than once if time permits.

 1. How long has that sick man .... in bed?
 2. You must .... still now.
 3. Yesterday I .... on the beach for an hour.
 4. Many dangers .... in the path of the early pioneers.
 5. You should not have .... in bed so late.
 6. Are the scissors .... on that table?
 7. Mother should have .... down after lunch.
 8. The bandit .... in hiding for a week.
 9. I must have .... there for an hour.
 10. The boat was .... at anchor.
 11. The Indians had .... in ambush behind the hills.
 12. How long did they .... there?
 13. Snow .... on the mountains all last winter.
 14. Were your glasses .... on the desk?

B. Write sentences on the board, leaving blanks to be filled with *lie, lay, lain,* or *lying.* Call on classmates to read the sentences, using the proper forms and naming any auxiliary verbs.

C. (1) Put these three statements on the board:

>   I can lie still.   I am lying still.   I have lain still.

(2) See how many other statements you can make by changing only the helping verbs. Turn to the list on page 283 if you like. Remember, you may combine two or more helping verbs. (3) Write each new statement in the right column. (4) When you can think of no more, practice reading the sentences in unison.

D. This is a geography lesson. Number your paper from 1 to 8. Opposite each number write *lie* or *lies*, whichever form is proper. *Do not write in this book.* Read these sentences orally in your small groups to check your answers.

1. Canada .... north of the United States.
2. San Diego .... at the southern edge of the California coast.
3. Many fertile farms .... in the Mississippi Valley.
4. The Black Hills .... in western South Dakota.
5. The Pacific and Atlantic coasts .... thousands of miles apart.
6. South of the Rio Grande .... the country of Mexico.
7. Which .... farther north, Maine or Minnesota?
8. Does St. Louis .... east of Minneapolis?

E. Make out a list of five true geographical statements about your state, using *lie* or *lies* in each sentence. Read your sentences to the class, leaving out the name of the place that you have in mind. The class will try to guess its name.

USING IRREGULAR VERBS—Continued

RULE 4. (*Break* and its forms)
Always use a helping verb with *broken;* never use one with *broke.*
Today I **break.**   Yesterday I **broke.**   Often I *have* **broken.**

READ AND THINK ABOUT

The other day, Harry and Raymond made up a jingle to help them remember the rule for using the forms of "break." They disagreed over the second line, however. Here is their "poem," with Harry's second line:

> Hurray for the independent *broke!*
> It travels on its own.
> But *broken* is the timid type
> And NEVER goes alone.

Raymond wanted the second line to be

> It needs no chaperone.

Which do you like better? After you decide, you may want to learn the jingle as an aid to remembering the correct use of *broke* and *broken.*

LEARNING ACTIVITIES IN USING *BROKE* AND *BROKEN*

A. Write these sentences, filling the blanks with the proper form of *break*. Read the sentences aloud and name any helping verbs. *Do not write in this book.*

1. John and I have not .... our promise.
2. The sun has not .... through the clouds all day.
3. The high-jump record was .... by Terry Mayo.
4. Three of the eggs in the girl's basket had ....
5. Eagerly the boy .... the seal on the letter.
6. The strong wind must have .... this window.
7. Jane .... the news to Father this morning.
8. Ground has just been .... for the new library.

B. Write two good sentences using *broke* and three using *broken*. Use inverted order (see point 1 on page 316) in at least two sentences. In your small groups, take turns at reading the sentences aloud.

★ **Spot Review**

(Based upon the sentences in A of the preceding activities)

1. How many girls are there in sentence 4? Prove your answer.
2. Spell the plural of *library* (sentence 8). Give the rule.
3. Which four sentences contain direct objects? Name these objects.
4. Why is *I*, not *me*, the standard form in sentence 1?
5. Rewrite sentence 2, using a contraction.

USING IRREGULAR VERBS—Continued

RULE 5. (*Run* and its forms)
  a) **Never use an auxiliary verb with** *ran*.
  b) **Use** *run* **in two ways: (1) with a helping verb and (2) by itself in present time.**
  Today I **run**.   Yesterday I **ran**.   Often I *have* **run**.

LEARNING ACTIVITIES IN USING *RAN* AND *RUN*

A. Take turns at completing the following sentences orally, using the proper form of *run* as a part of the sentence and using as many other words as you wish. To make sure that everyone listens, decide on some penalty for any person who completes a sentence exactly as someone else has given it.

1. I have never ...
2. As a boy, my father ...
3. Jim might have ...
4. That race was ...
5. After seeing me, the man ...
6. The child shouldn't have ...

B. (1) Find *run* in the dictionary. (2) Use in written sentences five different meanings of *run* as a verb. In each sentence use (*a*) *run* with a helping verb or (*b*) *ran*. In your small groups, take turns at reading your sentences aloud.

C. (1) Copy these sentences, filling the blanks with the proper form of *run*. (2) Underline each verb, including any helping verbs. (3) Exchange papers for checking. (4) *Proofread each sentence for careless errors in copying.* (5) Check the verbs as the sentences are read aloud.

1. In my first race, I .... a poor last.
2. That man's brother, a big-game hunter, must have .... many risks.
3. My Uncle Fred has .... for Congress twice.
4. Once upon a time, a busy road .... past our farm.
5. My alarm clock .... down last night.
6. Have you ever .... away from home?
7. At the Labor Day picnic last week, the boys .... races.
8. The color in this dress should not have ....
9. In the sixth inning of that game, our pitcher .... into trouble.
10. You must have .... this machine too fast.

Spot Review

(Based upon the sentences in C of the preceding activities)

1. How would you write the plural of the possessive in sentence 2?
2. How is *hunter* used in sentence 2? Explain the commas.
3. Why do *Uncle* (sentence 3) and *Day* (sentence 7) have capital letters?
4. Why is *have* the proper form in sentence 6?

ENRICHMENT

By yourself or with a friend, make up a jingle to help you remember (1) that *run* is used both by itself (to show present time) and with a helping verb; (2) that *ran* always stands alone. With your teacher's approval, say your jingle for the class. Be sure to apply the Guides to a Pleasing, Effective Voice, page 41.

A. Copy the following sentences. Underline each pronoun and label it according to its use in the sentence: *subject* (subj.), *predicate nominative* (p.n.), *direct object* (d.o.), *appositive* (app.). *Proofread to make sure you have made no errors in copying.*

1. He and I went to the ball game at Yankee Stadium.
2. A Yankee player, he with the number 12, hit a high foul ball.
3. The spectators closest to the ball were George and I.
4. The ball hit me on top of the head.

B. Read these sentences aloud, choosing the proper forms.

1. Tom chose Jim and (I, me).
2. Joe and (he, him) are great friends.
3. This is (she, her) speaking.
4. The boys and (we, us) will go with you.
5. Could it be (they, them) standing there?
6. No one called you and (I, me).
7. (We, Us) members of the committee need your help.
8. Will you tell (we, us) girls about the picnic?
9. Father called (we, us) children at six o'clock.
10. Every noon (we, us) boys play marbles.
11. The dog wagged (its, it's) tail.
12. Is this book (yours, your's)?
13. The next house is (ours, our's).
14. (They're, Their) car is a new one.

C. Read these sentences aloud, choosing the standard forms.

1. We (wasn't, weren't) waiting for anyone.
2. He (don't, doesn't) ever wear overshoes.
3. You (was, were) tired last night.
4. (Don't, Doesn't) she have brown eyes?
5. Where (was, were) you last Friday?
6. He (don't, doesn't) believe me.
7. They (was, were) busy in the kitchen.
8. (Wasn't, Weren't) you and Bill playing ball?
9. It (don't, doesn't) often snow here.

D. Copy these sentences, supplying the proper form of each verb. Go over the sentences orally.

1. That man (come) to this country forty years ago.
2. (Lie) here until dinnertime.

---

* Check Test 4 should be taken at this point. If the results show need for further study, students should do this review practice. They should then take Mastery Test 4.

3. Mother had (lie) down for a short rest.
4. The silence was (break) by a loud crash.
5. At the picnic last Friday, we (run) races.
6. The book (lie) on the table yesterday.
7. I (freeze) my ears last winter.
8. Many people have (come) to America from Europe.
9. The man had been (lie) in wait for us.
10. Mr. Blake has (run) for office many times.
11. Last night thieves (break) into Mr. Gray's store.
12. Now the ground has (freeze) hard.
13. Because of the hot sun, I (lie) in the shade.
14. Christmas Day had (come) again.
15. Whose farm (lie) straight north of here?
16. You (run) that race in record time.

Cumulative Review

CAPITALIZATION

Copy these sentences, inserting needed capital letters.

1. mexicans, canadians, and alaskans—all are americans. most of them live on a mainland, north america. people in ireland, england, and scotland live on islands.
2. Finally mother said, "on christmas day, let's show the slides of our trip to the east. we'll write uncle james and aunt alice to come."
3. father added, "that's a fine idea. we'll celebrate right here on good old emerson street. we'll have a good time."
4. bill and ben, who worked on a farm during june and july, wrote an airplane story that they called "landing in clover."
5. A pilot of the army air corps, captain n. b. dunn, made a forced landing in a clover field near which the boys were working.

PUNCTUATION

Copy these sentences, inserting needed punctuation.

1. Yes Son before I trust you to drive alone said Bobs father Id like to see you park the car
2. Thats easy Bob exclaimed with entirely too much confidence
3. Bob found a busy street tried to back into a parking place and scraped a fender
4. The next day Father Mother and Marge his older sister took Bob to a lonely street and made him practice parking over and over again
5. Then Marge gave him a book called How to Drive a Car by Captain O L Reyburn a member of the local traffic department

CONTRACTIONS

Write the correct contraction of each of these groups of words.

1. will not	3. does not	5. it is	7. you are
2. I will	4. they have	6. are not	8. have not

SPELLING

Copy the following words in a column on a sheet of paper. Beside each word write another word made from it by adding a suffix. These words are spelled by rules.

1. like	5. fool	9. hop	13. quit
2. swim	6. enter	10. skate	14. funny
3. open	7. lucky	11. write	15. refer
4. marry	8. argue	12. play	16. run

POSSESSIVE OF NOUNS

Write the correct possessive form of each of the nouns below and name the thing owned. For each common noun, put *a, an,* or *the* before it. For example, if the word were *team,* you might write *the team's captain.*

1. Charles	4. bears	7. firemen	10. Washington
2. oxen	5. children	8. girls	11. father-in-law
3. rabbit	6. Jane	9. authors	12. soprano

VERB-SUBJECT AGREEMENT

Read these sentences aloud, choosing the standard forms.

1. There (isn't, aren't) many boys in this class.
2. (Hasn't, Haven't) Fritz or Larry called you?
3. The men in the boat (was, were) fishing.
4. (Don't, Doesn't) the smell of those pies make you hungry?
5. George and Earl (has, have) been here before.
6. There (hasn't, haven't) been any letters for two days.
7. The pail of blueberries (wasn't, weren't) on the step.

TROUBLESOME VERBS

Read these sentences aloud, using the proper form of each verb.

1. Don has (do) the problem.
2. Have you (give) the answer?
3. I (know) him years ago.
4. The piece was (speak) well.
5. Have you (take) my eraser?
6. Once Bob (bring) us a lion.
7. I've (write) you before.
8. We (begin) work last week.
9. Have they (go)?
10. I have (see) that movie.
11. A queen was (choose).
12. At last he (give) up.
13. Only a pie was (take).
14. Dick had (go) early.
15. Has he (bring) a camera?
16. She has (write) twice.

Word Games to Test Your Thinking

CATCH ON TO THE TRICK

All the words defined below end in *ick* and rhyme with *trick*.

1. Not well
2. Sound of a watch
3. "Locking" sound
4. Piece of wood
5. A young chicken
6. Not thin
7. Baked block of clay
8. Give a blow with the foot
9. "It must be St. ...."
10. Slight cut
11. Nickname for *Richard*
12. Pass the tongue over
13. Select
14. Part of a candle
15. Fast
16. A cramp
17. To pierce lightly
18. Smooth
19. A quick light stroke
20. A stack of hay

FORWARD AND BACKWARD PUZZLE

Did you ever stop to think that many words are spelled the same forward as backward? Can you figure out the following? An example is *eve*, meaning "the night before."

1. Before (rhymes with *there*)
2. Even (rhymes with *bevel*)
3. Girl's name (rhymes with *banana*)
4. Boy's name (sounds like another word for *car*)
5. Past of *do*
6. A soft drink
7. A nickname for *Mother*
8. A small dog
9. Vigor
10. Distress signal
11. A name for *Father* (not *Pop*)
12. Not speaking
13. A small child
14. Girl's name (last name could be *Gardner*)

WOULD YOU LIKE TO KNOW—?

The encyclopedia answers to these questions may surprise you.

1. What strange weapon of offense has the *octopus?*
2. In what country was *oleomargarine* first produced?
3. What is the real name of the ship nicknamed *Old Ironsides?*
4. Why should *oleander* plants be kept away from little children?
5. In a race between an *ostrich* and a horse, which would win?

Copy the crossword puzzle. *Do not write in this book.*

Across

1. To fail to fulfill someone's hopes.
9. The sixtieth part of an hour.
10. The face of a clock.
11. Present form of *be*.
12. A girl's name.
13. Seven days.
14. Steamship (*abbr.*).
15. A person who has this never embarrasses anyone (rhymes with *fact*).
17. 1,102 (*Roman numerals*).
19. Grass-covered earth.
21. Present of *saw*.
22. Finish.
23. An act of pleading.
25. Payments charged for services.
28. Present tense of *went*.
29. Level; regular; opposite of *odd*.
30. Making use of.
32. Past of the verb *lead*.
33. Initials of "Honest Abe's" father.
34. One who does.
36. Said when you want someone to keep quiet.
37. What you hear in church.
39. Religious holiday.
42. To say again.
43. Comparative form of *dry*.
45. South Carolina (*abbr.*).
46. To try out something.

Down

1. To change from a solid into a liquid state; to melt.
2. Preposition.
3. A kind of wearing apparel.
4. A book of maps.
5. Opposite of *warlike*.
6. The same (*Latin abbr.*).
7. The daughter of one's brother.
8. Opposite of *giving*.
9. Spelled incorrectly.
16. Used in golf (*plural*).
18. An image to which worship is offered.
20. An act.
24. Indefinite article.
26. A kind of duck.
27. Noise made by some sleepers.
31. Jewels.
33. Opposite of *here*.
35. One way to cook meat.
36. Part of a stair.
38. New York City (*abbr.*).
40. A plural form of *be*.
41. "Sing a song of ......pence."
44. Yes (*Spanish and Italian*).

USING ADJECTIVES IN
BUILDING SENTENCES *

"ADJECTIVES MUST BE TO KEEP
SENTENCES FROM BEING TOO SHORT."

THINK IT OVER...

Should adjectives be used "to keep sentences from being too short"?
What *should* determine the use of adjectives?
Have you any idea how much use you yourself make of them?

*Pretest 5 should be taken at this point.

1. Recognizing Adjectives

Look again at the picture on page 329 and the sentence below it: "The boy hit the ball." Suppose it read like this:

One tall, slender boy hit *the first* ball.

What does that word *one* tell you? It tells *how many* boys. What do *tall* and *slender* tell you? They tell *what kind* of boy, or what he looked like. What do *the* and *first* tell you? They tell *which* ball the boy hit. The meaning of the nouns *boy* and *ball* is affected by those words *one, tall, slender, the,* and *first.* Such words are used as "adjectives."

One tall, slender boy hit **the first** ball.

As pointed out in earlier chapters, verbs, nouns, and pronouns are *parts of speech.* The adjective is another part of speech.

As you study this chapter, be sure to keep in mind that you cannot tell what part of speech a word is simply by looking at it. A word that is a noun in one sentence may be a verb in another sentence. In other words, <u>the part of speech of a word depends on the way that it is used in the sentence.</u> The word "farm," for example, may be used as a verb, a noun, or an adjective.

Did Jack *farm* all last summer? (*Farm* is a verb.)
His *farm* is located on Route 40. (*Farm* is a noun.)
Bob enjoys *farm* life. (*Farm* is an adjective.)

1. (DEFINITION) *True adjectives* are words that modify (*affect*) nouns by describing them, or telling *what kind*.

We need tall boys.   Red hair suits me.

A true adjective meets certain tests.

a) It will fit into the slots in this sentence:

The .... one seems very ....
The tall one seems very tall.   The red one seems very red.

b) It can take (1) **suffixes** or (2) the marking words *more* or *most* to show comparison.

(1) tall, taller, tallest   (2) useful, more useful, most useful

2. **Many adjectives are made from verbs.**

We crossed the frozen lake.   Freezing rain was falling.

3. **Adjectives may be compound.**

A loud and noisy crowd came.   Has he brown or blue eyes?

A small but strong man helped me.

LEARNING ACTIVITIES IN FINDING AND USING ADJECTIVES

A. To give a good idea of what adjectives can do, carry out this activity. (1) Here are five nouns: *river, tree, sky, man, coat.* (2) On your paper, write for each of those nouns five adjectives that might be used to describe it. (3) On the board list each noun and all the different adjectives that the members of the class wrote on their papers.

B. Use the tests in point 1 to decide which of the following words can be adjectives.

1. snowy	5. quickly	9. green	13. change
2. about	6. write	10. terrific	14. always
3. help	7. original	11. timidly	15. childish
4. different	8. lovely	12. blank	16. exciting

C. The way that a word is used determines its part of speech. Tell (1) whether each italicized word in these sentences is used as a noun, a verb, or an adjective and (2) how you know.

1. That song is a tale about three *blind* mice.
2. Did those headlights *blind* you?
3. I raised the *blind* to let in the sun.
4. The new store will *open* tomorrow.
5. He entered through that *open* window.
6. Come out into the *open*.
7. We are having *fine* weather.
8. The *fine* was a heavy one.
9. Did they *fine* that man?
10. A *brave* is an Indian warrior.
11. We must *brave* the storm.
12. That was a *brave* deed!

D. (1) Write an original paragraph in which you use these nouns: *boy, lake, storm, dog, wind, water.* Be sure to apply the Guides for Writing a Paragraph, page 214. With each noun use one or more adjectives that will give a clear and vivid picture. (2) *Be sure to proofread for careless errors;* review the Writing Chart, page 172. (3) Take turns reading paragraphs in class or in your small groups. As you listen, jot down adjectives that you think are especially well chosen. Compare notes afterwards. The drawing offers ideas for paragraphs.

★ **Spot Review**

(Based upon the sentences in C of the preceding activities)

1. Five of the sentences have verb phrases. Name the phrases.
2. Five sentences have direct objects. Name them.
3. Which one is an imperative sentence?
4. Give the pattern for each sentence.

2. Recognizing Predicate Adjectives

"IT LOOKS LIKE AN ADJECTIVE, BUT WHAT'S IT DOING AFTER THE VERB?"

Jack is honest.

THINK IT OVER...

Can an adjective come after the verb in a sentence?

Strange as it seems to the boy, *honest* is an adjective in *Jack is honest*. That is a *Pattern 4* sentence, explained in this lesson.

● **THESE ARE FACTS ABOUT PREDICATE ADJECTIVES**

1. **(DEFINITION)** **An adjective that completes the verb, or predicate, and modifies the subject is a** *predicate adjective*.

   The boy is tall.

   The word *tall* comes after and completes the predicate verb, *is*; it modifies the subject, *boy*. (It tells *what kind* of boy.)

2. **Predicate adjectives complete such linking verbs as** *am, is, are, was, were, be, been,* **or combinations, such as** *is being, will be, have been.*

   The children *were* sleepy.   The weather *has been* cold and wet.

3. **Predicate adjectives may also complete verbs like** *become, seem, feel, appear, look, taste,* **and** *smell.*

   The fruit *seems* ripe.   Mary *feels* ill.

4. **Sentences that have predicate adjectives are** *Pattern 4* **sentences. The formula is** $N + LV + A$.

N + LV + A	N + LV + A
Today was sunny.	Your desk looks neat.

393

LEARNING ACTIVITIES IN PREDICATE ADJECTIVES

A. Copy the following sentences. Underline each predicate adjective and draw an arrow to the word modified. Go over your papers orally.

1. This light is certainly brilliant.
2. Jack was late for breakfast.
3. The crowd appeared restless at first.
4. That man seems really busy.
5. Our dog becomes noisy sometimes.
6. The place looks much different now.
7. My brother is skillful at many things.
8. Those flowers smell sweet.
9. Mother felt better today.
10. We were almost sure of winning.

B. Copy the following sentences, completing each one so that it becomes a Pattern 4 sentence. (Be careful not to use a predicate noun by mistake.) In your small groups, take turns at reading sentences. Notice how the various predicate adjectives change the sentence picture. *Do not write in this book.*

1. That man certainly looks ....
2. Our neighbors are ....
3. Aunt Elsie is ....
4. The people have become ....
5. The air smells ....
6. The children were ....
7. The house looked ....
8. Both those men are ....
9. My head felt ....
10. I am ....

C. Write sentences using the following words in Pattern 4 sentences: *graceful, honest, sleepy, sweet, pleasant, beautiful.* Use a different linking verb in each sentence. Note the drawing. Read the sentences in class.

3. Recognizing Other Adjectival Words: I

Some words that are not true adjectives are used like adjectives; in other words, they modify nouns. *Determiners* form one group of such words. They are *adjectival words;* that is, words that are *used like adjectives.*

● **THESE ARE FACTS ABOUT ADJECTIVAL WORDS: I**

1. **(DEFINITION)** *Determiners* **are words that modify nouns but do not fit the tests for true adjectives.**

   a) **Some determiners point out** *which.*

   (1) **The articles** *a, an,* **and** *the* **always do so.**

   A man called.   I ate an apple.   The race is over.

   (2) *This, that, these,* **and** *those* **can do so.**

   This book is mine.   I like those plans.

   (3) *First, second, third,* **and so on can do so.**

   We took the first bus.   They live on the tenth floor.

   b) **Possessive nouns and pronouns are determiners that tell** *whose.*

   Henry's book is new.   My book is old.

   c) **Numerals (***one, two, three,* **...) are determiners that tell** *how many.*

   I ate two apples.   We need forty-six boys.

   d) **Special determiners limit nouns by telling** *which, how many,* **or** *how much.* **Here are some of them.**

all	both	enough	many	much	several
another	each	every	more	no	some
any	either	few	most	other	such

   Each girl helped.   Both men left.   I like most foods.

2. **If a noun has both determiners and true adjectives, the determiners always come first.**

   We bought two new tires.   It was a windy, rainy day.

   (*Two* comes before *new; a* comes before *windy* and *rainy.*)

The following words, taken from *B* of the Learning Activities, have interesting histories. Use your dictionary to find the story behind each word. With which word is the drawing connected?

lieutenant   mustang   dairy   vacation

LEARNING ACTIVITIES IN USING ADJECTIVES AND DETERMINERS

A. Many determiners can also be used as subjects, predicate nominatives, or direct objects. *His, her,* and *its; this, that, these,* and *those* can be. So can many of the words that are listed under subpoint *d* of point *1* on page 395.

Decide which italicized words in the following sentences are used as determiners and which are not. Tell as what sentence parts the latter are used. Make this an oral exercise.

1. *Much* money will be needed for *this* project.
2. Bill has *some* new books. *Several* look exciting.
3. *Many* people remember *her* very well.
4. *This* house must be *his.*
5. May I borrow *those* pliers? I haven't *any* of my own.
6. Where did you hear *that*?
7. *Which* day for the picnic suits you?
8. We can take *either* road. Both look very good.
9. *Each* player was a star in *that* game.
10. I don't know *much* about the *other* man.
11. *Most* days lately have had *some* sunshine.
12. *Another* girl has finished *her* report.

B. (1) Copy the following sentences, underlining each adjective or word used as an adjective. (2) Draw an arrow to the noun modified, as in the examples on page 391. (3) Exchange papers for checking. (4) *Proofread for careless errors in copying.* (5) Go over the sentences in class. Tell which words are true adjectives and which are determiners.

1. Three little girls wore white dresses.
2. Grandfather's new house has many beautiful rooms.
3. The howling wind drowned our voices.
4. Do many women become famous athletes?
5. Jim's throwing arm has been bothering him.
6. The noisy and excited crowd cheered their team.

7. The tall, thin, smiling lieutenant is my big brother.
8. Few men have ridden that wild mustang.
9. Those two boys have built several good carts.
10. Uncle Bill runs a large and spotless dairy.
11. Each team has won four thrilling games.
12. Have you seen Alfred's miniature camera?
13. These shoes are my favorite ones.
14. Both children have been enjoying their vacation.
15. The frightened child has lost his mother.

4. Recognizing Other Adjectival Words: II

Determiners, you have learned, are used like adjectives. This lesson deals with nouns that are used in that way; in other words, with nouns that function as modifiers.

● THESE ARE FACTS ABOUT OTHER ADJECTIVAL WORDS: II

1. **A word made from a proper noun can modify other nouns. Such a modifier is sometimes called a proper adjective.**
   The American flag waved in the breeze.

2. **A proper noun itself is sometimes a modifier.**
   My South Carolina uncle is visiting us.

3. **Common nouns sometimes are modifiers.**
   The package was tied with a paper ribbon.

LEARNING ACTIVITIES IN USING NOUN FORMS AS MODIFIERS

A. Write the following proper nouns and beside each write the modifying form made from it. If you are not sure of the spelling, check with the dictionary. *Do not write in this book.* Go over the list in class.

1. Canada	3. Japan	5. China	7. Turkey
2. Australia	4. Italy	6. Africa	8. Portugal

B. Write the following words and opposite each write the proper noun from which it comes. Check these in class.

1. English	4. Danish	7. Spanish	10. French
2. Norwegian	5. Swedish	8. Brazilian	11. Hungarian
3. Scottish	6. Belgian	9. Roman	12. Welsh

C. Write five sentences using as modifiers words from *B,* or others, if you prefer. *Be sure to proofread,* using the Writing Chart on page 172. In your small groups, read your sentences. Call on classmates to tell what word each of your choices modifies.

5. Using Vivid, Exact Adjectives

READ AND THINK ABOUT

Adjectives can be helpful in making what a person says both interesting and accurate. The trouble with many people is that they use the same adjectives again and again. For example, your father may have said to you last night, "Well, how was the game?" Depending upon which side won, of course, you may have replied with one of these remarks:

"It was grand."	"It was terrible."
"It was swell."	"It was awful."
"It was keen."	"It was rotten."

The left-hand answers indicate that you enjoyed the game; the other three, the opposite. Not one of them, however, gives a really good picture of what the game was like.

GUIDES FOR USING ADJECTIVES EFFECTIVELY

1. Avoid using such overworked adjectives as *grand, swell, keen, awful, nice, terrible,* or *wonderful.*
2. Use words that give an exact, vivid picture. Remember that vivid adjectives can be made from many verbs.

    WEAK: A *bad* hailstorm ruined our wheat.

    VIVID: A *slashing* hailstorm ruined our wheat.

    WEAK: An *old* car pulled up at the curb.

    VIVID: A *battered* car pulled up at the curb.

3. If your library has a dictionary of synonyms, use it to find strong substitutes for adjectives that you overuse.

Learn about words!

The following words, taken from *A* of the Learning Activities, have interesting histories. Use your dictionary to find the story behind each word. With which word is the drawing connected?

science   nice   carpenter   minstrel

LEARNING ACTIVITIES IN USING VIVID, EXACT ADJECTIVES

A. Make the following sentences more effective by substituting exact adjectives for the ones in italics. Go over your sentences in your small groups, making a list of the substituted adjectives.

1. It was a *wonderful* motion picture.
2. The trip into Canada was *great*.
3. They had a *grand* time at the minstrel show.
4. The Browns are *swell* people.
5. That certainly was an *awful* storm.
6. Our science teacher is *keen*.
7. We had a *terrible* time finding the carpenter.
8. John is a *nice* boy.
9. The dinner was *terrific*.

B. (1) Study the following sentences, all taken from Mark Twain's *The Adventures of Tom Sawyer*. (2) In an oral activity, point out and have listed on the board the vivid adjectives used by the author. Note that many are made from verbs. Notice also that in one sentence the adjectives follow the noun modified. (3) Point out any vivid nouns or verbs.

1. The balmy summer air, the restful quiet, the odor of the flowers, and the drowsing murmur of the bees had had their effect.
2. Away off in the flaming sunshine, Cardiff Hill lifted its soft green sides through a shimmering veil of heat.
3. The climbing fire lit up their faces and threw its ruddy glare upon the pillared tree-trunks ... and upon the varnished foliage and festooning vines.
4. One blinding flash after another came, and peal on peal of deafening thunder.
5. The boys cried out to each other, but the roaring wind and the booming thunderblasts drowned their voices utterly.
6. And that night there came on a terrific storm, with driving rain, awful claps of thunder, and blinding sheets of lightning.
7. Potter, pale and haggard, timid and hopeless, was brought in, ...
8. Tom was a glittering hero once more ...
9. The clanging bell had been calling for half an hour.

C. Write five original sentences in which you use adjectives that give a clear and exact picture. For example, describe a race, a fire, a new automobile, a good dinner, a picnic, a hot day, a cold day, a snowstorm, a crowd of people. Remember, adjectives that are verb forms (especially the *-ing* ones, such as *blazing*) often are good picture words. Take turns at reading sentences aloud. Have someone list on the board adjectives that seem to the class to be especially good.

FOLLOW-UP

Copy in your notebook the lists of vivid, exact adjectives that the class made in activities A, B, and C. Whenever you have a writing assignment, make use of this list.

USING ENGLISH IN ALL CLASSES

Go over papers that you are preparing for any of your classes. Check to see whether you are using the same vague or worn-out adjectives over and over. If you are, change them to words that give a clearer and more exact picture.

6. Comparing Adjectives

| THIS MAN IS FAT. | HIS BROTHER IS FATTER. | THEIR COUSIN IS FATTEST OF ALL. |

If an adjective could not take different forms, such as *fat, fatter, fattest,* comparing one thing with another would be almost impossible. Fortunately, adjectives *can* change their form to show various degrees of comparison.

● THESE ARE FACTS ABOUT COMPARING ADJECTIVES

1. Most adjectives have three degrees of comparison: (*a*) *positive*, (*b*) *comparative*, (*c*) *superlative*. Comparative **degree compares** *two* **things.** *Superlative* **degree compares** *more than two.*

Positive Degree	Comparative Degree	Superlative Degree
new	newer	newest
funny	funnier	funniest
noble	nobler	noblest

2. One-syllable adjectives and some two-syllable adjectives (especially ones ending in *y* or *le*) add *er* and *est* to form the comparative and the superlative, as in the examples above.* (For spelling changes that may take place, see Rule 2, page 190, and Rule 1, page 193.)

3. Many two-syllable adjectives and almost all those of more than two syllables use *more* and *most*.

Positive	Comparative	Superlative
helpless	more helpless	most helpless
important	more important	most important

4. A few adjectives are irregular in their comparison.

Positive	Comparative	Superlative
good	better	best
bad	worse	worst
much, many	more	most
little†	less	least

LEARNING ACTIVITY IN COMPARING ADJECTIVES

(1) In your small groups, divide the following words into two lists: (*a*) adjectives that are compared by adding *er* and *est* and (*b*) those compared by using *more* and *most*. (2) Compare lists in class. (3) Have the spelling of the comparisons in the *a* list written on the board. Give for each one the spelling rule that applies.

1. cheerful	6. clumsy	11. honest	16. prompt
2. jolly	7. splendid	12. steady	17. glad
3. flat	8. careless	13. big	18. muddy
4. delicious	9. cool	14. straight	19. simple
5. interesting	10. friendly	15. critical	20. dim

* The unabridged dictionary gives the comparative forms of most words that can be compared by adding *er* and *est*.

† The comparison here refers to *little* when applied to an amount: *little* money, *less* money, *least* money. *Little*, referring to *size*, is compared regularly: *little, littler, littlest*.

DIAGRAMMING ADJECTIVES

Here is how to fit adjectives into the diagram pattern.

One tall, slender boy hit *the first* ball.

You have learned that *one, tall,* and *slender* are adjectives modifying the subject, *boy;* and that *first* is an adjective modifying the object, *ball. The* is always an adjective; here, it modifies *ball.*

STEPS IN DIAGRAMMING ADJECTIVES

1. First, diagram the backbone of the sentence, as usual. Note that the words on the base line are the words of the sentence pattern.

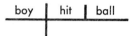

2. Place adjectives on slanting lines below the words that they modify:

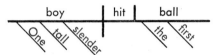

COMPOUND ADJECTIVES	POSSESSIVE ADJECTIVES
A *tall* **and** *slender* man met us.	*Tom's* sister often changes *her* mind.

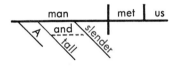 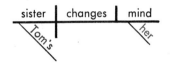

3. Diagram *predicate adjectives* as you do predicate nominatives. Place them on the main line with a slanted line pointing back to the subject.

Father is *tall.*   We were *tired* but *happy.*

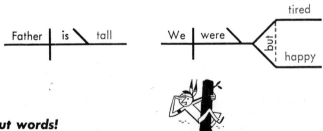

Learn about words!

The following words, taken from *A* of the Learning Activities, have interesting histories. Use your dictionary to find the story behind each word. With which word is the drawing connected?

acrobat   alert   carnival   champion

A. (1) Diagram the verb, the subject, any direct objects or predicate nominatives, and the adjectives in the following sentences. (2) Exchange papers. (3) Have the diagrams put on the board. (4) Check the papers as each diagram is explained orally. Be sure to follow a definite pattern. For example, one sentence in the sample diagrams might be explained thus: "The verb is an action verb, *changes*. The subject is a noun, *sister*. There is a direct object, the noun *mind*. *Tom's* is a possessive noun used to modify the subject, and *her* is a pronoun used as a possessive adjective to modify the direct object."

1. That old man reads many books.
2. Both girls are busy and happy.
3. Those men are our neighbors.
4. I need four carnival tickets.
5. The old champion has a new title.
6. The speech was long and dull.
7. Sue's young brother is noisy.
8. I have two new hats.
9. An acrobat must be alert.
10. This wall is old but strong.

B. For further practice, diagram the sentences in *B* on page 396 and in *A* on page 394. Be sure to explain the diagrams orally.

Spot Review ★

(Based upon the sentences in A *of the preceding activities)*
1. Account for the apostrophe in sentence 7.
2. Which sentences are Pattern 4 sentences?
3. Which sentences contain present tense verbs?
4. Compare the adjectives in sentence 6.

7. Using Standard English

PART ONE: USING ADJECTIVES PROPERLY

THINK IT OVER ...

This section deals with certain common problems in adjective usage. Learning and applying the rules on the next page will help you to make certain that your oral and written use of adjectives is in the realm of "standard" usage.

RULES FOR USING ADJECTIVES PROPERLY

RULE 1. Use *an* **before a word beginning with a vowel** (that is, *a, e, i, o,* or *u*) **or a vowel sound** (words beginning with silent *h,* as in *heir, honest,* and *hour*).

an apple   an honor   an egg   an orange

RULE 2. Use *a* **before a word beginning with a consonant sound.**

a house   a flower   a wreath   a storm

RULE 3. **When you speak about** *separate nouns,* **be sure to use** *a, an,* **or** *the* **before each. If only one person or thing is meant, do not repeat the article.**

He needed **a** stenographer and bookkeeper. (*one person*)
He needed **a** stenographer and **a** bookkeeper. (*two persons*)
She bought **a** green and brown dress. (*one dress*)
She bought **a** green and **a** brown dress. (*two dresses*)

RULE 4. **Use the singular** *this* **or** *that* **with** *kind* **or** *sort;* **use the plural** *these* **or** *those* **with** *kinds* **or** *sorts.*

this (or that) *kind* of shoes   these (or those) *kinds* of shoes
this (or that) *sort* of skates   these (or those) *sorts* of skates

RULE 5. **Do not use** *them* **for** *these* **or** *those.* *Them* is a personal pronoun that should be used only as an object.

STANDARD: Give me **those** books. NONSTANDARD: Give me ~~them~~ books.

RULE 6. **Use the** *superlative* **form of an adjective only if you are speaking of** *more than two.*

STANDARD: He is the **tallest** boy on the basketball team.
NONSTANDARD: This is the ~~newest~~ of the two books.

RULE 7. **Do not use double comparisons; that is, if you add** *-er* **and** *-est,* **omit** *more* **and** *most.*

STANDARD: I am **busier** than Dick.
NONSTANDARD: I am ~~more~~ busier than Dick.

LEARNING ACTIVITIES IN USING ADJECTIVES PROPERLY

A. (*Rules 1 and 2*) Write a list of ten nouns before which you should use the article *an.* Then do the same for *a.* Read your lists in class.

B. (*Rule 3*) In your small groups, go over the following sentences, choosing the proper or clearer forms. Explain your choice in each case.

1. Mr. Brown is (a physician and surgeon, a physician and a surgeon).
2. On the committee Bob put (a boy and girl, a boy and a girl).

3. I saw (a sailor and a soldier, a sailor and soldier) on the street.
4. Jack was wearing (a red and a blue, a red and blue) jacket.
5. The boys had (a bat and ball, a bat and a ball).
6. Marilyn wants to be (a teacher or nurse, a teacher or a nurse).
7. They are looking for a man to work as (a driver and mechanic, a driver and a mechanic).

C. (*Rule 4*) Copy these sentences, filling the blanks with *this, that, these, those,* or *them. Do not write in this book.* Exchange papers and check them as you read the sentences orally.

1. .... sort of desk is more convenient.
2. I like .... kind better now.
3. Are .... coats on sale?
4. I bought .... kind of dishes.
5. .... boys went with me.
6. .... sort of fish lives in fresh water.
7. Those shoes may be a bargain. I don't like ...., though.
8. .... kinds of matches are more expensive.
9. What did .... skates cost?
10. I like your glasses. How often have you worn ....?
11. Mother said that .... kinds of needles are best.
12. Do you ever wear .... sorts of dresses?

D. (*Rules 5 and 6*) (1) Copy the following sentences, using the proper adjective forms. (2) Exchange papers. (3) *Proofread for careless errors in copying.* (4) As they are read aloud, check the sentences for use of the proper adjective forms.

1. Which is the (taller, tallest) of you two boys?
2. I'm (more hungrier, hungrier) at dinner than at breakfast.
3. Of these two jackets, the blue one is the (better, best) value.
4. The (older, oldest) one of those four girls is a senior.
5. Last night we played our (worse, worst) game of all.
6. Is this the (shorter, shortest) of the two roads?

E. Write a paragraph in which you use *this, that, these,* and *those* in the right combinations with *kind* or *sort.* Perhaps thinking about the clothes that you wear will give you an idea for your paragraph. Refer to the Guides for Writing a Paragraph, page 214, as you plan your writing. Read the paragraphs in your small groups. Listen for the proper uses.

USING ENGLISH IN ALL CLASSES

Go over papers that you are preparing for any of your classes. Check to see whether you have misused any adjectives. If so, make the proper changes. If there is one usage that is a particular problem for you, review daily, for at least a week, the rule that applies.

READ AND THINK ABOUT

Knowing the standard forms of irregular verbs is not enough. You must *use* them outside school as well as in the classroom. The next five pages deal with such troublesome verbs as *drink, eat, throw, swim,* and *drive.*

USING IRREGULAR VERBS

RULE 1. (*Drink* and its forms)
Always use a helping verb with *drunk;* never use one with *drank.*

Today I drink.   Yesterday I drank.   Often I *have* drunk.

LEARNING ACTIVITIES IN USING DRANK AND DRUNK

A. Copy these sentences, filling each blank with the proper form of *drink.* Underline the verb that you use, including any helping verbs. Read the sentences aloud more than once. *Do not write in this book.*

1. Have you .... any milk today?
2. That was my glass of orange juice. Who .... it?
3. Ruth picked up the glass and .... the medicine quickly.
4. Someone has .... my tea.
5. Icy liquids should be .... slowly.
6. At last Friday's picnic, the boys .... lemonade.
7. We hurried to the spring and .... the clear, cold water.
8. Have you ever .... coconut milk?

B. In an oral activity, let one student read one of the following questions and then call on another student to answer, using *drank* or *drunk.* Do not use *did* in answering. Repeat the activity until everyone has had a chance to take part. So that everyone will listen, decide on a penalty for anyone who gives exactly the same answer as someone else has given.

1. Did you drink any milk?
2. Has anyone drunk from this glass?
3. Should we have drunk the tea first?
4. Did you drink root beer at the party?
5. How much milk did you drink yesterday?

C. Write five original sentences, two using *drank* and three using *drunk.* In your small groups, take turns at reading the sentences.

USING IRREGULAR VERBS—*Continued*

RULE 2. (*Eat* and its forms)
Always use a helping verb with *eaten;* never use one with *ate.* Remember that there is no such standard form as *et* or *aten.*

Today I eat.   Yesterday I ate.   Often I *have* eaten.

LEARNING ACTIVITIES IN USING *ATE* AND *EATEN*

A. Write each sentence below, filling the blank with the proper form of *eat*. Underline the form that you use and any helping verbs. In class, read the sentences aloud, more than once if you have time.

1. Jim .... his supper quickly and left for the game.
2. Rust had .... through the iron chain.
3. Who has .... the last piece of pie?
4. Last night I .... Chinese food for the first time.
5. Potatoes are .... in many forms.
6. Mary took the slice of cake and .... it quickly.
7. The bowlful of cherries was .... quickly.
8. A stray dog had .... the children's lunch.
9. John admitted he had never .... liver.
10. Yesterday my grandmother .... her breakfast at six A.M.
11. Before lunch June had .... several cookies.
12. The hungry animals .... quickly.

B. Write five sentences, leaving blanks to be filled with *ate* or *eaten*. Take turns at putting your sentences upon the board. Call upon some other student to read the sentences, supplying the standard forms.

C. (1) Write two questions using *ate* and two using *eaten*. (2) Choose sides. (3) Alternate in asking a question that must be answered in turn by someone on the other side. The answer must contain *ate* or *eaten*. Score a point for each question or answer that is properly expressed.

Spot Review

(*Based upon the sentences in* A *of the preceding activities*)
1. Give the rules for the three capital letters in sentence 4.
2. How would you spell the singular of the subject in sentence 5?
3. Why is the verb singular in sentence 7?
4. Explain the location of the apostrophe in sentence 8.

RULE 3. (*Throw* and its forms)
Always use a helping verb with *thrown;* **never use one with** *threw.*
There is no such standard form as *throwed.*

Today I **throw.**   Yesterday I **threw.**   Often I *have* **thrown.**

LEARNING ACTIVITIES IN USING *THREW* AND *THROWN*

A. (1) Copy these sentences, filling each blank with the proper form of *throw.* (2) Underline the verb, including any helping verbs. (3) Exchange papers for checking. (4) *Proofread for careless errors in copying.* (5) Mark the papers as the sentences are read aloud.

1. The pitcher .... his fast ball often in that game.
2. Suddenly George .... the door open and ran out.
3. The rock was .... with great force.
4. Have you .... away that large box?
5. Someone .... this note through the window. Who did it?
6. The smallest of the children has .... the ball over the house.
7. The general .... his best troops into the battle but still lost.
8. Daniel was .... into the lions' den.

B. Divide the class into two teams. Take turns giving sentences using *threw* and *thrown.* Listen to catch any nonstandard usage. Keep score on the board. Score a point for each proper sentence. Do not score a point, however, if someone gives a sentence that another player has already given. Thus, to help your team, you must listen carefully.

★ **Spot Review**

(*Based upon the sentences in A of the preceding activities*)

1. How do you spell the plural of the final word in sentence 4?
2. Why is *general* not capitalized in sentence 7?
3. Account for the apostrophe in sentence 8.

USING IRREGULAR VERBS—*Continued*

RULE 4. (*Swim* and its forms)
Always use a helping verb with *swum;* **never use one with** *swam.*

Today I **swim.**   Yesterday I **swam.**   Often I *have* **swum.**

LEARNING ACTIVITIES IN USING *SWAM* AND *SWUM*

A. (1) Go over these sentences orally, using *swam* or *swum* in each blank. (2) Practice reading the sentences in unison so that you can really hear the standard forms.

1. Yesterday I .... out to the raft.
2. Have you ever .... in any races?
3. Mary has never yet .... in the ocean.
4. The goldfish .... slowly around the bowl.
5. Long distances can be .... by an expert swimmer.
6. Just then a large shark .... past the ship.
7. Tom .... in the final race and won it.
8. Has anyone .... across Bear Lake?

B. Write sentences on the board, leaving blanks to be filled with *swam* or *swum*. Call on classmates to read the sentences, supplying the proper forms and identifying any helping verbs.

ENRICHMENT

Make a nonsense rhyme in which you use *swam* and *swum* correctly. Here is an example:

> I swam fast, and Bill swam fast;
> We swam with real perfection.
> But still we lost the race—and *why?*
> We'd swum the wrong direction!

USING IRREGULAR VERBS—Continued

RULE 5.   (*Drive* and its forms)
Always use an auxiliary verb with *driven;* never use one with *drove.*
Today I **drive**.   Yesterday I **drove**.   Often I *have* **driven**.

LEARNING ACTIVITIES IN USING *DROVE* AND *DRIVEN*

A. Copy these sentences, filling each blank with *drove* or *driven*. (2) Underline the verb, including any helping verbs. (3) Exchange papers. (4) *Proofread for careless errors in copying.* (5) Check the verb choices as the sentences are read aloud.

1. In a war many people are .... from their homes.
2. Last summer we .... to Crater Lake.

3. The owner of those cars has never .... a truck.
4. We girls .... to the lake for a picnic.
5. Tom may not have .... away yet.
6. Jim .... the sheep into the pasture yesterday.
7. I had never before .... this kind of car.
8. Fred has .... well lately.

B. Dictionaries give many meanings for the verb *drive*. In one dictionary, for example, *drive* has eight meanings as a transitive verb. Choose any five meanings and write sentences in which you use either *drove* or *driven*. Do not use any meaning more than once. In your small groups, read sentences aloud.

★ **Spot Review**

(*Based upon the sentences in* A *of the preceding activities*)
1. Why is *Lake* capitalized in sentence 2 and not in sentence 4?
2. What is the plural of the object in sentence 6?
3. Why is the verb singular in sentence 3? What is the direct object of the verb?

★ **Chapter Review** *

A. Copy the following sentences, underlining all words used as adjectives, including predicate adjectives. Draw an arrow from each adjective to the word that it modifies.

1. He drew four large pictures.
2. One child lost his parents.
3. My dog is a loud barker.
4. The fourth girl is short.
5. That cap is a pretty color.
6. We saw an English officer.
7. Did Ed bring his new skates?
8. Roger must be tired.
9. My father bought these shoes.
10. This banana tastes bitter.

B. Read the following sentences aloud, choosing the proper forms.

1. Have you seen (those, that) sort of skis before?
2. (Them, Those) bikes are parked in the wrong place.
3. I must be there in (a, an) hour.
4. (This, These) kind of sweaters is my favorite.
5. We needed (a pen and pencil, a pen and a pencil).
6. My job is (more easier, easier) than yours.
7. Which of these two watches is the (better, best)?
8. Mrs. Beggs is (a wife and mother, a wife and a mother).
9. (An, A) orange leaf fluttered to the ground.
10. Did you leave (those, them) magazines at school?

* Check Test 5 should be taken at this point. If the results show need for further study, students should do the review practice. They should then take Mastery Test 5.

C. Read these sentences aloud, supplying the proper form of each verb in parentheses.

1. For breakfast yesterday I (drink) a glass of milk but no coffee.
2. Have you ever (eat) mushrooms?
3. Tom (throw) hard and struck the batter out.
4. Mr. Smith has (drive) the same car for ten years.
5. I had often (swim) across the pool.
6. Yesterday I (eat) lunch at school.
7. The pitcher should have (throw) a curve.
8. We (drive) to Washington last year.
9. You should have (drink) some tomato juice.
10. He (swim) swiftly to the raft and climbed up on it.

Cumulative Review

CAPITALIZATION AND PUNCTUATION

Copy these sentences, supplying needed capital letters and punctuation.

1. a letter dated december 12 1962 arrived two years late at 4513 north sixth street miami florida 33109
2. no one captain smith passed over the bridge across the sangamon river while private hollis and i were on duty said private bell
3. our leader ann ames has been working with the girls club in california new mexico and colorado
4. yes everyone living near the ohio river was afraid of that flood
5. have you asked fred read the book mystery at laughing water jim

RECOGNIZING PARTS OF THE SENTENCE

Copy these sentences. Label each *verb*, (v.), *subject* (subj.), *direct object* (d.o.), or *predicate nominative* (p.n.).

1. The little girl stubbed her toe.
2. That boy is my brother.
3. Did Jack find his notebook?
4. I have not been working carefully.
5. Mother has never been president of the Hinsdale Flower Club.

VERB-SUBJECT AGREEMENT

Go over these sentences orally, choosing the standard forms.

1. A bunch of grapes (is, are) hanging from the tree.
2. It really (don't, doesn't) make much difference.
3. (Doesn't, Don't) the writer of these stories live in Ohio?
4. There (was, were) five peaches in that bowl this morning.
5. They (wasn't, weren't) at home.

6. He (don't, doesn't) know the tune.
7. The policemen (has, have) just arrived.
8. You (was, were) late this morning.
9. There (isn't, aren't) many cookies left.

PROPER USE OF PRONOUNS

Read these sentences aloud, choosing the standard forms.

1. Mary invited Ellen and (I, me) to the party.
2. Dick and (he, him) are good friends.
3. Scott and (we, us) found much to talk about.
4. They saw you and (I, me) at the show.
5. (We, Us) Scouts are meeting tonight.
6. Mother heard (we, us) boys.
7. The old cow swished (its, it's) tail.
8. This pen must be (yours, your's).
9. One of those cars is (ours, our's).
10. At the signal, all four elephants raised (they're, their) trunks at the same time.

TROUBLESOME VERBS

Read these sentences aloud, using the proper form of each verb in parentheses. Name any helping verbs.

1. The kittens (lie) in their basket all day today.
2. The milk (freeze) in the bottle this morning.
3. Who (see) the circus last week?
4. Haven't your parents (go) on a vacation?
5. Each boy (do) his best in our last contest.
6. The speaker had (come) all the way from Canada.
7. Has Edith (see) her friends?
8. Martha was (take) to the concert in the new car.
9. Mother (choose) new curtains yesterday.
10. My grandfather (give) me his watch.
11. Have you ever (run) for office before?
12. The ice almost (break) under the skaters last night.
13. My cousin (do) well in the last race.
14. The truth isn't (know) yet.

SPELLING

Write on your paper the new words made by using the prefix *dis* or *mis* or the suffix *ful,* as indicated.

1. (mis) take	5. peace (ful)	9. (dis) agree
2. spoon (ful)	6. (dis) solve	10. (mis) lead
3. (mis) spell	7. pocket (ful)	11. (mis) step
4. (dis) like	8. (mis) place	12. mouth (ful)

Word Games to Make You Think

HIDDEN NAMES OF DOGS

Each sentence below has hidden in it the name of one kind of dog.

EXAMPLE: Bill was wearing an **Ascot tie.** (*Scottie*)

1. Was Shep herding the cows?
2. I paired a leader in this class with one in the other.
3. We need someone who understands children.
4. Terrie ran for help immediately.
5. Will the president appoint Ernest to be the chairman?
6. While going past Bernard, he noticed that Bernie was crying.
7. You have set terms to which I cannot agree.
8. This pan I eliminated first of all.

WORD SQUARE

The words defined below have four letters each. Placed one under the other, they will spell the same down as across.

1. Take dinner.   2. Thought   3. Close by   4. A nobleman

HIS NAME WAS TOM

Can you name the "Toms" suggested below?

1. This Tom was small enough to stand on the palm of your hand.
2. This Tom was a Mother Goose character who disobeyed the law.
3. This Tom was one of our famous presidents.
4. This Tom was the hero of a book called *Tom* ....*'s School Days.*
5. This Tom, a Mother Goose character, sang for his supper.
6. Mark Twain made this Tom famous.

WOULD YOU LIKE TO KNOW—?

The encyclopedia answers to some of these questions may surprise you.

1. How do *pythons* kill their prey?
2. Why would you have a hard time buying *pineapple* seed?
3. For what does the *pelican* use its pouch?
4. About how long was *Pompeii* left buried after being destroyed by the volcano Vesuvius?

Copy the crossword puzzle. *Do not write in this book.*

1	2	■	3	4	■	5	6	7	8	■
9			■		10				11
12		■	13	14	■	15			
16	17	■	18			■	19		
20		■	21		■	22	■	23	
24		25		■	26		27		
■	28		■	29				30	
31	32		■		■	33	34
■	35			■	■	36		■
37		■	38		39			
40	41		■	42			■
■	■	43				

Across

1. Exclamation of surprise.
3. Something to be transacted.
9. Plural of *elf*.
10. A timepiece.
12. First two initials of the author of *Treasure Island*.
13. Exclamation showing pain.
15. A heavenly body that moves around the earth.
16. Contraction of *over*.
18. Present plural of *be*.
19. If you stub your ......, you might say No. 13 across.
20. The hand is quicker than the ....
21. Day before Saturday (*abbr.*).
23. Initials of the inventor of the electric light.
24. Sunday School (*abbr.*).
25. An error.
28. Film star, ... West.
29. Frosting.
31. Two things used by a fisherman (*two words*).
33. Nickname for *Joseph*.
35. Past tense of *pay*.
36. Preposition.
37. Third person pronoun.
39. A girl's name.
40. A riddle or puzzle.
42. A number.
43. A day of the week.

Down

1. The principal male character in a story (*plural*).
2. Narrow passageways.
3. Place for sleeping.
4. First person plural pronoun.
5. North Carolina (*abbr.*).
6. A kind of tree.
7. Black substance in chimneys.
8. Move quickly.
11. Joint between the thigh and the lower part of the leg (*plural*).
13. Rowing implements.
14. That which is written.
17. Second note of the scale.
21. A piece of open or cleared ground.
22. One of a pair worn in gliding over snow.
25. Present participle of *make*.
26. An aviator who has brought down five or more enemy planes.
27. Past tense of *enjoy*.
28. Extinct, flightless, large bird of New Zealand.
30. Present tense of *went*.
32. Not closed.
34. Each.
36. 2000 pounds (*plural*).
37. Feminine possessive pronoun.
38. Past tense of *sit*.
39. Same as 33 across.
41. Third person singular form of *be*.

USING ADVERBS IN BUILDING SENTENCES*

One tall, slender boy hit the first ball **hard**.

1. Recognizing Adverbs

READ AND THINK ABOUT

Compare the above picture with the one on page 390. What word has been added? How does it change the picture?

Words like "hard" are *adverbs,* another part of speech. Like adjectives (see page 390), they build up the basic sentence idea by giving exact or vivid details. In addition, adverbs can make a sentence mean the opposite (or nearly so) of what it means before the adverb is added.

He has come.   He has **not** come.
I have been there.   I have **never** been there.
I missed the turn.   I **almost** missed the turn.

* Pretest 6 should be taken at this time.

1. **(DEFINITION)** *Adverbs* are words used as modifiers to tell *manner* (how), *time* (when), *place* (where), **or** *degree* (how much) about other words.

He hit the ball hard. (*manner*) He hit the ball south. (*place*)
He hit the ball soon. (*time*)   He hit the ball too far. (*degree*)

2. **Adverbs modify, or affect the meaning of,** (*a*) *verbs,* (*b*) *adjectives,* **or** (*c*) *other adverbs.*

   a) The days go rapidly.
      ("Rapidly" tells *how* the days go; so it modifies the verb.)
   b) The train was very late.
      "Very" tells *how much* late; so it modifies the adjective.
   c) The boy hit the ball too hard.
      ("Too" tells *how much* hard, or the *degree* of force with which the boy hit the ball; so it modifies the adverb *hard.*)

3. **A word may be an adverb in one sentence, and another part of speech in some other sentence.** To know what part of speech a word is, find how it is used in a sentence.

   The boy hit the ball hard.

   ("Hard" is an adverb because it modifies the verb *hit.*)

   That was a hard rain.

   ("Hard" is an adjective because it modifies the noun *rain.*)

4. **"Not" is a special adverb because it really modifies the entire sentence.** *Not* **is usually classed as modifying the verb, however, for that is what carries the basic sentence idea.**

5. **Adverbs may be compound.**

   He speaks loudly and rapidly.   George works fast but well.

6. **Adverbs can shift position in a sentence.**

   I often agree with him.   I agree with him often.
   Often I agree with him.   I agree often with him.

LEARNING ACTIVITIES IN RECOGNIZING AND USING ADVERBS

A. Find the adverbs in these sentences and tell what word each one modifies. Make this an oral exercise. Give the sentence patterns.

   1. Harold does his work carefully but rather slowly.
   2. The club recently won this banner.

3. Yesterday this little boy seemed unusually restless.
4. The baby lay there very quietly.
5. He has called me once or twice.
6. Haven't they often visited here before?
7. Happy children seldom become really unhappy grown-ups.
8. Better specimens have never been found.
9. They have always been highly critical.
10. You shouldn't decide this important matter too quickly.

B. (1) Write ten sentences using adverbs that tell how you feel about certain things; for example, *hot weather, relatives, homework,* or *getting up in the morning.* (2) Recopy your sentences, but leave a blank for each adverb that you chose. (3) Exchange papers with a partner. (4) Fill the blanks with adverbs. (5) Compare your choices.

C. Shift the italicized adverbs in these sentences to as many other positions as they might sensibly occupy. Make this an oral activity.

1. He lived *then* in Millvale.
2. *Sometimes* we have held our picnic at Stone Lake.
3. You will wait for us, *surely*.
4. The road past our farm is *now* a four-lane highway.

D. In class, give the part of speech of each italicized word.

1. We usually arrive *early*.
2. The *early* train leaves at noon.
3. The *back* of the car was empty.
4. Won't you come *back?*
5. Did Father *back* the car into the garage?
6. Four of us rode in the *back* seat.
7. You must *right* this mistake by yourself.
8. Turn *right* at the corner.
9. That was not the *right* answer.
10. You have the *right* to vote.

ENRICHMENT

Copy the following paragraph, inserting adverbs before, after, or elsewhere near the italicized words. Compare work in your small groups to see how your choices of adverbs make the sentence pictures change.

An angry crowd of the natives, *armed* with war clubs and spears, *had gathered* on the shore. James Cook, *standing* in the bow of the boat, *faced* them. Four marines were at his back, but he *cautioned* them against using their muskets. He was *certain* that he *could settle* the trouble peacefully. As the boat *grounded,* Cook *sprang* into the shallow water and *marched* toward the angry mob. They *fell* back, *awed* by his steely glance.*

*Adapted from *Captain James Cook* by Armstrong Sperry; copyright 1953 by Row, Peterson and Company, Evanston, Illinois.

(Based upon the sentences in A *of the preceding activities)*

1. Which four sentences have direct objects? Name the objects.
2. Why is the verb *lay* correct in sentence 4?
3. How would you compare the adjectives in sentence 7?
4. What is the predicate nominative in sentence 7?

2. Forming Abverbs from Adjectives

● THESE ARE FACTS ABOUT ADVERBS: II

7. Most adverbs are formed from adjectives.

 a) **Many adverbs simply add** *ly* **to adjectives.**

ADJECTIVES:	slow	quick	useful
ADVERBS:	slow**ly**	quick**ly**	useful**ly**

 b) **Most adjectives that end in** *y* **change the** *y* **to** *i* **and then add** *ly.* **(See Rule 2b, page 116.)**

ADJECTIVES:	lazy	happy	mighty
ADVERBS:	laz**i**ly	happ**i**ly	might**i**ly

 c) **Most adjectives that have more than one syllable and end in** *le* **simply change the** *e* **to** *y.*

ADJECTIVES:	nob**le**	favorable	sensible
ADVERBS:	nob**ly**	favorab**ly**	sensib**ly**

8. Not all adverbs are formed from adjectives. *Never, not, here, there, then, when, where, always, very, too,* **and** *now* **are some common adverbs that do not come from adjectives.**

LEARNING ACTIVITIES IN FORMING AND USING ADVERBS

A. List the following adjectives and beside each write the adverb formed from it: *easy, large, busy, horrible, heavy, steady, careful, angry, weary, suitable, merry, hungry, equal, strange, considerable.* Go over the words in class and explain the spelling of each adverb.

B. Be prepared to give oral sentences using the adjectives named in *A.* Then give sentences using the adverbs formed from the adjectives; after giving a sentence, spell the adverb.

3. Comparing Adverbs

Since most adverbs are compared by using *more* and *most,* their comparisons are easy to form.

● THESE ARE FACTS ABOUT COMPARING ADVERBS

1. **Adverbs formed from adjectives use *more* and *most* to express comparison.**

   POSITIVE: slowly   lazily   comfortably
   COMPARATIVE: more slowly   more lazily   more comfortably
   SUPERLATIVE: most slowly   most lazily   most comfortably

2. **A few adverbs, including some words that also may be used as adjectives, add *er* and *est.*** Here are some examples.

   POSITIVE: soon   hard   early   fast   high
   COMPARATIVE: sooner   harder   earlier   faster   higher
   SUPERLATIVE: soonest   hardest   earliest   fastest   highest

3. **Some adverbs are compared irregularly.** Here are a few.

   POSITIVE: far   well   little   much   badly
   COMPARATIVE: farther   better   less   more   worse
   SUPERLATIVE: farthest   best   least   most   worst

4. **Adverbs like those in point 7, page 418, cannot be compared.**

LEARNING ACTIVITIES IN COMPARING ADVERBS

A. Using the numbered words, make four lists on your paper: (1) of the adverbs that use *more* and *most* in their comparison, (2) of those that use *er* and *est,* (3) of those that are irregular in their forms, and (4) of those that have no comparison. Exchange papers for checking.

1. softly	5. heavily	9. far	13. fairly	17. coldly
2. soon	6. easily	10. high	14. much	18. fast
3. now	7. well	11. badly	15. never	19. wildly
4. there	8. here	12. closely	16. not	20. quietly

B. For each adverb that can be compared in *A,* give oral sentences using the three degrees. Begin by having someone say a sentence using one of the words in its positive form. He will then call on another student to change the sentence so that it contains the comparative form of the same adverb. This student calls upon another student to change the sentence so that it contains the superlative form. He then calls upon someone to use another one of the words in its positive form, and so on. You may want to make this a team activity.

4. Using Vivid Adverbs

He smiled { *sneeringly.* *pityingly.* *timidly.* }

One good way to express yourself effectively is to use vivid (colorful), exact adverbs. Most vivid adverbs, like the ones in the drawing, end in *ly* and tell *how*.

LEARNING ACTIVITIES IN USING VIVID ADVERBS

A. In an oral activity, have listed on the board as many vivid adverbs as you can think of that show different ways of doing the following: (1) *laughing,* (2) *frowning,* (3) *driving,* (4) *singing,* (5) *dancing,* (6) *working,* (7) *running,* (8) *whispering.*

B. Copy the sentences below, filling each blank with one or more vivid adverbs. Think; do not write just the first word that pops into your head. Read the sentences orally to see how many different adverbs are used.

1. The whistle blew ....
2. The wind blew ....
3. Somewhere a dog barked ....
4. The rain fell ....
5. The man sat there ....
6. The crowd cheered ....

C. An author often uses adverbs of manner to show how a character feels as he makes a remark; for example, "What do you want?" the man asked *suspiciously.*

Using the adverbs as clues, read aloud in class these remarks from Dickens's *Our Mutual Friend.* Read only the quoted words.

1. "Well!" observed R. Wilfer cheerfully, "money and goods are certainly the best of references!"
2. "Nonsense, our age!" cried Bella, impatiently. "What's that got to do with him?"
3. "What did you say?" she asked sharply. "What did you say, Miss?"
4. "Please walk in," said Lavinia haughtily. "Our servant is out."
5. "Oh, I don't know what he said," cried Georgiana wildly, "but I hated him all the same for saying it."
6. "I alone know," returned the man, sternly shaking his head, "that your trumped-up story cannot possibly be true."

7. "Well?" retorted Mr. Venus snappishly. "If you hear it say the words, why don't you answer it?"
8. "My sister Lizzie," said the boy proudly, "wants no preparing, Mr. Headstone. What she is, she is, and shows herself to be."
9. "Ma," said Bella angrily, "you force me to say that I am truly sorry I did come home, and that I never will come home again."
10. "Why didn't you sit down before?" asked Mr. Boffin distrustfully.

D. Adverbs, like adjectives, can be overused, but they can help to sharpen the sentence picture. Here are more sentences, also from *Our Mutual Friend*. Which adverb in each parentheses do you think was the one that Dickens chose? Go over your choices in class. What does his word suggest in each case that the other does not?

1. The white face of the winter day came (slowly, sluggishly) on.
2. At this moment the greasy door is (violently, strongly) pushed.
3. A delicious wind ran with the stream, touching the surface (lightly, crisply).
4. In an instant, with a dreadful crash, flames shot (jaggedly, unevenly) across the air.
5. She rowed in (desperately, hard) for the nearest shallow water where she might run the boat aground.
6. The boat touched the edge of the patch of inn lawn, sloping (slightly, gently) to the water.
7. He now looked at him again—(carefully, stealthily) this time.
8. He sat looking (steadily, straight) before him at the vacant air.
9. Both Mrs. Wilfer and Lavinia were (greatly, ravenously) curious about every article of which the lodger stood possessed.
10. The little dressmaker stood up, humming her song, and nodded to him (brightly, pleasantly).

USING ENGLISH IN ALL CLASSES

A. Clear, exact adverbs are very important in science explanations or experiments. Notice these sentences from two science projects:

1. Do *not* stroke the knitting needle *back* and *forth*. Move the magnet *always* in the same direction.
2. Do *not* tilt the beaker *far enough* to let the pieces of dry ice fall *out*.

By leaving out the italicized adverbs, you will see how important a part of the directions they are.

Bring your science books to class. Turn to any lesson. See how many important uses of adverbs you can find on one page.

B. Read over any papers that you are preparing for other classes. Make any changes that you think will improve your selection of adverbs.

FOLLOW-UP

From *A* and *B*, copy into your notebook adverbs that you think are especially expressive. Refer to this list when you do original writing. Make your list grow as you discover vivid adverbs in your reading.

Diagramming Adverbs

Place an adverb on a slanting line below the word that it modifies, the same way as you do an adjective. As always, the words on the heavy base line are the parts of the basic sentence pattern.

Adverb Modifying the Verb

The boy hit the ball *hard*.

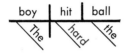

Adverb Modifying an Adjective

The train was *very* late.

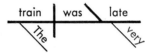

Adverb Modifying an Adverb

The boy hit the ball *too* hard.

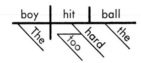

Compound Adverb

The snow fell *thickly* and *softly*.

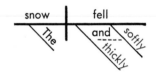

LEARNING ACTIVITIES IN DIAGRAMMING ADVERBS

A. Diagram all parts in the following sentences. Remember that the adverbs will go below the words they modify. Exchange papers for checking as the diagrams are put on the board. Be sure to explain orally and exactly each part of each diagram, using a regular pattern.

1. The new owner should arrive here soon.
2. My little sister has just had her sixth birthday.
3. We work well together.
4. A really old man came here yesterday.
5. My brother does not work very rapidly.
6. I have never taken so many pictures before.
7. Harry walked away slowly and very unhappily.
8. Your work is almost always very neat.
9. Tom is now our captain.
10. Have you made that trip often?

B. For additional drill in diagramming adverbs, turn back to the sentences in *A*, page 416. Be sure to go over the diagrams orally.

5. Using Standard English

PART ONE: AVOIDING ADJECTIVE-ADVERB CONFUSION

"I KNOW, DAD, BUT WHAT IF I DO SAY, 'RELMOND PLAYS GOOD,' AND NOT 'RELMOND PLAYS WELL'? YOU GET THE POINT EITHER WAY."

"OF COURSE. YOU MIGHT ALSO BE ABLE TO SWIM WITH A BOWLING BALL TIED TO YOUR ANKLE, BUT YOU PROBABLY WOULDN'T WIN VERY MANY RACES."

THINK IT OVER . . .

What the boy's father means is that "getting the point" is not enough, for nonstandard expression is likely to handicap a person, just as a bowling ball tied to a swimmer's ankle would. Remember that <u>people form opinions of you not only from the *ideas* that you express, but from the *language*</u> in which you express those ideas. Why handicap yourself with nonstandard language habits?

THE RULES FOR AVOIDING ADJECTIVE-ADVERB CONFUSION

RULE 1. Use *adjectives* to modify *nouns* or *pronouns*. Use *adverbs* to modify *verbs, adjectives,* or *adverbs.*

RULE 2. Do not use the adjective *sure* for the adverbs *surely, certainly, really.* Use *sure* only if those three words do not make sense.

Jack is **sure** of the time.
(*Sure* is a predicate adjective modifying the noun *Jack*. It would not make sense to say, "Jack is *surely* of the time.")

I **surely** am going.
(*Surely* is an adverb modifying the verb *am going.*)

RULE 3. Do not use the adjective *good* for the adverb *well.*

He had a **good** time.
(*Good* is an adjective; it tells *what kind* of *time.*)

He writes **well.**
(*Well* is an adverb modifying the verb *writes;* it tells *how.*)

RULE 4. Use *well* as an adjective only when it refers to health.

I feel **well.**
(*Well* is a predicate adjective modifying the pronoun *I.*)

RULE 5. Use the adverb *badly* to tell how something is done. Use the adjective *bad* in referring to health or feelings and to complete such linking verbs as *seem, look, taste, smell.*

I did my work **badly** yesterday.
(*Badly* is an adverb modifying the verb *did.*)

I felt **bad** about the news.
(*Bad* is a predicate adjective modifying the pronoun *I.*)

The weather looks **bad.**
(*Bad* is a predicate adjective; it tells *what kind* of *weather.*)

LEARNING ACTIVITIES IN USING ADVERBS PROPERLY

A. Copy these sentences, using either *good* or *well* in each blank. *Do not write in this book.* Read your sentences in class. Tell (1) which you used, an adjective or an adverb, and (2) what word it modifies.

1. Can't you see ....?
2. It was a .... game.
3. The chowder tastes ....
4. This biscuit looks ....
5. Don't you feel ....?
6. I like it very ....
7. Jim plays tennis ....
8. I am not feeling ....
9. That hot sun feels ....
10. Both boys did ....
11. She isn't at all ....
12. Ann really sings ....

B. Make this a team activity. Take turns at giving oral sentences using *good* as a predicate adjective and *well* as an adjective or an adverb. If a member of one team makes a mistake, the next person on the other team must correct it before giving his sentence. Keep track of the mistakes. The team with the smaller number of them is the winner.

C. Copy these sentences, filling the blanks with *bad* or *badly*. *Do not write in this book.* Go over the sentences orally in your small groups.

1. You behaved .... today.
2. Mary felt .... about it.
3. Her health has been ....
4. That pill didn't taste ....
5. The weather looks ....
6. I did .... on the first test.
7. The air smelled ....
8. He plays less .... now.

D. Supply the proper form from the words in parentheses in each of the following sentences. Remember, if the word tells *how* in connection with the verb, use the adverb form. Make this an oral exercise. Repeat it several times. *Do not write in this book.*

1. The team plays (good, well).
2. Ed played (bad, badly).
3. The car runs (well, good).
4. She seems (well, good) now.
5. The egg tasted (good, well).
6. That job was done (bad, badly).
7. Sue won (easy, easily).
8. I'm (surely, sure) sorry for you.
9. He felt (good, well) today.
10. News (sure, surely) travels fast.

PART TWO: AVOIDING DOUBLE NEGATIVES

"YOU DON'T NEVER HEAR MANY SENTENCES LIKE MINE!"

"HURRAY FOR THAT FACT!"

THINK IT OVER...

What is wrong with the first speaker's sentence? Can you see that putting *don't* and *never* together makes it mean just the opposite of what he is trying to say? It does!

THE RULES FOR AVOIDING DOUBLE NEGATIVES

RULE 1. **Do not use two negative words to limit one idea.**

STANDARD: I **never** need help.
STANDARD: I need **no** help.
NONSTANDARD: I **never** need ~~no~~ help.

(Both *never* and *no* give a negative meaning. Only one of them should be used.)

RULE 2. **Be especially careful to avoid using** *not* or *n't, no, never, none, scarcely, hardly,* **or** *nothing* **with another negative word.**

STANDARD: Sue **has no** book. Sue **hasn't a** book.
STANDARD: I **didn't** say **anything.** I said **nothing.**
NONSTANDARD: Sue ~~hasn't~~ **no** book. I ~~didn't~~ say **nothing.**

LEARNING ACTIVITIES IN AVOIDING DOUBLE NEGATIVES

A. Practice the following sentences orally, using the proper words from the parentheses. *Do not write in this book.*

1. I haven't (none, any) of the tickets.
2. This jacket isn't (nothing, anything) like mine.
3. I (can, can't) hardly wait.
4. This hasn't (ever, never) happened before.
5. I don't need (no, any) help.
6. We (haven't, have) scarcely any time left.
7. We're not (ever, never) going there again.
8. There has never been (anything, nothing) wrong.
9. Haven't you (no, any) other shoes?
10. You (don't hardly, hardly) look the same.

B. Write five "choice" sentences, similar to those in *A*. In your small groups, exchange papers and read the sentences aloud, making the right choices. Speak distinctly so that everyone in the group gets practice in hearing the standard forms.

ENRICHMENT

Draw a cartoon that shows people getting rid of double negatives in some way, such as by tossing them into a bonfire, putting them down the incinerator or into the garbage disposal unit, burying them, ... Use as many double negatives as you can: *don't never, haven't no, can't hardly,* and so on. Your work may be displayed on the bulletin board.

FOLLOW-UP

Look back over the rules on pages 424 and 426. Which ones are hardest for you to follow? Pick out one or two that you know are problems; then ask a friend to check your use of the forms covered. Building good speech habits is not really hard—if you really want to do so.

PART THREE: USING TROUBLESOME VERBS

Here are five more verbs that are sometimes used improperly. Most of the problems with these verbs come from using the past tense form when the past participle form is called for. (To review principal parts of verbs, go over point 16, page 291.)

USING IRREGULAR VERBS

RULE 1. (*Ride* and its forms)
Always use a helping verb with *ridden;* never use one with *rode*.
Today I ride.　　Yesterday I rode.　　Often I *have* ridden.

LEARNING ACTIVITIES IN USING *RODE* AND *RIDDEN*

A. Copy each sentence, filling the blank with the proper form of *ride*. Underline the form that you use. Underline also any auxiliary verbs. Practice reading the sentences aloud. *Do not write in this book.*

1. We had .... through some beautiful country.
2. That jockey has .... many winning horses.
3. Last winter I .... on a toboggan for the first time.
4. Have you ever .... on a streamlined train?
5. Jane's bicycle has been .... many miles.
6. At the rodeo last summer Jim .... an outlaw horse.
7. In the Bahamas bicycles are .... by almost everyone.
8. That horse was .... well in the last race.

B. Write five sentences, two using *rode* and three using *ridden*. You might write about (1) places that you have gone and how you traveled there or (2) rides at an amusement park. Take turns at reading sentences aloud. Call on classmates to identify any helping verbs.

RULE 2. (*Fly* and its forms)
Always use a helping verb with *flown;* **never use one with** *flew.*
Today I **fly**.   Yesterday I **flew**.   Often I *have* **flown**.

LEARNING ACTIVITIES IN USING *FLEW* AND *FLOWN*

A. Copy these sentences, filling each blank with the proper form of *fly*. Underline that form and any helping verbs. Read the sentences aloud.

1. Billy .... his first kite on a windy day last spring.
2. Every day much mail is .... across the country.
3. Have the birds .... south yet?
4. My uncle has .... test planes for the government.
5. The swarm of bees has .... into the hive.
6. Upon hearing the bad news, Uncle John .... into a rage.
7. Supplies were .... into Camp Whitney by airplane.
8. The flag of no other country should be .... above our own.

B. Choose some city or country in a far-off part of the world. Pretend that your class has just missed a chance to fly to that place. Go around the class, completing in turn one or the other of these sentences:

On that trip we'd have flown over . . .
On that trip we'd not have flown over . . .

USING IRREGULAR VERBS—Continued

RULE 3. (*Draw* and its forms)
Always use a helping verb with *drawn;* **never use one with** *drew.*
Remember that there is no such standard form as *drawed.*
Today I **draw**.   Yesterday I **drew**.   Often I *have* **drawn**.

LEARNING ACTIVITIES IN USING *DREW* AND *DRAWN*

A. (1) Copy these sentences, filling each blank with the proper form of *draw*. (2) Underline that form and any helping verbs. (3) *Proofread for careless errors in copying*. (4) Exchange papers for checking as the sentences are read aloud. Listen to be sure that the forms are standard.

1. The children's wagon had been .... up to the porch.
2. Yesterday my aunt .... these pictures for you and me.
3. Only one conclusion could be ....

4. Either Mary or June has .... this sketch.
5. The knight leaped from his horse and .... his sword.
6. Names of the winners will now be .... by this little boy.
7. The string should be .... tightly.
8. We shivered with fear but .... closer to the strange sight.
9. The horse had .... a heavy load up the hill.
10. The same person wrote the book and .... the pictures.

B. *Draw* is a verb with many meanings. Open your dictionary to the word; then write sentences using *drew* or *drawn* to illustrate five different meanings. Have sentences put on the board for criticism.

ENRICHMENT

From the sentences in *A,* choose three that show different meanings of *draw.* For each of the three, make a drawing to illustrate the sentence.

USING IRREGULAR VERBS—Continued

RULE 4. (*Rise* and its forms)
Always use a helping verb with *risen;* **never use one with** *rose.* **Remember that** *rise, rose,* **and** *risen* **are the only proper forms of this verb.**

Today I **rise.**　　　Yesterday I **rose.**　　　Often I *have* **risen.**

LEARNING ACTIVITIES IN USING *ROSE* AND *RISEN*

A. Write these sentences, filling each blank with the proper form of *rise.* Underline the verb, including any helping verbs. In class, read the sentences aloud, first individually and then together.

1. The sun had .... at five o'clock.
2. The fish .... to the top of the water and opened their mouths.
3. We should have .... earlier.
4. Ted .... from office boy to president of the company.
5. Tom has .... from private to sergeant.
6. Have you ever .... at 3:00 A.M.?
7. The moon had not yet ....
8. The price of eggs .... last month to its highest level this year.
9. The man .... slowly and started toward me.
10. By noon of that day, the river had .... two feet.

B. Write five sentences, two using *rose* and three using *risen.* In your small groups, take turns at reading sentences. Listen both to catch any nonstandard verbs and to get used to hearing the proper forms.

(Based upon the sentences in A *of the preceding activities)*

1. What is the reason for the colon in sentence 6?
2. Why is there no apostrophe in *its* in sentence 8?
3. Is the subject in sentence 8 singular, or plural?

USING IRREGULAR VERBS—Continued

RULE 5. (*Steal* and its forms)
Always use a helping verb with *stolen;* **never use one with** *stole.* **Remember that** *steal,* *stole,* **and** *stolen* **are the only standard forms.**

Today I **steal**. Yesterday I **stole**. Often I *have* **stolen**.

"OFFEN I HAVE STOLEN.
YESTERDAY I STOLE.
TODAY I AM IN JAIL."

LEARNING ACTIVITIES IN USING *STOLE* AND *STOLEN*

A. In an oral exercise, fill each blank with the proper form of *steal.* For each sentence that needs *stolen,* see how many other ways you could say the sentence by changing the helping verbs.

1. This necklace might have been ....
2. Jack .... softly from the room and tiptoed down the stairs.
3. That man's watch was .... last week.
4. The puppy had .... one of my shoes.
5. The thief .... a lady's purse but could not escape with it.
6. A box of valuable papers has been ....
7. He .... up behind me and grabbed my arm.
8. That elephant surely cannot have been ....
9. The last paragraph was .... from some famous book.
10. How many bases has he .... in the games this season?

B. Write five sentences using *stole* and *stolen* properly. Include different meanings of *steal.* In your small groups, take turns at reading sentences.

A. Copy these sentences. Draw a line under each adverb and from it draw an arrow to the word that the adverb modifies.

1. Soon John will be too busy and will need far more help.
2. We shall leave early.
3. Roger answered me nervously but clearly.
4. They are almost ready. Usually they are rather slow.
5. I sometimes walk more slowly.
6. We saw three much larger buildings yesterday.
7. I am too tired now. I really must not stay longer.

B. Read the following sentences aloud, choosing the proper forms from the parentheses.

1. He does his work (good, well) and (carefully, careful).
2. Joe fielded that liner (perfect, perfectly).
3. I (haven't hardly, have hardly) had time for my meals.
4. She feels (bad, badly) today.
5. Are you feeling (good, well)? You look much better than before.
6. This picnic (sure, surely) has been fun.
7. We sometimes do (bad, badly) on that kind of test.
8. Mr. Dee didn't say (anything, nothing) about a meeting.

C. Read these sentences orally, supplying the standard forms of the verbs in parentheses.

1. Have you ever (ride) in an airplane? I first (fly) last week.
2. Most of the birds had (fly) to warmer lands.
3. Jack (draw) and painted a picture of our house.
4. Tom had just (rise) to his feet.
5. We became tired and (steal) quietly away.
6. That picture was (draw) by a great artist.
7. The pony was (ride) by my little sister.

Cumulative Review

CAPITALIZATION AND PUNCTUATION

Supply needed capital letters and punctuation in this conversation.

milton have you seen that black calf since thursday asked paul
no milton replied ive been busy repairing the tractor
paul went on there seems to be something wrong with the calfs
left front leg

---

* Check Test 6 should be taken at this point. If the results show need
for further study, students should do this review practice. They
should then take Mastery Test 6.

lets go take a look suggested milton maybe its been cut on some barbed wire

wow look at that gash exclaimed paul wed better call father

Go over these sentences orally, supplying the needed verb forms.

1. Yesterday, for the first time, the boy (drink) from a spring.
2. Last month my grandmother (come) to live with us.
3. Why don't you (lie) down? You should not have (run) upstairs.
4. The lettuce in our garden had (freeze).
5. Has Henry (eat) his breakfast? Where has he (go)?
6. Has the book (come)? You should have (give) it to me.
7. Yesterday the postman (bring) two packages.
8. Henry (lie) on the davenport all last night.
9. Shouldn't you have (write) to Judy today?
10. Has someone (throw) away yesterday's paper?
11. She (give) me a smile but said nothing.
12. I (run) across a strange story in last night's *Daily News*.
13. The girls should have (drive) more slowly.
14. Are you (lie) on my hat?
15. Have you ever (swim) in a river?
16. Jim has (break) our only teapot. He should not have (take) it.

VERB-SUBJECT AGREEMENT

Read these sentences aloud, choosing the standard forms.

1. He (don't, doesn't) know the correct address.
2. (Was, Were) you waiting long?
3. They (was, were) there early.
4. It (don't, doesn't) matter much to me.
5. In the evening we (wasn't, weren't) at home.
6. (There's, There are) twenty boys coming to the picnic.
7. (Wasn't, Weren't) you and Ted born in Elmwood?
8. (Was, Were) you in that picture?
9. The Indians of that tribe (has, have) kept their old ways.

PROPER USE OF PRONOUNS

In an oral activity, choose the standard forms. Explain each choice.

1. Ray and (he, him) took off (their, they're) caps.
2. Bob and (me, I) walked up to the pup. It offered (its, it's) paw.
3. Were you and (she, her) at the door?
4. The teacher questioned Helen and (I, me).
5. May (we, us) three hikers cut across (your, you're) field?
6. At last Bob and (I, me) were ready for the trip.
7. (We, Us) girls remember you and (he, him).

Read these sentences aloud, choosing the standard forms.

1. I do not like (this, these) kind of apples.
2. My father is (an editor and publisher, an editor and a publisher).
3. (Them, Those) boys are here again.
4. Give me (an, a) apple.
5. I never watch (that, those) sort of programs.

Word Games to Test Your Thinking

SPELLING DEMONS BEGINNING WITH C

The blanks in the sentences below can be filled with words unscrambled from the italicized words. Each word begins with the letter *c*. How many can you unscramble? *Do not write in this book.*

EXAMPLE: Did you see that *eel clog*? He must go to ....! (*college*)

1. A .... wears a uniform, but it does not include *a tin cap*.
2. I would not call a *rat nice,* and that's for ....
3. If the *rich lend* too much money, their .... may inherit little.
4. *Tony* is a *cur* that lives in the ....
5. He sings in a ...., *or* some *such* group as that.
6. Dressed in men's ...., *she* was leading the *colt* to the barn.

FINDING WORDS IN THE WORD TRIANGLE

Many little words can be formed from the letters in the word *triangle*. Figure out those defined below; then see how many others you can find.

1. One who tells falsehoods.
2. Not imaginary.
3. A triangle has three.
4. A stove.
5. Opposite of *small.*
6. A very small insect. (The first letter is silent.)
7. Jack, the .... killer.
8. A messenger of God.
9. A strong, dazzling light.
10. Opposite of *boy.*
11. A part of a harness.
12. To rule (*homonym for No. 11*).
13. Used by carpenters.
14. Moisture falling from the clouds (*homonym for No. 11*).
15. Rock used in building.
16. Jungle cat.

You may be surprised at the answers the encyclopedia gives to some of the following questions.

1. Is it true that the first *tulips* came from Holland?
2. Did William *Tell* really shoot an apple off his son's head?
3. Is it correct to call a *termite* an ant?
4. When were *tanks* first used in warfare?
5. Would you be likely to meet a *tiger* in an African jungle?

ANOTHER "SPELLING DEMONS" CROSSWORD PUZZLE

Copy the crossword puzzle. *Do not write in this book.*

Across

1. Needful.
9. This goes around the neck.
10. A rather soft metal.
12. Preposition.
13. A church steeple.
14. Nine times ten.
17. Hotels.
18. East Central (*abbr.*).
19. Pronoun.
20. Cost.
25. Upon.
26. A club used in baseball.
28. Pain.
31. The air inhaled and exhaled in respiration.
33. Small child.
34. To inhale and exhale.
35. Short for *advertisement.*
36. General condition of the body.
37. Is fudge your favorite ......?
38. The night before.

Down

1. Observe.
2. East longitude (*abbr.*).
3. Anything that helps in solving a problem or mystery.
4. Each (*abbr.*).
5. Senior (*abbr.*).
6. Pertaining to the Alps.
7. Part of a harness.
8. Thread spun from wool.
9. A plant from which sugar is obtained.
11. Found in a schoolroom.
15. At that time.
16. Japanese coin.
21. Edgar Allan ....
22. Certainly.
23. You may take it in a tub.
24. Deadly.
26. To take a bath.
27. Opposite of *here.*
29. Collect on delivery (*abbr.*).
30. Height (*abbr.*).
31. A thin, flat nail.
32. Devour.
34. Short for *Benjamin.*
36. An exclamation.

USING PREPOSITIONS AND CONJUNCTIONS IN BUILDING SENTENCES *

1. Building Sentences with Prepositional Phrases

"I HAVEN'T ANY USE AT ALL IN MY LIFE FOR PREPOSITIONAL PHRASES."

THINK IT OVER ...

How many prepositional phrases has he actually used?
What do *you* know about prepositional phrases? Could you get along without them? If not, how are they useful?

PART ONE: RECOGNIZING PREPOSITIONAL PHRASES

Notice the sentences below. How important are the groups of words in parentheses? Try reading the sentences without them.

There was a great rush (of feet) (across the deck.)
A belt (of fog) had lifted (with the rising) (of the moon.)

Such word groups are *prepositional phrases,* so named because they begin with a *preposition,* another of the parts of speech. These phrases add important details to the sentence idea.

*Pretest 7 should be taken at this time.

1. (DEFINITION) A *preposition* is a word that shows relationship between a noun or a pronoun and some other word in a sentence.

   A *home* in *town* suits me.   A *home* near *town* suits me.

   (A home *in* town is very different from one *near* town.)

2. (DEFINITION) A *prepositional phrase* begins with a preposition and ends with a noun or a pronoun: *in town, with me.*

3. (DEFINITION) The noun or pronoun that completes a prepositional phrase is called the *object of the preposition.*

4. The object of a preposition may have adjective modifiers.

   A home *in a small town* suits me.

5. Here is a list of common prepositions.

about	at	beyond	from	on	toward
above	before	but (*except*)	in	out	under
across	behind	by	inside	outside	until
after	below	concerning	into	over	up
against	beneath	down	like	past	upon
along	beside	during	near	since	with
among	besides	except	of	through	within
around	between	for	off	to	without

6. **Some words in the above list may be used as more than one part of speech.** Remember, what part of speech a word is depends upon its use. To decide whether a word is a preposition, ask *whom* or *what* after the word. If a noun or a pronoun answers that question, the word is a preposition.

   I came **before** the storm.
   (*Before* what? *storm; before* is a preposition.)

   I have seen him **before**.
   (*Before* what? *nothing; before* is an adverb telling *when*.)

7. A prepositional phrase may have a compound object.

   I took a trip *to* Colombia and Brazil.

8. Prepositional phrases may be compound.

   I want a home on a farm or in a small town.

LEARNING ACTIVITIES

A. In a team activity, find the phrases in these sentences from *The Adventures of Tom Sawyer*. The list of prepositions above will help you. Note how many vivid and specific details the phrases add.

1. Tom drew a line in the dust with his big toe, . . .
2. The master, throned on high in his great splint-bottom armchair, was dozing, lulled by the drowsy hum of study.
3. Tom appeared on the sidewalk with a bucket of whitewash . . .
4. Half an hour later he was disappearing behind the Douglas mansion on the summit of Cardiff Hill.
5. Just here the blast of a toy tin trumpet came faintly down the green aisles of the forest.
6. Then the howl of a far-off dog rose on the night air, and was answered by a fainter howl from a remoter distance.
7. The doctor put the lantern at the head of the grave and came and sat down with his back against one of the elm trees.
8. A figure crept stealthily through a break in the other end of the ruined building, . . .
9. They lay around in the shade, after breakfast, . . . and then went off through the woods on an exploring expedition.
10. Now, for the first time, the deep stillness of the place laid a clammy hand upon the spirits of the children.

B. Go over the following sentences in class. Decide how each italicized word is used: as a *preposition,* a *verb,* a *noun,* an *adjective,* or an *adverb.* If a word is a preposition, name the object.

1. I *like* everything *about* that jacket *in* the window.
2. A *down* pillow *like* this one is really soft.
3. Who painted the *outside* of these bookshelves *before?*
4. I am *about* ready. Wait for me *outside.*
5. He ran *past* in a real hurry.
6. Come *out* and sit *down by* me.
7. The pitcher leaped *up* and caught the ball for the third *out.*
8. Does this team ever kick *before* fourth *down?*
9. The *past* week has slipped *by* too fast.
10. She hurried *down* the stairs and *out* the door.
11. The road *past* our house winds *up* a steep hill.
12. Come *in!* Don't stand *outside* the door.

PART TWO: USING PREPOSITIONAL PHRASES AS ADJECTIVES

READ AND DISCUSS

As is pointed out on page 398, expanding a sentence by adding descriptive adjectives helps to create an interesting and accurate sentence picture.

One tall, slender boy hit *the first* ball.

Now study this sentence:

One tall, slender boy *in a torn uniform* hit the first ball hard.

What is "in the torn uniform"? What does it tell you? Then as what kind of modifier is it used?

One tall, slender boy in a torn uniform hit the first ball hard.

● **THESE ARE FACTS ABOUT PREPOSITIONAL PHRASES USED AS ADJECTIVES**

1. Phrases used as adjectives modify nouns or pronouns.

The pears on this tree are ripe.   He helps each of us.

2. Prepositional phrases used as adjectives may be compound.

The road past our farm and beyond it is rough.

3. A phrase used as an adjective may modify the object in another prepositional phrase.

We made the trip *by the light* of the moon.

LEARNING ACTIVITIES

A. Go over the following sentences orally. Find the prepositional phrases used as adjectives and name the words modified.

1. I have forgotten the title of that book about birds.
2. The rules of the game demand fair play by one and all.
3. Our work in science covers many things.
4. The immense house on the corner was built recently.
5. That man in the blue suit is the umpire.
6. The grass beneath that tree and near the fence is dying.
7. I know that man with the carnation and the red tie.

8. The boy beside me plays a piccolo.
9. She has always been one of my best friends.
10. Have you a reason for your absence from the meeting?

B. Copy the following sentences. Add to each italicized preposition an object and enough adjectives to fill the rest of the blanks. In your small groups, read sentences aloud to see how the different choices change the picture. *Do not mark this book.*

    EXAMPLE: The man *in* .... is my father.
           The man *in the gray suit* is my father.

1. That boy *with* .... always comes early.
2. A letter *from* .... came this morning.
3. The road *past* .... was muddy.
4. Grandfather lives in a house *near* ....
5. The owner *of* .... gave it to me.

C. Write five sentences using prepositional phrases as adjectives. Use a different preposition each time. Let the phrases describe people or places you know, things you see on your way to school, things you like or dislike. Read the sentences in your small groups. Call on classmates to tell (1) the preposition, (2) its object, and (3) the word that each phrase modifies. You will need to listen carefully.

PART THREE: USING PREPOSITIONAL PHRASES AS ADVERBS

    One tall, slender boy in a torn uniform hit the first ball hard into left field.

THINK IT OVER . . .

What do the words "into left field" tell you?
What part of speech tells that same thing?
Then how is the phrase "into left field" used?

1. **Prepositional phrases may be used as adverbs to tell** (*a*) *how,* (*b*) *when,* (*c*) *where,* (*d*) *how much,* **or** (*e*) *why.* In other words, they tell (*a*) *manner,* (*b*) *time,* (*c*) *place,* (*d*) *degree,* or (*e*) *reason.*

   a) He ran like a frightened rabbit. (*how*)

   b) We left the house at dawn. (*when*)

   c) Meet me on this corner. (*where*)

   d) At least six people saw you. (*how much*)

   e) I wrote for information. (*why*)

2. **Most adverb phrases modify verbs.**

   Jack ran to first base.

   We were followed by Ted and Lee. (*compound objects*)

   See me at noon or after school. (*compound phrases*)

3. **Sometimes an adverb phrase modifies an adjective.**

   Are you ready for the trip?

LEARNING ACTIVITIES

A. In an oral activity, go over the following sentences. Locate each adverb phrase and name the word that it modifies.

1. The boys climbed quickly over the wall.
2. John is helpful in many ways.
3. The money was buried underneath a rock.
4. The children were already waiting for us.
5. I have come for my money.
6. John walked along the trail during the shower.
7. We are proud of our team and of their record.
8. The shadows stretched across the pool and the lawn.
9. On the hill stands an old tower.
10. William has come for the key.

B. Write a paragraph in which you use six prepositional phrases as adverbs. Choose a good topic sentence and then stick to it. (See page 214 for help.) In your small groups, read your paragraphs aloud. (Review first the Guides for Reading Aloud, page 57.) As paragraphs are read, jot down the adverb phrases and the words that they modify. Afterwards, compare lists. You will need to listen carefully. Perhaps one of the following phrases will suggest an idea around which to build a paragraph.

on the beach	along the highway	after the storm
across the desert	beyond the hill	in the haunted house
before Christmas	near the lake	during the game

PART FOUR: DISTINGUISHING ADJECTIVE FROM ADVERB
PHRASES

The boy is right. Most prepositional phrases can be used either as adverbs or as adjectives. The way a phrase is *used* in the sentence determines whether it is an adverb or an adjective phrase.

The boys ran around the track. (*adverb phrase*)

The fence around the track is high. (*adjective phrase*)

441

1. Adjective phrases tell *which* or *what kind* and modify nouns or pronouns.

The man with Bill is his uncle. (*which man*)

He is a man with many friends. (*what kind of man*)

2. Adverb phrases tell *how, when, where, how much,* or *why;* they usually modify verbs but sometimes modify adjectives.

We traveled in a jeep. (*how;* modifies the verb)

I'll arrive in an hour. (*when;* modifies the verb)

He lives in Canada. (*where;* modifies the verb)

I am older by a year. (*how much;* modifies an adjective)

She has come for your answer. (*why;* modifies the verb)

3. A phrase that modifies the object of another phrase is always an adjective phrase.

He stood on the top of the hill.

(*Of the hill* is an adjective phrase modifying *top,* the object in *on the top,* since it tells *which* top. *On the top* is itself an adverb phrase modifying *stood,* because it tells *where.*)

LEARNING ACTIVITIES

A. Go over the following sentences. Locate each prepositional phrase and tell (1) which word it modifies, and (2) what kind it is, adjective or adverb. Make this an oral exercise.

1. A band of savage warriors appeared at the edge of the forest.
2. In one cage we saw a huge bird from the jungles of Brazil.
3. She divided the candy among the children at the party.
4. Everyone in the class had finished at the same time.
5. We were awakened by a sudden clap of thunder.
6. Will you go to the hockey game with us?
7. A rosebush with sharp thorns grew beside the fence.
8. The airplane soared above the buildings on the field.
9. My uncle, the owner of the dog, walked slowly past the house.
10. We followed the fox by its tracks in the snow.

B. Write two sentences for each of the following prepositional phrases. In the first sentence use the phrase as an adjective; in the second, as an adverb. In your small groups, take turns at reading sentences. After you read a sentence, call on someone to tell (1) how the phrase is used and (2) what word it modifies. Use at least once each of these four basic sentence patterns: $N+V$, $N+LV+N$, $N+V+N$, and $N+LV+A$.

1. in the middle
2. beside the house
3. near us
4. on a boat
5. across the stream
6. with friends

(*Based upon the sentences in* A *of the preceding activities*)

1. Is the subject in sentence 1 singular or plural?
2. What is the direct object in sentence 3? Spell its plural.
3. Why is the subject in sentence 9 not capitalized? Explain the use of the commas.

DIAGRAMMING PREPOSITIONAL PHRASES

Like adjectives and adverbs themselves, prepositional phrases are placed below the words that they modify.

STEPS IN DIAGRAMMING PREPOSITIONAL PHRASES

1. Draw a slanting line from the word that the phrase modifies.
2. Write the preposition on the line.
3. Draw a horizontal line from the slanting line.
4. Write the object of the preposition on the horizontal line.
5. Place below the object any words that modify it.
6. Always begin the diagram in the same way. Find the verb and the subject first. Then see whether there is a direct object, a predicate nominative, or a predicate adjective. Last, diagram the modifiers—adjectives, adverbs, and prepositional phrases.

ADJECTIVE PHRASE	ADVERB PHRASE
The boy *in the new gray uniform* hit the ball.	The boy hit the ball *over the fence.*

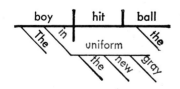   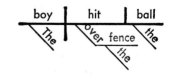

ADJECTIVE PHRASE MODIFYING THE OBJECT IN AN ADVERB PHRASE	COMPOUND OBJECT OF A PREPOSITION
The boy hit the ball *over the fence of the park.*	The boy was credited *with a home run, a double,* and *two singles.*

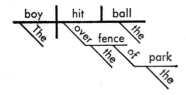

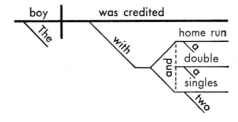

COMPOUND PHRASES

His performance *in the field* and *at bat* was sensational.

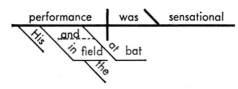

Note that only basic sentence-pattern parts go on the base line.

LEARNING ACTIVITIES IN DIAGRAMMING PREPOSITIONAL PHRASES

A. Diagram the following sentences. Be ready to explain your diagrams orally. Use a regular order, as in the following sample explanation for the first diagram on page 443: "In this sentence the verb is *hit*. The subject is the noun *boy*. *Ball* is a noun used as the direct object of the verb *hit*. *The* is a determiner modifying *boy*. *In the new gray uniform* is an adjective phrase modifying *boy*. The preposition is *in;* its object is the noun *uniform; the* is a determiner and *new* and *gray* are adjectives modifying *uniform*. *The* is a determiner modifying *ball*."

1. The ball shot over the fence and into some bushes.
2. The trail winds over the hill and through a wide valley.
3. A deep ditch was dug near the boundary of the field.
4. A little girl with long brown curls sat near Bob and me.
5. The four children listened carefully to every sound.
6. Do you still live in that brick house in the next block?
7. Heaps of wreckage were left after the storm.
8. The real owner of the property is not this stranger.
9. The sound of angry voices came faintly to our ears.
10. We have no time for excuses or delays.

B. If you wish further drill in diagramming phrases, use the sentences in *A*, page 438; *A*, page 440; and *A*, page 442.

READ AND DISCUSS

Which of these two sentences fits the picture below them?

He gave a watch *to the winner*.   He gave *the winner* a watch.

If both sentences fit the picture, what difference is there?

In the first sentence, *to the winner* is a prepositional phrase in which *winner* is the object. In the second, the preposition is understood, and *winner* is said to be an *indirect object*.

● THESE ARE FACTS ABOUT INDIRECT OBJECTS

1. **(DEFINITION) An** *indirect object* **is really a prepositional phrase in which the preposition** *to* **or** *for* **is understood, not stated. It tells** *to whom* **or** *for whom* **something is done.**

   She sent (to) **me** a gift.   He bought (for) **us** new shoes.

2. **An indirect object comes between the verb and the direct object. An indirect object always modifies the verb.**

   Mr. Jones *gave* the **winner** a *watch*.

3. **An indirect object may have modifiers.**

   She read *her little* **niece** a story.

4. **An indirect object may be compound.**

   He told **Ben** *and* **me** the truth.

5. **Only certain kinds of verbs take indirect objects.** Some that you probably use often are *give, tell, send, get, buy, show, build, do, make, save, read*. **Sentences that have indirect objects are** *Pattern 5* **sentences. Here is the pattern:** N + V-*give* + N + N. (V-*give* means that the pattern can be used only with verbs that function like *give*.)

   N + V-*give* + N + N
   He has given the winner a watch.

LEARNING ACTIVITIES IN FINDING AND USING INDIRECT OBJECTS

A. Copy the following sentences, placing parentheses around each indirect object. Underline with a wavy line each direct object. Go over the sentences in class.

1. Has anyone sent you a notice about the next meeting?
2. Father built us a picnic table.
3. The doctor will send you a bill for his services.
4. I sent Mr. Burns a birthday card.
5. Shall I get you a ticket to the game?
6. Doris bought me two new records.
7. Did Gary tell you and George his secret?
8. Give the man air.
9. The old road saved the hikers much time.
10. Has Elizabeth shown Jean and Jane her new dress?

B. Using the topic "Gifts," write an original paragraph that has in it at least five indirect objects. Think of a good topic sentence (see page 214) and then stick to it. Review the Guides for Reading Aloud, page 57; then read the paragraphs in your small groups. As you listen, jot down the indirect objects; then compare lists.

DIAGRAMMING INDIRECT OBJECTS

Indirect objects are diagrammed just like prepositional phrases, except that an (x) is used for the understood preposition.

Mr. Jones gave *Relmond* a watch.   He told *Ben* and *me* the truth.

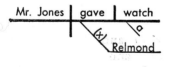
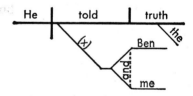

LEARNING ACTIVITIES IN DIAGRAMMING INDIRECT OBJECTS

A. Diagram the following sentences. Exchange papers for checking as the diagrams are put on the board and explained. Follow a specific, regular order in giving the explanations. See the example in *A,* page 444.

1. The salesman sold Father a blue suit.
2. The lawyer gave his client good advice.
3. Albert told the teacher his problem.
4. Yesterday I bought myself a new pair of shoes.
5. Has Jack offered you or Don a ride in his car?

6. Mother should have given Sandra and me more time.
7. The committee awarded each safe driver a certificate.
8. The pitcher threw me a fast ball.
9. I saved you a big piece of cake.
10. Has Coach Davis shown you and Tom that new play?

B. For additional practice, diagram the sentences in *A*, at the top of page 446. Explain the diagrams orally in class.

2. Building Sentences with Conjunctions

PART ONE: BUILDING COMPOUND PARTS OF SENTENCES *

● THESE ARE FACTS ABOUT CONJUNCTIONS

1. A *junction* is a place where two things join, and *con* means *with*. (DEFINITION) A *conjunction* is a word that *joins* one part of a sentence *with* another.

2. (DEFINITION) Sentence parts, or *elements*, that are joined by a conjunction are *compound parts*.

   SUBJECTS: *John* and *I* cut the grass.
   VERBS: Jean *hopped* and *skipped*.
   PREDICATE NOMINATIVES: The leader is *George* or *Bill*.
   PREDICATE ADJECTIVES: The clouds are *large* and *black*.
   DIRECT OBJECTS: We saw *Harry* and *Fred*.
   ADJECTIVES: He is a *thin* but *strong* man.
   ADVERBS: We scored *quickly* and *easily*.
   OBJECTS OF PREPOSITION: Wait for *Ann* and *me*.
   PREPOSITIONAL PHRASES: Go *up the path* and *over the hill*.
   INDIRECT OBJECTS: Julie gave *Pat* and *me* a surprise.
   APPOSITIVES: Mr. Carter, our *principal* and *friend*, is ill.

3. A compound element may have more than two parts.

   Joe, John, and *Jerry* came.   (Joe *and* John *and* Jerry came.)

4. Here are some common conjunctions: *and, but, either, or, neither, nor. Either* and *or* are often used as a pair, as are *neither–nor.* Other pairs are *both–and* and *not only–but also.*

   Either Ed *or* Ernie will go.   I want *both* you *and* him.

*This section sums up the teaching of compound parts of the simple sentence. For fuller treatment, see the Index.

LEARNING ACTIVITIES IN USING COMPOUND ELEMENTS

A. Locate the compound in each of the following sentences. Tell in which of the ways given on page 447 it is used. Make this an oral exercise.

1. A crowd of boys and girls followed us.
2. I shall choose either Helen or her brother.
3. The happy children laughed and sang.
4. Two hot drinks, coffee and tea, were served.
5. Our first visitors were Laura and Elaine.
6. I neither saw nor heard anything.
7. In our garden several small but sturdy trees are growing.
8. Jack waited for Carol, Barbara, and me.
9. You must leave quickly and quietly.
10. Apples and oranges were bought for the picnic.
11. After the game the boys were tired and hungry.
12. The kitten ran across the lawn and into the street.
13. The gardener gave Mother and me some helpful hints.

B. Write a paragraph containing compound elements of at least five kinds. Do not use *and* as the conjunction more than twice. As paragraphs are read, jot down the compound elements. Compare lists afterwards.

Diagramming Compound Elements

Compound elements are diagrammed on these pages: verbs and subjects, 324; predicate nominatives, 327; direct objects, 331; appositives, 335; adjectives, 402; adverbs, 422; prepositional phrases, 443–44; indirect objects, 446.

Here are some additional diagrams to help you.

The storm brought both *rain* and cold *weather*.

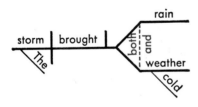

Mother visited in either *Iowa* or *Missouri*.

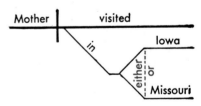

We saw *many* cities and towns. (*Many* modifies both *cities* and *towns*.)

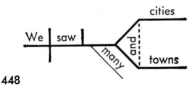

Susan works *not only* neatly *but also* quickly.

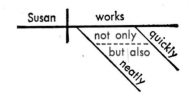

448

LEARNING ACTIVITIES IN DIAGRAMMING COMPOUND ELEMENTS

A. Diagram these sentences; then put them on the board and explain them. Be sure to name the conjunctions and the elements that they join.

1. Spot is an old but reliable watchdog.
2. Mary knits slowly but surely.
3. The boys raced down the alley and into the park.
4. The day was not only hot but also windy.
5. Jack visits often both Jones Beach and Coney Island.
6. The crowd whistled and applauded.
7. Either Letty or her mother will call you.
8. The water at the beach was very rough and cold.
9. The guilty one is neither Butch nor Bud.
10. Then Mother stopped at the station for some gas and oil.

B. For further practice, diagram the sentences in *A* on page 448. Be prepared to explain the diagrams orally.

PART TWO: BUILDING COMPOUND SENTENCES

Point 2, page 447, points out that conjunctions connect compound elements within a sentence. Conjunctions may also be used to make *compound sentences;* that is, to join two or more simple sentences.

Jim's favorite pie is apple. His second choice is berry.

Jim's favorite pie is apple, **and** his second choice is berry.

One tall, slender boy in a torn uniform hit the first ball hard into left field, **but the fielder there leaped up and caught it**

449

1. **(DEFINITION)** A *compound sentence* puts together two or more simple sentences.* This combining usually is done by using the conjunctions *and, but, or,* or *nor.*

   The boy hit the ball well. The shortstop caught it. (*two simple sentences*)
   The boy hit the ball well, *but* the shortstop caught it. (*compound sentence*)

2. **Only sentences closely related in thought should be joined.**

   GOOD: The boy hit the ball well, but the shortstop caught it.
   BAD: The boy hit the ball well, and the umpire was Mr. Bell.

3. **A comma usually separates the two parts of a compound sentence when they are joined by a conjunction. The comma goes before the conjunction.**

   The boy hit the ball well *but* the shortstop caught it.

   In very short compound sentences, the comma may be omitted, especially if the conjunction is *and*. (Even in such cases, use a comma if you feel a pause between the two parts.)

   I waited and soon Joe came.

4. **A compound sentence should not be confused with a simple sentence having compound parts.** (See point 2 on page 447.)

   To test, divide the sentence before and after the conjunction. Each part of a compound sentence is really a sentence.

   The boy hit a home run, | and | we scored four runs.
   (*Each part makes sense. The sentence is compound.*)

   The boy hit the ball | and | ran to first base.
   (*Only the first part makes sense. The sentence is simple.*)

   My little brother | and | his friend went to the game.
   (*Only the second part makes sense. The sentence is simple.*)

Learn about words!

The following words, taken from *A* of the Learning Activities, have interesting histories. Use your dictionary to find the story behind each word. To which word is the drawing related?

barbecue   colonel   hustle   parade

---

* Each simple sentence that becomes part of a compound sentence is known as an *independent clause* because it can stand alone.

LEARNING ACTIVITIES IN COMPOUND SENTENCES

A. (1) Copy the following compound sentences, inserting any needed commas. (2) Draw one line under subjects and two lines under verbs. (3) Enclose conjunctions in parentheses. (4) Exchange papers. (5) *Proofread for careless errors in copying.* (6) Go over the sentences in class. Name the two simple sentences that make up each compound sentence. Which four sentences have Pattern 3 (N+V+N) in both clauses?

1. Karen had planned the barbecue but she could not attend it.
2. Our players did not win the game nor did they score.
3. I leave for New York today and Sis is going with me.
4. Is he a colonel or don't you know?
5. Sara made the motion and Jon seconded it.
6. I should like that but I have a dental appointment.
7. I do not know him but Paul does.
8. We must hustle or the train will leave without us.
9. Mother baked the cookies and I made the pie.
10. Shall you watch the parade or haven't you decided?

B. Combine each pair of simple sentences into a compound sentence, using commas and conjunctions correctly. Exchange papers for checking as the sentences are put on the board.

1. You must pass the test. You cannot make the trip.
2. Frank is tall. He also is strong.
3. The boat filled with water. It did not sink.
4. Listen to me. You will be sorry.
5. I turned on the record player. We listened to records.
6. I must go to the store. We'll have nothing for dinner.
7. Joe went to the barbershop. Every barber was busy.
8. The car had stopped suddenly. It would have rammed the bus.
9. Jack is intelligent enough. He just did not think.
10. Gary walked bravely into the office. I followed him.

C. Write five compound sentences. Be sure that the two parts of each compound sentence are closely related. *Proofread for careless mistakes.*

D. These sentences are from James Fenimore Cooper's *Deerslayer* and *The Last of the Mohicans.* In an oral activity, decide which sentences are compound and which are simple sentences with compound parts.

1. Just at this instant, five or six rifles flashed, and the opposite hills flashed back the sharp reports.
2. Deerslayer adjusted his hard pillow, stretched out in the bottom of the canoe, and slept.
3. At the next instant, Judith and Hetty shrieked, and the air was filled with the yell of twenty savages.
4. Bullets whistled past him, and many cut twigs from the branches at his side, but not one touched him.

5. The canoe was gone, nor could he see any traces of it.
6. Their rifles were scattered about against the different trees, and their only weapons were their knives and tomahawks.
7. Then Deerslayer stepped from behind his own cover and hailed the Indian.
8. Once more the savage yells burst out of the woods, and the leaden hail whistled above the heads of the besieged.
9. The Hurons soon fired again, and a bullet struck the blade of Hawkeye's paddle.
10. Twenty knives gleamed in the air, and as many warriors sprang to their feet.

ENRICHMENT

Deerslayer and *The Last of the Mohicans* are not easy reading, but they tell exciting stories of life during the French and Indian Wars. Good readers will be thrilled by the daring bravery of Deerslayer, also known as "Hawkeye" and "Leatherstocking." The card catalogue in the library (see page 128) will help you to find these books. If you do read either book, perhaps you can tell the class one or more of the suspense-filled incidents in the story. In giving this talk, apply guides 2, 5, and 6, page 134, and use your Speech Chart.

DIAGRAMMING COMPOUND SENTENCES

STEPS IN DIAGRAMMING A COMPOUND SENTENCE

1. Diagram each part as a simple sentence, one below the other.
2. Join the two parts by a dotted line.
3. Write the conjunction on that line.

The boy hit the ball well, but the shortstop caught it.

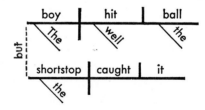

LEARNING ACTIVITIES IN DIAGRAMMING COMPOUND SENTENCES

A. Diagram these sentences. Exchange papers for checking as the diagrams are put on the board and explained step by step, giving each part its specific name. Begin, "This is a compound sentence."
1. Were you there, or didn't you go?
2. Mr. West flew to New York, but he will return by train.

3. Charles played golf, and Ann swam.
4. They should go, or they will miss a good play.
5. We had planned a picnic, but the weatherman predicted rain.
6. The plane left the ground, and we began our journey.
7. Jack gave the man a dollar, and he handed Jack two tickets.
8. Bill was studying English, and Bob was doing his arithmetic.
9. I had expected the pen, but the skates were a surprise.

B. For additional practice, diagram the sentences in *A,* page 451. Go over the diagrams orally.

3. Expressing Ideas in Effective Ways

Using vivid, exact words is one way to express ideas effectively, as explained on pages 292, 343, 398, and 420. In this lesson you will study other ways to improve expression.

The guides that follow apply especially to writing paragraphs, themes, stories, or letters. After doing the first quick writing of a piece, go back over it. Using the guides, make changes that will add variety and interest, or that will get rid of unnecessary words.

GUIDES FOR IMPROVING EXPRESSION

1. For emphasis or variety, move a phrase to the front of a sentence.
      At that very moment, Don walked in.
   In normal order, the sentence would read thus:
      Don walked in *at that very moment.*

2. Condense sentences by changing phrases to adjectives or adverbs.
   I like a face *with a smile.*   I like a *smiling* face.
   Meet me *at this place* tomorrow.   Meet me *here* tomorrow.

3. Change compound sentences to simple sentences by turning one part into modifying words or phrases.
   It was dark in the empty house, and I grew frightened.
   I grew frightened *in the dark, empty house.*

4. Change weak compound sentences to simple sentences by using an appositive.
   This dog is a toy poodle, and he has won many prizes.
   This dog, *a toy poodle,* has won many prizes.

LEARNING ACTIVITIES IN IMPROVING EXPRESSION

A. These sentences from *A Tale of Two Cities* by Charles Dickens are as he wrote them, except that phrases have been moved. Read the sentences orally as you think he wrote them. Does his way sound better?

1. The passenger opened the coach-door with those words and got in.
2. "I would do anything for you, and for any dear to you."
3. Taxers and taxed were fast asleep in the village.
4. The stone faces of the chateau, lion and human, stared blindly at the night for three heavy hours.
5. "Can I not save you without it, Mr. Carton?"
6. Some mortar and dust came dropping down in a few minutes.
7. "I have suffered a great deal on the road."
8. A group of officers at the gate were looking at the fire.
9. She arrived at the usual corner on a lightly-snowing afternoon.
10. Mr. Lorry sat at his desk on a steaming, misty afternoon.
11. There was a roar at every juryman's vote.
12. The death-carts rumble along the Paris streets, hollow and harsh.

B. (1) Shorten these sentences by changing one prepositional phrase or more to an adjective or an adverb. Do not change the sentence meaning. (2) On your paper, underscore the substituted words. (3) Exchange papers and compare sentences.

1. The boy ran into the room in a noisy manner.
2. Who lives in the house on the corner?
3. The train moved at a slow rate into the station.
4. In an angry voice, he ordered me out of the building.
5. Laura was wearing a dress with stripes in it.
6. A person with a friendly disposition usually is popular.
7. Have you seen that glass with a crack in it?
8. Roads with ice on them are dangerous.

C. In an oral activity, change these weak compound sentences to good simple sentences by applying either guide 3 or guide 4, page 453.

1. Barry helped me, and I soon finished the weeding.
2. We have a new car, and it is a yellow convertible.
3. Last night I watched a good television program, and it was a new kind of quiz show.
4. You can find him in the garage, or else he will be in the garden.
5. I built this cabin, and nobody helped me with it.
6. Mother made a new dessert today, and it was a lime-chiffon pie.
7. Dan Foley scored the winning basket, and he is a substitute guard.
8. Look for me in the library, or I might be in the gym.
9. This is David Ellis, and he is a good friend of mine.

D. Write five sentences beginning with prepositional phrases. Read the sentences in your small groups. After reading a sentence, call on a classmate to reword it in natural order. Decide which way sounds better.

4. Using Standard English

PART ONE: USING PREPOSITIONS PROPERLY

He walked around **in** the room.   He walked **into** the room.

"He walked around *in* the room," means that the boy walked while he was in the room, not that he walked from somewhere else into it.

The following rules will help you to use *in* and *into* correctly and to avoid other errors in using prepositions.

RULES FOR USING PREPOSITIONS PROPERLY

RULE 1. Use *into* for motion from outside to inside; use *in* for motion within: Sue jumped *into* the water.   She swam *in* the water.

RULE 2. Do not use *to* or *by* as substitutes for *at*.

STANDARD: He is not *at* home.   I stay *at* my aunt's house.
NONSTANDARD: He is not ~~to~~ home.   I stay ~~by~~ my aunt's house.

RULE 3. Do not use *off* or *off of* for *from*.

STANDARD: I bought it *from* him.
NONSTANDARD: I bought it ~~off~~ him.

RULE 4. Do not use *off of* for *off*.

STANDARD: Get *off* the train.   NONSTANDARD: Get *off* ~~of~~ the train.

RULE 5. Do not use unnecessary prepositions.

Where does she stay ~~at~~?   Where are you going ~~to~~?

LEARNING ACTIVITIES IN USING PREPOSITIONS PROPERLY

A. To get used to the sound of the proper forms, practice saying aloud the standard examples of the rules.

B. Copy the following sentences, choosing the proper forms from the parentheses. Read the sentences orally several times.

1. Get (off, off of) the roof immediately.
2. Is Grandmother (at, to) home?
3. Get (in, into) the car.
4. Where are you (living, living at)?
5. Mary visited (at, by) her grandparents' house.
6. I hurried (in, into) the room without knocking.
7. Tom bought the knife (off of, from) Ted.
8. For what man are you (looking for, looking)?
9. Where was your grandmother (going to, going)?
10. Were many people (to, at) the game?

C. Write sentences to illustrate Rules 1–4. In your small groups, take turns at reading sentences. Listen to get used to the standard forms.

PART TWO: USING OBJECTS OF PREPOSITIONS AND INDIRECT OBJECTS PROPERLY

READ AND THINK ABOUT

He ran by me.   He ran by Al and me.   Do Al and me a favor.

"Me" is the proper form in all three sentences. No doubt it sounds right to you in the first sentence, but how about in the other two? It may sound wrong in those sentences, but if you take out "Al and," you will see that "me" is right.

THE RULES

RULE 1. Use *me, her, him, us, them* as objects of a preposition. Do not so use *I, he, she, we, they.*

He sent *for* Joe and me   The candy was given *to* us boys.

RULE 2. Never use a nominative pronoun (*I, he, she, we,* or *they*) as an indirect object. Use *me, him, her, us,* or *them.*

Mother saved Jack and him some cookies.
Miss Bell gave her and me the last pencils.

RULE 3. In speaking of yourself and others, name yourself last, as a matter of politeness.

POLITE: He sent for Joe and me   POORER: He sent for me and Joe.

LEARNING ACTIVITIES IN USING OBJECTS OF PREPOSITIONS AND INDIRECT OBJECTS PROPERLY

A. Read the following sentences orally, choosing the standard forms. Make this a row contest in which you see which group can say the sentences properly twice in the shortest time.

1. The class gave Pam and (him, he) the prizes.
2. Everyone was ready except (we, us) three.
3. They saved (Grace and me, me and Grace) two seats.
4. This secret is between you and (me, I).
5. Mr. Bie told (them, they) and (us, we) the same story.
6. Will you show Meg and (me, I) your drawing?
7. The librarian will give you and (me, I) the information.
8. It was a vacation for (them, they) and (we, us).

B. (1) Using yourself and some friends as the topic, write five sentences to illustrate the rules above. Begin three sentences with an adverb phrase. (2) Put sentences on the board, leaving a blank for each objective pronoun. (3) Call on classmates to fill the blanks properly.

Spot Review ★

(*Based upon the sentences in* A *of the preceding activities*)

1. What is the tense of the verb in sentence 1? 6?
2. What part of speech is *Everyone* in sentence 2?
3. How would you spell the plural of the final word in sentence 5?
4. What are the principal parts of the verb in sentence 5?

PART THREE: USING <u>TO</u>, <u>TOO</u>, AND <u>TWO</u> CORRECTLY

Who sent you *to* me?
Don't stay *too* long at the zoo.
Twins are always *two*.

READ AND DO

If you have trouble with *to, too,* and *two,* copy the above sentences and practice reading them over and over. Do so while walking to school, doing dishes, running errands, . . .

THE RULES FOR USING *TO, TOO,* AND *TWO* CORRECTLY

RULE 1. Use an object with *to;* **it is a preposition:** I went to *town.*

RULE 2. Use *too,* **which is always an adverb, to modify verbs, adjectives, or other adverbs. When it modifies a verb,** *too* **means "also."**

May Harry *go,* too? (*Too* modifies the verb *may go.*)
John is too *tired.* (*Too* modifies the adjective *tired.*)
The time is going too *fast.* (*Too* modifies the adverb *fast.*)

RULE 3. *a*) **Use** *two* **as an adjective:** Those two *children* may go.
b) **Use** *two* **as a noun:** Two of the boys came early.

LEARNING ACTIVITIES IN USING *TO, TOO,* AND *TWO* CORRECTLY

A. Copy the following sentences, putting in each blank the correct form, *to, too,* or *two.* Check sentences in class. *Do not write in this book.*

1. I, ..., should like a visit .... those .... countries.
2. The boys went .... town .... hours ago.
3. Will you go .... the store, ...?
4. I have .... tickets .... the game.
5. .... boys are swimming .... the shore.
6. .... of my friends came .... the party .... late.
7. The work is not .... hard for us .... boys.
8. I am going .... the library and .... the bank, ...
9. .... trips .... the park in one day will be .... many.

B. Write five sentences using *to, too,* and *two* correctly. In your small groups, read sentences aloud. Call on someone to spell the forms needed. Say a sentence only once. Decide on a penalty for not listening.

PART FOUR: USING TROUBLESOME VERBS

The next few pages contain rules and practice for standard use of the forms of *sing, ring, blow, grow, fall,* and *wear.*

USING IRREGULAR VERBS

RULE 1. (*Sing, ring,* and their forms)
Never use an auxiliary verb with *sang* **or** *rang.*

Today I sing.	Yesterday I sang.	Often I *have* sung.
Today I ring.	Yesterday I rang.	Often I *have* rung.

A. (1) Copy each sentence below, supplying the proper form of the verb in parentheses. (2) Underline twice the complete verb. (3) In class, have the sentences read aloud several times. Stand when you read a sentence. If you get it right, sit down. If you miss, remain standing until the next time around.

1. How long have you (sing) in the chorus?
2. Your alarm clock must have (ring) early.
3. The bell should have (ring) ten minutes ago.
4. This line should be (sing) rapidly.
5. Neither June nor Jerry has ever (sing) on television before.
6. Suddenly a scream had (ring) out from behind the locked door.
7. You've never (sing) better!
8. Many sets of words have been (sing) to this music.
9. Has the bell (ring)?
10. A lullaby should be (sing) softly.
11. Nobody had (ring) the doorbell.

B. Make this a team contest. (1) One after the other, each person on each team will write on the board two sentences, one using *sang* or *sung* and one using *rang* or *rung*. Each sentence must have at least six words in it. The members of a team must go to the board in order, and not more than one person from a team may be out of his seat at once. (2) Stop the contest as soon as everyone on one team has written his sentences. (3) Credit each team with one point for each sentence it has on the board. (4) Go over the sentences orally. Reduce a team's score by one point for every nonstandard verb used.

Spot Review ★

(Based upon the sentences in A of the preceding activities)

1. How would you spell the plural of the last word in sentence 1?
2. What kind of sentence is sentence 7?
3. Is *better* in sentence 7 an adjective or an adverb? How do you know?
4. Why is *has* the proper auxiliary in sentence 5?

USING IRREGULAR VERBS—Continued

RULE 2. (*Blow* and its forms)
Always use a helping verb with *blown;* **never use one with** *blew.*
Remember that there is no standard form *blowed.*

Today I blow.   Yesterday I blew.   Often I *have* blown.

LEARNING ACTIVITIES IN USING *BLEW* AND *BLOWN*

A. In an oral activity, practice filling the blanks in these sentences, using the standard form of *blow*. Name any helping verbs.

1. Last night the wind .... hard.
2. In the storm, the roof was .... from our garage.
3. The children .... soap bubbles for an hour this morning.
4. The noon whistles have ....
5. Has the trouble .... over yet?
6. Who .... that whistle?
7. A strong wind had .... all week.
8. Jim .... the bugle for taps last night.

B. Write five sentences using *blew* and *blown* properly. Use a vivid adjective or adverb in each sentence. (See pages 398, 420.) The drawings on this page offer sentence ideas. In your small groups, take turns at reading sentences. Call on a listener to judge your sentences for standard usage and to name the vivid words.

C. Divide the class into two teams. Take turns at asking and answering questions about a big windstorm. Use one of these questions:

What blew away at your place?   Was anything blown away?

Have fun with your answers. For example, you might say, "The freckles on my sister's nose blew away," or "My dog's bark was blown away." If the person before you uses a nonstandard form, you must reword his sentence before giving your own. Score one point for each proper answer.

★ **Spot Review**

(*Based upon the sentences in* A *of the preceding activities*)

1. In sentence 1, what is *hard,* an adjective or an adverb? Explain.
2. How would you spell the plural of the subject in sentence 2?
3. Which three sentences have direct objects?

USING IRREGULAR VERBS—*Continued*

RULE 3. (*Grow* and its forms)
Always use an auxiliary verb with *grown;* **never use one with** *grew.*
Remember, there is no standard form *growed.*

Today I **grow.**   Yesterday I **grew.**   Often I *have* **grown.**

LEARNING ACTIVITIES IN USING *GREW* AND *GROWN*

A. (1) Write these sentences, filling the blanks with the proper form of *grow.* (2) Underline twice the verb, including any helping verbs. (3) Exchange papers. (4) *Proofread for careless errors in copying.* (5) Check the verb choices as the sentences are read aloud.

1. The corn .... several inches last week.
2. I have .... tired of doing nothing.
3. Bananas are .... in a hot, damp climate.
4. The grass .... well last spring.
5. This property has .... in value.
6. Where were these oranges ....?
7. We .... oats in this field last year.
8. A younger man would not have .... tired.
9. How you have ....!
10. My father .... up on a farm.

B. Pretend that each of you had a garden last year. Go around the class, telling what you grew and what you wished later that you had grown instead. Be ready to tell why, if anyone asks you. No crop may be named more than once.

Spot Review

(Based upon the sentences in A *of the preceding activities)*
1. In sentence 4, which is *well,* an adjective or an adverb? Explain.
2. How would you spell the plural of the subject in sentence 5?
3. What kind of sentence is sentence 9?

USING IRREGULAR VERBS—*Continued*

RULE 4. (*Fall* and its forms)
Always use a helping verb with *fallen;* **never use one with** *fell.*

Today I **fall.**   Yesterday I. **fell.**   Often I *have* **fallen.**

LEARNING ACTIVITIES IN USING *FELL* AND *FALLEN*

A. Write these sentences, supplying the standard forms of *fall*. Underline twice the verb, including helping verbs. Go over your work orally.

1. The baby had just .... asleep.
2. The responsibility for last month's play .... upon Jean and me.
3. By morning the river should have .... a foot or more.
4. Rain has .... steadily for hours.
5. Yes, Christmas .... upon Monday last year.
6. He might have .... heir to a large fortune.
7. The picture must have .... from its hook.

B. Go around the class rapidly, giving sentences with *fell* and *fallen*. See how long it takes for everyone to use each word properly.

USING IRREGULAR VERBS—Continued

RULE 5. (*Wear* and its forms)
Always use an auxiliary verb with *worn;* never use one with *wore*. Remember, there is no standard form *weared*.

Today I **wear.**   Yesterday I **wore.**   Often I *have* **worn.**

LEARNING ACTIVITIES IN USING *WORE* AND *WORN*

A. In an oral activity, practice the following sentences, using *wore* or *worn* in each blank. When you use *worn,* name the auxiliary verbs.

1. These two colors shouldn't be .... together.
2. Mary .... a new kind of hat yesterday.
3. This dress surely has .... well.
4. My red coat is badly ....
5. At the party last Friday, those girls .... dresses just alike.
6. Everyone had .... new shoes except Jack and him.
7. Are skirts being .... longer this year?
8. This coat can be .... either in summer or in winter.

B. (1) Make a class list on the board of as many combinations of *worn* and helping verbs as you can. (2) Give oral sentences with each combination in order. (3) After you give a sentence, call on someone else.

★ **Spot Review**

(*Based upon the sentences in* A *of the preceding activities*)

1. Why are *surely* and *well* the proper forms in sentence 3?
2. Why should you say *those* girls, not *them* girls, in sentence 5?
3. Why is *him* the proper pronoun in sentence 6?

A. (1) Copy these sentences; *proofread to be sure you have copied accurately.* (2) Underline each prepositional phrase and draw an arrow to the word modified. (3) If the phrase is used as an adjective, write *adj.* after the sentence. If it is used as an adverb, write *adv.* (4) Put parentheses around each indirect object. Name the sentence patterns.

1. The boys were playing in the street.
2. The librarian gave Lucy a list of new books.
3. We did the work with great care.
4. After supper we played games.

B. (1) Copy each of the following sentences; *proofread to be sure you have copied accurately.* (2) Put parentheses around each compound. (3) Decide how each is used in the sentence. After the sentence, put one or more of these marks: *v.* for compound parts used as verbs; *subj.,* as subjects; *d.o.,* as direct objects; *p.n.,* as predicate nominatives; *p.a.,* as predicate adjectives; *o.p.,* as objects of a preposition; *i.o.,* as indirect objects; *adj.,* as adjectives; *adv.,* as adverbs; and *pr. ph.,* as prepositional phrases. *Do not write in this book.*

1. Jane lost or mislaid her book.
2. The owners are Mr. Smith and Mr. Haines.
3. A new and better plan was offered by Phil and Fred.
4. Martha or Alice will give you and Ann the money.
5. We saw many lakes and rivers.
6. John writes slowly but neatly.
7. Father was tired and cold from the ride.
8. Mickey hit the ball over the fence and into the street.

C. Number your paper from 1 to 5. After each number, write *Compound* for each compound sentence and *Simple* for each simple sentence.

1. We were watching television, but they were studying.
2. Frances and Cynthia are making cookies in the kitchen.
3. The dentist did not pull the tooth, nor did he even fill it.
4. We had better run, or we'll miss part of the game.
5. The reporter wrote the story and gave it to the editor.

D. Read the following sentences aloud, choosing the proper forms.

1. John crawled (in, into) the wagon.
2. Please get (off, off of) the steps.
3. Ruth visited last week (by, at) her cousin's house.
4. Is Joe (at, to) home? I borrowed this book (from, off) him.
5. Where did you (stay at, stay)? Where will you (go, go to) next?
6. Did the (two, too, to) boys go (to, too, two) town, (too, to, two)?

*Check Test 7 should be taken at this point. If the results show need for further study, students should do this review practice. They should then take Mastery Test 7.

E. Read these sentences aloud, choosing the standard pronouns.

1. Mother gave a party for Ellen and (me, I).
2. Lou sent Alice and (I, me) postcards.
3. That job is not for (me and you, you and me).
4. Between you and (me, I), there should be no secrets.
5. Mrs. Jones gave you and (him, he) good advice.
6. The letter was addressed to (us, we) two boys.

F. Read these sentences aloud, supplying the proper form of each verb.

1. Have you ever (sing) in public?
2. The wind (blow) hard last night.
3. The corn has not (grow) well this year.
4. He had (wear) a hat, but it had (fall) off.
5. The noon whistles have (blow), and the bell has (ring).

★ **Cumulative Review**

PARTS OF THE SENTENCE

Copy these sentences, leaving extra space between lines. Label *verbs* (v.), *subjects* (subj.), *predicate nominatives* (p.n.), *direct objects* (d.o.), *appositives* (app.), *adjectives* (adj.), and *adverbs* (adv.).

1. Is that watermelon ripe? Our first one was a beauty.
2. My mother has a new coat.
3. The tree, a tall pine, was swaying wildly in the terrific wind.

TROUBLESOME VERBS

Read these sentences aloud, supplying the standard form of each verb.

1. I (eat) a sandwich, (drink) some milk, and then went to school.
2. My feet were almost (freeze). Why had I (come) without boots!
3. The man had (drive) up in a cart. It was (draw) by a mule.
4. Why have you (ride) that horse? You have (break) your word.
5. We had (steal) away to the beach and had (swim) out to the float.
6. Have the prices of plane tickets (rise)? I've not (fly) lately.
7. That rock should not be (lie) there. Who (throw) it?

PROPER USE OF PRONOUNS

Go over these sentences aloud, choosing the standard forms.

1. My dog and (I, me) like (your, you're) woods.
2. One day (we, us) boys were fishing in (their, they're) pond.
3. Jean and (she, her) watched the kitten chasing (its, it's) tail.
4. Yes, it was (he, him), and he saw (we, us) boys.
5. Can it be (they, them)? That car is (there's, theirs).

Read these sentences aloud, choosing the standard forms.

1. (This, These) kind of cookies tastes (good, well).
2. Jack has (sure, surely) found (a, an) interesting book.
3. How (good, well) does he sing?
4. Mary hasn't (ever, never) liked (them, those) shoes.
5. (Them, Those) gloves (sure, surely) are pretty.
6. Jim (has, hasn't) hardly ever felt (bad, badly).

VERB-SUBJECT AGREEMENT

Read these sentences aloud, choosing the standard forms.

1. He (don't, doesn't) know me. It (don't, doesn't) matter, though.
2. (Was, Were) you at the party? Neither Ed nor I (was, were).
3. The noise of the explosions (doesn't, don't) carry far.
4. A bushel of peaches (has, have) just been delivered.
5. Either the Smiths or the Grays (was, were) there.

SPELLING

Figure out the scrambled *ie* or *ei* words in the following sentences.

1. The hospital (pteitan) was very (tique).
2. The (fithe) dropped a (dankrichfeeh) as he ran off.
3. I (veelibe) you (gihew) more than I do.

Word Games to Test Your Thinking
ALPHABET ADDITION OR SUBTRACTION

EXAMPLES: Take *n* from *close by* and leave *part of the body*. (near-ear)
Add *p* to *automobile* and have a *kind of fish*. (car-carp)

1. Take *a* from *once more* and leave *profit*.
2. Take *s* from *talk* and leave the *top of a mountain*.
3. Take *t* from a *pronoun* and leave *stockings*.
4. Take *p* from *gave wages to* and leave *help*.
5. Add *s* to a *female deer* and have a *form of "do."*
6. Add *y* to a *public vehicle* and have *not idle*.
7. Add *m* to a *chum* and have a *kind of tree*.

Find the answers that the encyclopedia gives to these questions.

1. How did *Death Valley* get its name?
2. Were the first *dams* built to supply power, or to irrigate land?
3. When was *daylight-saving* time first used?
4. You have heard the expression "dead as a *dodo.*" Was there ever a real creature of that name?
5. Is the *dragonfly* a harmful, or a useful, insect?

"I" BEFORE "E" PUZZLE

Copy the crossword puzzle. *Do not write in this book.*

Across

1. Your sister's daughter.
4. Part of something.
8. A preposition.
9. Credit (*abbr.*).
10. Used by fishermen.
12. Pertaining to a chorus.
14. Opposite of *give.*
16. A preposition.
19. Textile used to stiffen or shape clothes.
21. Eisenhower's nickname.
23. One's relatives.
24. Legal term meaning *unless.*
26. Contraction of *even.*
27. Anything that happens.
29. Six (Roman numerals).
30. "Anchors ......" (Navy song).
31. Half an *em.*
32. Suffix that forms the comparative of adjectives.
33. George (*abbr.*).
35. Fastened to a horse's bit.
36. If you are polite, you will say, "Yes, ...," to a man.

Down

1. Short sleep.
2. Pronoun.
3. Company (*abbr.*).
4. Make angry.
5. Period of history.
6. Used after the salutation in a business letter.
7. Nickname for *Edward.*
9. Part of the jaw.
11. To mislead or trick.
12. The overhead part of a room.
13. The medicine helps to ...... the pain.
15. Same as 9 across.
17. One who lives near you.
18. Eleven (Roman numerals).
20. Seventh-...... stretch (*plural*).
22. Past form of *know.*
25. Fishing net.
28. "Now and ......" means the same as *occasionally.*
30. Present form of *be.*
34. East Indies (*abbr.*).

IMPROVING WHAT YOU WRITE

1. Reviewing the Sentence and Its Parts

● REVIEW OF FACTS ABOUT SENTENCES

1. *Verbs, nouns, pronouns, adjectives, adverbs, prepositions,* **and** *conjunctions* are the parts of speech from which sentences are built.*

2. **The work of each part of speech is to help build sentences.** To see how each sentence part affects sentence meaning, study in order the drawings on pages 280, 313, 329, 362, 390, 415, 438, 439, and 449. Note what each part adds to the sentence.

3. **As this book points out over and over, the same word may be used as more than one part of speech.**
   Walk past him. (*prep.*)   The past week was rainy. (*adj.*)
   Forget the past. (*n.*)   Who just went past? (*adv.*)

4. **Two parts of speech, the** *noun* **and the** *pronoun,* **may be used in sentences in various ways.** They may be used as (*a*) subjects, (*b*) predicate nominatives, (*c*) direct objects, (*d*) appositives, (*e*) objects of prepositions, or (*f*) indirect objects.

5. **(DEFINITION) A** *simple sentence* **is a group of words used to make a statement, ask a question, or give a command. It contains a subject and a predicate, either or both of which may be compound.**

6. **(DEFINITION) Two or more simple sentences joined together form a** *compound sentence.*

* There is another part of speech, called the *interjection,* which is a word or a word group that shows feeling. It usually comes at the beginning of a sentence, and is set off by a comma or an exclamation point, depending upon how strong the speaker's feeling is.
   Oh, there they go.   *Hurrah!* I won a prize!

REVIEW OF WORD ORDER, SENTENCE PATTERNS, MODIFIERS

1. **The normal order of the basic sentence parts is as follows:**
   Pattern 1: **N** + **V** (*subject* + *verb*)
   Pattern 2: **N** + **LV** + **N** (*subject* + *linking verb* + *predicate noun*)
   Pattern 3: **N** + **V** + **N** (*subject* + *verb* + *direct object*)
   Pattern 4: **N** + **LV** + **A** (*subject* + *linking verb* + *predicate adjective*)
   Pattern 5: **N** + **V**-*give* + **N** + **N** (*subject* + *verb* + *indirect object* + *direct object*)

2. **Modifiers are used to expand the basic patterns.**
   a) **Adjectives, determiners, and nouns used as modifiers describe or limit nouns and pronouns.**
   b) **Adverbs tell** *how, where, when,* **or** *how much* **about verbs, adjectives, or other adverbs.** (Adverbs that tell *how much* are called "qualifiers.")
   c) **Prepositional phrases function as do adjectives or adverbs.**

REVIEW ACTIVITIES IN SENTENCE STRUCTURE

A. Identify the basic sentence patterns in the following sentences.
1. The man in the middle must be the leader.
2. Jim surely played well in the final game.
3. Our class will hold its annual picnic soon.
4. I wrote Joan a letter today.
5. Our tulips look really beautiful now.
6. My favorite dessert is pie with ice cream.
7. The first day of spring was cloudy.
8. Someone gave me the wrong address.
9. My father has many cousins in Ireland.
10. The boy on the end came here from Canada.

B. In an oral activity, compose sentences that fit these basic patterns.
1. Pattern 1, using a compound subject
2. Pattern 3, including compound modifiers
3. Pattern 2 and Pattern 4, combining them in a compound sentence
4. Pattern 5, including at least one determiner and one adverb phrase

C. Copy the following sentences, filling each blank with a determiner or a qualifying adverb. Use a different qualifier each time.
1. .... busy people are .... happy.
2. .... day of summer was .... cold.
3. .... boys have been working .... hard.
4. Last night I .... had .... strange dreams.

2. Handling Sentence Fragments

"THAT'S ONLY PART OF A SENTENCE."

"BUT IT HAS A SUBJECT AND A VERB."

After Hazel had made the candy.

THINK IT OVER . . .

Why do you think the "sentence" really is only a fragment?

Sentence fragments covered in point 2, page **337**, are fragments because they lack either a subject or a verb or both. Sometimes, however, a group of words may have a subject and a verb and still be only a sentence fragment.

After Hazel had made the candy.

That group of words has a verb, *had made,* and a subject, *Hazel.* It is not a sentence, however, because it does not give a *complete* thought. You want to know something more—*what happened* after Hazel had made the candy. In other words, the main idea is missing. For a complete sentence, that main idea must be added:

After Hazel had made the candy, I washed the dishes.*

Learn about words!

The following words, taken from *A* of the Learning Activities, have interesting histories. Use your dictionary to find the story behind each word. With which word is the drawing connected?

chapel   normal   journey   pill

---

* This is what is known as a *complex sentence.* You will study more about this kind of sentence next year.

A. (1) Copy the following groups of words. (2) Write *S* beside each complete sentence and *F* beside each fragment. (3) Make complete sentences of all the fragments. If you put the fragment first, use a comma after it. Compare work in class.

1. Before he went to school.
2. While I sat in the car.
3. You should take this pill.
4. Since she moved to Texas.
5. We sent him on a journey.
6. If we build a new chapel.
7. Because I was hungry.
8. His temperature is normal.
9. As I said in my letter.
10. So that we could leave early.

B. Here is a paragraph that is well written except that some fragments have been punctuated as if they were complete sentences. Copy the paragraph as it should be written. Read your work aloud, showing, by the way that you read, how the paragraph should be written.

One summer four friends and I decided to put on a cowboy show. Because we were feeling bored. We had a hard time getting started, though. For every one of us wanted to be the cowboy hero. Who killed the rustlers. Finally my buddy and I gave in and agreed to be rustlers. After we had practiced for several days. We gave our one and only performance. Since we were charging only a penny admission, we had sold a lot of tickets. Most of which our parents had bought. We sold tickets to boys and girls, too, but made the mistake of not insisting on cash payment in advance. After the play was over. We were not sure whether it had been a success. Because all the paid admissions (our parents) had stayed home, and all the unpaid ones had shown up.

3. Getting Rid of Run-on Sentences Effectively

READ AND DISCUSS

Pages 170–71 and 340–41 of this book explain what run-on sentences are and how you can correct them. If you need to review run-on sentences, go over those pages now. How would you correct the following run-on sentence?

The door of the small house was open and so I walked inside and I saw a little boy and he was playing with a dog.

Your first idea might be to break it into separate sentences:

> The door of the small house was open. I walked inside. I saw a little boy there. He was playing with a dog.

Now the little paragraph is correct enough, but why is it still a poor one? Why is the following one better?

> The door of the small house being open, I walked inside. There I saw a little boy playing with a dog.

Two sentences have been made from four, and an adverb has been moved. Now think about the words themselves. What vivid or exact substitutes might be used? What modifiers might be added?

> The door of the small gray cabin being invitingly open, I stepped inside. There I saw a curly-headed little boy playing with a fat brown puppy.

What words have been changed? What words have been added?

STEPS IN DEALING EFFECTIVELY WITH RUN-ON SENTENCES

1. Break run-ons into separate sentences.

2. Combine and improve the sentences by using the Guides for Improving Expression, page 453.

3. Go back over the revised sentences. Substitute or add vivid or exact words wherever you can do so effectively. (See pages 292, 343, 398, and 420 for help.)

ACTIVITIES IN DEALING EFFECTIVELY WITH RUN-ON SENTENCES

A. In class, break the following run-on sentences into separate sentences. Have these written on the blackboard. See that each sentence is correctly punctuated and begins with a capital letter. Then make the sentences more effective with the aid of steps 2 and 3 above.

1. In the winter the wind often blows, it blows around our house and at night the branches of the trees hit against the windows and when I am alone in the house the noise sometimes frightens me.

2. The fire engine went past our house and four of us boys were playing in our yard and so we ran after it, we were soon left behind.

3. Snow had been falling all night and so Jack put on his overshoes and took the snow shovel from its hook in the basement and his little brother went out into the cold air with him.

B. (1) On scratch paper, correct and improve the following paragraph by following the steps on page 471. (2) Copy the paragraph neatly on good paper. (3) *Proofread for careless errors.*

I like all outdoor sports very much and so I spend most of my spare time outdoors, in summer I like to play tennis and I play tennis more than anything else, I also play on a softball team and we practice three times a week what I like best is swimming and so I go to the beach every chance I get, in the winter I like to skate and ski, and I spend most of my time skating the rink is close by and so it is easy to get there, to go skiing Father must take me in the car the nearest hill for skiing is fifteen miles from our house.

USING ENGLISH IN ALL CLASSES

Bring to English class papers written for other classes recently. Correct any fragments or run-on sentences.

4. Correcting and Revising What You Write

"YOU MEAN YOU'RE REWRITING IT FOR THE THIRD TIME?"

"WHY NOT? DON'T FORGET— MISS LEE SAID THAT EVEN SHAKESPEARE REWROTE THINGS!"

THINK IT OVER...

Really good written expression almost always is the result of writing and rewriting. A writer first puts his ideas down on paper as quickly as he can. After doing so, he goes back over his work. He scratches out words, substitutes or inserts new words, rearranges sentences, and makes any other changes that he thinks will best express what he has to say.

Whether you are writing just for fun or for some practical reason (such as improving your marks in school), you will find that revising and polishing is worth the time that it takes.

LEARNING ACTIVITY IN CORRECTING AND REVISING A THEME

(1) In class, examine and talk over this one-paragraph story. Find the many mistakes in capitalization, punctuation, spelling, and grammatical usage. (2) Using every other line on your paper, copy the story, but correct the mistakes and break it up into separate sentences. (3) Combine and improve sentences by applying the Guides for Improving Expression, page 435. Cross out the parts that you want to change; write the changes above them. (4) Insert or substitute vivid, exact language wherever you see the chance. (5) Copy your work neatly. (6) *Proofread for careless mistakes.* (7) Exchange papers and have several read aloud to see how they compare.

When we were younger my brother and I boxed quiet alot, my father was interest in boxing, and so he liked to show us off, often when company come at night he would get us out of bed to box. The company allmost allways give us some money. Probly because they felt it was to bad that we should loose our sleep. One year we were invided to box at the matche's the American legion had planed. For the forth of July. We was suposed to take a nap that afternoon befor are match, when the afternoon was just starting we could here the noise from the selabration and we whent out the back way and run down the ally and got to were the fun was going on and so we got are share of the candy pop popcorn and ice cream, and about five oclock we whent home and are parents dident no we had ben away. That night we boxed alright anyway and had a wonderfull time. Recieving over six dollers apeice for are fight. After we was in bed we felt badly about decieving are parants, and so we whoke them up and tolled them wat we had did. They was cross at us at first for being whoke up, but they forgive us, and we whent back to bed.

FOLLOW-UP

If you have not already formed the habit of doing your first writing on scratch paper, begin to build that habit now. Then revise and polish to say things in the best way that you know how.

Cumulative Review *

★

CAPITALIZATION AND PUNCTUATION

Copy these sentences, supplying needed capitalization and punctuation.

1. yes said mrs brown our neighbor weve let the boys raise rabbits pigeons and now hamsters

* After this final review, take the Last Test in the test booklet.

2. sue didnt you live at 1142 lake street sandusky ohio asked meg
3. while we were in the west last summer we visited captain and mrs c h black we also spent two days in yellowstone national park
4. my grandmother said that she was born at 1 30 AM on may 14 1900

PARTS OF THE SENTENCE

Copy these sentences. Above each italicized word, write its use. You may abbreviate. After each sentence, name its pattern.

1. That *man* in the gray suit is a *stranger* to my family and *me*.
2. A box of *oranges* blocked the *doorway*.
3. Mary and *Helen* sang the opening song.
4. The night was *cold but clear*.
5. Fred, my older *brother, finally* told *me* the news.

VERB-SUBJECT AGREEMENT

Go over the following sentences orally, choosing the standard forms from the parentheses.

1. (Was, Were) you in school yesterday?
2. That sort of movies (doesn't, don't) appeal to me.
3. (Don't, Doesn't) Jim want a score card?
4. Either James or Tom (is, are) in the house.
5. It (don't, doesn't) matter to them.
6. They (was, were) waiting for me at the corner.
7. The list of names (is, are) posted on the board.
8. That box of books (look, looks) heavy.
9. (Is, Are) there many people in the room?

TROUBLESOME VERBS

Go over the following sentences orally, choosing the standard forms from the parentheses.

1. Who (sits, sets) here? Where has he (gone, went)?
2. Will you (borrow, lend) me that lamp? Just (set, sit) it here.
3. I (lay, laid) there for an hour. Nobody (saw, seen) me.
4. John (come, came) up to me and (begun, began) a long speech.
5. I've neither (saw, seen) him nor (wrote, written) to him.
6. Joe has (rode, ridden) off. I might have (knew, known) it!
7. Who (give, gave) you that book? I'd not have (chose, chosen) it.
8. Billy (brung, brought) in the paper and then (run, ran) outdoors.
9. When was the race (run, ran)? Was the record (broke, broken)?
10. I've (taken, took) many trips, but I've never (flew, flown).
11. Have you (ate, eaten) here before? The prices have (rose, risen).
12. We had (drove, driven) to the lake and had (swum, swam) for an hour.

13. I had (drawn, drawed) a walk and later had (stole, stolen) home.
14. Who (learned, taught) you that song? I've (sung, sang) it often.
15. It's (grown, grew) cold! I should have (wore, worn) a coat.
16. He had not (spoke, spoken) but had (threw, thrown) me a smile.
17. The temperature had (fallen, fell), and the lake was (froze, frozen).
18. Has Phil (come, came), or have you (begun, began) without him?
19. Who (drank, drunk) my iced tea? You must have (done, did) it.
20. The bell had (rung, rang), and the whistle had (blew, blown).

PROPER USE OF PRONOUNS

In an oral activity, choose the standard forms. Explain each choice.

1. Leaders will be you and (him, he). (You're, Your) our choice.
2. (We, Us) two came early. (It's, Its) the first time!
3. (I and Ray, Ray and I) have been looking for you and (him, he).
4. Wait for Ruth and (me, I). Did you forget (us, we) girls?
5. Mother gave (he, him) and (me, I) some cake.
6. (Him, He) and (I, me) usually walk to school together.
7. Is this hat (yours, your's)? I really like (its, it's) color.
8. Sally and (she, her) will come later. (Their, They're) busy.

PROPER USE OF ADJECTIVES AND ADVERBS

Go over these sentences orally, choosing the standard forms.

1. Don't do (anything, nothing) now. Wait at least (a, an) hour.
2. Are (them, those) books yours? They (sure, really) look exciting.
3. John hasn't (no, any) ticket. I'm (certainly, sure) sorry, too.
4. You (surely, sure) played (well, good) in that game.
5. Ed is hardly (ever, never) ill, but today he feels (bad, badly).
6. I don't feel (good, well). I haven't eaten (nothing, anything).
7. We can win (easy, easily). Just ask (them, those) boys.

PROPER USE OF PREPOSITIONS

Go over these sentences orally, choosing the standard forms.

1. She is not (to, at) home. Where has she (gone, gone to)?
2. He fell (off of, off) that bicycle. He had borrowed it (off, from) me.
3. The (two, too, to) boys were (too, to, two) late for the game.
4. Did you visit (at, by) your uncle's farm, (too, two, to)?
5. Where will you (stay, stay at)?
6. He jumped (in, into) the car and drove away.

MASTERY TESTS IN SPELLING

At the beginning of Chapter 9, you took two Pretests in spelling. At the end of that chapter, you took Check Tests. Take those tests again as Mastery Tests. Follow the plan for the Pretests, page 178.

APPENDIX

Principal Parts of Troublesome Verbs

Present Tense	Past Tense	Past Participle	Present Tense	Past Tense	Past Participle
attack	attacked	attacked	ride	rode	ridden
beat	beat	beaten	ring	rang, rung *	rung
become	became	become			
begin	began	begun	rise	rose	risen
blow	blew	blown	run	ran	run
break	broke	broken	see	saw	seen
bring	brought	brought	set	set	set
burst	burst	burst	shake	shook	shaken
choose	chose	chosen	shrink	shrank, shrunk *	shrunk
climb	climbed	climbed			
come	came	come	sing	sang, sung *	sung
do	did	done			
drag	dragged	dragged	sink	sank, sunk *	sunk
draw	drew	drawn			
drink	drank	drunk	sit	sat	sat
drive	drove	driven	sneak	sneaked	sneaked
drown	drowned	drowned	speak	spoke	spoken
eat	ate	eaten	spring	sprang, sprung *	sprung
fall	fell	fallen			
fly	flew	flown	steal	stole	stolen
freeze	froze	frozen	swim	swam	swum
give	gave	given	take	took	taken
go	went	gone	tear	tore	torn
grow	grew	grown	throw	threw	thrown
know	knew	known	wear	wore	worn
lay	laid	laid	write	wrote	written
lie	lay	lain			

* The first form is preferred.

Verb Conjugations

A conjugation begins with the principal parts of the verb, since the verb tenses are formed from them. The present participle (see the footnote on page 291) is included in the principal parts of the following two conjugations.

Both active and passive forms of "to draw" are given; when the verb is passive, the subject simply *receives* the action: "He *was given* a pencil."

Conjugation of TO DRAW

Principal Parts

Present: draw	*Present Participle:* drawing
Past: drew	*Past Participle:* drawn

ACTIVE		PASSIVE	

Present Tense

SINGULAR	PLURAL	SINGULAR	PLURAL
1. I draw	we draw	I *am* drawn	we *are* drawn
2. you draw	you draw	you *are* drawn	you *are* drawn
3. he* draws	they draw	he *is* drawn	they *are* drawn

Past Tense

1. I drew	we drew	I *was* drawn	we *were* drawn
2. you drew	you drew	you *were* drawn	you *were* drawn
3. he drew	they drew	he *was* drawn	they *were* drawn

Future Tense

1. I *shall* draw	we *shall* draw	I *shall be* drawn	we *shall be* drawn
2. you *will* draw	you *will* draw	you *will be* drawn	you *will be* drawn
3. he *will* draw	they *will* draw	he *will be* drawn	they *will be* drawn

Present Perfect Tense

1. I *have* drawn	we *have* drawn	I *have been* drawn	we *have been* drawn
2. you *have* drawn	you *have* drawn	you *have been* drawn	you *have been* drawn
3. he *has* drawn	they *have* drawn	he *has been* drawn	they *have been* drawn

She and *it* and *singular nouns* are used just as *he* is.

SINGULAR	PLURAL	SINGULAR	PLURAL
1. I *had* drawn	we *had* drawn	I *had been* drawn	we *had been* drawn
2. you *had* drawn	you *had* drawn	you *had been* drawn	you *had been* drawn
3. he *had* drawn	they *had* drawn	he *had been* drawn	they *had been* drawn

Future Perfect Tense

SINGULAR	PLURAL	SINGULAR	PLURAL
1. I *shall have* drawn	we *shall have* drawn	I *shall have been* drawn	we *shall have been* drawn
2. you *will have* drawn	you *will have* drawn	you *will have been* drawn	you *will have been* drawn
3. he *will have* drawn	they *will have* drawn	he *will have been* drawn	they *will have been* drawn

CONJUGATION OF TO BE

PRINCIPAL PARTS

Present: be   *Present Participle:* being
Past: was   *Past Participle:* been

Present Tense

SINGULAR	PLURAL
1. I am	we are
2. you are	you are
3. he is	they are

Present Perfect Tense

SINGULAR	PLURAL
I have been	we have been
you have been	you have been
he has been	they have been

Past Tense

SINGULAR	PLURAL
1. I was	we were
2. you were	you were
3. he was	they were

Past Perfect Tense

SINGULAR	PLURAL
I had been	we had been
you had been	you had been
he had been	they had been

Future Tense

SINGULAR	PLURAL
1. I shall be	we shall be
2. you will be	you will be
3. he will be	they will be

Future Perfect Tense

SINGULAR	PLURAL
I shall have been	we shall have been
you will have been	you will have been
he will have been	they will have been

Suggestions for Good Handwriting

1. Slant all letters in the same direction.
   Do not write this way.

2. Make your writing a good size.
   Do not write too large. Do not write too small.

3. Write on a straight line.
   Do not have some letters high and others low.

4. Avoid crowding your writing.
   See how hard to read this kind of writing is.

5. Make capitals and tall letters tall.
   Do not make them the height of the small letters.

6. Keep small letters even in height.
   Notice how uneven these letters are.

7. Use dots, not circles, above _i_'s and _j_'s; really cross _t_'s.
   This just isn't the way to do it.

8. Be sure to close the letters _a_, _d_, _g_, _k_, _o_, and _s_.
   Not closing them makes the words look
   bad and hard to read.

9. Loop the letters _b_, _e_, _f_, _g_, _h_, _j_, _k_, _l_, _p_, _q_, _y_, _z_.
   Never let a loop cut through a word above or below.

   You make your writing hard to read if you
   loop carelessly and have letters crossing other lines.

10. Make the final stroke of _a_, but not of _o_,
    touch the line.
    Do not make them hard to tell apart.

11. Round the tops of _m_'s and _n_'s.
    They must not look like _w_'s or _v_'s.

Glossary of Terminology in Linguistic Grammar

EXPLANATORY NOTE

This glossary contains (1) terms that are alternatives for ones used in the textbook and (2) supplementary linguistic terms used in various linguistic grammars.

Adword. An adword is one that can be compared, either by means of the suffixes *-er, -est* or of *more, most.*

Affix. An affix is any prefix or suffix.

Bound morpheme. A bound morpheme is a meaningful language unit that cannot stand alone as a word. *Dis* in *disagree* and *ful* in *cupful* are examples.

Completer. A completer is (1) the direct object of a transitive verb; or (2) the predicate nominative, predicate adjective, or place adverb completing a linking verb.

Consumer sentence. A consumer sentence, also called a *matrix sentence* or a *receiver sentence,* is what is known in traditional grammar as an independent clause. In linguistic terminology, it is a sentence into which is inserted a construction that is a transformation of another sentence.

Contact clause. A contact clause is a relative clause from which the relative is omitted. In "The house [that] we live in is old," omitting the relative *that* makes "we live in" a contact clause.

Deep structure. Deep structure is what seems to underlie surface structure in a sentence. Two sentences, for example, may seem to have the same structure, but a detailed analysis will reveal that the two must somehow be different. "He seems difficult to help" and "He seems glad to help" appear to have the same structure, but you cannot rearrange them in the same ways. You can say, "It seems difficult to help him," but not "It seems glad to help him." You can say, "He seems glad to help us," but not "He seems difficult to help us."

Derivational suffix. A derivational suffix is one that changes a word (1) from one part of speech to another or (2) to a variation that is the same part of speech as the word was before. As examples, the suffix *-able* changes the verb *laugh* to the adjective *laughable;* the suffix *-ful* changes the noun *house* to another noun, *houseful.*

Derived sentence. A derived sentence is one resulting from a transformation.

Double arrow. A double arrow ($\Rightarrow$) is the symbol in transformational grammar that means "is rewritten as."

Double-base transformation. A double-base transformation is one that blends two or more sentences into one.

Embed (*imbed*). To embed is to transform a sentence and insert the result into another sentence. In "I have a new coat. It is blue," for example, the second sentence can be embedded in the first: "I have a new *blue* coat."

First position. The first position in a sentence is the subject position.

Form class words. Form class words are ones that can change their form. They include verbs, nouns (and pronouns), adjectives, and adverbs.

Free morpheme. A free morpheme is one that can stand alone as a word; the *turn* in *return* is an example.

Functional shift. Functional shift is the movement, over the years, of a word from one part of speech to another. The word *change,* for instance, began as a verb, but now has noun uses as well.

Function word. A function word is a structure word; that is, a *determiner,* an *auxiliary,* a *qualifier,* a *preposition,* or a *conjunction.*

Immediate constituents. The immediate constituents of a sentence or of its parts are the two divisions into which they can be broken down. In "Many friends helped us," *Many friends* and *helped us* are the immediate constituents of the sentence; *Many* and *friends* are the immediate constituents of the noun cluster *Many friends*; *helped* and *us* are those of the predicate *helped us.*

Inflectional affix. An inflectional affix is one that makes plurals or possessives of nouns; that produces the tense forms of verbs; or that shows comparison of adjectives and of some adverbs.

Input sentence. An input sentence is one that is transformed and put into another sentence.

Intensifier. The term *intensifier* is sometimes used as a synonym for *qualifier.* It seems better restricted to the labeling of qualifiers that make stronger what they modify; for example, the *extremely* in "Today was extremely cold" is an intensifier; the *rather* in "Today was rather cold" is a qualifier.

Interrogators. Interrogators are the structure words *who, whose, whom, what, where, when, how,* and *why* when they are used to form questions.

Kernel sentence. A kernel sentence is a sentence built to fit any of the basic sentence patterns of the English language.

Matrix sentence. *See* Consumer sentence.

Modal auxiliary. A modal auxiliary is one that shows shades of meaning. *Shall, should, will, would, may, might, must, can, could* are examples.

Morpheme. A morpheme is a meaningful unit of speech; it may be a word or only a part of a word.

Nominal. A nominal is any word or word group used in a noun position.

Nominalization. Nominalization is the process of creating a noun or a word group that is used as a noun.

Noun adjunct. A noun adjunct is a noun that modifies another noun; for example, *country* in *country roads; London* in *London fog.*

Noun-headed structure. A noun-headed structure is a noun with its modifiers; it is a noun cluster.

Noun phrase. In transformational grammar, a noun phrase is any noun or word group used as a noun, along with any affixes or modifiers that it has.

Null sign. *See* Zero.

Output sentence. *See* Derived sentence.

Particle. A particle is a preposition that joins with a verb to produce a "two-word verb": He *turned down* my offer.

P-group. A P-group is a prepositional phrase.

Phoneme. A phoneme is any one of the more than forty basic sounds in the English language. A phoneme is merely a sound; it has no meaning by itself. Here is a chart of the phonemes.

Consonants

voiceless:	/p/ *p*ut	/t/ *t*ake	/č/ *ch*at	/k/ *k*ill
voiced:	/b/ *b*ut	/d/ *d*oes	/ǰ/ *j*ury	/g/ *g*one
voiceless:	/f/ *f*in	/θ/ *th*in	/s/ *s*ing	/š/ *sh*out
voiced:	/v/ *v*an	/ð/ *th*at	/z/ *z*ing	/ž/ vi*s*ion
nasal:	/m/ *m*et	/n/ *n*ot	/ŋ/ si*ng*	
liquids:	/l/ *l*ove	/r/ *r*un		

Vowels

high:	/i/ h*i*t	/ɨ/ j*u*st *	/u/ b*oo*k
mid:	/e/ s*e*t	/ə/ b*u*t	/o/ h*o*pe
low:	/æ/ c*a*t	/a/ n*o*t	/ɔ/ l*a*w

Semivowels

/y/ *y*et	/h/ *h*er	/w/ *w*ere

Diphthongs

/iy/ b*ea*t	/aw/ b*ou*t	/ah/ c*al*m	/ɨw/ n*ew*
/ey/ b*ai*t	/uw/ b*oo*t	/ɔh/ h*aw*k	/ih/ d*ea*r
/ay/ *I*	/ow/ b*oa*t	/oy/ b*oy*	

Postdeterminer. A postdeterminer is one that follows any other determiners used before a noun. Examples are ordinal or cardinal numbers and the "comparing" determiners (*more, most, fewer,* ...).

Prearticle. A prearticle is a determiner that can precede the article *the;* for example, in *both the boys, both* is a prearticle.

Predeterminer. A predeterminer is a determiner that has an *of* between it and the following determiner, as in "*some* of *this* money."

Receiver sentence. *See* Consumer sentence.

482

Second position. The second position is the place that the verb fills in normal sentence order in the English language.

S-group. An S-group is a dependent clause.

Single-base transformation. A single-base transformation (sometimes called a *singular transformation*) is one that operates on the material of one basic sentence. It may be a passive transformation, a *there* transformation, a question (*or* request) transformation, a negative transformation, an indirect-object transformation, or simply a shifting of the elements in the sentence.

Structure word. A structure word (also called *function word*) is one that serves as a marker for a sentence element. Structure words have little meaning in themselves; they include *determiners, auxiliary verbs, qualifying adverbs, prepositions,* and *conjunctions.*

Subject complement. A subject complement is a predicate nominative or a predicate adjective.

Subordinator. A subordinator is a subordinate conjunction.

Syntax. Syntax studies the ways in which sentences are constructed from words; it bears close relation to morphology.

Tag question. A tag question is one added to a declarative or an imperative sentence: He has left, *hasn't he?* Wait a minute, *will you?*

Third position. The third position is the place in a sentence that is filled by a complement; in other words, by a *direct object, a predicate nominative,* or *a predicate adjective.*

Transformation. A transformation is an operation on a basic-pattern sentence that produces a different arrangement or a changed sentence. *See also* Single-base transformation; Double-base transformation.

Two-word verb. *See* Particle.

V-*en* form. A V-*en* form is the verb form that is known in traditional grammar as the *past participle.*

Verb-headed structure. A verb-headed structure is one made up of a verb and its modifiers; it is a verb cluster.

Verb phrase. In transformational grammar a verb phrase is the verb or the verb and any affixes or words used with it to form the predicate.

Wh-**nominal.** A *wh*-nominal is a noun clause.

Wh-**word.** The *wh*-words are *who, whom, whose, what, which, that, why, how, when, where,* and their compounds with *-ever.* They are used in questions and in noun clauses.

Zero (*also* zero morph, zero form, zero affix, null sign). The zero symbol is ∅. It signifies a lack or an omission. It might be, for example, the lack of an inflectional ending; it would be used with *sheep* to show that the word is the same in the plural as well as in the singular: sheep + ∅.

INDEX

A

A, an, the (articles), 395
A, an, using properly, 404
Abbreviations
  avoiding in address, 253, 254
  capitalization in titles of persons, 146
  period to show, 151
  used in dictionary, 121
Accent marks in dictionary, 114
Accepting an invitation, guides, 261
Action verbs, 279–82
Activities, extra. *See* Just for Fun
Address
  commas in, 153
  envelope, 254–55
  inside, 265
Address, nominative of (direct address), 153
Adjectives and other adjectival words, 389–405
  a, an, the, 395, 404
  adverbs, confusion with, avoiding, 423–25
  articles, 395, 404
  common nouns as, 397–98
  comparison of, 193, 391, 400–401
    double, avoiding, 404
    irregular, 401
    shown in dictionary, 112
  compound, 234
  determiners, 309, 395–96; defined, 395
    See also Determiners
  diagramming, 402–403
  hyphen in compound, 159
  in Pattern 4 sentence, 393
  limiting (determiners), 395–96
  made from proper nouns, 397
  made from verbs, 391
  nouns as, 395–98
  numerals as, 395
  order of, 395
  possessive noun as, 395–96
  predicate adjective, 393–94; defined, 393
  prepositional phrase as, 437–39
  pronoun as, 391
  proper noun as, 397–98
  proper usage of, 403–405, 410, 433, 465, 475
  recognizing, practice in, 268, 392, 394, 396–97, 410, 437, 444, 464
  this, that, these, those as, 395

Adjectives—*Continued*
  true, 333–34; defined, 391
  vivid, exact, 398–400; guides, 398
Adjective phrase, 437–39
  diagramming, 443–44
  distinguishing from adverb phrase, 441
Adverbs, 415–17; defined, 416
  adding suffixes to form, 190
  adjectives, confusion with, avoiding, 423
  comparison, 419; given in dictionary, 112
  diagramming, 422
  double negatives, 425–26
  forming from adjectives, 418
  prepositional phrase as, 439–41
  proper usage, rules, 424, 426
    practice, 424–25, 426, 431, 465, 475
  recognizing, practice in, 416–17, 421, 431, 444, 465
  vivid, 420
Adverb phrase, 439–41; diagramming, 443
  distinguishing from adjective phrase, 442
Adword, 480
Affix, 480
Agreement
  verb with noun subject, 345–51
  verb with pronoun subject, 374–76
Ain't, avoiding, 347–48, 375
Almanacs, 122–26
Alphabetical order
  guides, 111
  in dictionary, 110–12
  in encyclopedias, 124
A.M. and P.M., periods in, 151
And, in compound sentence, 450
Angel and *angle,* 201
Antecedent, defined, 363
Apostrophe, 161–65
  avoiding in possessive pronouns, 373
  in contractions, 163
  in possessive nouns, 161
  to form plurals, 165
Appendix of a book, 132
Appositives, 332–35; defined, 153
  comma to set off, 153, 333
  diagramming, 335
  distinguishing from predicate nominative, 333
  pronoun as, 365–66
  to improve expression, 333, 453

Library, 120–131
   almanacs, 122; atlases, 122–23
   books, how shelved, 127
   books on special subjects, 123
   card catalogue, 128–31; guides, 130
   Dewey Decimal System, 126–27
   encyclopedias, 123
   fiction books, how indexed, 128
   Readers' Guide, 123, 125
   special sources of information, 120–31
Lie, lay, lain, 380–81
   review practice, 384–85, 412, 432, 464, 474
Linguistics, defined, 271
   adjectives
      articles (determiners), 395–96, 404
      as noun markers, 395–96, 397–98
      in sentence patterns, 393–94
      true, 391–92; defined, 391
   auxiliaries, as markers, 283
   count nouns, 310–12
   determiners. *See main entry*
   English sentence patterns, 275, 318–19, 322,
      325–27, 328–30, 393–94, 443, 445, 468
      expanding basic patterns, 468
      Pattern 1 (N + V), 318–19, 322, 325
      Pattern 2 (N + LV + N), 325–27
      Pattern 3 (N + V + N), 328–30
      Pattern 4 (N + LV + A), 393–94
      Pattern 5 (N + V-*give* + N + N), 445
      pronouns in, 365
   markers (signal words)
      auxiliaries as, 283
      determiners as, 309–11
      more, most, as, 394
   mass nouns, 310–12
   "nonsense" words, 309
   nouns, 308–51
      as determiners, 397
      changes in form (plurals), 309
      cluster, 313
      count and mass classes of, 310–12
      markers for, 309
   qualifiers (adverbs) as markers, 468
   slot sentences (test frames)
      for adjectives, 394
      for nouns, 309
      for verbs, 280
   spoken and written language, 276–78
   verbs
      auxiliaries as markers, 283
      cluster, 283
      form changes, 280
      phrase, 283
   word order, importance of, 275

Linking verb, 326
   defined, 326
Listening, 25–31
   guides to improving, 26, 29
   television, radio, and films, 30–31
   to assignments, 29
   to directions and explanations, 29
   See also Maintenance practice, listening
Literature, quotations from, 15, 45–56, 58–60,
   85, 105–106, 106–107, 212, 233, 236,
   237, 275–76, 278, 293, 311–12, 323,
   339, 344, 399, 421, 437, 451–52, 454

M

Magazines, using, 123–26
   practice, 40, 97, 103, 126, 145, 155, 160, 209,
      233, 234, 241, 249, 260, 267
Maintenance practice
   adjective usage, 410, 433, 465, 466, 475
   adverb usage, 431, 465, 475
   capitalization, 173–74, 202, 228, 249, 268,
      305, 341, 358–59, 385, 411, 431, 473–
      74
   card catalogue, 56, 133, 135, 260, 452
   choral reading, 56, 249, 293
   dictionary, 43, 58, 95, 106, 119, 121, 183,
      184, 198, 207, 383, 397, 410, 429
      See also Learn about words!
   effective expression, 37, 95, 135, 194, 232,
      247, 260, 300, 333, 345, 400, 422, 460,
      471, 473
   encyclopedias, using, 134, 176, 307, 361,
      387, 413, 434, 466
   handwriting, 140, 162, 191, 196, 201, 210,
      234, 256, 266, 290, 342
   letter writing, 125, 126, 345
   listening, 33, 34, 42, 57, 58, 60, 66, 68, 73,
      87, 92, 95, 98, 155, 156, 160, 164, 187,
      223, 248, 288, 296, 301, 311, 338, 353,
      354, 356, 361, 373, 376, 382, 407, 408,
      439, 441, 459, 460
   oral discussions, 27, 30, 31, 34, 37, 40, 47,
      66, 67, 82, 91, 92, 102, 124, 125, 160,
      198, 204, 237, 240, 244, 247, 262, 293
      See also Discussions, introductory
   outlining, 33, 66, 134, 135, 204, 240, 244
   paragraph building, 27, 30, 31, 134, 164,
      182, 187, 204, 205, 234, 260, 288, 312,
      315, 344, 392, 405, 441, 446, 448
   parts of speech, 310, 392, 417, 437
   parts of the sentence, recognizing, 357, 411,
      464, 474